Fodor's 97

London

"When it comes to information on regional history, what to see and do, and shopping, these guides are exhaustive."

—*USAir Magazine*

"Usable, sophisticated restaurant coverage, with an emphasis on good value."

—Andy Birsh, *Gourmet Magazine* columnist

"Valuable because of their comprehensiveness."

—*Minneapolis Star-Tribune*

"Fodor's always delivers high quality...thoughtfully presented...thorough."

—*Houston Post*

"An excellent choice for those who want everything under one cover."

—*Washington Post*

Fodor's Travel Publications, Inc.
New York • Toronto • London • Sydney • Auckland
http://www.fodors.com/

Fodor's London

Editor: Caroline Haberfeld

Author: Kate Sekules

Editorial Contributors: Robert Andrews, Robert Blake, Judy Blumenberg, Audra Epstein, Jane Moss, Ann Saunders, Heidi Sarna, Helayne Schiff, Mary Ellen Schultz, M. T. Schwartzman, Dinah Spritzer

Creative Director: Fabrizio La Rocca

Cartographer: David Lindroth

Cover Photograph: Richard T. Norwitz

Text Design: Between the Covers

Copyright

ISBN 0-679-03245-2

Special Sales

Fodor's Travel Publications are available at special discounts for bulk purchases for sales promotions or premiums. Special editions, including personalized covers, excerpts of existing guides, and corporate imprints, can be created in large quantities for special needs. For more information contact your local bookseller or write to Special Markets, Fodor's Travel Publications, 201 East 50th Street, New York, NY 10022. Inquiries from Canada should be directed to your local Canadian bookseller or sent to Random House of Canada, Ltd., Marketing Department, 1265 Aerowood Drive, Mississauga, Ontario L4W 1B9. Inquiries from the United Kingdom should be sent to Fodor's Travel Publications, 20 Vauxhall Bridge Road, London, England SW1V 2SA.

PRINTED IN THE UNITED STATES OF AMERICA

10 9 8 7 6 5 4 3 2 1

CONTENTS

Maps

ON THE ROAD WITH FODOR'S

WE'RE ALWAYS THRILLED to get letters from readers, especially one like this:

It took us an hour to decide what book to buy and we now know we picked the best one. Your book was wonderful, easy to follow, very accurate, and good on pointing out eating places, informal as well as formal. When we saw other people using your book, we would look at each other and smile.

Our editors and writers are deeply committed to making every Fodor's guide "the best one"—not only accurate but always charming, brimming with sound recommendations and solid ideas, right on the mark in describing restaurants and hotels, and full of fascinating facts that make you view what you've traveled to see in a rich new light.

About Our Writer

Our success in achieving our goals—and in helping to make your trip the best of all possible vacations—is a credit to the hard work of our extraordinary writer.

A native Londoner, **Kate Sekules** writes about travel, food, and fitness for many magazines, including *Vogue, The New Yorker, BBC Holidays,* and *Health & Fitness,* and for the *Time Out Guide to Eating and Drinking in London.* She also writes fiction and is a longtime Fodor's contributor.

Our editor, **Caroline Haberfeld,** is half British and has spent a good portion of her life in London doing everything from relaxing in friends' living rooms and seeking out new shops for knitting wool to scouring Indian restaurants for the perfect tandoori.

New This Year

This year we've reformatted our guides to make them easier to use. *London '97* has brand-new walking tours and a timing section that tells you exactly how long to allot for each tour—and what time of day, day of the week, or season of the year is optimal. You may also notice our fresh graphics, new in 1996. More readable and more helpful than ever? We think so—and we hope you do, too.

On the Web

Also check out Fodor's Web site (http://www.fodors.com/), where you'll find travel information on major destinations around the world and an ever-changing array of travel-savvy interactive features.

How to Use This Book

Organization

Up front is the **Gold Guide.** Its first section, **Important Contacts A to Z,** gives addresses and telephone numbers of organizations and companies that offer destination-related services and detailed information and publications. **Smart Travel Tips A to Z,** the Gold Guide's second section, gives specific information on how to accomplish what you need to in London as well as tips on savvy traveling. Both sections are in alphabetical order by topic.

The Exploring chapter is subdivided by neighborhood; each subsection recommends a walking or driving tour and lists neighborhood sights alphabetically. Off the Beaten Path sights appear after the places from which they are most easily accessible. The remaining chapters are arranged in alphabetical order by subject (dining, lodging, nightlife and the arts, outdoor activities and sports, shopping, and side trips).

At the end of the book you'll find Portraits, wonderful essays about the theater scene, the historic Great Fire, and a chronology, followed by suggestions for pretrip reading, both fiction and nonfiction.

Icons and Symbols

★ Our special recommendations
✕ Restaurant
🏨 Lodging establishment
✕🏨 Lodging establishment whose restaurant warrants a detour
🐤 Rubber duckie (good for kids)
☞ Sends you to another section of the guide for more info
✉ Address
☎ Telephone number
FAX Fax number
⏲ Opening and closing times
🎟 Admission prices (those we give apply only to adults; substantially reduced fees are almost always available for children, students, and senior citizens)

Numbers in white and black circles–② and ❷, for example—that appear on the maps, in the margins, and within the tours correspond to one another.

Restaurant Reservations and Dress Codes

Reservations are always a good idea; we note only when they're essential or when they are not accepted. Book as far ahead as you can, and reconfirm when you get to town. Unless otherwise noted, the restaurants listed are open daily for lunch and dinner. We mention dress only when men are required to wear a jacket or a jacket and tie.

Credit Cards

The following abbreviations are used: **AE,** American Express; **DC,** Diners Club; **MC,** MasterCard; and **V,** Visa.

Please Write to Us

You can use this book in the confidence that all prices and opening times are based on information supplied to us at press time; Fodor's cannot accept responsibility for any errors. Time inevitably brings changes, so always confirm information when it matters—especially if you're making a detour to visit a specific place. In addition, when making reservations be sure to mention if you have a disability or are traveling with children, if you prefer a private bath or a certain type of bed, or if you have specific dietary needs or any other concerns.

Were the restaurants we recommended as described? Did our hotel picks exceed your expectations? Did you find a museum we recommended a waste of time? If you have complaints, we'll look into them and revise our entries when the facts warrant it. If you've discovered a special place that we haven't included, we'll pass the information along to our correspondents and have them check it out. So send your feedback, positive *and* negative, to the London Editor at 201 East 50th Street, New York, New York 10022—and have a wonderful trip!

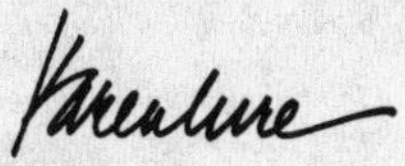

Karen Cure
Editorial Director

Central London

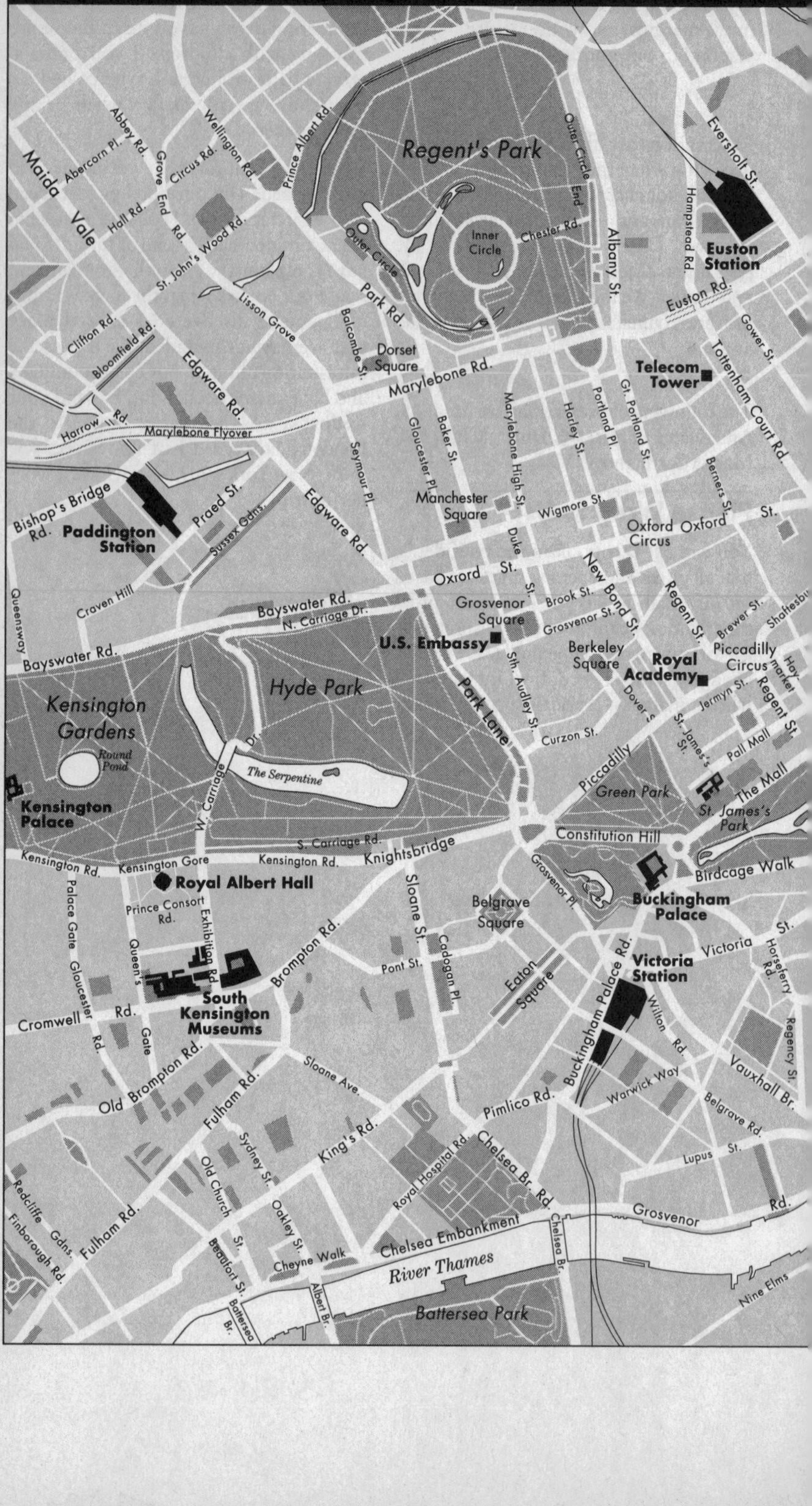

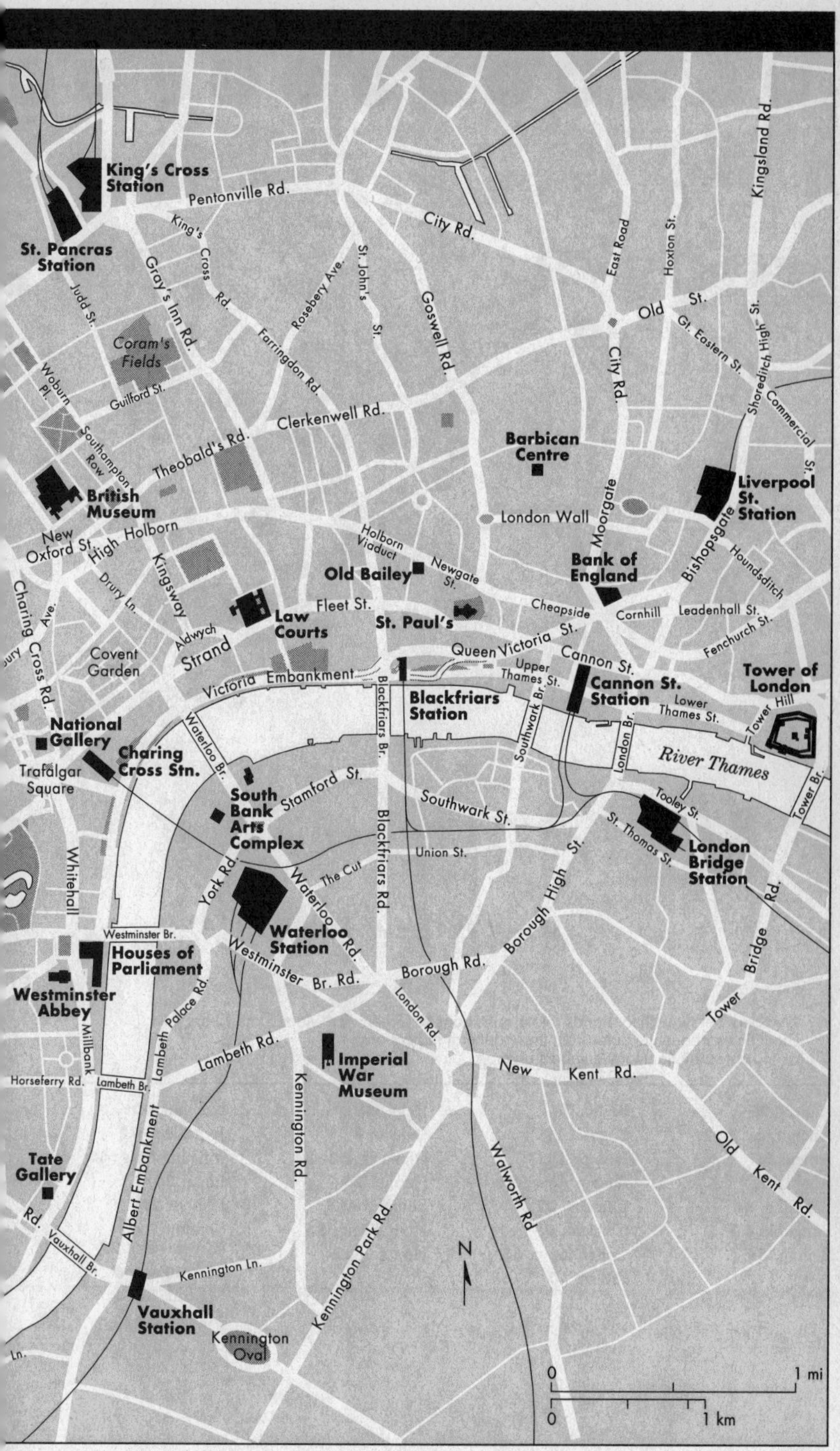
King's Cross Station
St. Pancras Station
Pentonville Rd.
City Rd.
King's Cross Rd.
Gray's Inn Rd.
Judd St.
Rosebery Ave.
St. John's St.
Goswell Rd.
East Road
Hoxton St.
Kingsland Rd.
Old St.
Gt. Eastern St.
Shoreditch High St.
Commercial St.
Coram's Fields
Woburn Pl.
Guilford St.
Farringdon Rd.
Clerkenwell Rd.
Southampton Row
Theobald's Rd.
Barbican Centre
Liverpool St. Station
British Museum
London Wall
Moorgate
New Oxford St.
High Holborn
Holborn Viaduct
Newgate St.
Old Bailey
Bank of England
Bishopsgate
Houndsditch
Drury Ln.
Kingsway
Charing Cross Rd.
Ave.
Law Courts
Fleet St.
St. Paul's
Cheapside
Cornhill
Leadenhall St.
Fenchurch St.
Covent Garden
Aldwych
Strand
Queen Victoria St.
Cannon St.
Upper Thames St.
Tower of London
Victoria Embankment
Blackfriars Br.
Blackfriars Station
Cannon St. Station
Lower Thames St.
Tower Hill
National Gallery
Waterloo Br.
Southwark Br.
London Br.
River Thames
Charing Cross Stn.
Trafalgar Square
Stamford St.
South Bank Arts Complex
Southwark St.
Tooley St.
Tower Br.
St. Thomas St.
London Bridge Station
Union St.
Whitehall
York Rd.
The Cut
Waterloo Rd.
Blackfriars Rd.
Borough High St.
Waterloo Station
Westminster Br.
Houses of Parliament
Westminster Br. Rd.
Borough Rd.
Tower Bridge Rd.
Westminster Abbey
Lambeth Palace Rd.
London Rd.
Millbank
Lambeth Rd.
Imperial War Museum
Horseferry Rd.
Lambeth Br.
New Kent Rd.
Kennington Rd.
Albert Embankment
Tate Gallery
Old Kent Rd.
Walworth Rd
Kennington Park Rd.
Vauxhall Br.
N
Kennington Ln.
Vauxhall Station
Kennington Oval
Ln.
0
1 mi
0
1 km

World Time Zones

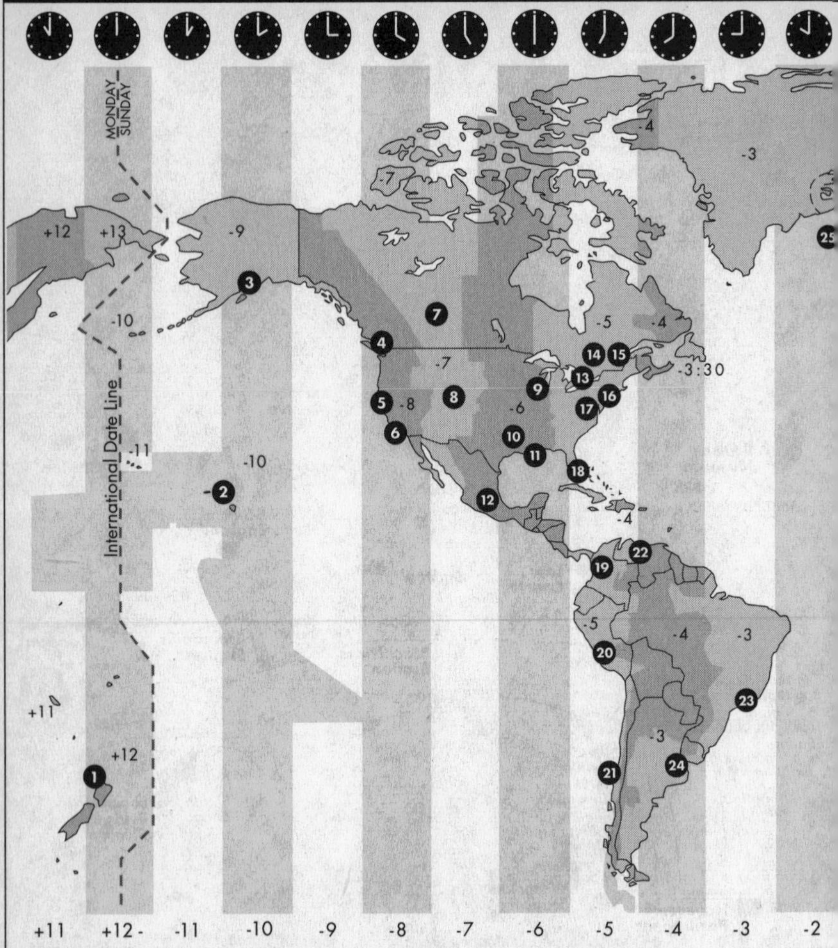

Numbers below vertical bands relate each zone to Greenwich Mean Time (0 hrs.).
Local times frequently differ from these general indications,
as indicated by light-face numbers on map.

Algiers, **29**
Anchorage, **3**
Athens, **41**
Auckland, **1**
Baghdad, **46**
Bangkok, **50**
Beijing, **54**

Berlin, **34**
Bogotá, **19**
Budapest, **37**
Buenos Aires, **24**
Caracas, **22**
Chicago, **9**
Copenhagen, **33**
Dallas, **10**

Delhi, **48**
Denver, **8**
Djakarta, **53**
Dublin, **26**
Edmonton, **7**
Hong Kong, **56**
Honolulu, **2**

Istanbul, **40**
Jerusalem, **42**
Johannesburg, **44**
Lima, **20**
Lisbon, **28**
London (Greenwich), **27**
Los Angeles, **6**
Madrid, **38**
Manila, **57**

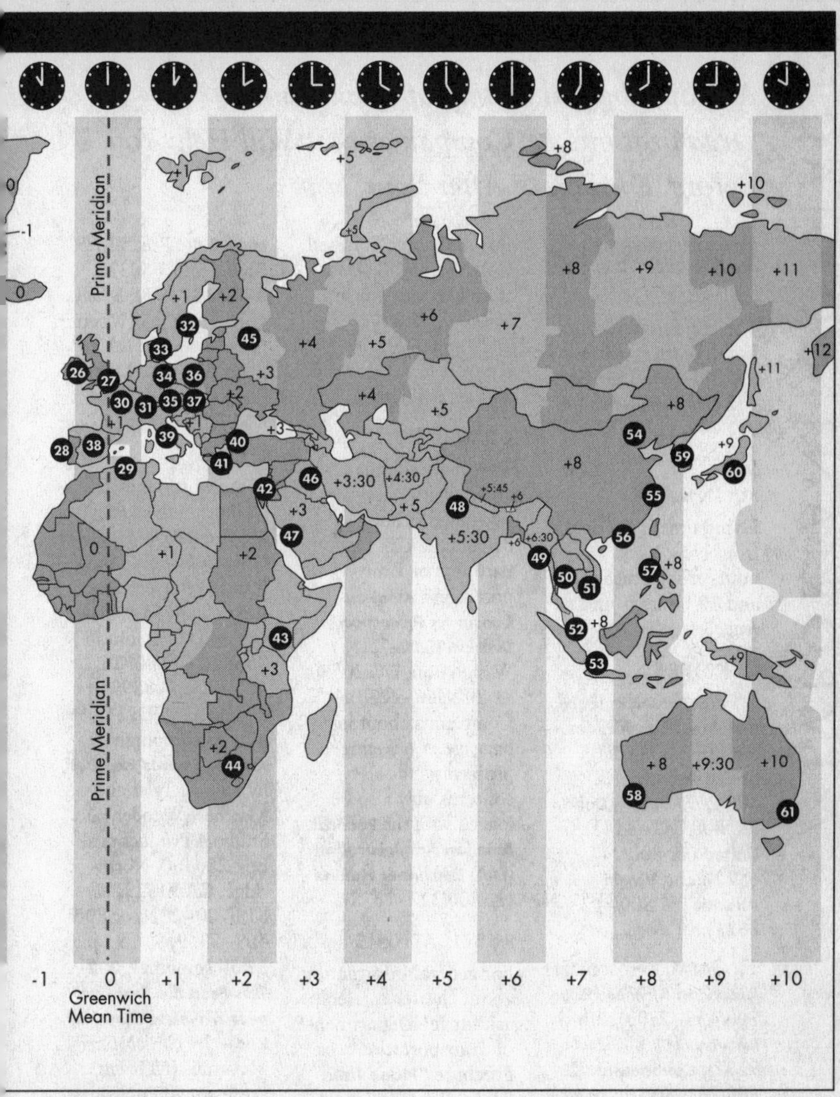
Prime Meridian
Prime Meridian
-1
0
+1
+2
+3
+4
+5
+6
+7
+8
+9
+10
Greenwich
Mean Time

IMPORTANT CONTACTS A TO Z

An Alphabetical Listing of Publications, Organizations, & Companies that Will Help You Before, During, & After Your Trip

A

AIR TRAVEL

The major gateways to London are **Heathrow** (☎ 011–44–181/759–4321) and **Gatwick** (☎ 011–44-12931/535–353).

FLYING TIME

Flying time is 6½ hours from New York, 7½ hours from Chicago, and 10 hours from Los Angeles.

CARRIERS

TO HEATHROW➢ Contact **American Airlines** (☎ 800/433–7300), **British Airways** (☎ 800/247–9297), **Delta** (☎ 800/241–4141), **United** (☎ 800/241–6522), and **Virgin Atlantic** (☎ 800/862–8621).

TO GATWICK➢ Contact **American Airlines** (☎ 800/433–7300), **British Airways** (☎ 800/247–9297), **Continental** (☎ 800/231–0856), **Delta** (☎ 800/241–4141), **Northwest Airlines** (☎ 800/447–4747), **TWA** (☎ 800/892–4141), and **Virgin Atlantic** (☎ 800/862–8621).

FROM THE U.K

British Airways (☎ 0181/897–4000; outside London, 0345/222–111); from Stansted **Air UK** (☎ 0345/666–777) flies to Scotland, Newcastle, and the Channel Islands; **Jersey European** (☎ 0345/676–676) to Bristol, Exeter, Stansted, Gatwick, and Belfast; from Heathrow **British Midland** (☎ 0181/754–7321 or 0345/554–554) serves Belfast, Scotland, and the Midlands.

COMPLAINTS

To register complaints about charter and scheduled airlines, contact the U.S. Department of Transportation's **Aviation Consumer Protection Division** (✉ C-75, Washington, DC 20590, ☎ 202/366–2220). Complaints about lost baggage or ticketing problems and safety concerns may also be logged with the **Federal Aviation Administration (FAA) Consumer Hotline** (☎ 800/322–7873).

PUBLICATIONS

For general information about charter carriers, ask for the Department of Transportation's free brochure **"Plane Talk: Public Charter Flights"** (✉ Aviation Consumer Protection Division, C-75, Washington, DC 20590, ☎ 202/366–2220). The Department of Transportation also publishes a 58-page booklet, **"Fly Rights,"** available from the Consumer Information Center (✉ Supt. of Documents, Dept. 133B, Pueblo, CO 81009; $1.75).

For other tips and hints, consult the Consumers Union's monthly **"Consumer Reports Travel Letter"** (✉ Box 53629, Boulder, CO 80322, ☎ 800/234–1970; $39 1st year) and the newsletter **"Travel Smart"** (✉ 40 Beechdale Rd., Dobbs Ferry, NY 10522, ☎ 800/327–3633; $37 per year).

Some worthwhile publications on the subject are ***The Official Frequent Flyer Guidebook,*** by Randy Petersen (✉ Airpress, 4715-C Town Center Dr., Colorado Springs, CO 80916, ☎ 719/597–8899 or 800/487–8893; $14.99 plus $3 shipping); ***Airfare Secrets Exposed,*** by Sharon Tyler and Matthew Wunder (✉ Studio 4 Productions, Box 280400, Northridge, CA 91328, ☎ 818/700–2522 or 800/408–7369; $16.95 plus $2.50 shipping); ***202 Tips Even the Best Business Travelers May Not Know,*** by Christopher McGinnis (✉ Irwin Professional Publishing, 1333 Burr Ridge Pkway., Burr Ridge, IL 60521, ☎ 800/634–3966; $11 plus $3.25 shipping); and ***Travel Rights,*** by Charles Leocha (✉ World Leisure Corporation, 177 Paris St., Boston, MA 02128, ☎ 800/444–2524; $7.95 plus $3.95 shipping).

For information on how to avoid jet lag, there are two publications: ***Jet Lag, A Pocket Guide to Modern Treatment*** (✉ MedEd Publishers, 1421 W. 3rd Ave., Columbus, OH 43212, ☎ 800/875-8489; $5.95) and ***How to Beat Jet Lag*** (✉ Henry Holt, 115 W. 18th St., New York, NY 10011, ☎ 800/288-2131; $14.95).

Travelers who experience motion sickness or ear problems in flight should get the brochures **"Ears, Altitude, and Airplane Travel"** and **"What You Can Do for Dizziness & Motion Sickness"** from the American Academy of Otolaryngology (✉ 1 Prince St., Alexandria, VA 22314, ☎ 703/836-4444, FAX 703/683-5100, TTY 703/519-1585).

B

BETTER BUSINESS BUREAU

For local contacts in the hometown of a tour operator you may be considering, consult the **Council of Better Business Bureaus** (✉ 4200 Wilson Blvd., Suite 800, Arlington, VA 22203, ☎ 703/276-0100, FAX 703/525-8277).

BUS TRAVEL

For details on bus service within London, contact **London Transport** (☎ 0171/222-1234). Travelcards (*see* Underground Travel, *below*) are good for both tube and bus.

C

CAR RENTAL

The major car-rental companies represented in London are **Alamo** (☎ 800/327-9633; in the U.K., 0800/272-2000), **Avis** (☎ 800/331-1084; in Canada, 800/879-2847), **Budget** (☎ 800/527-0700; in the U.K., 0800/181181), **Dollar** (☎ 800/800-4000; in the U.K., 0990/565656, where it is known as Eurodollar), **Hertz** (☎ 800/654-3001; in Canada, 800/263-0600; in the U.K., 0345/555888), and **National InterRent** (sometimes known as Europcar InterRent outside North America; ☎ 800/227-3876; in the U.K., 01345/222-525). Rates in London begin at $27 a day and $103 a week for an economy car with unlimited mileage. This does not include tax on car rentals, which is 17.5%.

RENTAL WHOLESALERS

Contact **Auto Europe** (☎ 207/828-2525 or 800/223-5555), **Europe by Car** (☎ 800/223-1516; in CA, 800/252-9401), or the **Kemwel Group** (☎ 914/835-5555 or 800/678-0678).

THE CHANNEL TUNNEL

For information, contact **Le Shuttle** (in the U.S., ☎ 800/388-3876; in the U.K., 0990/353535), which transports cars, or **Eurostar** (in the U.S., ☎ 800/942-4866; in the U.K., 0345/881881), the high-speed train service between London (Waterloo) and Paris (Gare du Nord). Eurostar tickets are available in the U.K. through **InterCity Europe,** the international wing of BritRail (✉ Victoria Station, London, ☎ 0171/834-2345 or 0171/828-0892 for credit-card bookings), and in the United States through **Rail Europe** (☎ 800/942-4866) and **BritRail Travel** (☎ 800/677-8585).

CHILDREN & TRAVEL

BABY-SITTING

First check with the hotel desk for recommended child-care arrangements. Local agencies: **Nanny Service** (✉ 9 Paddington St., London W1M 3LA, ☎ 0171/935-3515), **The Nanny Co. Ltd.** (✉ Stern House, 85 Gloucester Rd., London SW7 4SS, ☎ 0171/835-2277), **Universal Aunts** (✉ 19 The Chase, London SW4 ONP, ☎ 0171/738-8937).

FLYING

Look into **"Flying with Baby"** (✉ Third Street Press, Box 261250, Littleton, CO 80163, ☎ 303/595-5959; $4.95 includes shipping), cowritten by a flight attendant. **"Kids and Teens in Flight,"** free from the U.S. Department of Transportation's Aviation Consumer Protection Division (✉ C-75, Washington, DC 20590, ☎ 202/366-2220), offers tips on children flying alone. Every two years the February issue of ***Family Travel Times*** (☞ Know-How, *below*) details children's services on three dozen airlines. **"Flying Alone, Handy Advice for Kids Traveling Solo"** is available free from the American Automobile Association (AAA) (✉ send stamped, self-addressed, legal-size envelope: Flying Alone, Mail Stop 800, 1000 AAA Dr., Heathrow, FL 32746).

GAMES

Milton Bradley has games to help keep little (and not so little) children from fidgeting while in planes, trains, and automobiles. Try packing the Travel Battleship sea-battle game ($7); Travel Connect Four, a vertical strategy game ($8); the Travel Yahtzee dice game ($6), the Travel Trouble dice and board game ($7), and the Travel Guess Who mystery game ($8). Parker Brothers has travel versions of Clue!, Sorry, and Monopoly.

KNOW-HOW

Family Travel Times, published quarterly by Travel with Your Children (✉ TWYCH, 40 5th Ave., New York, NY 10011, ☎ 212/477–5524; $40 per year), covers destinations, types of vacations, and modes of travel.

The ***Family Travel Guides*** catalog (✉ Carousel Press, Box 6061, Albany, CA 94706, ☎ 510/527–5849; $1 postage) lists about 200 books and articles on traveling with children. Also check ***Take Your Baby and Go! A Guide for Traveling with Babies, Toddlers and Young Children,*** by Sheri Andrews, Judy Bordeaux, and Vivian Vasquez (✉ Bear Creek Publications, 2507 Minor Ave. E, Seattle, WA 98102, ☎ 206/322–7604 or 800/326–6566; $5.95 plus $1.50 shipping).

LOCAL INFORMATION

For information and advice when in London, call **Kidsline** (☎ 0171/222–8070).

The ***Children's Guide to London,*** by Christopher Pick (✉ Cadogan Books, 16 Lower Marsh, London SE1 7RJ; £3.50), and ***Kids' London,*** by Elizabeth Holt and Molly Perham (✉ St. Martin's Press, 175 5th Ave., New York, NY 10010; $5.95), cover the subject. Up-to-date information is available in ***Capital Radio's London for Kids*** magazine, available at newsstands (£1.50).

The booklet ***Children's London*** (available free from the London Tourist Board, Tourist Information Centre, Victoria Station Forecourt, London SW1V 1JT) gives a complete story.

LODGING

Hotels that are noticeably family- and child-friendly include **Forte Hotels** (☎ 0171/836–7744), **Basil Street Hotel** (✉ Basil St., Knightsbridge, London SW3 1AH, ☎ 0171/581–3311), and **Edward Lear** (✉ 28 Seymour St., London W1H 5WD, ☎ 0171/402–5401).

PEN PALS

For addresses of children in London to whom your children can write before your trip, send a self-addressed, stamped envelope to **International Friendship League** (✉ 55 Mt. Vernon St., Boston, MA 02108, ☎ 617/523–4273).

TOUR OPERATORS

Contact **Grandtravel** (✉ 6900 Wisconsin Ave., Suite 706, Chevy Chase, MD 20815, ☎ 301/986–0790 or 800/247–7651), which has tours for people traveling with grandchildren ages 7–17; **Families Welcome!** (✉ 4711 Hope Valley Rd., Durham, NC 27707, ☎ 919/489–2555 or 800/326–0724); or **Rascals in Paradise** (✉ 650 5th St., Suite 505, San Francisco, CA 94107, ☎ 415/978–9800 or 800/872–7225).

CUSTOMS

IN THE U.S.

The **U.S. Customs Service** (✉ Box 7407, Washington, DC 20044, ☎ 202/927–6724) can answer questions on duty-free limits and publishes a helpful brochure, "Know Before You Go." For information on registering foreign-made articles, call 202/927–0540.

COMPLAINTS➢ Note the inspector's badge number and write to the commissioner's office (✉ 1301 Constitution Ave. NW, Washington, DC 20229).

CANADIANS

Contact **Revenue Canada** (✉ 2265 St. Laurent Blvd. S, Ottawa, Ontario K1G 4K3, ☎ 613/993–0534) for a copy of the free brochure **"I Declare/Je Déclare"** and for details on duty-free limits. For recorded information (within Canada only), call 800/461–9999.

D

DISABILITIES & ACCESSIBILITY

COMPLAINTS

To register complaints under the provisions of

the Americans with Disabilities Act, contact the U.S. Department of Justice's **Disability Rights Section** (✉ Box 66738, Washington, DC 20035, ☎ 202/514–0301 or 800/514–0301, FAX 202/307–1198, TTY 202/514–0383 or 800/514–0383). For airline-related problems, contact the U.S. Department of Transportation's **Aviation Consumer Protection Division** (☞ Air Travel, *above*). For complaints about surface transportation, contact the Department of Transportation's **Civil Rights Office** (☎ 202/366–4648).

LOCAL INFORMATION

Contact **London Transport's Unit for Disabled Passengers** (✉ 172 Buckingham Palace Rd., London SW1W 9TN ☎ 0171/918–3312) for details on **Stationlink,** a wheelchair-accessible "midibus" service, as well as information on other access information. **Artsline** (☎ 0171/388–2227) provides information on the accessibility of arts events.

ORGANIZATIONS

TRAVELERS WITH HEARING IMPAIRMENTS➢ The **American Academy of Otolaryngology** (✉ 1 Prince St., Alexandria, VA 22314, ☎ 703/836–4444, FAX 703/683–5100, TTY 703/519–1585) publishes a brochure, "Travel Tips for Hearing Impaired People."

TRAVELERS WITH MOBILITY PROBLEMS➢ Contact the **Information Center for Individuals with Disabilities** (✉ Box 256, Boston, MA 02117, ☎ 617/450–9888; in MA, 800/462–5015; TTY 617/424–6855); **Mobility International USA** (✉ Box 10767, Eugene, OR 97440, ☎ and TTY 503/343–1284, FAX 503/343–6812), the U.S. branch of a Belgium-based organization (☞ *below*) with affiliates in 30 countries; **MossRehab Hospital Travel Information Service** (☎ 215/456–9600, TTY 215/456–9602), a telephone information resource for travelers with physical disabilities; the **Society for the Advancement of Travel for the Handicapped** (✉ 347 5th Ave., Suite 610, New York, NY 10016, ☎ 212/447–7284, FAX 212/725–8253; membership $45); and **Travelin' Talk** (✉ Box 3534, Clarksville, TN 37043, ☎ 615/552–6670, FAX 615/552–1182) which provides local contacts worldwide for travelers with disabilities.

TRAVELERS WITH VISION IMPAIRMENTS➢ Contact the **American Council of the Blind** (✉ 1155 15th St. NW, Suite 720, Washington, DC 20005, ☎ 202/467–5081, FAX 202/467–5085) for a list of travelers' resources or the **American Foundation for the Blind** (✉ 11 Penn Plaza, Suite 300, New York, NY 10001, ☎ 212/502–7600 or 800/232–5463, TTY 212/502–7662), which provides general advice and publishes "Access to Art" ($19.95), a directory of museums that accommodate travelers with vision impairments.

IN THE U.K.

Contact the **Royal Association for Disability and Rehabilitation** (✉ RADAR, 12 City Forum, 250 City Rd., London EC1V 8AF, ☎ 0171/250–3222) or **Mobility International** (✉ rue de Manchester 25, B-1080 Brussels, Belgium, ☎ 00–322–410–6297, FAX 00–322–410–6874), an international travel-information clearing-house for people with disabilities.

PUBLICATIONS

Several publications for travelers with disabilities are available from the **Consumer Information Center** (✉ Box 100, Pueblo, CO 81009, ☎ 719/948–3334). Call or write for its free catalog of current titles. The Society for the Advancement of Travel for the Handicapped (☞ Organizations, *above*) publishes the quarterly magazine **"Access to Travel"** ($13 for 1-year subscription).

The 500-page ***Travelin' Talk Directory*** (✉ Box 3534, Clarksville, TN 37043, ☎ 615/552–6670, FAX 615/552–1182; $35) lists people and organizations who help travelers with disabilities. For travel agents worldwide, consult the ***Directory of Travel Agencies for the Disabled*** (✉ Twin Peaks Press, Box 129, Vancouver, WA 98666, ☎ 360/694–2462 or 800/637–2256, FAX 360/696–3210; $19.95 plus $3 shipping).

TRAVEL AGENCIES & TOUR OPERATORS

The Americans with Disabilities Act requires

that all travel firms serve the needs of all travelers. That said, you should note that some agencies and operators specialize in making travel arrangements for individuals and groups with disabilities, among them **Access Adventures** (✉ 206 Chestnut Ridge Rd., Rochester, NY 14624, ☎ 716/889–9096), run by a former physical-rehab counselor.

TRAVELERS WITH MOBILITY PROBLEMS➤ Contact **Accessible Journeys** (✉ 35 W. Sellers Ave., Ridley Park, PA 19078, ☎ 610/521–0339 or 800/846–4537, FAX 610/521–6959), a registered nursing service that arranges vacations; **Flying Wheels Travel** (✉ 143 W. Bridge St., Box 382, Owatonna, MN 55060, ☎ 507/451–5005 or 800/535–6790), a travel agency specializing in European cruises and tours; **Hinsdale Travel Service** (✉ 201 E. Ogden Ave., Suite 100, Hinsdale, IL 60521, ☎ 708/325–1335 or 800/303–5521), a travel agency that benefits from the advice of wheelchair traveler Janice Perkins; **Nautilus Tours** (✉ 5435 Donna Ave., Tarzana, CA 91356, ☎ 818/344–3640 or 800/345–4654); and **Wheelchair Journeys** (✉ 16979 Redmond Way, Redmond, WA 98052, ☎ 206/885–2210 or 800/313–4751), which can handle arrangements worldwide.

TRAVELERS WITH DEVELOPMENTAL DISABILITIES➤ Contact the nonprofit **New Directions** (✉ 5276 Hollister Ave., Suite 207, Santa Barbara, CA 93111, ☎ 805/967–2841).

TRAVEL GEAR

The **Magellan's** catalog (☎ 800/962–4943, FAX 805/568–5406), includes a range of products designed for travelers with disabilities.

DISCOUNTS & DEALS

AIRFARES

For the lowest airfares to London, call ☎ 800/FLY-4-LESS.

CLUBS

Contact **Entertainment Travel Editions** (✉ Box 1068, Trumbull, CT 06611, ☎ 800/445–4137; $28–$53, depending on destination), **Great American Traveler** (✉ Box 27965, Salt Lake City, UT 84127, ☎ 800/548–2812; $49.95 per year), **Moment's Notice Discount Travel Club** (✉ 163 Amsterdam Ave., Suite 137, New York, NY 10023, ☎ 212/486–0500; $25 per year, single or family), **Privilege Card** (✉ 3391 Peachtree Rd. NE, Suite 110, Atlanta, GA 30326, ☎ 404/262–0222 or 800/236–9732; $74.95 per year), **Travelers Advantage** (✉ CUC Travel Service, 49 Music Sq. W, Nashville, TN 37203, ☎ 800/548–1116 or 800/648–4037; $49 per year, single or family), or **Worldwide Discount Travel Club** (✉ 1674 Meridian Ave., Miami Beach, FL 33139, ☎ 305/534–2082; $50 per year for family, $40 single).

HOTEL ROOMS

For hotel room rates guaranteed in U.S. dollars, call **Steigenberger Reservation Service** (☎ 800/223–5652).

PASSES

See Train Travel and Underground Travel, *below.*

STUDENTS

Members of Hostelling International–American Youth Hostels (☞ Students, *below*) are eligible for discounts on car rentals, admissions to attractions, and other selected travel expenses.

PUBLICATIONS

Consult ***The Frugal Globetrotter,*** by Bruce Northam (✉ Fulcrum Publishing, 350 Indiana St., Suite 350, Golden, CO 80401, ☎ 800/992–2908; $15.95). For publications that tell how to find the lowest prices on plane tickets, *see* Air Travel, *above.*

Also see Fodor's ***Affordable London*** (available in bookstores, or ☎ 800/533–6478; $12.00).

G

GAY & LESBIAN TRAVEL

ORGANIZATIONS

The **International Gay Travel Association** (✉ Box 4974, Key West, FL 33041, ☎ 800/448–8550, FAX 305/296–6633), a consortium of more than 1,000 travel companies, can supply names of gay-friendly travel agents, tour operators, and accommodations.

PUBLICATIONS

The premier international travel magazine for gays and lesbians is

Our World (✉ 1104 N. Nova Rd., Suite 251, Daytona Beach, FL 32117, ☎ 904/441–5367, FAX 904/441–5604; $35 for 10 issues). The 16-page monthly **"Out & About"** (☎ 212/645–6922 or 800/929–2268, FAX 800/929–2215; $49 for 10 issues and quarterly calendar) covers gay-friendly resorts, hotels, cruise lines, and airlines.

TOUR OPERATORS

Hanns Ebensten Travel (✉ 513 Fleming St., Key West, FL 33040, ☎ 305/294–8174), one of the nation's oldest operators in the gay market, and **Toto Tours** (✉ 1326 W. Albion St., Suite 3W, Chicago, IL 60626, ☎ 312/274–8686 or 800/565–1241) offer group tours to worldwide destinations.

TRAVEL AGENCIES

The largest agencies serving gay travelers are **Advance Travel** (✉ 10700 Northwest Fwy., Suite 160, Houston, TX 77092, ☎ 713/682–2002 or 800/695–0880), **Islanders/Kennedy Travel** (✉ 183 W. 10th St., New York, NY 10014, ☎ 212/242–3222 or 800/988–1181), **Now Voyager** (✉ 4406 18th St., San Francisco, CA 94114, ☎ 415/626–1169 or 800/255–6951), and **Yellowbrick Road** (✉ 1500 W. Balmoral Ave., Chicago, IL 60640, ☎ 312/561–1800 or 800/642–2488). **Skylink Women's Travel** (✉ 3577 Moorland Ave., Santa Rosa, CA 95407, ☎ 707/588–9961 or 800/225–5759) serves lesbian travelers.

H

HEALTH ISSUES

MEDICAL ASSISTANCE COMPANIES

The following companies are concerned primarily with emergency medical assistance, although they may provide some insurance as part of their coverage. For a list of full-service travel insurance companies, ☞ Insurance, *below.*

Contact **International SOS Assistance** (✉ Box 11568, Philadelphia, PA 19116, ☎ 215/244–1500 or 800/523–8930; ✉ Box 466, Pl. Bonaventure, Montréal, Québec H5A 1C1, ☎ 514/874–7674 or 800/363–0263; ✉ 7 Old Lodge Pl., St. Margarets, Twickenham TW1 1RQ, England, ☎ 0181/744–0033), **Medex Assistance Corporation** (✉ Box 10623, Baltimore, MD 21285, ☎ 410/453–6300 or 800/573–2029), **Traveler's Emergency Network** (✉ 3100 Tower Blvd., Suite 3100A, Durham, NC 27702, ☎ 919/490–6065 or 800/275–4836, FAX 919/493–8262), **TravMed** (✉ Box 5375, Baltimore, MD 24094, ☎ 800/732–5309), or **Worldwide Assistance Services** (✉ 1133 15th St. NW, Suite 400, Washington, DC 20005, ☎ 202/331–1609 or 800/821–2828, FAX 202/828–5896).

I

INSURANCE

IN CANADA

Contact **Mutual of Omaha** (✉ Travel Division, 500 University Ave., Toronto, Ontario M5G 1V8, ☎ 800/268–8825 or 416/598–4321).

IN THE U.S.

Travel insurance covering baggage, health, and trip cancellation or interruptions is available from **Access America** (✉ Box 90315, Richmond, VA 23286, ☎ 804/285–3300 or 800/284–8300), **Carefree Travel Insurance** (✉ Box 9366, 100 Garden City Plaza, Garden City, NY 11530, ☎ 516/294–0220 or 800/323–3149), **Near Travel Services** (✉ Box 1339, Calumet City, IL 60409, ☎ 708/868–6700 or 800/654–6700), **Tele-Trip** (✉ Mutual of Omaha Plaza, Box 31716, Omaha, NE 68131, ☎ 800/228–9792), **Travel Guard International** (✉ 1145 Clark St., Stevens Point, WI 54481, ☎ 715/345–0505 or 800/826–1300), **Travel Insured International** (✉ Box 280568, East Hartford, CT 06128, ☎ 203/528–7663 or 800/243–3174), and **Wallach & Company** (✉ 107 W. Federal St., Box 480, Middleburg, VA 22117, ☎ 703/687–3166 or 800/237–6615).

L

LODGING

For information on hotel consolidators, ☞ Discounts, *above.*

APARTMENT & VILLA RENTAL

Among the companies to contact are **At Home Abroad** (✉ 405 E. 56th St., Suite 6H, New York, NY 10022, ☎ 212/421–9165,

FAX 212/752–1591), **Europa-Let** (✉ 92 N. Main St., Ashland, OR 97520, ☎ 541/482–5806 or 800/462–4486, FAX 541/482–0660), **Hometours International** (✉ Box 11503, Knoxville, TN 37939, ☎ 615/588–8722 or 800/367–4668), **Interhome** (✉ 124 Little Falls Rd., Fairfield, NJ 07004, ☎ 201/882–6864, FAX 201/808–1742), **Property Rentals International** (✉ 1008 Mansfield Crossing Rd., Richmond, VA 23236, ☎ 804/378–6054 or 800/220–3332, FAX 804/379–2073), **Rental Directories International** (✉ 2044 Rittenhouse Sq., Philadelphia, PA 19103, ☎ 215/985–4001, FAX 215/985–0323), **Rent-a-Home International** (✉ 7200 34th Ave. NW, Seattle, WA 98117, ☎ 206/789–9377 or 800/488–7368, FAX 206/789–9379, hmaria@aol.com), **Vacation Home Rentals Worldwide** (✉ 235 Kensington Ave., Norwood, NJ 07648, ☎ 201/767–9393 or 800/633–3284, FAX 201/767–5510), **Villas and Apartments Abroad** (✉ 420 Madison Ave., Suite 1003, New York, NY 10017, ☎ 212/759–1025 or 800/433–3020, FAX 212/755–8316), and **Villas International** (✉ 605 Market St., Suite 510, San Francisco, CA 94105, ☎ 415/281–0910 or 800/221–2260, FAX 415/281–0919). Members of the travel club **Hideaways International** (✉ 767 Islington St., Portsmouth, NH 03801, ☎ 603/430–4433 or 800/843–4433, FAX 603/430–4444, info@hideaways.com; $99 per year) receive two annual guides plus quarterly newsletters and arrange rentals among themselves.

HOME EXCHANGE

Some of the principal clearinghouses are **HomeLink International/Vacation Exchange Club** (✉ Box 650, Key West, FL 33041, ☎ 305/294–1448 or 800/638–3841, FAX 305/294–1148; $70 per year), which sends members three annual directories, with a listing in one, plus updates; **Intervac International** (✉ Box 590504, San Francisco, CA 94159, ☎ 415/435–3497, FAX 415/435–7440; $65 per year), which publishes four annual directories.

M

MAIL

The **London Chief Post Office** at Trafalgar Square (✉ 24–28 William IV St., London WC2N 4DL) is open Monday–Saturday 8–8. They will hold international mail for one month. The **Trafalgar Square Post Office** (✉ 24–28 William IV St., WC2N 4DL, ☎ 0171/930–9580) is open Monday–Saturday 8–8. Most other post offices are open weekdays 9–5:30, Saturday 9–12:30 or 1.

MONEY MATTERS

ATMS

For specific foreign **Cirrus** locations, call 800/424–7787; for foreign **Plus** locations, consult the Plus directory at your local bank.

CURRENCY EXCHANGE

If your bank doesn't exchange currency, contact **Thomas Cook Currency Services** (☎ 800/287–7362 for locations). **Ruesch International** (☎ 800/424–2923 for locations) can also provide you with foreign banknotes before you leave home and publishes a number of useful brochures, including a "Foreign Currency Guide" and "Foreign Exchange Tips."

WIRING FUNDS

Funds can be wired via **MoneyGram℠** (for locations and information in the U.S. and Canada, ☎ 800/926–9400) or **Western Union** (for agent locations or to send money using MasterCard or Visa, ☎ 800/325–6000; in Canada, 800/321–2923; in the U.K., 0800/833833; or visit the Western Union office at the nearest major post office).

P

PACKING

For strategies on packing light, get a copy of ***The Packing Book,*** by Judith Gilford (✉ Ten Speed Press, Box 7123, Berkeley, CA 94707, ☎ 510/559–1600 or 800/841–2665, FAX 510/524–4588; $7.95).

PASSPORTS & VISAS

IN THE U.S.

For fees, documentation requirements, and other information, call the State Department's **Office of Passport Services** information line (☎ 202/647–0518).

CANADIANS

For fees, documentation requirements, and other

information, call the Ministry of Foreign Affairs and International Trade's **Passport Office** (☎ 819/994–3500 or 800/567–6868).

PHOTO HELP

The **Kodak Information Center** (☎ 800/242–2424) answers consumer questions about film and photography. The ***Kodak Guide to Shooting Great Travel Pictures*** (available in bookstores; or contact Fodor's Travel Publications, ☎ 800/533–6478; $16.50) explains how to take expert travel photographs.

S

SAFETY

"Trouble-Free Travel," from the AAA, is a booklet of tips for protecting yourself and your belongings when away from home. Send a stamped, self-addressed, legal-size envelope to Flying Alone (✉ Mail Stop 75, 1000 AAA Dr., Heathrow, FL 32746).

SENIOR CITIZENS

ORGANIZATIONS

Contact the **American Association of Retired Persons** (✉ AARP, 601 E St. NW, Washington, DC 20049, ☎ 202/434–2277; annual dues $8 per person or couple). Its Purchase Privilege Program secures discounts for members on lodging, car rentals, and sightseeing.

Additional sources for discounts on lodgings, car rentals, and other travel expenses, as well as helpful magazines and newsletters, are the **National Council of Senior Citizens** (✉ 1331 F St. NW, Washington, DC 20004, ☎ 202/347–8800; annual membership $12) and Sears's **Mature Outlook** (✉ Box 10448, Des Moines, IA 50306, ☎ 800/336–6330; annual membership $9.95).

PUBLICATIONS

The 50+ Traveler's Guidebook: Where to Go, Where to Stay, What to Do, by Anita Williams and Merrimac Dillon (✉ St. Martin's Press, 175 5th Ave., New York, NY 10010, ☎ 212/674–5151 or 800/288–2131; $13.95), offers many useful tips. **"The Mature Traveler"** (✉ Box 50400, Reno, NV 89513, ☎ 702/786–7419; $29.95), a monthly newsletter, covers all sorts of travel deals.

SIGHTSEEING

BY CANAL

During summer, narrow boats and barges cruise London's two canals, the Grand Union and Regent's Canal; most vessels (they seat about 60) operate on the latter, which runs between Little Venice in the west (nearest tube: Warwick Avenue on the Bakerloo Line) and Camden Lock (about 200 yards north of Camden Town tube station). **Jason's Trip** (☎ 0171/286–3428) operates one-way and round-trip narrow-boat cruises on this route. During April, May, and September, there are two cruises per day; from June to August, there are four. Trips last 1½ hours and cost £3.75 for adults, £2.50 for children and senior citizens round-trip.

London Waterbus Co. (☎ 0171/482–2550) offers the Zoo Waterbus service daily from March to September, on weekends in winter. A round-trip canal cruise, London Zoo—Camden Lock, costs £3.20 for adults, £1.90 for children. Combined zoo entrance—waterbus tickets are also available.

Canal Cruises (☎ 0171/485–4433) also offers cruises from March to October on the *Jenny Wren* (£3.90), and all year on the floating restaurant *My Fair Lady* (Tues.–Sat. dinner and entertainment, £26.95; Sun. lunch, £16.95).

BY RIVER

From April to October, boats cruise the Thames, offering a different view of the London skyline. Most leave from Westminster Pier (☎ 0171/930–4097), Charing Cross Pier (Victoria Embankment, ☎ 0171/839–3572), and Tower Pier (☎ 0171/488–0344). Downstream routes go to the Tower of London, Greenwich, and the Thames Barrier; upstream destinations include Kew, Richmond, and Hampton Court. Most of the launches seat between 100 and 250 passengers, have a public-address system, and provide a running commentary on passing points of interest. Depending upon the destination, river trips may last from one to four hours. For more information, call **Catamaran Cruisers** (☎ 0171/839–3572), **Tidal Cruises** (☎ 0171/928–9009), or **Westminster Passenger**

Services Association (☎ 0171/930–4097).

STUDENTS

GROUPS

The major tour operators specializing in student travel are **Contiki Holidays** (✉ 300 Plaza Alicante, Suite 900, Garden Grove, CA 92640, ☎ 714/740–0808 or 800/466–0610) and **AESU Travel** (✉ 2 Hamill Rd., Suite 248, Baltimore, MD 21210–1807, ☎ 410/323–4416 or 800/638–7640).

HOSTELING

In the United States, contact **Hostelling International–American Youth Hostels** (✉ 733 15th St. NW, Suite 840, Washington, DC 20005, ☎ 202/783–6161 or 800/444–6111 for reservations at selected hostels, FAX 202/783–6171); in Canada, **Hostelling International–Canada** (✉ 205 Catherine St., Suite 400, Ottawa, Ontario K2P 1C3, ☎ 613/237–7884); and in the United Kingdom, the **Youth Hostel Association of England and Wales** (✉ Trevelyan House, 8 St. Stephen's Hill, St. Albans, Hertfordshire AL1 2DY, ☎ 01727/855215 or 01727/845047). Membership (in the U.S., $25; in Canada, C$26.75; in the U.K., £9.30) gives you access to 5,000 hostels in 77 countries that charge $5–$30 per person per night.

I.D. CARDS

To be eligible for discounts on transportation and admissions, get either the **International Student Identity Card,** if you're a bona fide student, or the **GO 25: International Youth Travel Card,** if you're not a student but under age 26. Each includes basic travel-accident and illness coverage, plus a toll-free travel hot line. In the United States, either card costs $18; apply through the Council on International Educational Exchange (☞ Organizations, *below*). In Canada, cards are available for $15 each ($16 by mail) from Travel Cuts (☞ Organizations, *below*), and in the United Kingdom for £5 each at student unions and student travel companies.

ORGANIZATIONS

A major contact is the **Council on International Educational Exchange** (mail orders only: ✉ CIEE, 205 E. 42nd St., 16th Floor, New York, NY 10017, ☎ 212/661–1450), with walk-in locations in Boston (✉ 729 Boylston St., 02116, ☎ 617/266–1926), Miami (✉ 9100 S. Dadeland Blvd., 33156, ☎ 305/670–9261), Los Angeles (✉ 10904 Lindbrook Dr., 90024, ☎ 310/208–3551), 43 other college towns in the U.S., and in the United Kingdom (✉ 28A Poland St., London W1V 3DB, ☎ 0171/437–7767). Twice per year, it publishes *Student Travels* magazine. The CIEE's Council Travel Service offers domestic air passes for bargain travel within the United States and is the exclusive U.S. agent for several student discount cards.

The **Educational Travel Centre** (✉ 438 N. Frances St., Madison, WI 53703, ☎ 608/256–5551 or 800/747–5551, FAX 608/256–2042) offers rail passes and low-cost airline tickets, mostly for flights that depart from Chicago.

In Canada, also contact **Travel Cuts** (✉ 187 College St., Toronto, Ontario M5T 1P7, ☎ 416/979–2406 or 800/667–2887).

PUBLICATIONS

Check out the ***Berkeley Guide to London*** (available in bookstores; or contact Fodor's Travel Publications, ☎ 800/533–6478; $12.00).

SUBWAY TRAVEL

In London, the transportation system is known as the Underground or, more affectionately, the "Tube." For details, ☞ Underground Travel, *below.*

T

TELEPHONE MATTERS

The country code for Britain is 44. There are two area codes in London, 0171 for inner London and 0181 for outer London. For local access numbers abroad, contact **AT&T** USA Direct (☎ 800/874–4000), **MCI** Call USA (☎ 800/444–4444), or **Sprint** Express (☎ 800/793–1153).

TOUR OPERATORS

Among the companies that sell tours and packages to London, the following are nationally known, have a proven reputation, and offer plenty of options.

GROUP TOURS

SUPER-DELUXE➢ **Abercrombie & Kent**

(✉ 1520 Kensington Rd., Oak Brook, IL 60521-2141, ☎ 708/954–2944 or 800/323–7308, FAX 708/954–3324) and **Travcoa** (✉ Box 2630, 2350 S.E. Bristol St., Newport Beach, CA 92660, ☎ 714/476–2800 or 800/992–2003, FAX 714/476–2538).

DELUXE➢ **Globus** (✉ 5301 S. Federal Circle, Littleton, CO 80123-2980, ☎ 303/797–2800 or 800/221–0090, FAX 303/795–0962), **Maupintour** (✉ Box 807, 1515 St. Andrews Dr., Lawrence, KS 66047, ☎ 913/843–1211 or 800/255–4266, FAX 913/843–8351), and **Tauck Tours** (✉ Box 5027, 276 Post Rd. W, Westport, CT 06881, ☎ 203/226–6911 or 800/468–2825, FAX 203/221–6828).

FIRST CLASS➢ **Brendan Tours** (✉ 15137 Califa St., Van Nuys, CA 91411, ☎ 818/785–9696 or 800/421–8446, FAX 818/902–9876), **British Airways Holidays** (☎ 800/247–9297), **Caravan Tours** (✉ 401 N. Michigan Ave., Chicago, IL 60611, ☎ 312/321–9800 or 800/227–2826), **CIE Tours** (✉ 108 Ridgedale Ave., Morristown, NJ 07960, ☎ 201/292–3438 or 800/243–8687), **Collette Tours** (✉ 162 Middle St., Pawtucket, RI 02860, ☎ 401/728–3805 or 800/832–4656, FAX 401/728–1380), **Insight International Tours** (✉ 745 Atlantic Ave., #720, Boston, MA 02111, ☎ 617/482–2000 or 800/582–8380, FAX 617/482–2884 or 800/622–5015), and **Trafalgar Tours** (✉ 11 E. 26th St., New York, NY 10010, ☎ 212/689–8977 or 800/854–0103, FAX 800/457–6644).

BUDGET➢ **Cosmos** (☞ Globus, *above*) or **Trafalgar** (☞ *above*).

PACKAGES

Just about every airline that flies to London sells packages that include round-trip airfare and hotel accommodations. Carriers to contact include **American Airlines Fly AAway Vacations** (☎ 800/321–2121), **British Airways Holidays** (☞ *above*), **Continental Vacations** (☎ 800/634–5555), **Delta Dream Vacations** (☎ 800/872–7786), and **United Vacations** (☎ 800/328–6877). Other packagers are **Celtic International Tours** (✉ 1860 Western Ave., Albany, NY 12203, ☎ 518/463–5511 or 800/833–4373), **CIE Tours** (✉ Box 501, 100 Hanover Ave., Cedar Knolls, NJ 07927-0501, ☎ 201/292–3899 or 800/243–8687), **DER Tours** (✉ 11933 Wilshire Blvd., Los Angeles, CA 90025, ☎ 310/479–4140 or 800/782–2424), and **Jet Vacations** (✉ 1775 Broadway, New York, NY 10019, ☎ 212/474–8740 or 800/538–2762). **Funjet Vacations,** based in Milwaukee, Wisconsin, and **Gogo Tours,** based in Ramsey, New Jersey, sell packages only through travel agents.

Regional operators specialize in putting together London packages for travelers in their local area. Arrangements may include charter or scheduled air. Contact **Travel Impressions** (✉ 465 Smith St., Farmingdale, NY 11735, ☎ 516/845–8000 or 800/284–0044, FAX 516/845–8095).

For independent self-drive itineraries, contact **Budget WorldClass Drive** (☎ 800/527–0700; in the U.K., 0800/181181).

FROM THE U.K.➢ Contact the **London Travel Service** (✉ Bridge House, High Rd., Broxbourne, Hertfordshire EN10 7DT, ☎ 01992/456–177) for centrally situated hotels, theater, and entertainment; or call **Highlife** (✉ Box 139, Leeds LS2 7TE, ☎ 0800/700–400).

THEME TRIPS

Travel Contacts (✉ Box 173, Camberley, England GU15 1YE, ☎ 27667–7217, FAX 2766–3477), which represents 150 tour operators, can satisfy virtually any special interest in London. **Great British Vacations** (✉ 4800 S.W. Griffith Dr., #125, Beaverton, OR 97005, ☎ 503/643–8080 or 800/452–8434) creates custom-designed itineraries that include walking and visting gardens and stately homes.

ANTIQUES➢ **Travel Keys Tours** (✉ Box 162266, Sacramento, CA 95816, ☎ 916/452–5200) specializes in tours to the antique fairs and flea markets of Europe.

COOKING➢ If you want to learn French cooking, **Le Cordon Bleu** (✉ 404 Irvington St., Pleasantville, NY 10570, ☎ 800/457–2433 in U.S.), one of the world's best-known cooking schools, has courses for beginners and connoisseurs.

HOMES AND GARDENS➢ **Coopersmith's England** (✉ Box 900, Inverness, CA 94937, ☎ 415/669–1914, FAX 415/669–1942) will wine and dine you with gourmet meals and book your accommodations in castles, historic country inns, and manor houses. **Expo Garden Tours** (✉ 101 Sunrise Hill Rd., Norwalk, CT 06851, ☎ 203/840–1441 or 800/448–2685, FAX 203/840–1224) visits the annual Chelsea Flower Show.

PERFORMING ARTS➢ **Dailey-Thorp Travel** (✉ 330 W. 58th St., #610, New York, NY 10019-1817, ☎ 212/307–1555 or 800/998–4677, FAX 212/974–1420) specializes in classical music and opera programs throughout Europe. **Keith Prowse Tours** (✉ 234 W. 44th St., #1000, New York, NY 10036, ☎ 212/398–1430 or 800/669–8687, FAX 212/302–4251, tickets@keithprowse.com, http://www.keithprowse.com) arranges theater, flower-show, and horse-racing programs in London.

TENNIS➢ **Championship Tennis Tours** (✉ 7350 E. Stetson Dr., #106, Scottsdale, AZ 85251, ☎ 602/990–8760 or 800/468–3664, FAX 602/990–8744, mike@tennistours.com, http://www.tennis-tours.com), **Sportstours** (✉ 2301 Collins Ave., #A1540, Miami Beach, FL 33139, ☎ 800/879–8647, FAX 305/535–0008), and **Steve Furgal's International Tennis Tours** (✉ 11828 Rancho Bernardo Rd., #123–305, San Diego, CA 92128, ☎ 619/487–7777 or 800/258–3664) have packages to Wimbledon, held each summer in London.

VILLA RENTALS➢ Contact **Villas International** (✉ 605 Market St., San Francisco, CA 94105, ☎ 415/281–0910 or 800/221–2260, FAX 415/281–0919).

ORGANIZATIONS

The **National Tour Association** (✉ NTA, 546 E. Main St., Lexington, KY 40508, ☎ 606/226–4444 or 800/755–8687) and the **United States Tour Operators Association** (✉ USTOA, 211 E. 51st St., Suite 12B, New York, NY 10022, ☎ 212/750–7371) can provide lists of members and information on booking tours.

PUBLICATIONS

Contact the USTOA (☞ Organizations, *above*) for its **"Smart Traveler's Planning Kit."** Pamphlets in the kit include the "Worldwide Tour and Vacation Package Finder," "How to Select a Tour or Vacation Package," and information on the organization's consumer protection plan. Also get copy of the Better Business Bureau's **"Tips on Travel Packages"** (✉ Publication 24–195, 4200 Wilson Blvd., Arlington, VA 22203; $2).

TRAIN TRAVEL

DISCOUNT PASSES

BritRail Passes are available from most travel agents or from **BritRail Travel International** offices (✉ 1500 Broadway, New York, NY 10036, ☎ 212/575–2667; ✉ 94 Cumberland St., Toronto, Ontario M5R 1A3, ☎ 416/482–1777). Note that EurailPasses are not valid in Britain.

In London, contact the British Rail Travel Centre (✉ Euston Station, London NW1 1DF, ☎ 0171/387–7070).

TRAVEL AGENCIES

For names of reputable agencies in your area, contact the **American Society of Travel Agents** (✉ ASTA, 1101 King St., Suite 200, Alexandria, VA 22314, ☎ 703/739–2782), the **Association of Canadian Travel Agents** (✉ Suite 201, 1729 Bank St., Ottawa, Ontario K1V 7Z5, ☎ 613/521–0474, FAX 613/521–0805) or the **Association of British Travel Agents** (✉ 55-57 Newman St., London W1P 4AH, ☎ 0171/637–2444, FAX 0171/637–0713).

TRAVEL GEAR

For travel apparel, appliances, personal-care items, and other travel necessities, get a free catalog from **Magellan's** (☎ 800/962–4943, FAX 805/568–5406), **Orvis Travel** (☎ 800/541–3541, FAX 703/343–7053), or **TravelSmith** (☎ 800/950–1600, FAX 415/455–0554).

ELECTRICAL CONVERTERS

Send a self-addressed, stamped envelope to the **Franzus Company** (✉ Customer Service, Dept. B50, Murtha Industrial Park, Box 142, Beacon Falls, CT

06403, ☎ 203/723-6664) for a copy of the free brochure "Foreign Electricity Is No Deep, Dark Secret."

U

UNDERGROUND TRAVEL

PASSES

Several passes for tube and bus travel are available at tube and rail stations, as well as some newsstands. The **One Day Travelcard** allows unrestricted travel on both bus and tube and is valid weekdays after 9:30 AM, weekends, and all national holidays (cost: £2.80–£3.80). The **LT Card** is the same as above, but without the time restrictions (cost: £3.90–£6.50). There are also weekly and monthly **Travelcards** valid for bus and tube travel; the cost varies according to distance and the number of zones covered. The **Visitor's Travelcard** may be bought in the United States and Canada for three, four, and seven days' travel; it is the same as the LT Card and has a booklet of discount vouchers to London attractions. In the United States, the Visitor's Travelcard costs $25, $32, and $49, respectively; in Canada, C$29, C$36, and C$55, respectively. Apply to travel agents or, in the United States, to BritRail Travel International (✉ 1500 Broadway, New York, NY 10036, ☎ 212/382-3737).

U.S. GOVERNMENT TRAVEL BRIEFINGS

The U.S. Department of State's American Citizens Services office (✉ Room 4811, Washington, DC 20520; enclose SASE) issues **Consular Information Sheets** on all foreign countries. These cover issues such as crime, security, political climate, and health risks as well as listing embassy locations, entry requirements, currency regulations, and providing other useful information. For the latest information, stop in at any U.S. passport office, consulate, or embassy; call the interactive hot line (☎ 202/647-5225, FAX 202/647-3000); or, with your PC's modem, tap into the department's computer bulletin board (☎ 202/647-9225).

V

VISITOR INFORMATION

Contact the **British Tourist Authority (BTA)** in the United States (✉ 551 5th Ave., Suite 701, New York, NY 10176, ☎ 212/986-2200 or 800/462-2748; ✉ 625 N. Michigan Ave., Suite 1510, Chicago, IL 60611, ☎ 312/787-0490; ✉ World Trade Center, 350 S. Figueroa St., Suite 450, Los Angeles, CA 90071, ☎ 213/628-3525; ✉ 2580 Cumberland Pkwy., Suite 470, Atlanta, GA 30339, ☎ 404/432-9635), in Canada (✉ 111 Avenue Rd., 4th floor, Toronto, Ontario M5R 3J8, ☎ 416/925-6326), and in the United Kingdom (✉ Thames Tower, Black's Rd., London W6 9EL).

IN THE U.K.

In London go in person to the **London Tourist Information Centre** at Victoria Station Forecourt for general information Monday–Saturday 8–7 and Sunday 8–5, or to the **British Travel Centre** (✉ 12 Regent St., SW1Y 4PQ) for travel, hotel, and entertainment information weekdays 9–6:30, weekends 10–4.

The London Tourist Board's **Visitorcall** (☎ 0839/123456) phone guide to London gives information about events, theater, museums, transport, shopping, and restaurants. A three-month events calendar (☎ 0839/401279) and an annual version (☎ 0839/401278) are available by fax (set fax machine to polling mode, or press start/receive after the tone). Visitorcall charges are 39p–49p per minute, depending on the time of the call.

W

WEATHER

For current conditions and forecasts, plus the local time and helpful travel tips, call the **Weather Channel Connection** (☎ 900/932-8437; 95¢ per minute) from a Touch-Tone phone.

The ***International Traveler's Weather Guide*** (✉ Weather Press, Box 660606, Sacramento, CA 95866, ☎ 916/974-0201 or 800/972-0201; $10.95 includes shipping), written by two meteorologists, provides month-by-month information on temperature, humidity, and precipitation in more than 175 cities worldwide.

SMART TRAVEL TIPS A TO Z

Basic Information on Traveling in London & Savvy Tips to Make Your Trip a Breeze

A

AIR TRAVEL

If time is an issue, **always look for nonstop flights,** which require no change of plane. If possible, **avoid connecting flights,** which stop at least once and can involve a change of plane, even though the flight number remains the same; if the first leg is late, the second waits.

For better service, **fly smaller or regional carriers,** which often have higher passenger satisfaction ratings. Sometimes they have such in-flight amenities as leather seats or greater legroom and they often have better food.

CUTTING COSTS

The Sunday travel section of most newspapers is a good place to look for deals.

MAJOR AIRLINES➢ The least-expensive airfares from the major airlines are priced for round-trip travel and are subject to restrictions. Usually, you must **book in advance and buy the ticket within 24 hours** to get cheaper fares, and you may have to **stay over a Saturday night.** The lowest fare is subject to availability, and only a small percentage of the plane's total seats is sold at that price. It's smart to **call a number of airlines, and when you are quoted a good price, book it on the spot**—the same fare may not be available on the same flight the next day. Airlines generally allow you to change your return date for a $25 to $50 fee. If you don't use your ticket, you can apply the cost toward the purchase of a new ticket, again for a small charge. However, most low-fare tickets are nonrefundable. To get the lowest airfare, **check different routings.** If your destination has more than one gateway, **compare prices to different airports.**

CONSOLIDATORS➢ Consolidators buy tickets for scheduled flights at reduced rates from the airlines, then sell them at prices below the lowest available from the airlines directly—usually without advance restrictions. Sometimes you can even get your money back if you need to return the ticket. Carefully read the fine print detailing penalties for changes and cancellations. If you doubt the reliability of a consolidator, **confirm your reservation with the airline.**

ALOFT

AIRLINE FOOD➢ If you hate airline food, **ask for special meals when booking.** These can be vegetarian, low-cholesterol, or kosher, for example; commonly prepared to order in smaller quantities than standard fare, they can be tastier.

JET LAG➢ To avoid this syndrome, which occurs when travel disrupts your body's natural cycles, try to maintain a normal routine. At night, **get some sleep.** By day, move about the cabin to **stretch your legs, eat light meals, and drink water—not alcohol.**

SMOKING➢ Smoking is banned on all flights of less than six hours' duration within the United States and on all Canadian flights; the ban also applies to domestic segments of international flights aboard U.S. and foreign carriers. Delta has banned smoking system-wide. On U.S. carriers flying to London and other destinations abroad, a seat in a no-smoking section must be provided for every passenger who requests one, and the section must be enlarged to accommodate such passengers as long as they have complied with the airline's deadline for check-in and seat assignment. If smoking bothers you, request a seat far from the smoking section.

Foreign airlines are exempt from these rules but do provide no-smoking sections; British Airways has banned smoking, as has Virgin Atlantic on most international flights. Some countries have banned smoking on all domestic flights, and others may not allow smoking on some flights. Talks continue on the feasibility of broadening no-smoking policies.

B

BUS TRAVEL

London's bus system consists of bright red double- and single-deckers, plus other buses of various colors. Destinations are displayed on the front and back, and the bus number is on the front, back, and side. Not all buses run the full length of their route at all times. Some buses still have a conductor whom you pay after finding a seat, but there are a lot of "one-man" buses on the road, in which you pay the driver upon boarding. One-way fares start at 90p in the central zone.

Buses stop only at clearly indicated stops. Main stops—at which the bus *should* stop automatically—have a plain white background with a red *LT* symbol on it. There are also request stops with red signs, a white symbol, and the word "Request" added; at these you must hail the bus to make it stop. Smoking is not allowed on any bus. Although you can see much of the town from a bus, ***don't take one if you want to get anywhere in a hurry;*** traffic often slows to a crawl, and during rush hour you may find yourself waiting 40 minutes for a bus and then not being able to get on it once it arrives. If you do go by bus, ask at a Travel Information Centre for a free London Bus Map.

FARES

One-way fares start at 90p in the central zone. Travelcards (☞ Undergound Travel *in* Important Contacts A to Z) are good for both tube and bus.

C

CAMERAS AND CAMCORDERS

PHOTOGRAPHY

If your camera is new or if you haven't used it for a while, **shoot and develop a few rolls of film** before you leave. Always **store film in a cool, dry place**—never in your car's glove compartment or on the shelf under the rear window.

Select the right film for your purpose—**use print film if you plan to frame or display your pictures,** but **use slide film if you hope to publish your shots.** Also, **consider black-and-white film** for different and dramatic images. For best results, **use a custom lab** for processing; use a one-hour lab only if time is a factor.

The chances of your film growing cloudy increase with each pass through an X-ray machine. To protect against this, carry it in a clear plastic bag and **ask for hand inspection at security.** Such requests are virtually always honored at U.S. airports, and are usually accommodated abroad. Don't depend on a lead-lined bag to protect film in checked luggage—the airline may increase the radiation to see what's inside.

Keep a skylight or haze filter on your camera at all times to protect the expensive (and delicate) lens glass from scratches. Better yet, **use an 81B warming filter,** which—unlike skylight or haze filters—really works in overcast conditions and will pump up those sunrises and sunsets.

VIDEO

Before your trip, **test your camcorder, invest in a skylight filter to protect the lens, and charge the batteries.** (Airport security personnel may ask you to turn on the camcorder to prove that it's what it appears to be.) The batteries of most newer camcorders can be recharged with a universal or worldwide AC adapter-charger (or multivoltage converter), whether the voltage is 110 or 220. All that's needed is the appropriate plug.

Videotape is not damaged by X-rays, but it may be harmed by the magnetic field of a walk-through metal detector, so **ask that videotapes be hand-checked.** Prerecorded videotape sold in Great Britain is based on the PAL standard, which will not play back in the United States. Blank tapes bought in London can be used for camcorder taping, but they are pricey. Some U.S. audiovisual shops convert foreign tapes to U.S. standards; contact an electronics dealer to find the nearest.

CAR RENTAL

When considering a rental car, it's worth

noting that unless you are going to be traveling extensively outside London, a car in the city is often more of a liability than an asset. Remember that Britain drives on the left, and the rest of Europe on the right. Therefore, you may want to leave your rented car in Britain and pick up a left-side drive if you cross the Channel. ☞ Driving, *below.*

CUTTING COSTS

To get the best deal, **book through a travel agent who is willing to shop around.** When pricing cars, **ask where the rental lot is located.** Some off-airport locations offer lower rates—even though their lots are only minutes away from the terminal via complimentary shuttle. You also may want to **price local car-rental companies,** whose rates may be lower still, although service and maintenance standards may not be as high as those of a national firm. Ask your agent to **look for fly-drive packages,** which also save you money, and **ask if local taxes are included** in the rental or fly-drive price. These can be as high as 20% in some destinations. Don't forget to find out about required deposits, cancellation penalties, drop-off charges, and the cost of any required insurance coverage.

Also **ask your travel agent about a company's customer-service record.** How has it responded to late plane arrivals and vehicle mishaps? Are there often lines at the rental counter, and—if you're traveling during a holiday period—does a confirmed reservation guarantee you a car?

Always **find out what equipment is standard** at your destination before specifying what you want; automatic transmission and air-conditioning are usually optional—and very expensive. You may, however, consider paying extra for an automatic if you are unfamiliar with manual transmissions. Driving on the "wrong" side of the road will probably be enough to worry about.

Be sure to **look into wholesalers**—companies that do not own their own fleets but rent in bulk from those that do and often offer better rates than traditional car-rental operations. Prices are best during off-peak periods; rentals booked through wholesalers must be paid for before you leave the United States.

INSURANCE

When driving a rented car, you are generally responsible for any damage to or loss of the rental vehicle. Before you rent, **see what coverage you already have** under the terms of your personal auto insurance policy and credit cards.

If you do not have auto insurance or an umbrella insurance policy that covers damage to third parties, purchasing CDW or LDW is highly recommended.

Collision policies that car-rental companies sell for European rentals typically do not cover stolen vehicles. Before you buy additional coverage for theft, find out if your credit card or personal auto insurance will cover the loss.

LICENSE REQUIREMENTS

In London your own driver's license is acceptable. An International Driver's Permit is a good idea; it's available from the American or Canadian automobile associations, or, in the United Kingdom, from the AA or RAC.

SURCHARGES

Before you pick up a car in one city and leave it in another, **ask about drop-off charges or one-way service fees,** which can be substantial. Note, too, that some rental agencies charge extra if you return the car before the time specified on your contract. To avoid a hefty refueling fee, **fill the tank just before you turn in the car**—but be aware that gas stations near the rental outlet may overcharge.

THE CHANNEL TUNNEL

The "Chunnel" is the fastest way to cross the English Channel short of flying—35 minutes from Folkestone to Calais, 60 minutes from motorway to motorway, or 3 hours from Waterloo, London, to Paris's Gare du Nord. It consists of two large 50-kilometer- (31-mile-) long train tunnels, and a smaller service tunnel running between them.

CHILDREN & TRAVEL

When traveling with children, **plan ahead** and **involve your youngsters** as you outline your trip. When packing, **include a supply of things to keep them busy** en route (☞ Children & Travel *in* Important Contacts A to Z). On sightseeing days, try to **schedule activities of special interest to your children,** like a trip to a zoo or a playground. If you **plan your itinerary around seasonal festivals,** you'll never lack for things to do. In addition, **check local newspapers for special events** mounted by public libraries, museums, and parks.

BABY-SITTING

For recommended local sitters, **check with your hotel desk.**

DRIVING

If you are renting a car, don't forget to **arrange for a car seat when you reserve.** Sometimes they're free.

FLYING

Always **ask about discounted children's fares.** On international flights, infants under 2 not occupying a seat generally travel free or for 10% of the accompanying adult's fare; the fare for children ages 2–11 is usually half to two-thirds of the adult fare. On domestic flights, children under 2 not occupying a seat travel free, and older children are charged at the lowest applicable adult rate.

BAGGAGE➢ In general, the adult baggage allowance applies to children paying half or more of the adult fare. If you are traveling with an infant, **ask about carry-on allowances** before departure. In general, for infants charged 10% of the adult fare you are allowed one carry-on bag and a collapsible stroller; you may be limited to less if the flight is full.

SAFETY SEATS➢ According to the FAA, it's a good idea to **use safety seats aloft** for children weighing less than 40 pounds. Airline policies vary. U.S. carriers allow FAA-approved models but usually require that you buy a ticket, even if your child would otherwise ride free, since the seats must be strapped into regular seats. Foreign carriers may not allow infant seats, may charge a child rather than an infant fare for their use, or may require you to hold your baby during takeoff and landing—defeating the seat's purpose.

FACILITIES➢ When making your reservation, **request for children's meals or freestanding bassinets** if you need them; the latter are available only to those seated at the bulkhead, where there's enough legroom. If you don't need a bassinet, **think twice before requesting bulkhead seats**—the only storage space for in-flight necessities is in inconveniently distant overhead bins.

LODGING

Most hotels allow children under a certain age to stay in their parents' room at no extra charge; others charge them as extra adults. Be sure to **ask about the cutoff age.**

CUSTOMS & DUTIES

IN LONDON

There are two levels of duty-free allowance for travelers entering Great Britain: one for goods bought outside the EU, the other for goods bought in the EU (Belgium, Greece, the Netherlands, Denmark, Italy, Portugal, France, the Irish Republic, Spain, Germany, or Luxembourg).

In the first category, you may import duty-free: 200 cigarettes or 100 cigarillos or 50 cigars or 250 grams of tobacco; 2 liters of table wine and, in addition, (a) 1 liter of alcohol over 22% by volume (most spirits), (b) 2 liters of alcohol under 22% by volume (fortified or sparkling wine or liqueurs), or (c) 2 more liters of table wine; 50 milliliters of perfume; ¼ liter of toilet water; and other goods up to a value of £136, but not more than 50 liters of beer or 25 cigarette lighters.

In the second category, the EU has set guidelines for the import of certain goods. Following side trips entirely within the EU, you no longer need to go through customs on your return to the United Kingdom; however, if you exceed the guideline amounts, you may be required to prove that the goods are for your personal use only ("personal use" includes gifts). The guideline levels are: 800 cigarettes, 400 cigarillos, 200 cigars, and 1 kilogram of smoking tobacco, plus 10 liters of spirits, 20 liters of fortified wine, 90 liters of wine, and 110 liters of beer, plus goods to the value of £71. No animals or pets of any kind can be brought into the United Kingdom without a lengthy quarantine. The penalties are severe and are strictly enforced. Similarly, fresh meats, plants and vegetables, controlled drugs, and firearms and ammunition may not be brought into Great Britain.

You will face no customs formalities if you enter Scotland or Wales from any other part of the United Kingdom, though anyone coming from Northern Ireland should expect a security check.

IN THE U.S.

You may bring home $400 worth of foreign goods duty-free if you've been out of the country for at least 48 hours and haven't already used the $400 allowance, or any part of it, in the past 30 days.

Travelers 21 or older may bring back 1 liter of alcohol duty-free, provided the beverage laws of the state through which they reenter the United States allow it. In addition, regardless of their age, they are allowed 100 non-Cuban cigars and 200 cigarettes. Antiques and works of art more than 100 years old are duty-free.

Duty-free, travelers may mail packages valued at up to $200 to themselves and up to $100 to others, with a limit of one parcel per addressee per day (and no alcohol or tobacco products or perfume valued at more than $5); on the outside, the package should be labeled as being either for personal use or an unsolicited gift, and a list of its contents and their retail value should be attached. Mailed items do not affect your duty-free allowance on your return.

IN CANADA

If you've been out of Canada for at least seven days, you may bring in C$500 worth of goods duty-free. If you've been away for fewer than seven days but for more than 48 hours, the duty-free allowance drops to C$200; if your trip lasts between 24 and 48 hours, the allowance is C$50. You cannot pool allowances with family members. Goods claimed under the C$500 exemption may follow you by mail; those claimed under the lesser exemptions must accompany you.

Alcohol and tobacco products may be included in the seven-day and 48-hour exemptions but not in the 24-hour exemption. If you meet the age requirements of the province or territory through which you reenter Canada, you may bring in, duty-free, 1.14 liters (40 imperial ounces) of wine or liquor *or* 24 12-ounce cans or bottles of beer or ale. If you are 16 or older, you may bring in, duty-free, 200 cigarettes, 50 cigars or cigarillos, and 400 tobacco sticks or 400 grams of manufactured tobacco. Alcohol and tobacco must accompany you on your return.

An unlimited number of gifts with a value of up to C$60 each may be mailed to Canada duty-free. These do not affect your duty-free allowance on your return. Label the package "Unsolicited Gift—Value Under $60." Alcohol and tobacco are excluded.

D

DISABILITIES & ACCESSIBILITY

When discussing accessibility with an operator or reservationist, **ask hard questions.** Are there any stairs, inside *or* out? Are there grab bars next to the toilet *and* in the shower/tub? How wide is the doorway to the room? To the bathroom? For the most extensive facilities, meeting the latest legal specifications, **opt for newer accommodations,** which more often have been designed with access in mind. Older properties or ships must usually be retrofitted and may offer more limited facilities as a result. Be sure to **discuss your needs before booking.**

DISCOUNTS & DEALS

You shouldn't have to pay for a discount. In fact, you may already be eligible for all kinds of savings. Here are some time-honored strategies for getting the best deal.

LOOK IN YOUR WALLET

When you **use your credit card to make travel purchases,** you may get free travel-accident insurance, collision damage insurance, medical or legal assistance, depending on the card and bank that issued it. Visa and MasterCard provide one or more of these services, so **get a copy of your card's travel benefits.** If you are a member of the AAA or an oil-company-sponsored road-assistance plan, always **ask hotel or car-rental reservationists for auto-club discounts.** Some clubs offer additional discounts on tours, cruises, or admission to attractions. And don't forget that auto-club membership entitles you to free maps and trip-planning services.

SENIORS CITIZENS & STUDENTS

As a senior-citizen traveler, you may be eligible for special rates, but you should mention your senior-citizen status up front. If you're a students or under 26 can also get discounts, especially if you have an official ID card (☞ Senior-Citizen Discounts *and* Students on the Road, *below*).

DIAL FOR DOLLARS

To save money, **look into "1-800" discount reservations services,** which often have lower rates. These services use their buying power to get a better price on hotels, airline tickets, and sometimes even car rentals. When booking a room, always **call the hotel's local toll-free number** (if one is available) rather than the central reservations number—you'll often get a better price. Ask the reservationist about special packages or corporate rates, which are usually available even if you're not traveling on business.

JOIN A CLUB?

Discount clubs can be a legitimate source of savings, but you must use the participating hotels and visit the participating attractions in order to realize any benefits. Remember, too, that you have to pay a fee to join, so **determine if you'll save enough to warrant your membership fee.** Before booking with a club, **make sure the hotel or other supplier isn't offering a better deal.**

GET A GUARANTEE

When shopping for the best deal on hotels and car rentals, **look for guaranteed exchange rates,** which protect you against a falling dollar. With your rate locked in, you won't pay more even if the price goes up in the local currency.

DRIVING

The best advice on driving in London is: **don't.** Because the capital grew up as a series of villages, there never was a central plan for London's streets, and the result is a winding mass of chaos, aggravated by a passion for one-way streets.

If you must risk life and limb, however, note that the speed limit is 30 mph in the royal parks, as well as (theoretically) in all streets—unless you see the large 40 mph signs (and small repeater signs attached to lampposts) found only in the suburbs. Other basic rules: Pedestrians have right-of-way on "zebra" crossings (those black-and-white stripes that stretch across the street between two Belisha beacons—orange-flashing globe lights on posts). The curb on each side of the zebra crossing has zigzag markings. It is illegal to park within the zigzag area, or to pass another vehicle at a zebra crossing. At other crossings pedestrians must yield to traffic, but they do have right-of-way over traffic turning left at controlled crossings—if they have the nerve.

Traffic lights sometimes have arrow-style lights directing left or right turns; it is therefore important not to get into the turn lane if you mean to go straight ahead, so try to catch a glimpse of the road markings in time. The use of horns is prohibited between 11:30 PM and 7 AM.

You can park at night in 30-mph zones, provided you are within 25 yards of a lighted street lamp, but not within 15 yards of a road junction. To park on a bus route, you must show side (parking) lights, but you'll probably get a ticket anyway. On "Red Routes"—busy stretches with red lines painted in the gutter—you may not even stop to let a passenger out. During the day—and probably at all times—it is safest to believe that you can park nowhere except at a meter, in a garage, or where you are sure there are no lines or signs; otherwise, you run the risk of a towing cost of about £100, or a wheel clamp, which costs about the same, since you pay to have the clamp removed, plus the one or two tickets you'll have earned first. It is also illegal to park on the sidewalk.

LONDON DISTRICTS

Greater London is divided into 32 boroughs—33, counting the City of London, which has all the powers of a London borough. More useful for finding your way around, however, are the subdivisions of London into various postal districts. Throughout the guide we've listed the full postal code for places you're likely to be contacting by mail, although you'll find the first half of the code more important. The first one or two letters give the location: N=north, NW=northwest, etc. Don't expect the numbering to be logical, however. You won't, for example, find W2 next to W3.

I

INSURANCE

Travel insurance can protect your monetary investment, replace your luggage and its contents, or provide for medical coverage should you fall ill during your trip. Most tour operators, travel agents, and insurance agents sell specialized health-and-accident, flight, trip-cancellation, and luggage insurance as well as comprehensive policies with some or all of these coverages. Comprehensive policies may also reimburse you for delays due to weather—an important consideration if you're traveling during the winter months. Some health-insurance policies do not cover preexisting conditions, but waivers may be available in specific cases. Coverage is sold by the companies listed in Important Contacts A to Z; these companies act as the policy's administrators. The actual insurance is usually underwritten by a well-known name, such as The Travelers or Continental Insurance.

Before you make any purchase, **review your existing health and homeowner's policies** to find out whether they cover expenses incurred while traveling.

BAGGAGE

Airline liability for baggage is limited to $1,250 per person on domestic flights. On international flights, it amounts to $9.07 per pound or $20 per kilogram for checked baggage (roughly $640 per 70-pound bag) and $400 per passenger for unchecked baggage. Insurance for losses exceeding the terms of your airline ticket can be bought directly from the airline at check-in for about $10 per $1,000 of coverage; note that it excludes a rather extensive list of items, shown on your airline ticket.

COMPREHENSIVE

Comprehensive insurance policies include all the coverages described above plus some that may not be available in more specific policies. If you have purchased an expensive vacation, especially one that involves travel abroad, comprehensive insurance is a must; **look for policies that include trip delay insurance,** which will protect you in the event that weather problems cause you to miss your flight, tour, or cruise. A few insurers will also sell you a waiver for preexisting medical conditions. Some of the companies that offer both these features are Access America, Carefree Travel, Travel Insured International, and TravelGuard (☞ Important Contacts A to Z).

FLIGHT

You should **think twice before buying flight insurance.** Often purchased as a last-minute impulse at the airport, it pays a lump sum when a plane crashes, either to a beneficiary if the insured dies or sometimes to a surviving passenger who loses his or her eyesight or a limb. Supplementing the airlines' coverage described in the limits-of-liability paragraphs on your ticket, it's expensive and basically unnecessary. Charging an airline ticket to a major credit card often automatically provides you with coverage that may also extend to travel by bus, train, and ship.

HEALTH

Medicare generally does not cover health care

costs outside the United States; nor do many privately issued policies. If your own health insurance policy does not cover you outside the United States, **consider buying supplemental medical coverage.** It can reimburse you for $1,000–$150,000 worth of medical and/or dental expenses incurred as a result of an accident or illness during a trip. These policies also may include a personal-accident, or death-and-dismemberment, provision, which pays a lump sum ranging from $15,000 to $500,000 to your beneficiaries if you die or to you if you lose one or more limbs or your eyesight, and a medical-assistance provision, which may either reimburse you for the cost of referrals, evacuation, or repatriation and other services, or automatically enroll you as a member of a particular medical-assistance company.

TRIP

Without insurance, you will lose all or most of your money if you cancel your trip regardless of the reason. Especially if your airline ticket, cruise, or package tour is nonrefundable and cannot be changed, it's essential that you **buy trip-cancellation-and-interruption insurance.** When considering how much coverage you need, look for a policy that will cover the cost of your trip plus the nondiscounted price of a one-way airline ticket should you need to return home early. Read the fine print carefully, especially sections that define "family member" and "preexisting medical conditions." Also **consider default or bankruptcy insurance,** which protects you against a supplier's failure to deliver. Be aware, however, that if you buy such a policy from a travel agency, tour operator, airline, or cruise line, it may not cover default by the firm in question.

L

LODGING

APARTMENT & VILLA RENTAL

If you want a home base that's roomy enough for a family and comes with cooking facilities, **consider taking a furnished rental.** This can also save you money, but not always—some rentals are luxury properties (economical only when your party is large). Home-exchange directories list rentals—often second homes owned by prospective house swappers—and some services search for a house or apartment for you (even a castle if that's your fancy) and handle the paperwork. Some send an illustrated catalog; others send photographs only of specific properties, sometimes at a charge; up-front registration fees may apply.

HOME EXCHANGE

If you would like to find a house, an apartment, or some other type of vacation property to exchange for your own while on holiday, **become a member of a home-exchange organization,** which will send you its updated listings of available exchanges for a year, and will include your own listing in at least one of them. Arrangements for the actual exchange are made by the two parties involved, not by the organization.

M

MAIL

Stamps may be bought from main or subpost offices (the latter are located in stores), from stamp machines outside post offices, and from many newsagents stores and newsstands. Mailboxes are known as post or letter boxes and are painted bright red; large tubular ones are set on the edge of sidewalks, while smaller boxes are set into post-office walls.

RATES

Postal rates are: airmail letters up to 10 grams to North America, 41p; postcards 35p, aerogrammes 36p. Letters within Britain are 25p for first class, 19p for second class. Always check rates in advance, however, as they are subject to change.

RECEIVING MAIL

If you're uncertain where you'll be staying, you can have mail sent to you c/o Poste Restante, **London Chief Post Office** (✉ Trafalgar Square, 24–28 William IV St., London WC2N 4DL). Hours are Monday–Saturday 8–8. The service is free and mail will be held for 30 days. You'll need your passport or some other form of identification to claim your mail. You can also collect letters at **American Express** (✉ 6 Haymarket, SW1Y 4BS, ☎ 0171/930–4411, or any other branch). The service is free to cardholders and travelers check holders; all others pay a small fee.

MONEY & EXPENSES

The units of currency in Great Britain are pound sterling (£) and pence (p): £50, £20, £10, and £5 bills; £1 (100p), 50p, 20p, 10p, 5p, 2p, and 1p coins. At press time, the exchange rate was about U.S. $1.71 and Canadian $2.35 to the pound sterling.

ATMS

CASH ADVANCES➢ Cirrus, Plus, and many other networks that connect automated teller machines operate internationally. Chances are that you can **use your bank card, MasterCard, or Visa at ATMs** to withdraw money from an account or get a cash advance.

Before leaving home, **check on frequency limits** for withdrawals and cash advances. Also **ask whether your card's PIN must be reprogrammed** for use in London. Four-digit numbers are commonly used overseas. Note that Discover is accepted mostly in the United States.

TRANSACTION FEES➢ On credit-card cash advances you are charged interest from the day you receive the money, whether from a teller or an ATM. Although fees charged for ATM transactions may be higher abroad than at home, Cirrus and Plus exchange rates are excellent, because they are based on wholesale rates offered only by major banks.

COSTS

A movie in the West End costs £5–£9.50 (less on Mondays and at matinees); a theater seat, from £6 to about £20, more for hit shows; admission to a museum or gallery, around £3 (though many are free and others request a "voluntary contribution"); coffee, £1–£2; a pint of light (lager) beer in a pub, £1.70–£2.20; whiskey, gin, vodka, and so forth, by the glass in a pub, £1.50 and up (the measure is smaller than in the United States); house wine by the glass in a pub or wine bar, around £2, in a restaurant, £3.50 or more; a Coke, around 50p; a ham sandwich from a sandwich bar in the West End, £2; a 1-mile taxi ride, £4; an average Underground or bus ride, £1.30, a longer one, £2.30.

EXCHANGING CURRENCY

For the most favorable rates, **change money at banks.** You won't do as well at exchange booths in airports or rail and bus stations, in hotels, in restaurants, or in stores, although you may find their hours more convenient. To avoid lines at airport exchange booths, **get a small amount of the local currency before you leave home.**

TAXES

AIRPORT➢ As of November 1, 1994, all travelers departing the United Kingdom must now pay a £5–£10 Airport Departure Tax.

VAT➢ The British sales tax (VAT, Value Added Tax) is 17½%. The tax is almost always included in quoted prices in shops, hotels, and restaurants.

You can **get a VAT refund** by either the Over the Counter or the more cumbersome Direct Export method. Most large stores provide these services, but only if you request them, and will handle the paperwork. For the Over the Counter method, you must spend more than £75 in one store. Ask the store for Form VAT 407 (you must have identification—passports are best), to be given to customs when you leave the country. (Lines at major airports can be long, so allow plenty of time.) The refund will be forwarded to you in about eight weeks, minus a small service charge, either in the form of a credit to your charge card or as a British check, which American banks usually charge you to convert. With the Direct Export method, the goods go directly to your home; you must have a Form VAT 407 certified by customs, police, or a notary public when you get home and then sent back to the store, which will refund your money.

TRAVELER'S CHECKS

Whether or not to buy traveler's checks depends on where you are headed; **take cash to rural areas and small towns, traveler's checks**

to cities. The most widely recognized checks are issued by American Express, Citicorp, Thomas Cook, and Visa. These are sold by major commercial banks for 1%–3% of the checks' face value—it pays to **shop around.** Both American Express and Thomas Cook issue checks that can be countersigned and used by either you or your traveling companion, and they both provide checks, at no extra charge, valued in pounds. So you won't be left with excess foreign currency, **buy a few checks in small denominations** to cash toward the end of your trip. Before leaving home, **contact your issuer for information on where to cash your checks** without a incurring a transaction fee. Record the numbers of all your checks, and keep this listing in a separate place, crossing off the numbers of checks you have cashed.

WIRING MONEY

For a fee of 3%–10%, depending on the amount of the transaction, you can have money sent to you from home through MoneyGram[SM] or Western Union (☞ Money Matters *in* Important Contacts A to Z). The transferred funds and the service fee can be charged to a MasterCard or Visa account.

P

PACKING FOR LONDON

London can be cool, damp, and overcast, even in summer. You'll need a heavy coat for winter and a lightweight coat or warm jacket for summer. Always **bring a raincoat and an umbrella.** Pack as you would for an American city: coats and ties for expensive restaurants and nightspots, casual clothes elsewhere. Jeans are popular in London and are perfectly acceptable for sightseeing and informal dining. Tweeds and sport jackets are popular here with men. For women, ordinary street dress is acceptable everywhere. If you plan to stay in budget hotels, take your own soap. Many do not provide soap, and some give guests only one tiny bar per room.

Bring an extra pair of eyeglasses or contact lenses in your carry-on luggage, and if you have a health problem, **pack enough medication** to last the trip or have your doctor write you a prescription using the drug's generic name, because brand names vary from country to country (you'll then need a duplicate prescription from a local doctor). It's important that you **don't put prescription drugs or valuables in luggage to be checked,** for it could go astray. To avoid problems with customs officials, carry medications in the original packaging. Also, don't forget the addresses of offices that handle refunds of lost traveler's checks.

ELECTRICITY

To use your U.S.-purchased electric-powered equipment, **bring a converter and an adapter.** The electrical current in Great Britain is 220 volts, 50 cycles alternating current (AC); wall outlets take plugs with three prongs.

If your appliances are dual-voltage, you'll need only an adapter. Hotels sometimes have 110-volt outlets for low-wattage appliances near the sink, marked FOR SHAVERS ONLY; don't use them for high-wattage appliances like blow-dryers. If your laptop computer is older, carry a converter; new laptops operate equally well on 110 and 220 volts, so you need only an adapter.

LUGGAGE

Airline baggage allowances depend on the airline, the route, and the class of your ticket; ask in advance. In general, on domestic flights and on international flights between the United States and foreign destinations, you are entitled to check two bags. A third piece may be brought on board, but it must fit easily under the seat in front of you or in the overhead compartment. In the United States, the FAA gives airlines broad latitude regarding carry-on allowances, and they tend to tailor them to different aircraft and operational conditions. Charges for excess, oversize, or overweight pieces vary.

If you are flying between two foreign destinations, note that baggage allowances may be determined not by piece but by weight—generally 88 pounds (40 kilograms) in first class, 66 pounds (30 kilograms) in business class, and 44 pounds (20 kilograms) in economy. If your flight between two cities abroad *connects* with your transatlantic or transpacific flight, the piece method still applies.

SAFEGUARDING YOUR LUGGAGE➤ Before leaving home, **itemize your bags' contents** and their worth, and label them with your name, address, and phone number. (If you use your home address, cover it so that potential thieves can't see it readily.) Inside each bag, **pack a copy of your itinerary.** At check-in, **make sure that each bag is correctly tagged** with the destination airport's three-letter code. If your bags arrive damaged—or fail to arrive at all—file a written report with the airline before leaving the airport.

PASSPORTS & VISAS

If you don't already have one, **get a passport.** It is advisable that you **leave one photocopy of your passport's data page** with someone at home and keep another with you, separated from your passport, while traveling. If you lose your passport, promptly call the nearest embassy or consulate and the local police; having the data page information can speed replacement.

IN THE U.S.

All U.S. citizens, even infants, need only a valid passport to enter Great Britain for stays of up to three months. Application forms for both first-time and renewal passports are available at any of the 13 U.S. Passport Agency offices and at some post offices and courthouses. Passports are usually mailed within four weeks; allow five weeks or more in spring and summer.

CANADIANS

You need only a valid passport to enter Great Britain for stays of up to three months. Passport application forms are available at 28 regional passport offices, as well as post offices and travel agencies. Whether for a first or a renewal passport, you must apply in person. Children under 16 may be included on a parent's passport but must have their own to travel alone. Passports are valid for five years and are usually mailed within two to three weeks of application.

S

SENIOR-CITIZEN DISCOUNTS

To qualify for age-related discounts, **mention your senior-citizen status up front** when booking hotel reservations, not when checking out, and before you're seated in restaurants, not when paying the bill. Note that discounts may be limited to certain menus, days, or hours. When renting a car, **ask about promotional car-rental discounts**—they can net even lower costs than your senior-citizen discount.

STUDENTS ON THE ROAD

To save money, **look into deals available through student-oriented travel agencies.** To qualify, you'll need to have a bona fide student ID card. Members of international student groups are also eligible (☞ Students *in* Important Contacts A to Z).

T

TAXIS

Those big black taxicabs are as much a part of the London streetscape as the red double-decker buses, yet many have been replaced by the new boxy, sharp-edged model, while the beauty of others is marred by the advertising they carry on their sides. Hotels and main tourist areas have cab stands (just take the first in line), but you can also **flag one down from the roadside.** If the yellow FOR HIRE sign on the top is lit, the taxi is available. Many cab drivers often cruise at night with their FOR HIRE signs unlit; this is to enable them to choose their passengers and avoid those they think might cause trouble. If you see an unlit, passengerless cab, hail it: You might be lucky.

FARES

Fares start at £1 for the first 582 yards and increase by units of 20p per 291 yards or 60 seconds. A 40p surcharge is added on weekday nights 8–midnight and until 8 PM on Saturday. The surcharge rises to 60p on

Saturday night, Sunday, and national holidays—except over Christmas and New Year's Eve, when it rises to £2. Fares are usually raised in June of each year.

TELEPHONES

There are three types of phones: those that accept (a) only coins, (b) only British Telephone (BT) phonecards, or (c) BT phonecards and credit cards.

The coin-operated phones are of the push-button variety; most take all but 1p and 2p coins. Insert the coins *before* dialing (minimum charge is 10p). If you hear a repeated single tone after dialing, the line is busy; a continual tone means the number is unobtainable (or that you have dialed the wrong—or no—prefix). The indicator panel shows you how much money is left; add more whenever you like. If there is no answer, replace the receiver and your money will be returned.

Card phones operate with special cards that you can buy from post offices or newsstands. They are ideal for longer calls, are composed of units of 10p, and come in values of £2, £4, £10, and more. To use a card phone, lift the receiver, insert your card, and dial the number. An indicator panel shows the number of units used. At the end of your call, the card will be returned. Where credit cards are taken, slide the card through, as indicated.

For long-distance calls within Britain, dial the area code (which begins with 01), followed by the number.

London has two area codes, 0171 for inner London and 0181 for outer London. You don't have to dial either if you are calling inside the same zone. Drop the 0 from the prefix and dial only 171 or 181 when calling from overseas.

All calls are charged according to the time of day. Standard rate is weekdays 8 AM–6 PM; cheap rate is weekdays 6 PM–8 AM and all day on weekends.

LONG-DISTANCE

The long-distance services of AT&T, MCI, and Sprint make calling home relatively convenient, but in many hotels you may find it impossible to dial the access number. The hotel operator may also refuse to make the connection. Instead, the hotel will charge you a premium rate—as much as 400% more than a calling card—for calls placed from your hotel room. To avoid such price gouging, travel with more than one company's long-distance calling card—a hotel may block Sprint but not MCI. If the hotel operator claims that you cannot use any phone card, ask to be connected to an international operator, who will help you to access your phone card. You can also dial the international operator yourself. If none of this works, try calling your phone company collect in the United States. If collect calls are also blocked, call from a pay phone in the hotel lobby. Before you go, **find out the local access codes** for your destinations.

TIPPING

Many restaurants and large hotels (particularly those belonging to chains) will automatically add a 10%–15% service charge to your bill, so **always check in advance before you hand out any extra money.** You are, of course, welcome to tip on top of that for exceptional service. If you are dissatisfied with the service, however, refuse to pay the service charge, stating your reasons for doing so; you will be within your rights legally.

Do not tip movie or theater ushers, elevator operators, or bar staff in pubs—although you may buy them a drink if you're feeling generous. Washroom attendants may display a saucer, in which it's reasonable to leave 20p or so.

Here's a guide for other tipping situations: **Restaurants:** 10%–15% of the check for full meals if service is not already included; a small token if you're just having coffee or tea. **Taxis:** 10%–15%, or perhaps a little more for a short ride. **Porters:** 50p–£1 per bag. **Doormen:** £1 for hailing taxis or for carrying bags to check-in desk. **Bellhops:** £1 for carrying bags to rooms, £1 for room service. **Hairdressers:** 10%–15% of the bill, plus £1–£2 for the hair-washer.

TOUR OPERATORS

A package or tour to London can make your

vacation less expensive and more hassle-free. Firms that sell tours and packages reserve airline seats, hotel rooms, and rental cars in bulk and pass some of the savings on to you. In addition, the best operators have local representatives available to help you at your destination.

A GOOD DEAL?

The more your package or tour includes, the better you can predict the ultimate cost of your vacation. Make sure you know exactly what is covered, and **beware of hidden costs.** Are taxes, tips, and service charges included? Transfers and baggage handling? Entertainment and excursions? These can add up.

Most packages and tours are rated deluxe, first-class superior, first class, tourist, or budget. The key difference is usually accommodations. If the package or tour you are considering is priced lower than in your wildest dreams, **be skeptical.** Also, **make sure your travel agent knows the accommodations** and other services. Ask about the hotel's location, room size, beds, and whether it has a pool, room service, or programs for children, if you care about these. Has your agent been there in person or sent others you can contact?

BUYER BEWARE

Each year a number of consumers are stranded or lose their money when operators—even very large ones with excellent reputations—go out of business. To avoid becoming one of them, take the time to **check out the operator**—find out how long the company has been in business and ask several agents about its reputation. Next, **don't book unless the firm has a consumer-protection program.** Members of the USTOA and the NTA are required to set aside funds for the sole purpose of covering your payments and travel arrangements in case of default. Nonmember operators may instead carry insurance; look for the details in the operator's brochure—and for the name of an underwriter with a solid reputation. Note: When it comes to tour operators, **don't trust escrow accounts.** Although there are laws governing those of charter-flight operators, no governmental body prevents tour operators from raiding the till.

Next, **contact your local Better Business Bureau and the attorney general's offices** in both your own state and the operator's; have any complaints been filed? Finally, **pay with a major credit card.** Then you can cancel payment, provided that you can document your complaint. Always **consider trip-cancellation insurance** (☞ Insurance, *above*).

BIG VS. SMALL➢ Operators that handle several hundred thousand travelers per year can use their purchasing power to give you a good price. Their high volume may also indicate financial stability. But some small companies provide more personalized service; because they tend to specialize, they may also be more knowledgeable about a given area.

USING AN AGENT

Travel agents are excellent resources. In fact, large operators accept bookings made only through travel agents. But it's good to **collect brochures from several agencies** because some agents' suggestions may be skewed by promotional relationships with tour and package firms that reward them for volume sales. If you have a special interest, **find an agent with expertise in that area;** ASTA can provide leads in the United States. (Don't rely solely on your agent, though; agents may be unaware of small-niche operators, and some special-interest travel companies only sell direct.)

SINGLE TRAVELERS

Prices are usually quoted per person, based on two sharing a room. If traveling solo, you may be required to pay the full double-occupancy rate. Some operators eliminate this surcharge if you agree to be matched up with a roommate of the same sex, even if one is not found by departure time.

TRAIN TRAVEL

London is served by no fewer than 15 railroad stations, so be absolutely certain of the station for your departure or arrival. All have Underground stations either in the train station or within a few minutes' walk, and most are served by several bus routes. British Rail still controls all major railroad services, but it is in the process of splitting into seven divisions that are due to be sold to private operators (little about this operation was certain at press time). The principal routes that connect London to other major towns and cities are on an Inter-City network; unlike its European counterparts, British Rail imposes no extra charge for the use of this express-service network.

FARES

Generally speaking, **it is less expensive to buy a return (round-trip) ticket,** especially for day trips not far from London; always inquire about discount fares for your route. Buying a ticket on the train is the most expensive way to go, since you must pay the full one-way fare. Inquire about APEX fares; there are substantial discounts for those booking 1 to 2 weeks in advance. You can hear a recorded summary of timetable and fare information to many InterCity destinations by dialing the appropriate "dial and listen" numbers listed under British Rail in the telephone book.

MAJOR STATIONS

Charing Cross serves southeast England, including Canterbury, Margate, and Dover/Folkestone. **Euston/St. Pancras** serves East Anglia, Essex, the northeast, the northwest, and northern Wales, including Coventry, Stratford-upon-Avon, Birmingham, Manchester, Liverpool, Windermere, Glasgow, and Inverness. **King's Cross** serves the east Midlands; the northeast, including York, Leeds, and Newcastle; and north and east Scotland, including Edinburgh and Aberdeen. **Liverpool Street** serves Essex and East Anglia. **Paddington** serves the south Midlands, west and south Wales, and the West Country, including Reading, Bath, Bristol, Oxford, Cardiff, Swansea, Exeter, Plymouth, and Penzance. **Victoria** serves southern England, including Gatwick Airport, Brighton, Dover/Folkestone, and the south coast. **Waterloo** serves the southwest, including Salisbury, Bournemouth, Portsmouth, Southampton, and the isles of Wight, Jersey, and Guernsey, and is the departure point for the Channel Tunnel.

PASSES

If you plan to travel outside of London by train, **consider purchasing a BritRail Pass.** Prices begin at $235 for eight days of second-class travel and $325 for eight days of first-class travel. Passes good for longer periods of time are also available, as are a Flexipass, a BritRail Senior Pass, and a BritRail Kids Pass. Remember that EurailPasses are not honored in Great Britain.

Many travelers assume that rail passes guarantee them seats on the trains they wish to ride. Not so. You need to **book seats ahead even if you are using a rail pass**; seat reservations are required on some European trains, particularly high-speed trains, and are a good idea on trains that may be crowded—particularly in summer on popular routes. You will also need a reservation if you purchase sleeping accommodations.

SEAT RESERVATIONS

Seats cannot be reserved by phone. You should **apply in person** to any British Rail Travel Centre or directly to the station from which you depart. Seat reservations cost £1.

TRAVEL GEAR

Travel catalogs specialize in useful items that can **save space when packing** and make life on the road more convenient. Compact alarm clocks, travel irons, travel wallets, and personal-care kits are among the most common items you'll find. They also carry dual-voltage appliances, currency converters and foreign-language phrase books. Some catalogs even carry miniature coffeemakers and water purifiers.

U

UNDERGROUND TRAVEL

Known colloquially as "the tube," London's extensive Underground system is by far the most widely used form of city transportation. Trains run both beneath and aboveground out into the suburbs, and **all stations are clearly marked** with the London Underground circular symbol. (In Britain, the word "subway" means "pedestrian underpass.") Trains are all one class; smoking is *not* allowed on board or in the stations.

There are 10 basic lines—all named—plus the East London line, which runs from Shoreditch and Whitechapel across the Thames and south to New Cross, but which is currently closed indefinitely (a replacement bus service is in operation); and the Docklands Light Railway, which runs from Stratford in east London and from Bank and Tower gateway to Greenwich, with an extension to the Royal Docks that should be completed by the time you read this. The not-yet-built Metro Express, which will run from Haringey to Wimbledon underneath Soho and Fulham, may start appearing on maps, too—it's the light green line. The Central, District, Northern, Metropolitan, and Piccadilly lines all have branches, so **be sure to note which branch is needed for your particular destination.** Electronic platform signs tell you the final stop and route of the next train, and some signs conveniently indicate how many minutes you'll have to wait for the train to arrive.

FARES

For both buses and tube fares, London is divided into six concentric zones; the fare goes up the farther out you travel. Ask at Underground ticket counters for the London Transport booklets that give details of all the various ticket options for the tube. Traveling without a valid ticket makes you liable for an on-the-spot fine (£10 at press time), so always pay your fare before you embark.

For one trip between any two stations, you can buy an ordinary single (one-way ticket) for travel anytime on the day of issue; if you're coming back on the same route the same day, an ordinary return (round-trip ticket) costs twice the single fare. Singles vary in price from 70p to £3.10—expensive if you're making several journeys in a day. There are several passes good for both the tube and the bus; ☞ Important Contacts A to Z, *above.*

HOURS

From Monday to Saturday, trains begin running just after 5 AM; the last services leave central London between midnight and 12:30 AM. On Sundays, trains start two hours later and finish about an hour earlier. Frequency of trains depends on the route and the time of day, but normally you should not have to wait more than 10 minutes in central areas.

INFORMATION

A pocket map of the entire tube network is available free from most Underground ticket counters. There is a large map on the wall of each platform.

There are LT (London Transport) Travel Information Centres at the following tube stations: Heathrow, daily, varying times at each terminal; Victoria, daily 8:15 AM–9:30 PM; Piccadilly Circus, daily 8:15–6; Oxford Circus, Monday–Saturday 8:15–6; Euston, Monday–Thursday and Saturday 7:15–6, Friday 7:15 AM–7:30 PM, Sunday 8:15–6; and King's Cross, Monday–Thursday 8:15–6, Friday 7:15 AM–7:30 PM, Saturday 7:15–6. For information on all London bus and tube times, fares, and so forth, call 0171/222–1234; the line is operated 24 hours.

W

WHEN TO GO

The heaviest tourist season in Britain runs from mid-April to mid-October, with another peak around Christmas—though the tide never really ebbs. The spring is the time to see the countryside and the London gardens at their freshest; early summer to catch the roses and full garden splendor; the fall for near-ideal exploring conditions. The British take their vacations mainly in July and August, and the resorts are crowded. London in summer, however, though full of visitors, is also full of interesting things to see and do. But be warned: Air-conditioning is *very* rare in London, and in a hot summer you'll swelter. The winter can be rather dismal and is frequently wet and usually cold, but all the theaters, concerts, and exhibitions go full speed.

CLIMATE

London's weather has always been contrary, and in recent years it has become positively erratic, with hot summers and mild winters proving that the greenhouse effect is running rampant over Britain. It is virtually impossible to forecast what the pattern might be, but you can be fairly certain that it will not be what you expect! The main feature of the British weather is that it is generally mild—with some savage exceptions, especially in summer. It is also fairly damp—though even that has been changing in recent years, with recurring periods of drought.

What follows are the average daily maximum and minimum temperatures for London.

Climate in London

Jan.	43F	6C	May	62F	17C	Sept.	65F	19C
	36	2		47	8		52	11
Feb.	44F	7C	June	69F	20C	Oct.	58F	14C
	36	2		53	12		46	8
Mar.	50F	10C	July	71F	22C	Nov.	50F	10C
	38	3		56	14		42	5
Apr.	56F	13C	Aug.	71F	21C	Dec.	45F	7C
	42	6		56	13		38	4

1 Destination: London

THE CITY OF VILLAGES

LONDON IS AN ENORMOUS CITY—600 square miles—on a tiny island, hosting about 7 million Londoners, ⅛ of the entire population of England, Scotland, and Wales; but it has never felt big to me. It is fashioned on a different scale from other capital cities, as if, given the English penchant for modesty and understatement, it felt embarrassed by its size. Each of the 32 boroughs that comprise the whole has its own attitude, and most are subdivided into yet smaller enclaves exhibiting yet more particular behaviors, so that there is really no such person as a generic Londoner. Stay here long enough, and Professor Higgins's feat of deducing Eliza Dolittle's very street of birth from the shape of her vowels will seem like nothing special. It's a cliché, but London really is a city of villages.

I have lived in several of these, and am fluent in the language of a few others, but my village, Holland Park, is the one I know best, and it illustrates as well as any how London is changing. Holland Park is small—just a few streets surrounding the former grounds of Holland House, a Jacobean mansion whose remains (it was bombed during World War II) now house a restaurant, a gallery, an open-air theater, and a youth hostel. North of the park, Holland Park Avenue metamorphoses into the windy local high street, Notting Hill Gate, then into bleak Bayswater Road, abutted on its right by Kensington Gardens and Hyde Park before breaking, where the main London gallows once stood, into irritating, commercial Oxford Street. But here, for a few West Eleven moments (postal-district terminology you'd do well to master, to help with navigation), it is a broad, plane tree–lined boulevard, strung with vast white-stuccoed late-Victorian houses and looking an awful lot like Paris.

In our sophisticated age, the European ambience of Holland Park Avenue has been seized upon by niche-marketeers, and we now have two French patisseries, three international newsstands, a BMW showroom, and a candlelit Provençale restaurant within a couple of blocks. The history racket is doing similar things all over town, history being what London has to sell now that it no longer cuts much ice in the world economy. It would be sentimental to prefer the avenue's old hardware store and late-night family grocer (open till 9!) to the fancy Continental shops that have replaced them—London's got to move with the times, after all.

Both good and bad come with the new territory. The Pakistani family who used to take turns minding the grocery store bought the block a decade later. Those Patels are now a well-known London dynasty, with most of the capital's newsstands in their empire—a satisfying reversal of roles from the British Raj days. Meanwhile, homeless Londoners (the number is about 100,000, and rising) work the overpriced yuppie supermarket threshold selling their magazine, *The Big Issue,* for a profit of 25p per guilty conscience. As one of the many villages built during Victoria's reign, Holland Park is a neighborhood unaccustomed to urban blight. But much of London has weathered several centuries of coping with the indigent population.

That's one of the best things about the city: Everything has been seen before, and history is forever poking its nose in. Whatever you're doing, you're doing it on top of a past layered like striated rock. You can see the cross sections clearly sometimes, as in the City, where lumps of Roman wall nest in the postmodern blocks of the street helpfully named London Wall. Walk toward the Thames to Cheapside, which you can tell was the medieval marketplace if you know the meaning of "ceap" ("to barter"), and there's the little Norman church of St. Mary-le-Bow, rebuilt by Wren and then again after the Blitz, but still ringing the Bow Bells. Then look to your right, and you'll be gobsmacked by the dome of St. Paul's. Of course, all you really wanted was to find a place for lunch—nearly impossible on a weekend in this office wasteland.

Instead of going weak-kneed at the sights, Londoners are apt to complain about such privations, while pretending simultaneously that no other city in the United Kingdom exists. Edinburghers and Liverpudlians can complain till Big Ben tolls 13, but Londoners continue to pull rank with a complacency that amuses and infuriates visitors in about equal measure. London definitely *used* to be important. The vein of water running through its center has always linked the city with the sea, and it once gave British mariners a head start in the race to mine the world's riches and bring them home. The river proved convenient for building not only palaces (at Westminster, Whitehall, Hampton Court, Richmond, Greenwich) but an empire, too.

The empire dissolved, but the first Thames bridge is still there, in almost the same spot that the emperor Claudius picked in AD 43, and although the current drab concrete incarnation dates only from 1972, it's still called London Bridge. The Tudor one was much better—something I learned before I was 10 from visits to the Museum of London, which used to live nearby in Kensington Palace. I liked the old bridge because of the row of decapitated heads stuck on poles above the gatehouse, which you could see on the model. It added a frisson to history, which more recent exhibitions, like the amazingly popular London Dungeon, have rather cynically packaged.

The old London Bridge lasted 600 years. Lined with shops and houses, it presided over a string of fairs *on* the Thames, when winters were colder and the water froze thick. Nowadays we rarely see a snowfall, though we'll talk endlessly about its possibility. We are genuinely obsessed by the weather, because we have so much of it, though most of it is damp. Snow varies the scenery, stops any tube train with an overground route, makes kids of everyone with a makeshift toboggan and access to a park (99% of the population), and fosters a community spirit normally proscribed by the city's geography and its citizens' cool. Winters were colder as recently as the '60s, when waiting for the crust to thicken enough to skate on the Round Pond in Kensington Gardens—now good only for model-boat sailors and duck feeders—was only a matter of time.

The corollary to our temperate winter, though, is a fresh confidence in summer sufficient to support herds of sidewalk tables. Holland Park Avenue no longer has the monopoly on Parisian ambience. All over town, an epidemic of Continental-style café chains serving croissants and *salade frisée* has devoured the traditional tobacco-stained pubs serving warm bitter and bags of pork scratchings. Most of the remaining pubs have turned into faux-Edwardian parlors with coffee machines and etchings or, more recently, wood-floored bars serving flavored vodkas and Tuscan food. The change has been going on for about a decade, and it suits London, as does its momentous discovery that restaurants are allowed to serve good food in smart surroundings and not charge the earth.

London is increasingly a European city, as if England were no longer stranded alone in the sea. In fact, ever since airplanes superseded ships, this island race has been undergoing an identity crisis, which reached its apogee in the '70s when Prime Minister Edward Heath sailed us irrevocably into the Common Market. Occasionally Britain still holds out against some European Community legislation or other, attempting to reassert differences that are following executions at the Tower and British Colonial supremacy into history. But however much the social climate changes, London is built on a firm foundation. Until the ravens desert the Tower of London—which is when, they say, the kingdom will fall—we have Westminster Abbey, and St. Paul's and the Houses of Parliament, the Georgian squares and grand Victorian houses, the green miles of parks, the river, the museums and galleries and theaters, and 32 boroughs of villages to keep us going.

–Kate Sekules

WHAT'S WHERE

Bloomsbury

The British Museum and the University of London dominate this area, but it's hard to get images of Virginia Woolf, T.S. Eliot, E.M. Forster, Vanessa and Clive Bell, et al out of your mind even if there is nothing but imagination left of the Bloomsbury Group.

Chelsea
Former bohemia, this southwest "village" was all artists and writers, then mods and hippies, then punks in the '70s when the King's Road had its final heyday. Now fabulously expensive Chelsea is great for strolling and the Royal Hospital and Physic Garden are essential stops for gardeners especially during the Chelsea Flower Show in May.

The City
The heart of financial Britain, the oldest square mile of London, winds down quickly after the bankers go home, so leave youself enough time when you're done with the Tower of London.

Covent Garden
A nest of narrow streets, arcades, and pedestrian malls, this area is dominated by the Piazza. Originally a vegetable market in the 1830s, then a flower market from the 1870s, the indoor/outdoor structure has been converted into clothing shops and crafts stalls, with great little stores in the surrounding area, and the London Transport Museum and the famous Royal Opera House nearby. Eliza "My Fair Lady" Dolittle wasn't the only one singing in the neighborhood.

The East End
In certain respects London's real center, since a true Cockney must be born within the sound of Bow bells, the East End contains some of the best street markets, the Bethnal Green Museum of Childhood, the Geffrye Museum, and a bloody past—this was Jack the Ripper territory.

Greenwich
A quick 8-mile jaunt down the Thames (25 minutes on a boat) will bring you past the Naval Maritime Museum and the *Cutty Sark* to Greenwich's Old Royal Observatory, where if time stood still, the whole world's watches would be off. If you tire of straddling the hemispheres, take a walk through the acres of parkland that blanket the area or the weekend crafts and antiques markets.

Hampstead
Hampstead's characteristic Georgian houses, tidiness, and picturesque village atmosphere has always attracted writers, musicians, and artists. Then there's also Hampstead Heath, a bigger asset than the Freud Museum and Keats House.

Hyde Park, Kensington Gardens
Together these two connected parks form the biggest acreage of green in central London. Within the gates are Kensington Palace and the Serpentine Lake and Gallery, plus the city's horseback riding route Rotten Row.

Knightsbridge and Kensington
Harrods is the first thought you have when you think of Knightsbridge, but consider also all the other expensive shops, then continue on to Kensington where the scale is smaller as are the price tags (except in the antique stores up Kensington Church Street).

Notting Hill and Holland Park
Notting Hill, around Portobello Road, is full of restaurants, galleries, small exciting shops and is populated by the local hip youth. Neighboring Holland Park is entirely the opposite—its leafy streets are full of expensive white stucco Victorians that lead to bucolic Holland Park itself.

Regent's Park
Regent's Park is home to the much-loved zoo, the much-loved rose garden, and the much-loved outdoor theater; of course, it's a favorite hangout of mothers with strollers, too. Watch out for those balls—soft-, foot-, and cricket.

St. James's and Mayfair
St. James's Palace isn't available for comment, though it certainly adds cachet to one of the ritziest addresses in town. Mayfair vies for the honor with its verdant squares, luxury hotels, and the exclusive shops of Savile Row and Old and New Bond streets.

Soho
Soho has an international flavor that many of central London's neighborhoods lack and has long been one of the leading bohemian enclaves and is now crammed with restaurants, bars, cafés, and nightclubs. Cozy Chinatown nestles on its edge.

The South Bank
You won't say "How very British" in this part of town across the Thames from London Bridge, for the bombs of World

War II flattened medieval Southwark. However, what's cropped up in its place includes the Design Museum and a reconstruction of Shakespeare's Globe Theater, with the South Bank Arts Complex, England's chief arts center not far away.

The Thames Upstream

The royal palaces and country houses of Chiswick, Kew, Richmond, and Putney all have serenity and beautiful rolling greenery that explain the astronomical prices that real estate brings here. Stroll around and get lost in a daydream breathing the rural air or find your way out of the famous maze at Hampton Court Palace.

Westminster and Royal London

This is one of two centers of London and a visit here is essential for contained in this area are perhaps some of the most famous sites anywhere in the world: Westminster Abbey, Buckingham Palace, the National Gallery, and the Houses of Parliament, with Big Ben dominating the view.

PLEASURES AND PASTIMES

Dining

London now ranks—and longtime absentees must suspend disbelief here—among the world's top dining scenes. A new generation of chefs has precipitated a fresh approach to food preparation, which you could call "London-style" though most refer to it as "Modern British." Everyone seems to have an opinion about it, and newspapers and magazines now devote columns if not pages to food and restaurant reviews. Everyone reads them and everyone dines out to the point where London has become a significant foodies' town.

This healthy scene rests on a solid foundation of ethnic cuisines. Thousands of (mostly northern) Indian restaurants have long ensured that Londoners view a tasty tandoori as a birthright. Chinese—Cantonese, primarily—outposts in London's tiny Chinatown have been around a long time, as have Greek tavernas; now, Thai eateries are proliferating. Places serving Malaysian, Spanish, Russian, Ko... and a trace of Japanese (with more o... way?) are adding to the density of din... choices. After all this, traditional British food, lately revived from its deathbed, appears as one more exotic cuisine in the pantheon.

As for cost, the democratization of restaurants means lighter checks than during the '80s, partly due to the popularity of fixed-price menus; still, London is not an inexpensive city for dining. Damage-control methods include having lunch as your main meal—many top places feature good-value lunch menus, halving the price of evening à la carte—and ordering a pair of appetizers instead of an entrée, to which few places object. Seek out fixed-price menus, but watch for hidden extras added to the check, including a "cover," bread and vegetables charged separately, and a service tariff. Many restaurants exclude service charges from the printed menu (which the law obliges them to display outside), then add 10%–15% to the check, or else stamp SERVICE NOT INCLUDED along the bottom, in which case you should add the 10%–15% yourself. Just don't pay twice for service—unscrupulous restaurateurs have been known to add service, but leave off the total on the credit card slip blank.

A final caveat: Beware of Sundays. Many restaurants are closed on this day, especially for dinner; likewise, on public holidays. Over the Christmas period, the London restaurant community all but shuts down—only hotels will be prepared to feed you. When in doubt, call ahead.

The Pub

Londoners could no more live without their "local" than they could forgo dinner. The pub—or public house, to give it its full title—is ingrained in the British psyche as social center, bolt-hole, second home. Pub culture—revolving around pints, pool, darts, and sports—is still male-dominated; however, as a result of the gentrification trend that started in the late '80s by the major breweries (which own most pubs), transforming many ancient smoke- and spittle-stained dives into fantasy Edwardian drawing rooms, women have been entering their welcoming doors in increasing numbers. This decade, the trend has been toward The Bar, superficially identified by its cocktail list, creative paintwork, bare floorboards, and chrome fittings, but the social consequences are the same: these are English pubs, but not as we formerly knew them.

When doing a London pub crawl, you must remember one thing: Arcane licensing laws forbid the serving of alcohol after 11 PM (10:30 on Sunday; there are different rules for restaurants)—a circumstance you see in action at 10 minutes to 11, when the "last orders" bell signals a stampede to the bar. After many decades, however, some relaxation of these unpopular laws are in evidence, with weekend "extensions" being granted, especially in Soho, plus a slew of clubs/bars/pubs that get around it by charging a moderate cover after 11 PM.

The Arts

There isn't *a* London "arts scene"—there is an infinite variety of them. As long as there are audiences for Feydeau revivals, drag queens, obscure teenaged rock bands, hit musicals, body-painted Parisian dancers, and improvised stand-up comedy, someone will figure out how to stage them. Admission prices are not always bargain-basement, but when you consider the cost of a London hotel room, the city's arts and entertainment are easily affordable.

To find out what's showing during your stay, the weekly magazine *Time Out* (it comes out every Wednesday; Tuesday in central London) is an invaluable resource. The *Evening Standard*—especially the Friday edition—also carries listings, as do the "quality" Sunday papers and the Friday and Saturday *Independent, Guardian,* and *Times*. You'll find racks overflowing with leaflets and flyers in most cinema and theater foyers, and you can pick up the free fortnightly *London Theatre Guide* leaflet from most hotels as well as tourist information centers.

THEATER➢ From Shakespeare to the umpteenth year of *Les Misérables* (or *The Glums,* as it's affectionately known), London's West End has the cream of the city's theater offerings. But there's much more to see in London than the offerings of Theaterland and the national companies: Of the 100 or so legitimate theaters operating in the capital, only about half are officially "West End," while the remainder fall under the blanket title of "Fringe." Much like New York's Off- and Off-Off-Broadway, Fringe Theater encompasses everything from off-the-wall "physical theater" pieces to premiers of new plays and revivals of old ones. ☞ Chapter 9: "The True Heart of London," by Jane Moss.

If you're a theater junkie, and want to put together a West End package, the *Complete Guide to London's West End Theatres* has seating plans and booking information for all of the houses. It costs £9.95 from the Society of London Theatres.

MUSIC➢ London is home to four world-class orchestras. The London Symphony Orchestra is in residence at the Barbican Centre, while the London Philharmonic lives at the Royal Festival Hall—one of the finest concert halls in Europe. Between the Barbican and South Bank, there are concert performances almost every night of the year. The Barbican also present chamber music concerts in partnership with such celebrated orchestras as the City of London Sinfonia. The Royal Albert Hall during the Promenade Concert season—July to September—is an unmissable pleasure. Also look for the lunchtime concerts held throughout the city in either smaller concert halls, arts-center foyers, or churches; they usually cost under £5 or are free. St. John's, Smith Square, and St. Martin-in-the-Fields are the major venues and also present evening concerts.

MOVIES➢ Aside from the multiplexes and big screens, there are movie clubs and repertory cinemas in London that offer a wider range of movies, including classic, Continental, and underground, as well as underestimated masterpieces. The king of this culture is the National Film Theatre, where the London Film Festival is based in the fall; there are also lectures and presentations here.

Walking

London's a great walking city, since so many of its treasures are to be found as untouted details—tiny alleyways barely visible on the map; garden squares; churchyards; shop windows; sudden vistas of skyline or park. However, it is big, VERY BIG. And often rather damp. With the obvious precautions of comfortable, weatherproof shoes and an umbrella, this least expensive of tourist activities might well become your favorite pastime.

NEW AND NOTEWORTHY

Why are the streets deserted around 7 PM on a Saturday night? Where is everyone? Well, nearly every Londoner is indulging in sanctified gambling—watching one Anthea Turner (the original "Why Am I Famous?," or W.A.I.F) plucking balls on television for the **National Lottery.** Whatever may be the moral implications of so much money being printed, London is a better place for it. Among the capital's beneficiaries of Lottery money are megaliths of the arts, like the **South Bank Centre,** due to be canopied in undulating glass by Sir Richard Rogers (architect of the Paris Pompidou Centre and the Lloyd's building here), and the **Tate Gallery,** which is going to split in two at the Millennium. Underway now is the conversion of the former Bankside Power Station, opposite St. Paul's Cathedral, into the **Tate Gallery of Modern Art.** When that's open, we'll be able to see more of the national collection of British art, currently shown in bits and pieces at the Millbank Tate—which is 100 years old on July 21, 1997—where space is limited, and much is kept in the vaults. Pre-10th century work will remain, however.

Another vast chunk of cash—almost £80 million—is going to the **Royal Opera House,** which needs some spit and polish, having had its last major renovation over 90 years ago. The work will not only bring the existing Opera House up to snuff, but also improve the nearby Covent Garden Piazza, though the biggest tranche of money goes into building a brand new home for the **Royal Ballet,** a second auditorium, and a less formal studio performance space. The only national center of the arts we haven't yet mentioned is the **Barbican,** which, though it hadn't been awarded any cash by press time, had just secured the services of **Richard Corrigan,** one of London's most talented chefs, to perform major surgery on its sorry catering operations.

A further two new Thames-side features are not Lottery-funded. The former stock cube processing plant, which has long been a London landmark for its Art Deco tower, known as the **OXO Tower** (you'll see why as soon as you look at it) has become a hotbed of design, retail, residential, and riverfront dining action, with yet another hip restaurant opening on the 8th floor, run by the hip and foodie **Fifth Floor** at Harvey Nichols crew. Upstream from there, the apparently endless saga of **County Hall** is apparently ending in a three-act drama. Firstly, a big chunk of this former Greater London Council administration building next to Westminster Bridge is being sold off as private apartments; secondly, there will be a 318-room bargain riverside hotel kindly donated to London by **Travel Inn,** due for completion in 1998; thirdly, Europe's largest **Aquarium** is supposedly being installed in the subterranean regions. Watch that space. Travel Inn is also building a hotel upstream at picturesque **Putney Bridge.**

Much else has been happening in the cultural centers of London. The **Victoria & Albert** pioneered a move that will surely spread to all the major museums, with its Wednesday night **Late View.** One of the first innovations of new Director, Alan Borg, this isn't merely extended opening hours, but a tiny party, with wine bars, gallery talks, and high-profile lecture series. The **Commonwealth Institute** wins this year's prize for the biggest changes, though, with a complete renovation underway that includes the addition of the **Wonders of the World** dark ride, through rain forest, safari, and glacier. Down the road from there, **Kensington Palace** has reopened with its state rooms refurbished to appear just as they did when young Princess Victoria was growing up. Miles away in the City, the **Museum of London** has added yet another bit, the Roman London Gallery, complete with Roman street, and several Roman interiors, both patrician and working class. Less edifying, but more attractive to the kids, is a bunch of high tech new stuff. The biggest thing is Windsor Castle's new neighbor, the **Legoland Theme Park,** with gadzillions of Lego and Duplo bricks formed into a "Miniland" version of Europe, a fairy tale boat ride, a wild woods adventure park and pirate treasure trail and—believe it—a children's driving school. Smaller, but more virtually real, **Segaworld** entered the Trocadero's collection of internet age rides, with six separate virtual experiences, like the **VR2** where you battle aliens in space. It's the biggest virtual theme ride outside Japan, they claim.

Finally, we must pay homage to the continuing rise of the restaurant as all things to all people in this increasingly continental city. Everyone's a foodie, and—although a national newspaper propounded the theory that it is in fact the same 900 people who are keeping every one of London's restaurants going—everyone eats out. Among the bigger, newer places we do and don't list are **Coast, The Avenue, Mezzo, L'Odeon, Vong, The Astral, The Criterion, The People's Palace,** and . . . Well, sorry, but the crystal ball's a little cloudy. You'll have to come and see for yourself.

FODOR'S CHOICE

No two people will agree on what makes a perfect vacation, but it's fun and helpful to know what others think. We hope you'll have a chance to experience some of Fodor's Choices yourself while visiting London. For detailed information about each entry, refer to the appropriate chapters within this guidebook.

Views

If London's been kind enough to provide you with a bright day, take advantage of the view afforded you of the city from **Parliament Hill Fields.**

Look **down the Mall to Buckingham Palace,** from underneath Admiralty Arch and see what the queen sees during all those royal ceremonies.

Cross the river to Jubilee Gardens to see **The Houses of Parliament at sunset.**

A dramatically floodlit **Tower Bridge** confronts you as you come out of the Design Museum on a winter's night.

Walks

Stroll across **Regent's Park at sunset,** east (Cumberland Terrace) to west (the Mosque), pausing in summer to watch (or play) softball.

Even on a wet day, the walk along the **South Bank of the Thames,** from Lambeth Palace to Blackfriars Bridge is enjoyable.

Just like John Le Carré, you can climb the rolling hills of **Hampstead Heath,** from Hampstead Village to Kenwood, perhaps in time for a summer concert.

Museums

The serene 18th-century mansion, Hertford House, which houses the **Wallace Collection,** is as much a part of the appeal as the rich array of porcelain, paintings, furniture, and sculpture.

Eccentric architect of the Bank of England, **Sir John Soane** left his **house** to the nation on condition nothing be changed and the result is a phantasmagoria of colors, unusual perspectives, and artifacts from many centuries.

You could move into the **British Museum** and never tire of all that it has to offer, from the Rosetta Stone and the Elgin Marbles to the British Library's hundreds of original manuscripts.

Hotels

★ **Claridges.** The same fine qualities that attracted the King of Morocco, among many others, to this world-renowned Mayfair hotel are sure to make you feel right at home too. **$$$$**

★ **The Dorchester.** It's a true accomplishment that so much gold leaf and marble, linens and brocades have managed the effect of sophisticated intimacy in this hotel that has all of Hyde Park as its front garden. **$$$$**

★ **The Savoy.** Secure a river suite at this historic, late-Victorian hotel overlooking the Thames, and you'll get one of the best stays—and views—in London. **$$$$**

★ **The Beaufort.** It's fair to use this set of Victorian houses, run by a wonderfully friendly all-female staff, as a home away from home, especially if you live practically next door at Harrods. **$$$**

★ **The Franklin.** Everything is romantic here from the quiet garden to tea in the lounge to the sweet smell of the Floris cosmetics that you'll find in your room. **$$$**

★ **The Pelham.** Here there is the comforting feel of a country house with all the advantages of being in the center of South Kensington. **$$$**

★ **Basil Street.** So many people return to this Knightsbridge hotel that there is a standard discount for repeat guests—what more need be said. **$$**

★ **The Commodore.** Secreted in a quiet square behind Bayswater Road, this family-run hotel has some great value duplex-style rooms.**$$**

★ **The Vicarage.** Friendly and homey, this Kensington B&B has kept high standards for years.**$**

Restaurants

★ **La Tante Claire.** Pierre Kaufman is probably London's best chef.**$$$$**

★ **Le Caprice.** This glamorous place has stood the test of time—the food is great, the ambience even better.**$$$**

★ **Quaglino's.** This isn't the biggest, but it is still the best of Sir Terence Conran's London hot spots.**$$$**

★ **St. John.** Here you can enjoy refrectory-style dining in a brash and British mode.**$$**

★ **Wódka.** Laid back and stylish, this serves London's only modern Polish food.**$$**

★ **Geales.** Fish and chips as you always imagined it.**$**

FESTIVALS AND SEASONAL EVENTS

Top seasonal events in and around London include the Chelsea Flower Show in May, Derby Day at Epsom Racecourse, Wimbledon Lawn Tennis Championships and Henley Regatta in June, and a new innovation, the London Arts Season, which combines many events in theater, art and music with good deals on hotels and meals out. There is a complete list of ticket agencies in *Britain Events,* available from the **British Travel Centre** (☒ 12 Regent St., London SW17 4PQ, in person only).

WINTER

MID-DEC.➢ **Olympia International Show Jumping Championships,** international equestrian competition in Olympia's Grand Hall. For information, call ☏ 0171/370–8209.

JAN 1➢ **The London Parade** is a good ole US-style extravaganza complete with cheerleaders, floats, and marching bands, led by the Lord Mayor of Westminster. It starts on the south side of Westminster Bridge at 12:30, finishing in Berkeley Square around 3 PM. No tickets required.

JAN. 3–12➢ **43rd London International Boat Show,** the largest boat show in Europe. ☒ *Earl's Court Exhibition Centre, Warwick Rd., London SW5 9TA,* ☏ *01784/473377.*

Feb.–Mar.➢ **London Arts Season,** showcases the city's extensive arts scene, with bargain-priced tickets and special events. ☒ *British Travel Centre, 12 Regent St., SW1Y 4PQ,* ☏ *(for Arts Season only) 0171/839–6181.*

SPRING

MAR. 13–22 AND SEPT. 11–20➢ **Chelsea Antiques Fair,** a twice-yearly fair with wide range of pre-1830 pieces for sale. Old Town Hall, King's Rd., Chelsea SW3 4PW, ☏ 01444/482–514.

MAR. 13–APR. 7➢ **Daily Mail Ideal Home Exhibition** is a consumer show of new products and ideas for the home. ☒ *Earl's Court Exhibition Centre, Warwick Rd., London SW5 9TA, tel. 01895/ 677–677.*

MAR.➢ **Camden Jazz Festival** is 10 days of concerts sponsored by the Borough of Camden. For information, call ☏ 0171/860–5866.

MID-APR.➢ **London Marathon,** a New York–style marathon through

London's streets. Runners from 68 countries start in Greenwich and Blackheath 9–9:30 AM, then run via Docklands and Canary Wharf, the Tower of London and Paliament Square to finish in the Mall.

MAY 8–15➢ **British Antique Dealers' Association Fair,** the newest of the major fairs, is large and prestigious, with many affordable pieces. ☒ *Duke of York's Headquarters, King's Rd., Chelsea SW3,* ☏ *0171/589–6108.*

MID–MAY➢ **Royal Windsor Horse Show,** a major show-jumping event attended by some members of the Royal Family. ☒ *Show Box Office, 4 Grove Parade, Buxton, Derbyshire SK17 6AJ,* ☏ *01298/72272.*

MAY 20–23➢ **Chelsea Flower Show,** Britain's major flower show, covers 22 acres. ☒ *Royal Hospital Rd., Chelsea SW3,* ☏ *0171/630–7422.*

SUMMER

LATE MAY–LATE AUG.➢ **Glyndebourne Festival Opera** is a unique opportunity to see international stars in a bucolic setting and a brand-new theater. Tickets go fast and early. ☒ *Glyndebourne Festival Opera, Lewes, Sussex BN8 5UU,* ☏ *01273/ 812–321.*

EARLY JUNE➢ **Beating Retreat by the Guards Massed Bands,** when more than 500 musicians parade at Horse Guards, Whitehall. ☒ *Tickets from Household Division Fund, Block 8, Wellington Barracks, Birdcage Walk, London SW1E 6HQ,* ☏ *0171/414–3253.*

JUNE 7➢ **Derby Day** is the best-known event in the horse-racing calendar. ☒ *Information from United*

Racecourses Ltd., Racecourse Paddock, Epsom, Surrey KT18 5NJ, ☎ *013727/26311.*

June 14➢ **Trooping the Colour,** Queen Elizabeth's colorful official birthday parade, is held at Horse Guards, Whitehall. Write for tickets *only* between January 1 and February 28, enclosing a self-addressed stamped envelope: ✉ *Ticket Office, Headquarters, Household Division, Chelsea Barracks, London SW1H 8RF,* ☎ *0171/414–2497.*

June 12–21➢ **The Grosvenor House Antiques Fair** is one of the most prestigious antiques fairs in Britain. ✉ *Grosvenor House Hotel, Park La., London W1A 3AA,* ☎ *0171/499–6363.*

June 23–July 6➢ **Wimbledon Lawn Tennis Championships,** held at the All England Lawn Tennis and Croquet Club in Wimbledon. Write early to enter the lottery for tickets for Centre and Number One courts; tickets for outside courts available daily at the gate. ✉ *Church Rd., Wimbledon, London SW19 5AE,* ☎ *0181/946–2244.*

June 25–29➢ **Henley Royal Regatta,** an international rowing event and top social occasion, at Henley-upon-Thames, Oxfordshire. For information, call ☎ 01491/572–153.

Mid-July–mid-Sept.➢ **Henry Wood Promenade Concerts,** a marvelous series of concerts at the Royal Albert Hall. ✉ *Box Office, Royal Albert Hall, Kensington Gore SW7 2AP,* ☎ *0171/589–8212.*

July 15–26➢ **The Royal Tournament** features military displays and pageantry by the Royal Navy, the Royal Marines, the Army, and the Royal Air Force. ✉ *Earl's Court Exhibition Centre, Warwick Rd., London SW5 9TA,* ☎ *0171/370–8226.*

AUTUMN

Sept 20➢ **The Great River Race** is a festive 22-mile race sailed by 150-odd traditional boats (curraghs, shallops, wherries, Viking longboats . . .) at 2:15 PM from Ham House, Richmond, downstream to Island Gardens, Greenwich. ☎ 0181/398–9057.

Nov. 2➢ **London to Brighton Veteran Car Run,** a run from Hyde Park in London to Brighton in East Sussex. No tickets required. For information, call ☎ 01753/681–736.

Nov. 8➢ **Lord Mayor's Procession and Show.** At the lord mayor's inauguration, a procession takes place from the Guildhall in the City to the Royal Courts of Justice. No tickets required. For information, call ☎ 0171/606–3030.

2 Exploring London

LONDON GREW FROM A WOODEN BRIDGE built over the Thames in the year AD 43 to its current 7 million souls and 1,554 square kilometers (600 square miles) in haphazard fashion, meandering from its two official centers: Westminster, seat of government and royalty, and the City, site of finance and commerce. Many a tourist meanders the same way, and below are comprehensive sections on the famous parts of **Westminster and Royal London** and the **City.**

However, London's *un*official centers multiply and mutate year after year, and it would be a shame to stop only at the postcard views. Life is not lived in monuments, as the patrician patrons of the great Georgian architects understood when they commissioned the elegant squares and town houses of **St. James's** and **Mayfair** for newly rich merchants. Thanks to World War II bombs and today's newly rich merchants, the West End's elegance is patchy now. On its border, the once-seedy **Soho** still pleasures the flesh (gastronomically these days); and Westminster Abbey's original vegetable patch (or convent garden), which became the site of London's first square, **Covent Garden,** is now an unmissable stop on any agenda.

If the great, green parks (☞ Hyde Park, Kensington Gardens, and Notting Hill and Regent's Park and Hampstead, *below*) are, as in Lord Chatham's phrase, "the lungs of London," then the River Thames is its backbone. The river underlies the commercial success that made London great, and along its banks stand reminders from every century. Though there was traffic as far east as the **Docklands** from Roman times, they had their first boom in the Victorian era; today they are undergoing a peculiar stop-start renaissance. It's said that only cockneys "born within the sound of Bow Bells" in the adjacent **East End** are authentic Londoners, and so our tour around one of London's most diverse and least known areas may be the quintessential local experience.

Back on the river, the **South Bank** section absorbs the Southwark stews of Shakespeare's day—and the current reconstruction of his original Globe theatre, the concert hall from the '50s Festival of Britain, the arts complex from the '70s, and—farther downstream—the gorgeous 17th- and 18th-century symmetry of **Greenwich,** where the world's time is measured.

WESTMINSTER AND ROYAL LONDON

This tour is London For Beginners. If you went no farther than these few acres, you would have seen many of the famous sights, from the Houses of Parliament, Big Ben, Westminster Abbey, and Buckingham Palace, to two of the world's greatest art collections, the National and the Tate galleries. It might be possible to do it all in a day, but picking a highlight or two is a better idea. The galleries alone deserve a day apiece, and if you're going to the Abbey in summer, queuing up will consume most of your stamina. This is concentrated sightseeing, so pace yourself.

Westminster is by far the younger of the capital's two centers, postdating the City by some 1,000 years. Edward the Confessor put it on the map when he packed up his court from its cramped City quarters and went west a couple of miles, founding the abbey church of Westminster—the minster west of the City—in 1050. Subsequent kings continued to hold court there until Henry VIII decamped to Whitehall Palace in 1512, leaving Westminster to the politicians. And there they still are, not in the palace, which was burned almost to the ground in 1834, but in the Vic-

Central London Exploring *(Boxes Refer to Detail Maps)*

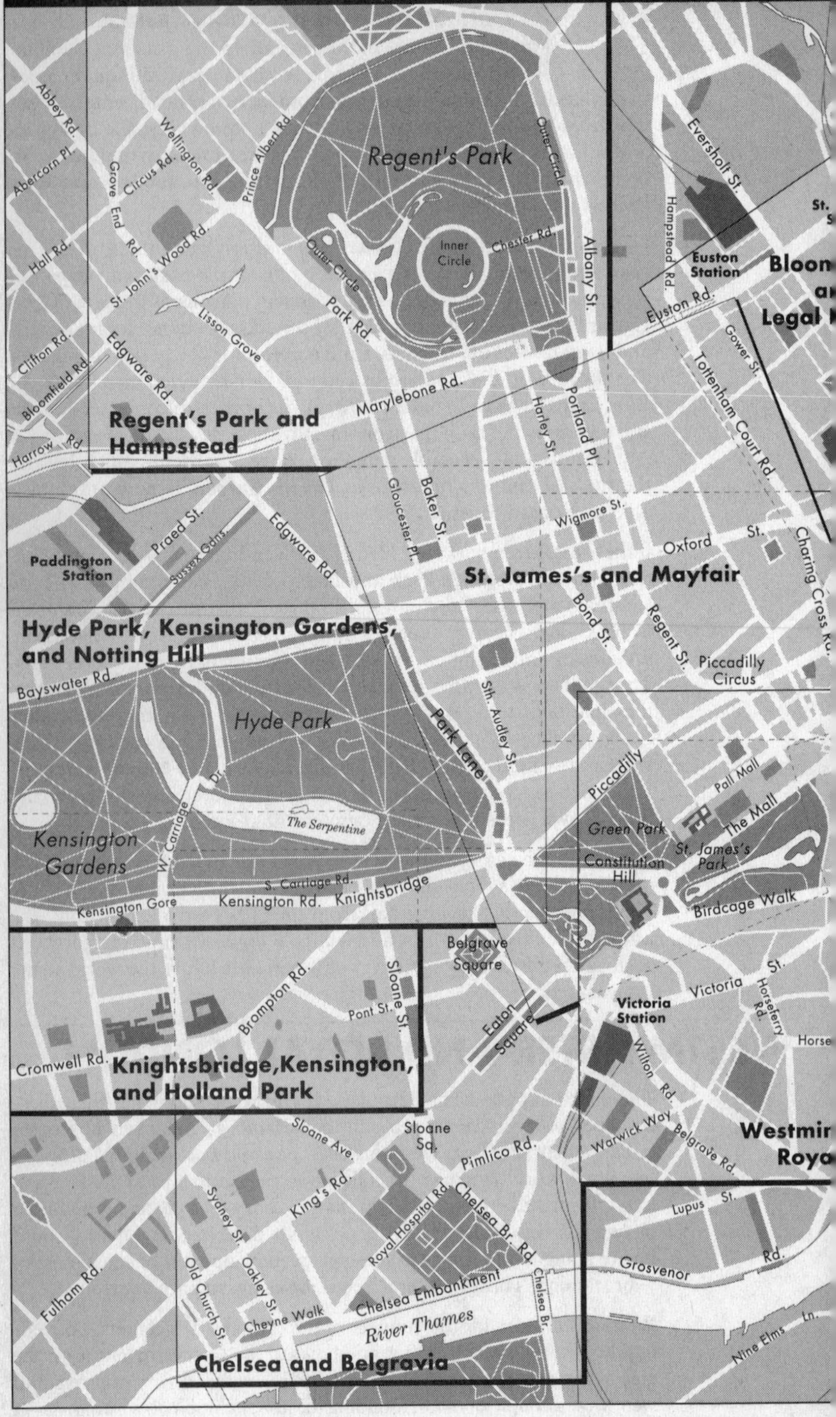

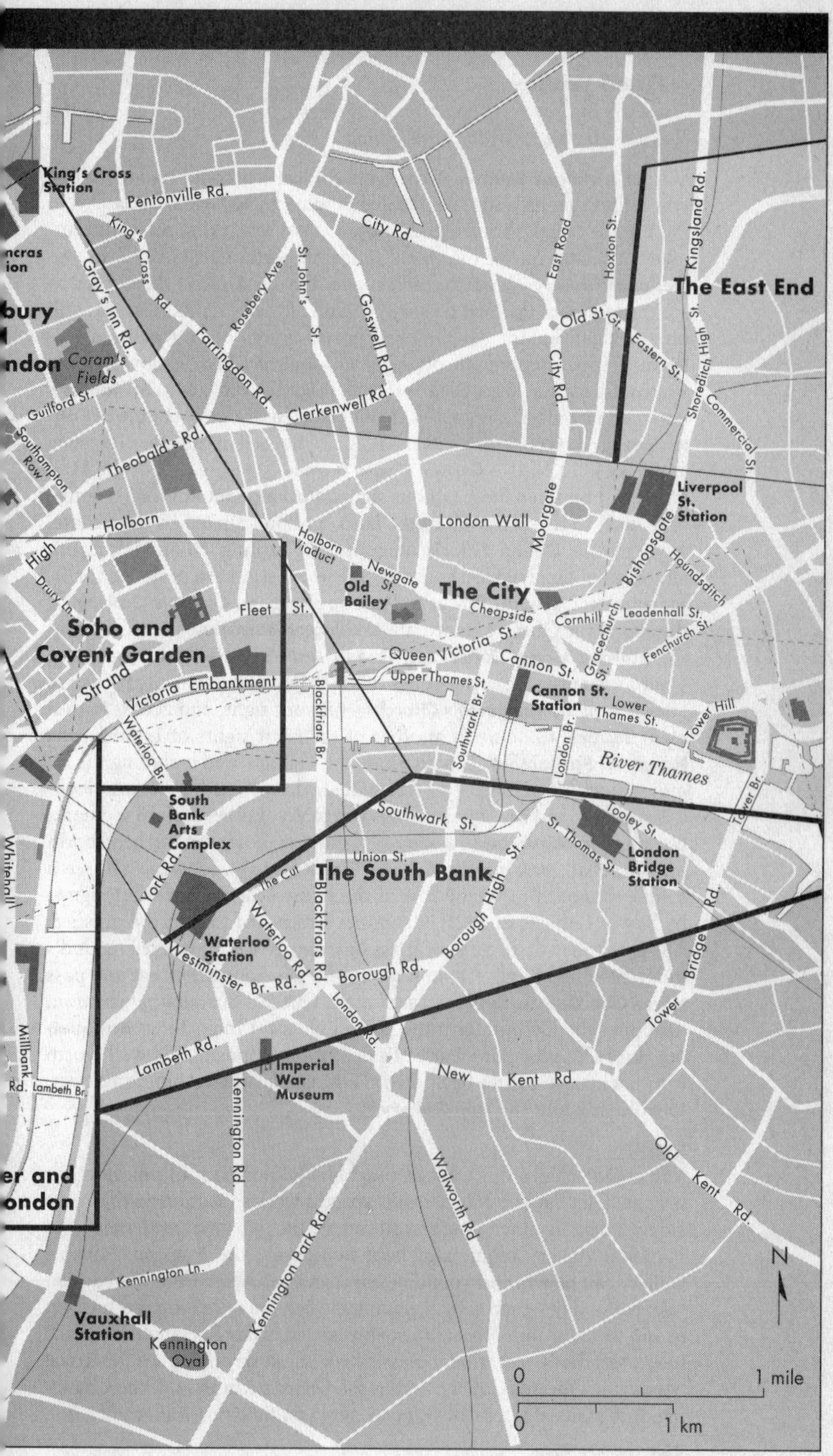
King's Cross Station
Pentonville Rd.
City Rd.
King's Cross Rd.
Gray's Inn Rd.
Rosebery Ave.
St. John's St.
Goswell Rd.
East Road
Hoxton St.
Kingsland Rd.
The East End
Old St.
Gt. Eastern St.
Shoreditch High St.
City Rd.
Commercial St.
Farringdon Rd.
Clerkenwell Rd.
Coram's Fields
Guilford St.
Southampton Row
Theobald's Rd.
Holborn
Moorgate
London Wall
Liverpool St. Station
Bishopsgate
Houndsditch
Holborn Viaduct
Newgate St.
Old Bailey
The City
High
Drury Ln.
Fleet St.
Cheapside
Cornhill
Leadenhall St.
Fenchurch St.
Soho and Covent Garden
Strand
Queen Victoria St.
Cannon St.
Gracechurch St.
Victoria Embankment
Upper Thames St.
Cannon St. Station
Lower Thames St.
Tower Hill
Blackfriars Br.
Southwark Br.
London Br.
Waterloo Br.
River Thames
Tower Br.
Southwark St.
South Bank Arts Complex
Tooley St.
St. Thomas St.
London Bridge Station
Whitehall
York Rd.
The Cut
Union St.
The South Bank
Borough High St.
Waterloo Rd.
Blackfriars Rd.
Waterloo Station
Westminster Br. Rd.
Borough Rd.
London Rd.
Tower Bridge Rd.
Millbank
Lambeth Rd.
Lambeth Br.
Imperial War Museum
New Kent Rd.
Kennington Rd.
Old Kent Rd.
Walworth Rd.
Kennington Park Rd.
Kennington Ln.
Vauxhall Station
Kennington Oval
N
0
1 mile
0
1 km

torian mock-Gothic Houses of Parliament, whose 320-foot Clock Tower is as much a symbol of London as the Eiffel Tower is of Paris.

A Good Walk

Numbers in the text correspond to numbers in the margin and on the Westminster and Royal London map.

Start at **Trafalgar Square** ①, the geographical center of London, where you'll find the instantly identifiable landmark, **Nelson's Column** ② in the middle (read about the area on a plaque marking its 150th anniversary), and one of the world's most important art collections, the **National Gallery** ③, on the north side. Detour around the corner to see the **National Portrait Gallery** ④. East of the National Gallery, still on Trafalgar Square, see the much-loved church of **St. Martin-in-the-Fields** ⑤ then, stepping through grand **Admiralty Arch** ⑥ down on the southwest corner, enter the royal pink road, **the Mall,** with **St. James's Park** running along the south side. On your right is the **Institute of Contemporary Arts** ⑦, known as the ICA and housed in the great Regency architect John Nash's **Carlton House Terrace** ⑧ At the foot of the Mall is one of London's most famous sights, **Buckingham Palace** ⑨, home, of course, to the monarch of the land, and punctuated by the ornate, white marble **Queen Victoria Memorial** ⑩. Turning left and left again, almost doubling back on yourself, follow the southern perimeter of St. James's Park around Birdcage Walk, passing the **Queen's Gallery** ⑪, the HQ of the Queen's Guard, the **Wellington Barracks** ⑫ on your right, the hulking **Home Office** and **Queen Anne's Gate** ⑬. Cross Horse Guard's Road at the eastern edge of the Park, walk down Great George Street, with **St. Margaret's Church** ⑭ on your right, and across **Parliament Square,** to come to another of the great sights of London, the **Houses of Parliament** ⑮, built along the Thames, and including the famous Clock Tower, usually (erroneously) known as Big Ben. A clockwise turn around the Square brings you to yet another major landmark, breathtaking **Westminster Abbey** ⑯. Complete the circuit and head north up Whitehall, passing the **Cabinet War Rooms** ⑰, where you'll see a simple monolith in the middle of the street—the **Cenotaph,** designed by Edwin Lutyens in 1920 in commemoration of the 1918 Armistice. The gated alley there on your left is **Downing Street** ⑱, where England's modest "White House" stands at number 10. Soon after that you pass **Horse Guards Parade** ⑲, setting for the Queen's birthday celebration, Trooping the Colour, with the perfect classical Inigo Jones **Banqueting House** ⑳, scene of Charles I's execution, opposite. It's well worth it to backtrack a little back down Whitehall, down Abington Street, to Millbank and the **Tate Gallery** ㉑.

TIMING

You could achieve this walk of roughly 4.8 kilometers (3 miles) in just over an hour, but you could equally spend a week's vacation on this route alone. Allow as much time as you can for the two great museums—the National Gallery requires at *least* two hours; the National Portrait Gallery can be whizzed round in less than one. Westminster Abbey can take half a day—especially in summer, when lines are long, both to get in and to get around. In summer, you can get inside Buckingham Palace too, a half day's operation increased to a whole day if you see the Royal Mews, the Queen's Gallery, and/or the Guards' Museum. If the Changing of the Guard is a priority, make sure you time this walk right.

Sights To See

6 **Admiralty Arch.** Standing on the southwest corner of Trafalgar Square, this was designed in 1910 by Sir Aston Webb as part of a ceremonial route to Buckingham Palace and named after the adjacent Royal Navy headquarters. As you pass under the enormous triple archway—though

not through the central arch, opened only for state occasions—the atmosphere changes along with the color of the road, for you are exiting frenetic Trafalgar Square and entering The Mall (rhymes with "shall"), which derives its name from a croquetlike 17th century sport, and which leads to the Palace.

20 **Banqueting House.** All that remains today of the Tudor Palace of Whitehall, which was (according to one foreign visitor) "ill-built, and nothing but a heap of houses" and therefore due for a grand remodeling at the hands of Inigo Jones, commissioned by James I. Jones (1573–1652), one of England's great architects, had been influenced by Andrea Palladio's work during a sojourn in Tuscany and had brought that sophistication and purity back with him to London. The graceful and disciplined classical style of Banqueting House must have stunned its early occupants. James I's son, Charles I, enhanced the interior by employing the Flemish painter Peter Paul Rubens to glorify his father all over the ceiling. As it turned out, these allegorical paintings, depicting a wise monarch being received into heaven, were the last thing Charles saw before he was beheaded by Cromwell's Parliamentarians on a scaffold outside in 1649. But his son, Charles II, was able to celebrate the restoration of the monarchy here 20 years later. ✉ *Whitehall,* ☎ *0171/930–4179.* 🎫 *£3.* ⏲ *Mon.–Sat. 10–5; closed Good Friday, Dec. 24–26, Jan. 1, and at short notice for banquets, so call first. Tube: Westminster.*

9 **Buckingham Palace.** Although the building itself is no masterpiece and has housed the monarch only since Victoria moved here from Kensington Palace at her accession in 1837, this tops the must-see lists. When Victoria moved in, the place was a mess. George IV, at *his* accession in 1820, had fancied the idea of moving to Buckingham House, his parents' former home, and had employed John Nash, as usual, to remodel it. The government authorized only "repair and improvement"; Nash, who had other ideas, overspent his budget by about half a million pounds. George died, Nash was dismissed, and Edward Blore finished the building, adding the now familiar east front (facing the Mall). Victoria arrived to faulty drains and sticky doors and windows nevertheless, but they did not mar her affection for the place, nor that of her son, Edward VII. The Portland stone facade dates only from 1913 (it, too, was part of the Aston Webb scheme), and the interior was renovated and redecorated only after World War II bomb damage.

The palace contains some 600 rooms, including the State Ballroom and, of course, the Throne Room. The royal apartments are in the north wing; when the queen is in, the royal standard flies at the masthead. Until recently all were off limits to the public, but a 1992 fire at Windsor Castle created an urgent need for cash. And so the state rooms are now on show—on something of an experimental basis through 1997—for eight weeks in August and September, when the royal family is away. Without an invitation to one of the queen's garden parties, however, you won't see much of the magnificent 45-acre grounds. ✉ *Buckingham Palace Rd.,* ☎ *0171/799–2331.* 🎫 *£8.* ⏲ *Call for hours, which had not been set at press time. Tube: St. James's Park, Victoria.*

17 **Cabinet War Rooms.** In back of the hulking **Foreign Office** (which was built in the 1860s by Sir Giles Gilbert Scott, better known for such fantastical Gothic Revival buildings as the House of Commons), this is an essential visit for World War II buffs. During air raids the War Cabinet met in this warren of 17 bomb-proof chambers. The Cabinet Room is still arranged as if a meeting were about to convene; in the Map Room, the Allied campaign is charted; the Prime Minister's Room holds the desk from which Churchill made his morale-boosting broadcasts; and the Telephone Room has his hot line to FDR. ✉ *Clive Steps,*

Westminster and Royal London

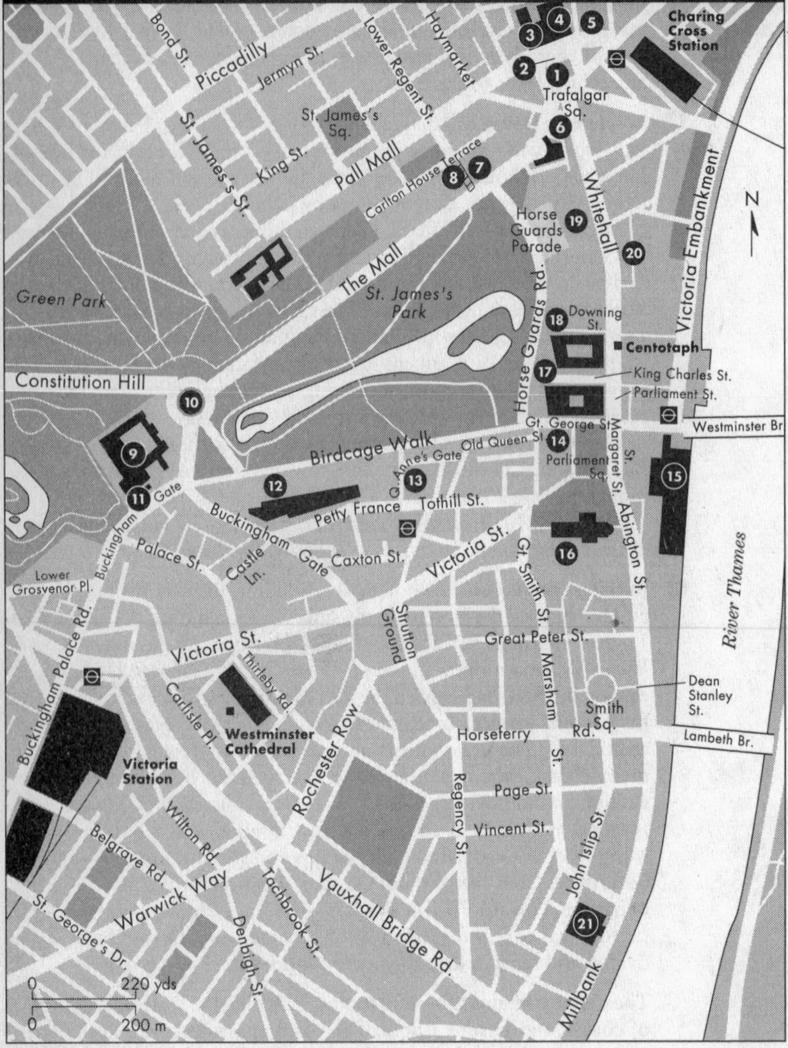

Admiralty Arch, **6**
Banqueting House, **20**
Buckingham Palace, **9**
Cabinet War Rooms, **17**
Carlton House Terrace, **8**
Downing Street, **18**
Horse Guards Parade, **19**
Houses of Parliament, **15**
Institute of Contemporary Arts (ICA), **7**
National Gallery, **3**
National Portrait Gallery, **4**
Nelson's Column, **2**
Queen Anne's Gate, **13**
Queen Victoria Memorial, **10**
Queen's Gallery, **11**
St. Margaret's Church, **14**
St. Martin-in-the-Fields, **5**
Tate Gallery, **21**
Trafalgar Square, **1**
Wellington Barracks, **12**
Westminster Abbey, **16**

King Charles St., ☏ 0171/930–6961. £4. Daily 10–5:15; closed Good Friday, May Day, Dec. 24–26, Jan. 1. Tube: Westminster.

8 **Carlton House Terrace.** This is a glorious example of Regency architect John Nash's genius. Between 1812 and 1830, under the patronage of George IV (Prince Regent until George III's death in 1820), Nash was responsible for a series of West End developments, of which these white-stucco facades and massive Corinthian columns may be the most imposing. It was a smart address, needless to say, and one that prime ministers Gladstone (1856) and Palmerston (1857–75) enjoyed. Today Carlton House Terrace is home to the Royal College of Pathologists, the Royal Society, the Turf Club, and, at No. 12, the ☞ **Institute of Contemporary Arts** better known as the ICA. *Tube: Charing Cross.*

18 **Downing Street.** Looking like an unassuming alley, but barred by iron gates at both its Whitehall and Horse Guards Road ends, this is where London's modest version of the White House stands at **10 Downing Street.** Only three houses remain of the terrace built circa 1680 by Sir George Downing, who spent enough of his youth in America to graduate from Harvard—the second man ever to do so. **No. 11** is the residence of the chancellor of the exchequer (secretary of the treasury), **No. 12** the party whips' office. No. 10 has officially housed the prime minister since 1732. (The gates were Margaret Thatcher's brainwave.) Just south of Downing Street, in the middle of Whitehall, you'll see the **Cenotaph,** a stark white monolith designed in 1920 by Edward Lutyens to commemorate the 1918 armistice. On Remembrance Day (the Sunday nearest November 11) it is strewn with blood-red poppies to honor the dead of both world wars, with the first wreath laid by the queen. (Wherever you are on that day, you'll be inveigled to buy a plastic poppy to support veterans' charities.)

Duke of York Steps. Bisecting Carlton House Terrace on the north side of The Mall, these are surmounted by the 124-foot Duke of York's Column (☞ Waterloo Place, *below*), from which an 1834 bronze of George III's second son, Frederick, gazes toward the Whitehall War Office. The Duke was popular among his troops until each man in the army had one day's pay extracted to fund this £25,000 tribute, which was perched so high, said the wits, to keep him away from creditors. He owed £2 million at his death.

19 **Horse Guards Parade.** This large square faces Horse Guards Road, opposite St. James's Park, at one end, and Whitehall on the other. Once the tilt-yard of Whitehall Palace, where jousting tournaments were held, it is now notable mainly for the annual Trooping the Colour ceremony, in which the queen takes the Royal Salute, her official birthday gift, on the second Saturday in June. (Like Paddington Bear, the queen has two birthdays; her real one is on April 21.) There is pageantry galore, with marching bands and the occasional guardsman fainting clean away in his busby, and throngs of people. The ceremony is televised and also broadcast on Radio 4. You can also attend the queenless rehearsals on the preceding two Saturdays. At the Whitehall facade of Horse Guards, two mounted sentries known as the Queen's Life Guard provide what may be London's most frequently taken up photo opportunity. They change, quietly, at 11 AM Monday–Saturday, 10 on Sunday. On a site reaching from here to the Thames and from Trafalgar to Parliament squares once stood Whitehall Palace, established by Henry VIII, who married two of his six wives (Anne Boleyn and Jane Seymour) and breathed his last there. The sheer scale of this 2,000-room labyrinth in red Tudor brick must have been breathtaking, but we won't dwell on it, as it burned to the ground in 1698, thanks to a fire started by a Dutch laundress whose name has not made it to posterity.

★ ⑮ **Houses of Parliament.** Here is arguably London's most famous and photogenic sight, with the Clock Tower, which everyone mistakenly calls Big Ben, keeping watch on the corner and Westminster Abbey ahead of you across Parliament Square, in which stand statues of Lord Palmerston and Benjamin Disraeli (prime ministers under Victoria); Sir Robert Peel (founder of the Metropolitan Police Force–the first "bobbies"); a hulking, hunched 1973 bronze Churchill; Richard the Lionheart; Oliver Cromwell; and Abraham Lincoln.

The Palace of Westminster, as the complex is still properly called, was established by Edward the Confessor during the 11th century, when he moved his court from the City, and has been the seat of English administrative power ever since. In 1512, Henry VIII abandoned it for Whitehall. It ceased to be an official royal residence after 1547: At the Reformation, the Royal Chapel was secularized and became the first meeting place of the Commons. The Lords settled in the White Chamber. These, along with everything but the **Jewel Tower** and **Westminster Hall,** were destroyed in 1834 when "the sticks"—the arcane abacus beneath the Lords' Chamber on which the court had kept its accounts until 1826—were incinerated and the fire got out of hand.

The same cellar had seen an earlier attempt to raze the palace: the infamous Gunpowder Plot of November 5, 1605, perpetrated by the Catholic convert Guy Fawkes and his fellow conspirators. If you are in London in late October or early November, you may see children with dressed-up teddy bears demanding a "penny for the guy!" They do it because, to this day, November 5 is Guy Fawkes Day (a.k.a. Bonfire Night), when fireworks bought with the pennies accompany pyres of these makeshift effigies of Guy Fawkes, and anyone who still knows it recites: "Remember, remember/The 5th of November,/The Gunpowder Treason and plot./There isn't a reason/Why gunpowder treason/Should ever be forgot."

After the 1834 fire, architects were invited to submit plans for new Houses of Parliament in the grandiose "Gothic or Elizabethan style." Charles Barry's were selected from among 97 entries, partly because Barry had invited the architect and designer Augustus Pugin to add the requisite neo-Gothic curlicues to his own Renaissance-influenced style. As you can see, it was a happy collaboration, with Barry's classical proportions offset by Pugin's ornamental flourishes—although the latter were toned down by Gilbert Scott when he rebuilt the bomb-damaged House of Commons after World War II.

The two towers were Pugin's work. The **Clock Tower,** now virtually the symbol of London, was completed in 1858 after long delays due to bickering over the clock's design. (Barry designed the faces himself in the end.) It contains the 13-ton bell that chimes the hour (and the quarter) known as Big Ben. Some say Ben was "Big Ben" Caunt, heavyweight champ; others, Sir Benjamin Hall, the far-from-slim Westminster building works commissioner. At the other end is the 336-foot-high **Victoria Tower,** which contains the 3-million-document parliamentary archives and now gleams from its recent restoration and cleaning. The rest of the complex was scrubbed down some years ago; the revelation of the honey stone under the dowdy, smog-blackened facades, which seemed almost symbolic at the time, cheered London up no end.

There are two Houses, the Lords and the Commons. The former consists of more than 1,000 peers (nowadays there are more "life peers," with recently bestowed titles, than aristocrats; there are also 26 Anglican bishops who are "spiritual peers"), the latter of 650 elected Members of Parliament (MPs). The party with the most MPs forms the government, its leader becoming Prime Minister; other parties form the Opposition. Since 1642, when Charles I tried to have five MPs arrested, no monarch has been allowed into the House of Commons. The State Opening of Parliament in November consequently takes place in the House of Lords, after a ritual inspection of the cellars in case a modern Guy Fawkes lurks.

Visitors aren't allowed many places in the Houses of Parliament, though the Visitors' Galleries of the House of Commons do afford a fine view of the surprisingly cramped debating chambers. The opposing banks of green leather benches seat only 346 MPs—not that this is much of a problem, since absentees far outnumber the diligent. When MPs vote, they exit by the "Aye" or the "No" corridor, counted by the party "whips" (yes, it is a fox hunting term); when they speak, it is not directly to each other but through the Speaker, who also decides who will get the floor each day. Elaborate procedures notwithstanding, debate is often drowned out by the amazingly immature jeers and insults familiar to TV viewers since 1989, when cameras were first allowed into the House of Commons.

The House of Lords was televised first, perhaps because its procedures are more palatably dignified, with the Lord Chancellor, or Chief Justice, presiding from his official seat, the Woolsack (England's economy was once dependent on this commodity) over a few gently slumbering peers. Or perhaps the Lords were first because of their telegenic gold and scarlet chamber, Pugin's masterpiece. The Upper House remains the highest court of appeal in the land, though its parliamentary powers are restricted to delaying or suspending passage of a bill. It is separated from the Lower House by the octagonal **Central Lobby,** which is where constituents wait for their MPs and also where the press is received—hence the term "lobby correspondent" for a domestic political reporter. Other public areas of the 1,100-room labyrinth are rather magnificently got up in high neo-Gothic style and punctuated with stirring frescoes commissioned by Prince Albert. You pass these en route to the Visitors Galleries—if, that is, you are patient enough to wait in line for hours (the Lords line is shorter) or have applied in advance through your embassy. ✉ *St. Stephen's Entrance, St. Margaret St., SW1,* ☎ *0171/219–3000.* 💳 *Free. Commons open Mon.–Thurs. 2:30–10, Fri. 9:30–3; Lords open Mon.–Thurs. 2:30–10. Closed Easter wk, May bank holiday, July–Oct., 3 wks at Christmas. Tube: Westminster.*

❼ **Institute of Contemporary Arts (ICA).** Behind its incongruous white-stucco facade, at No. 12 Carlton House Terrace, the ICA has provided a stage for the avant-garde in performance, theater, dance, visual art, and music since it was established in 1947. There are two cinemas, an underused library of video artists' works, a bookshop, a café and a bar, and a team of adventurous curators. ✉ *The Mall,* ☎ *0171/930–3647.* 💳 *1-day membership: £1.50. An additional charge is made for entry to specific events.* ⏲ *Daily noon–9:30, later for some events; closed Dec. 24–27, Jan. 1. Tube: Charing Cross.*

NEED A BREAK?

The **ICAfé** is windowless but brightly spotlighted, with a self-service counter offering good hot dishes, salads, quiches, and desserts. The bar upstairs, which serves baguette sandwiches, has a picture window overlooking the Mall. Both are packed before popular performances, and are subject to the £1.50 one-day membership fee.

The Mall. This street was laid out around 1660 for the game of *pell mell* that also gave Pall Mall its name, and quickly became the place to be seen. Samuel Pepys, Jonathan Swift, and Alexander Pope all wrote about it, and it continued as the beau monde's social playground into the early 19th century, long after the game it was built for had gone out of vogue. Something of the former style survives on those summer days when the queen is throwing a Buckingham Palace garden party: hundreds of her subjects throng The Mall, from the grand and titled to the humble and hardworking, all of whom have donned hat and frock to take afternoon tea with her—or somewhere near her—on the lawns of Buck House. The old Mall still runs alongside the graceful pink 115-foot-wide avenue that replaced it in 1904 for just such occasions.

★ ❸ **National Gallery.** The low, gray, colonnaded neo-classical facade of London's greatest art collection fills the north side of Trafalgar Square. The institution was founded in 1824, when George IV and a connoisseur named Sir George Beaumont persuaded a reluctant government to spend £57,000 on part of the recently deceased philanthropist John Julius Angerstein's collection. These 38 paintings, including works by Raphael, Rembrandt, Titian, and Rubens, were augmented by 16 of Sir George's own and exhibited in Angerstein's Pall Mall residence until 1838, when William Wilkin's building was completed. By the end of the century, enthusiastic directors and generous patrons had turned the National Gallery into one of the world's foremost collections, with works from painters of the Italian Renaissance and earlier, from the Flemish and Dutch masters, the Spanish school, and of course the English tradition, including Hogarth, Gainsborough, Stubbs, and Constable.

In 1991, following years of wrangling and the rehanging of the entire collection, the Sainsbury Wing was opened. It had been financed by the eponymous British grocery dynasty to house the early Renaissance collection, and designed—eventually—by the American architect Robert Venturi after previous plans were abandoned. (Prince Charles hadn't liked them. "A monstrous carbuncle on the face of a much-loved friend" was his infamous comment.)

The collection is really too overwhelming to absorb in a single viewing. It is wise to acquaint yourself with the layout—easy to negotiate compared with other European galleries—and plot a route in advance. The **Micro Gallery**, a computer information center in the Sainsbury Wing, might be the place to start. You can access in-depth information on any work here, choose your favorites, and print out a free personal tour map that marks the paintings you most want to see. Careful, though—you could spend hours in here scrolling through the colorful potted history of art.

Among the 2,200-odd paintings, most of them on permanent display, many are instantly recognizable. What follows is a list of 10 of the most familiar to jog your memory, whet your appetite, and offer a starting point for your own exploration. The first five are in the Sainsbury Wing. In chronological order: (1) **van Eyck** (c. 1395–1441), *The Arnolfini Marriage.* A solemn couple hold hands, the fish-eye mirror behind them mysteriously illuminating what can't be seen from the front. (2) **Uccello** (1397–1475), *The Battle of San Romano.* In a work commissioned by the Medici family, the Florentine commander on a rearing white warhorse leads armored knights to battle with the Sienese. (3) **Bellini** (c.1430–1516), *The Doge Leonardo Loredan.* The artist captured the Venetian doge's beatific expression (and snail-shell "buttons") at the beginning of his 20 years in office. (4) **Botticelli** (1445–1510), *Venus and Mars.* Mars sleeps, exhausted by the love goddess, oblivious to the lance wielded by mischievous putti and the buzzing of wasps. (5) **Leonardo da Vinci** (1452–1519), *The Virgin and Child.* This haunting black chalk cartoon is partly famous for having been attacked at gunpoint, and now gets extra protection behind glass and screens. (6) **Caravaggio** (1573–1610), *The Supper at Emmaus.* A cinematically lighted, freshly resurrected Christ blesses bread in an astonishingly domestic vision from the master of chiaroscuro. (7) **Velázquez** (1599–1660), *The Toilet of Venus.* "The Rokeby Venus," named for her previous home in Yorkshire, has the most famously beautiful back in any gallery. She's the only surviving female nude by Velázquez. (8) **Constable** (1776–1837), *The Hay Wain.* Rendered overfamiliar by too many birthday cards, this is the definitive version of rural England. (9) **Turner** (1775–1851), *The Fighting Téméraire.* Most of the collection's other Turners were moved to the Tate Gallery; the final voyage of the great French battleship into a livid, hazy sunset stayed here. (10) **Seurat** (1859–1891), *Bathers at Asnières.* This static summer day's idyll is one of the pointillist extraordinaire's best-known works.

Glaring omissions from the above include Titian, Holbein, Bosch, Brueghel, Rembrandt, Vermeer, Rubens, Canaletto, Claude, Teipolo, Gainsborough, Ingres, Monet, Renoir, Van Gogh . . . you get the picture. As you leave, look on the sloping lawn in front for Grinling Gibbons's statue of James II, who failed to return Britain to Catholicism during his short reign (1685–88). Gibbons, "Master Carver in Wood to the Crown," was much in vogue at the end of the 17th century (see his choir-stall carvings at St. Paul's). At the other end of the lawn is a bronze of George Washington presented to the British by the Commonwealth of Virginia in 1921. ✉ *Trafalgar Sq.,* ☎ *0171/839–3321; 0171/839–3526 (recorded general information); 0171/389–1773 (recorded exhibition information).* 🎫 *Free; admission charge for special exhibitions. Free 1-hr guided tours start at the Sainsbury Wing weekdays at 11:30 and 2:30, Sat. 2 and 3:30.* ⊙ *Mon.–Sat. 10–6, Sun. 2–6; June–Aug., also Wed. until 8; closed Good Friday, May Day, Dec. 24–26, Jan. 1. Tube: Charing Cross.*

NEED A BREAK? The **Brasserie** in the Sainsbury Wing of the National Gallery offers a fashionable lunch—mussels, gravlax, charcuterie, salads, a hot dish—plus baguette sandwiches, pastries, tea, coffee, and wine, in a sophisticated, spacious room on the second floor.

❹ **National Portrait Gallery.** An idiosyncratic collection that presents a potted history of Britain through its residents, past and present. As an art collection it is eccentric, as the subject, not the artist, is the point, and there are notable works (a Holbein portrait of Henry VIII, Stubbs and Hockney self-portraits) mixed up with photographs, busts, caricatures, and amateur paintings. (The miniature of Jane Austen by her sister Cassandra, for instance, is the only likeness we have of the great novelist.) Many of the faces are obscure and will be just as unknown to English visitors, because the portraits outlasted their sitters' fame. But the annotation is comprehensive, and there is a new, separate research center for those who get hooked on particular personages—part of an expansion that includes a streamlined layout (still chronological, with the oldest at the top) and a photography gallery. ✉ *St. Martin's Pl., WC2,* ☎ *0171/306–0055.* 🎫 *Free.* ⊙ *Weekdays 10–5, Sat. 10–6, Sun. 2–6. Closed public holidays. Tube: Charing Cross, Leicester Square.*

❷ **Nelson's Column.** The famous column is the 145-foot granite perch from which E. H. Baily's 1843 statue of Admiral Lord Horatio Nelson, one of England's favorite heroes keeps watch; three bas-reliefs depicting his victories at Cape St. Vincent, the Battle of the Nile, and Copenhagen (and a fourth, his death at Trafalgar itself in 1805) around the base–all four were cast from cannons he captured. The four majestic lions, designed by the Victorian painter Sir Edwin Landseer, were added in 1867. The calling cards of generations of picturesque pigeons have been a corrosive problem for the statue, which may have been finally solved by the statue's new gel coating.

⓭ **Queen Anne's Gate.** Standing south of Birdcage Walk, by St. James's Park, are these two pretty 18th-century closes, once separate but now linked by a statue of the last Stuart monarch. (Another statue of Anne, beside St. Paul's, inspired the doggerel "Brandy Nan, Brandy Nan, you're left in the lurch,/Your face to the gin shop, your back to the church,"—proving that her attempts to disguise her habitual tipple in a teapot fooled nobody.) Also here is the Henry Moore bronze *Mother and Child.*

❿ **Queen Victoria Memorial.** You can't overlook this if you're near Buckingham Palace, which it faces from the traffic island at the west end of the Mall. The monument was conceived by Sir Aston Webb as the nucleus of his ceremonial route down The Mall to the Palace, and executed by the sculptor Thomas Brock, who was knighted on the spot when it was revealed to the world in 1911. Many wonder why he was, since the thing is Victoriana incarnate: The frumpy queen glares down the Mall, with golden-winged Victory overhead and her siblings Truth, Justice, and Charity, plus Manufacture, Progress-and-Peace, War-and-Shipbuilding, and so on—in Osbert Sitwell's words, "tons of allegorical females . . . with whole litters of their cretinous children"—surrounding her. Climbing it is not encouraged, even though it's the best vantage point for viewing the daily **Changing of the Guard,** which, with all the pomp and ceremony monarchists and children adore, remains one of London's best free shows. ✉ *Guard leaves Wellington Barracks 11 AM, arrives at Buckingham Palace 11:30. Daily Apr.–July; alternate days Aug.–Mar. Tube: St. James's Park, Victoria.*

⓫ **Queen's Gallery.** This is the former chapel at the south side of Buckingham Palace, which has been open to visitors since 1962. On display here are paintings from her majesty's collection—the country's largest by far—including works by Vermeer, Leonardo, Rubens, Rembrandt, Canaletto . . . and Queen Victoria, though by no means all at the same time. Sign-of-the-times note: Now that she is a taxpayer, HRH's artwork, along with all her other possessions (for example, Buckingham Palace), are officially part of a business known as Royal Collection Enterprises. ✉ *Buckingham Palace Rd.,* ☎ *0171/799–2331.* 🎫 *£3.50. Combined ticket for Queen's Gallery and Royal Mews: £6.££* ⏲ *Tues.–Sat. 10–5, Sun. 2–5; closed Dec. 24–Mar. 4, Good Friday. Tube: St. James's Park, Victoria.*

Royal Mews. Designed by John Nash, these stand nearly next door to the Queen's Gallery, close to Buckingham Palace. Mewses were originally falcons' quarters (the name comes from their "mewing," or feather shedding), but horses gradually eclipsed birds of prey. Now some of the magnificent royal beasts live here alongside the fabulous bejeweled, glass, and golden coaches they draw on state occasions. The place is unmissable children's entertainment. ✉ *Buckingham Palace Rd.,* ☎ *0171/799–2331.* 🎫 *£3.50. Combined ticket for Queen's Gallery and Royal Mews: £6.* ⏲ *Oct.–Mar., Wed. noon–4; Apr.–Oct., Tues.–Thurs. noon–4; closed Mar. 25–29, Oct. 1–5, Dec. 23–Jan. 5. Tube: St. James's Park, Victoria.*

St. James's Park. London's smallest, most ornamental park, and the oldest of its royal ones. Henry VIII drained a marsh that festered here next to the lepers' hospital that St. James's Palace replaced, and bred his deer on the newly dry land. Later kings tinkered with it further, James

I installing aviary and zoo (complete with crocodiles); Charles I laying formal gardens, which he then had to cross to his execution at the Banqueting House in 1649; and Charles II employing André Lenôtre, Louis XIV's Versailles landscaper, to remodel it completely with avenues, fruit orchards, and a canal. Its present shape more or less reflects what John Nash designed under George IV, turning the canal into a graceful lake (which was cemented in at a depth of 4 feet in 1855, so don't even think of swimming) and generally naturalizing the gardens.

More than 30 species of birds—including flamingos, pelicans, geese, ducks, and swans (which belong to the queen)—now congregate on Duck Island at the east end of the lake, attracting ornithologists at dawn. Later on summer days the deck chairs (which you must pay to use) are crammed with office lunchers being serenaded by music from the bandstands. The best time to stroll the leafy walkways, though, is after dark, with Westminster Abbey and the Houses of Parliament rising above the floodlit lake, and peace reigning.

14 **St. Margaret's Church.** Dwarfed by its northern neighbor, Westminster Abbey, this church was founded during the 12th century and rebuilt between 1486 and 1523. St. Margaret's is the parish church of the Houses of Parliament and much sought after for weddings; Samuel Pepys married here in 1655, Winston Churchill in 1908. The east Crucifixion window celebrates another union, the marriage of Prince Arthur and Catherine of Aragon. Unfortunately, it arrived so late that Arthur was dead and Catherine had married his brother, Henry VIII. Sir Walter Raleigh is among the notables buried here, only without his head, which had been removed at Old Palace Yard, Westminster, and kept by his wife, who was said to be fond of asking visitors, "Have you met Sir Walter?" as she produced it from a velvet bag.

5 **St. Martin-in-the-Fields.** One of Britain's best-loved churches, this was completed in 1726; James Gibbs's classical-temple-with-spire design became familiar as the pattern for churches in early Colonial America. Though it seems dwarfed by the surrounding structures of Trafalgar Square, the spire is actually slightly taller than Nelson's Column, which it overlooks. It is a welcome sight for the homeless, who have sought soup and shelter here since 1914. The church is also a haven for music lovers, since the internationally known Academy of St. Martin-in-the-Fields was founded here, and a popular program of lunchtime (free) and evening concerts continues today. St. Martin's is often called the royal parish church, partly because Charles II was christened here—not because his mistress, Nell Gwyn, lies under the stones, alongside William Hogarth, Thomas Chippendale (the cabinetmaker), and Jack Sheppard, the notorious highwayman. Also in the crypt is the **London Brass-Rubbing Centre,** where you can make your own souvenir knight from replica tomb brasses, with metallic waxes, paper, and instructions provided, and the **St. Martin's Gallery** showing contemporary work. There is also a crafts market in the courtyard behind the church. ✉ *St. Martin-in-the-Fields, Trafalgar Sq.,* ☎ *0171/930–0089. Credit card bookings for evening concerts,* ☎ *0171/839–8362. Brass rubbing fee from £1. Church open daily 8–8; crypt open Mon.–Sat. 10–8, Sun. noon–6. Tube: Charing Cross, Leicester Square.*

NEED A BREAK? St. Martin's **Café-in-the-Crypt** serves full meals, sandwiches, snacks, and even a glass of wine, Monday–Saturday 10–8; noon–6 on Sunday.

Smith Square. An elegant enclave of perfectly preserved early 18th-century town houses which still looks like the London of Dr. Johnson. The address is much sought-after by MPs, especially of the Tory persuasion; No. 32 is the Conservative Party Headquarters. The Baroque church of **St. John's, Smith Square,** completed around 1720, dominates charmingly. It is well known to Londoners as a chamber-music venue; its popular lunchtime concerts are often broadcast on the radio.

NEED A BREAK? In the crypt of St. John's is **The Footstool**—about the only place to find refreshment around here. It has an interesting and reasonably priced lunchtime menu and also serves evening meals on concert nights.

21 **Tate Gallery.** By the river, on traffic-laden Millbank, the Tate Gallery of Modern British Art, to give it its full title, opened in 1897, funded by the sugar magnate Sir Henry Tate. "Modern" is slightly misleading, since one of the three collections here consists of British art from 1545 to the present, including works by William Hogarth, Thomas Gainsborough, Sir Joshua Reynolds, and George Stubbs from the 18th century, and by John Constable, William Blake (a mind-blowing collection of his visionary works), and the pre-Raphaelite painters from the 19th century. Also from the 19th century is the second of the Tate's collections, the Turner Bequest, consisting of J. M. W. Turner's personal collection; he left it to the nation on condition that the works be displayed together. The James Stirling–designed **Clore Gallery** (to the right of the main gallery) has fulfilled his wish since 1987, and should not be missed.

The Tate's modern collection is international and so vast that it is never all on display at once. The current director, Nicholas Serota, instigated the strategy of annual rehanging, which goes some way toward solving the dilemma of the gallery's embarrassment of riches, but also means that a favorite work may not be on view; although, the most famous and popular works are on permanent display. Come the year 2000, the Tate's space dilemma will be solved with the opening of the new gallery, opposite St. Paul's, in the former Bankside Power Station, currently undergoing a £100 million transformation to the plans of Swiss architects, Herzog & de Meuron. Even now, though, you can see work by an abundance of late 19th- and 20th-century artists, and a good deal more besides. Your tour will deal you multiple shocks of recognition (Rodin's *The Kiss,* Lichtenstein's *Whaam!*), and you can rent a "Tate-inform" hand-held audio guide, with commentaries by curators, experts, and some of the artists themselves, to enhance the picture. Here's a short list of names: Matisse, Picasso, Braque, Léger, Kandinsky, Mondrian, Dalí, Bacon, de Kooning, Pollock, Rothko, Moore, Hepworth, Warhol, Freud, Hockney. ✉ *Millbank,* ☎ *0171/821–1313 or 0171/821–7128 (recorded information).* 💵 *Free; personal audio guide rental, admission charged for special exhibitions.* ⏲ *Mon.–Sat. 10–5:50, Sun. 2–5:50; closed Good Friday, May Day, Dec. 24–26, Jan. 1.*

1 **Trafalgar Square.** This is the center of London, by dint of a plaque on the corner of the Strand and Charing Cross Road from which distances on U.K. signposts are measured. It is the home of ☞ **the National Gallery** and of one of London's most distinctive landmarks, ☞ **Nelson's Column;** also of many a political demonstration, a raucous New Year's party, and the highest concentration of bus stops and pigeons in the capital. In short, it is London's most famous square.

Long ago the site housed the Royal Mews, where Edward I (1239–1307) kept his royal hawks and lodged his falconers. (Not the numberless Edward the Confessor of Westminster Abbey fame, who died in 1066, this one was known as "Longshanks" and died of dysentery in 1307.) Later, all the kings' horses were stabled here, in increasingly smart quarters, until 1830, when John Nash had the buildings torn down as part of his Charing Cross Improvement Scheme—which he did not live to complete. The baton was passed to Sir Charles Barry, archi… of the Houses of Parliament, and in 1840 the Square was paved, with the fountains added five years later. (Sir Edwin Lutyens remodeled them in 1939, and they were further enhanced with cavorting sea creatures after World War II.)

There's a pathetic history attached to the **equestrian statue of Charles I,** which stands near Whitehall on the southern slope of the Square (on a pedestal *possibly* designed by Sir Christopher Wren and *possibly* carved by Grinling Gibbons). After Charles's High Treasurer ordered it (from Hubert le Sueur), the Puritan Oliver Cromwell tumbled Charles from the throne and commissioned a scrap dealer with the appropriate name of Rivett to melt the king down. Rivett made a fortune peddling knickknacks wrought, he claimed, from its metal, only to produce the statue miraculously unscathed after the restoration of the monarchy—and to make more cash reselling it to the authorities. In 1767 Charles II had it placed where it stands today, near the spot where his father was executed in 1649.

Today, street performers enhance the square's intermittent atmosphere of celebration, which is strongest in December, first when the lights on the gigantic Christmas tree (an annual gift from Norway to thank the British for harboring their royal family during World War II) are turned on, and then—less festively, especially during the recent year when two people were crushed to death by the crowds—when thousands see in the New Year.

⓬ **Wellington Barracks.** These are the headquarters of the Guards Division, the queen's five regiments of elite foot guards (Grenadier, Coldstream, Scots, Irish, and Welsh) who protect the sovereign and patrol her palace dressed in tunics of gold-purled scarlet and tall fur "busby" helmets of Canadian brown bearskin. (The two items cost more than £4,000 for the set.) If you want to learn more about the guards, you can visit the **Guards Museum;** the entrance is next to the Guards Chapel. ✉ *Wellington Barracks, Birdcage Walk,* ☎ *0171/930–4466, ext. 3430.* 🎫 *£2.* ⏲ *Sat.–Thurs. 10–4; closed national holidays. Tube: St. James's Park.*

★ ⓰ **Westminster Abbey.** Announced by the teeming human contents of herds of tour buses, off the south side of Parliament Square, this is where nearly all of England's monarchs were crowned, amid vast pomp and circumstance, and most are buried here, too. The place is crammed with spectacular medieval architecture and impressive and moving monuments. It is worth pointing out, though, that the Abbey is still a place of worship, and while attending a service is not something to undertake purely for sightseeing reasons, it provides a glimpse of the Abbey in its full majesty, accompanied by music from the Westminster choristers and the organ that Henry Purcell once played. Some parts are closed on Sunday except to worshipers.

The origins of Westminster Abbey are uncertain. The first church on the site may have been built as early as the 7th century by the Saxon King Sebert (who may be buried here, alongside his queen and sister); a Benedictine abbey was established during the 10th century. There were certainly pre-existing foundations when Edward the Confessor was crowned in 1040, moved his palace to Westminster, and began building a church. Only traces have been found of that incarnation, which was consecrated eight days before Edward's death in 1065. (It appears in the Bayeaux Tapestry.) Edward's canonization in 1139 gave a succession of kings added incentive to shower the Abbey with attention and improvements. Henry III, full of ideas from his travels in

Confess…
Henry V's Chantry, **14**
Chapter House, **21**
Coronation Chair, **15**
Henry VII Chapel, **9**
High Altar, **12**
Norman Undercroft and Museum, **20**
North Entrance, **16**
Organ Loft, **5**
Poet's Corner, **8**
Pyx Chamber, **19**
Royal Airforce Chapel, **12**
St. George Chapel, **4**
Sanctuary, **6**
Sir Winston Churchill Memorial, **2**
Stairs to Library, **18**
Tomb of Elizabeth I, **13**
Tomb of Henry II, **11**
Tomb of Mary, Queen of Scots, **10**
Tomb of the Unknown Warrior, **3**
West Entrance and Bookshop, **1**

Westminster Abbey

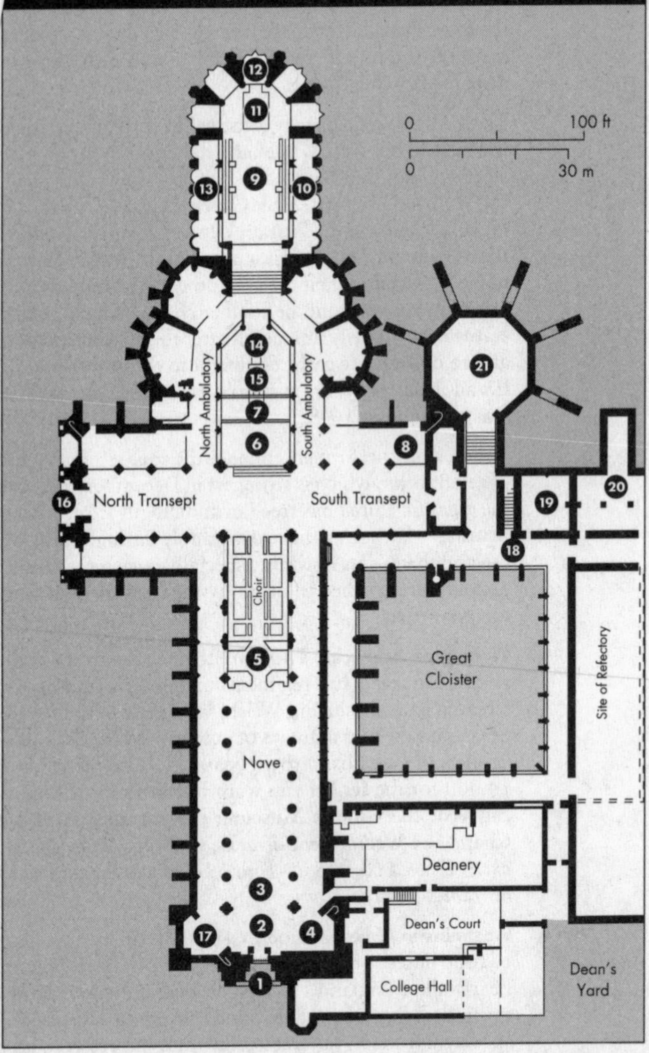

France, pulled it down and started again with Amiens and Rheims in mind. In fact it was the master mason Henry de Reyns ("of Rheims") who, between 1245 and 1254, put up the transepts, north front, and rose windows, as well as part of the cloisters and Chapter House; and it was his master plan that, funded by Richard II, was resumed 100 years later. Henry V (reigned 1413–1422) and Henry VII (1485–1509) were the chief succeeding benefactors. The Abbey was eventually completed in 1532. After that, Sir Christopher Wren had a hand in shaping the place; his West Towers were completed in 1745, 22 years after his death. The most riotous elements of the interior were, similarly, much later affairs.

The Nave is your first sight on entering; you need to look up to gain a perspective on the awe-inspiring scale of the church, because the eye-level view is obscured by the 19th- (and part 13th-) century choir screen, past which point admission is charged. Before paying, look at the poignant **Tomb of the Unknown Warrior,** an anonymous World

War I martyr who lies buried here in memory of the soldiers fallen in both world wars. Nearby is one of the very few tributes to a foreigner, a plaque to Franklin D. Roosevelt.

There is only one way around the Abbey, and as there will almost certainly be a crocodile of shuffling visitors at your heels, you'll need to be alert to catch the highlights. Pass through the Choir, with its mid–19th-century choir stalls, into the North Transept. Look up to your right to see the painted-glass Rose Window, the largest of its kind; left for the first of the extravagant 18th-century monuments in the North Transept chapels. You then proceed into the **Henry VII Chapel,** passing the huge white marble tomb of Elizabeth I, buried with her half sister, "Bloody" Mary I; then the tomb of Henry VII with his queen, Elizabeth of York, by the Renaissance master Torrigiano (otherwise known for having been banished from Florence after breaking Michelangelo's nose). All around are magnificent sculptures of saints, philosophers, and kings, with wild mermaids and monsters carved on the choir stall misericords (undersides), and exquisite fan vaulting above—one of the miracles of Western architecture.

Next you enter the **Chapel of Edward the Confessor,** where beside the royal saint's shrine stands the **Coronation Chair,** which has been briefly graced by nearly every regal posterior. Edward I ordered it around 1300, and it shelters the Stone of Scone (pronounced *skoon*), a brown sandstone block upon which Scottish kings had been crowned since time began, and which Edward I symbolically stole in 1296. Scottish Nationalists borrowed it back for about six months in 1950; otherwise, only Oliver Cromwell (who took it to Westminster Hall to "crown" himself Lord Protector) and wartime caution have removed it from here.

The tombs and monuments for which Westminster Abbey is probably best loved appeared at an accelerated rate starting in the 18th century. One earlier occupant, though, was Geoffrey Chaucer, who in 1400 became the first poet to be buried in **Poets' Corner.** Most of the other honored writers have only their memorials here, not their bones: William Shakespeare and William Blake (who both had a long wait before the dean deemed them holy enough to be here at all), John Milton, Jane Austen, Samuel Taylor Coleridge, William Wordsworth, Charles Dickens. All of Ben Jonson is here, though—buried upright in accord with his modest demand for a two-foot-by-two-foot grave. ("O rare Ben Jonson," reads his epitaph, in a modest pun on the Latin *orare,* "to pray for.") Sir Isaac Newton, James Watt, and Michael Faraday are among the scientists with memorials. There is only one painter: Godfrey Kneller, whose dying words were "By God, I will not be buried in Westminster."

After the elbow battle you are guaranteed in Poets' Corner, you exit the Abbey by a door from the South Transept. Outside the west front is an archway into the quiet green **Dean's Yard** and the entrance to the **Cloisters,** where the monks strolled in contemplation. You may do the same, and catch a fine view of the massive flying buttresses above in the process. You may also, for a modest fee, take an impression from one of the tomb brasses in the **Brass-Rubbing Centre** (☎ 0171/222–2085). Also here is the entrance to Westminster School, formerly a monastic college, now one of Britain's finest public (which means the exact opposite) schools; Christopher Wren and Ben Jonson number among the old boys. The **Chapter House,** a stunning octagonal room supported by a central column and adorned with 14th-century frescoes, is where the King's Council and, after that, an early version of the Commons met between 1257 and 1547. In the **Undercroft,** which survives from Edward the Confessor's original church, note the deliciously macabre effigies made from the death masks and actual clothing of Elizabeth I, Charles II, and Admiral Lord Nelson (complete with eye patch), among others. Finally, the **Pyx Chamber** next door contains the Abbey's treasure, just as it used to when it became the royal strongroom during the 13th century. ✉ *Broad Sanctuary,* ☎ *0171/222–5152.* 🎫 *Nave: free; Royal Chapels and Poets' Corner: £4.* ⏲ *Mon., Tues., Thurs., and Fri. 9–4; Wed. 9–7:45; Sat. 9–2 and 3:45–5; Sun. all day for services only; closed weekdays to visitors during services. Tube: Westminster. Undercroft, Pyx Chamber, Chapter House, and Treasury,* ☎ *0171/222–5152. Joint* 🎫 *£2.50.* ⏲ *Daily 10:30–4; closed Good Friday, Dec. 24–26. Tube: Westminster.*

Westminster Cathedral. This massive cathedral is hard to miss—once you are almost upon it, that is. It's set back from the left side of the street in a 21-year-old paved square that has fallen on hard times. Westminster Council, the local authority, would like to turn it into the Piazza San Marco of London, but until funding is found, it remains the windy haunt of homeless people and pigeons.

The cathedral is the seat of the Cardinal of Westminster, head of the Roman Catholic Church in Britain; consequently it is London's principal Roman Catholic church. The asymmetrical redbrick Byzantine hulk, dating only from 1903, is banded with stripes of Portland stone and abutted by a 273-foot campanile at the northwest corner, which you can scale by elevator. Faced with the daunting proximity of the heavenly Westminster Abbey, the architect, John Francis Bentley, flew in the face of fashion by rejecting neo-Gothic in favor of the Byzantine idiom, which still provides maximum contrast today—not only with the great church, but with just about all of London.

The interior is partly unfinished but worth seeing for its atmosphere of broody mystery; for its walls, covered in mosaic of a hundred different marbles from all over the world; and for a majestic nave—the widest in England—distinguished by a series of Eric Gill reliefs depicting the Stations of the Cross. ✉ *Ashley Pl.,* ☎ *0171/834–7452. Admission to tower: £2.* ⏲ *Cathedral daily, tower daily Apr.–Sept.*

ST. JAMES'S AND MAYFAIR

These neighboring areas (together with part of the following section, Soho and Covent Garden) make up the West End, which is the real center of London nowadays. Here is the highest concentration of grand hotels, department stores, exclusive shops, glamorous restaurants, commercial art galleries, auction houses, swanky offices—all the accoutrements of a capital city.

A late-17th-century ghost in the streets of contemporary St. James's would not need to bother walking through walls, because practically none have moved since he knew them. Its boundaries, clockwise from the north, are Piccadilly, Haymarket, The Mall, and Green Park: a neat rectangle, with a protruding spur satisfyingly located at Cockspur Street. The rectangle used to describe "gentlemen's London," where Sir was outfitted head and foot (but not in between, since the tailors were, and still are, north of Piccadilly in Savile Row) before repairing to his club. In fact, this has been a fashionable part of town from the first, largely by dint of the eponymous palace, St. James's, which was a royal residence—if not *the* palace—from the time of Henry VIII until the beginning of the Victorian era.

Mayfair, like St. James's, is precisely delineated—a trapezoid contained by Oxford Street and Piccadilly on the north and south, Regent Street and Park Lane on the east and west. Within its boundaries are streets broad and narrow, but mostly unusually straight and gridlike for London, making it fairly easy to negotiate. Real estate here is exorbitant, so this is embassy country and the site of luxury shops and swank hotels.

A Good Walk

Numbers in the text correspond to numbers in the margin and on the St. James's and Mayfair map.

Starting in Trafalgar Square, you'll find Cockspur Street off the southwest corner; follow it to the foot of **Haymarket.** On your right is London's earliest shopping arcade, the splendid Regency Royal Opera Arcade, which John Nash finished in 1818. Now you come to **Pall Mall** ①, a showcase of 18th- and 19th-century patrician architecture, and home to such famous gentleman's retreats as the Reform Club, halfway along on the right, from which Phineas Fogg set out Around the World. At the end of Pall Mall, you collide with the small Tudor brick **St. James's Palace** ② Continue along Cleveland Row by the side of the palace to spy on York House, home of the duke and duchess of Kent, then turn left into Stable Yard Road to Lancaster House, built for the Duke of York in the 1820s but more notable recently as the venue for the 1978 conference that led to the end of white rule in Rhodesia/Zimbabwe, and Clarence House, designed by John Nash and built in 1825 for the Duke of Clarence, who became William IV, and now home to the Queen Mother.

Go south on Stable Yard Road, left on the Mall, and left again up Marlborough Rd, until you reach St. James's Street, then turn right into King Street—No. 8 is Christie's, the fine-art auctioneers who got £25 million for Van Gogh's *Sunflowers*; Duke Street on the left harbors further exclusive little art salons—but straight ahead is **St. James's Square** ③, one of London's oldest, and home of the London Library. Leave the square by Duke of York Street to the north, and turn left on **Jermyn Street** ④, the world center of gentlemen's paraphernalia shops. Set back from the street is the lovely **St. James's Church** ⑤. A right on Duke Street brings you to Piccadilly. Turn right again, and you'll pass the exclusive department store that supplies the queen's groceries, Fortnum and Mason, on the right, and the **Royal Academy of Arts** ⑥ opposite, with famous **Piccadilly Circus** ⑦ ahead. Turn around (**Wellington Arch** ⑧ and **Apsley House** ⑨ are ahead in the distance), cross the street and head north up the shopping mecca of **Bond Street** ⑩, with **Burlington Arcade** ⑪ to the right. You could detour by turning right before you reach Oxford Street into Burlington Gardens, where you'll find the **Museum of Mankind** ⑫, or go into Brook Street (the composer Handel lived at No. 25), which leads to Hanover Square. Turning right down St. George Street brings you to the porticos of St. George's Church, where Percy Shelley and George Eliot, among others, had their weddings. A right turn after the church down Mill Street brings you into the tailors' mecca of Savile Row, the fashionable spot for the bespoke suit since the mid-19th century. Alternatively, hit Oxford Street from New Bond Street, (**Selfridges** ⑬, Marks & Spencer, and **Marble Arch** ⑭ are to the left) cross it, and make your way to Manchester Square, and the wonderful **Wallace Collection** ⑮.

TIMING

Although this walk doesn't cover an enormous distance, you'll probably do a lot of doubling back and detouring down interesting alleys—and into interesting shops. If you want to do more than window shop, we suggest most emphatically a weekday jaunt, starting in the morning, so you get time for the Royal Academy too, and maybe visits to the Wallace Collection, or the Museum of Mankind and some of the commercial art galleries in and around Cork Street. Walking the walk alone should take under two hours. Add at least two more for the RA, depending on the exhibition, another two for the Wallace Collection, and one to two for the Museum of Mankind. Any of those could easily consume an afternoon, if you have one to spare. Shopping could take all week.

Sights To See

9 **Apsley House.** Built by Robert Adam in the 1770s and later refaced and extended, this was where the Duke of Wellington lived from the 1820s until his death in 1852. As the Wellington Museum, it has been kept as the Iron Duke liked it, his uniforms and weapons, his porcelain and plate, and his extensive art collection, partially looted during military campaigns, displayed heroically. Unmissable, in every sense, is the gigantic Canova statue of a nude (but fig-leafed) Napoléon Bonaparte, Wellington's archenemy. Apsley House got iron shutters in 1830 after rioters, protesting the Duke's opposition to the Reform Bill (he was briefly prime minister), broke the windows. Yes, the British loved him for defeating Napoléon, but mocked him with the name "Iron Duke"—it referred not to his military prowess, but to those shutters. ✉ *149 Piccadilly,* ☎ *0171/499–5676.* 🎫 *£3.* ⏲ *Tues.–Sun. 11–5.*

Berkeley Square. As anyone who's heard the song knows, the word is pronounced to rhyme with "starkly." Not many of its original mid-18th-century houses are left, but look at Nos. 42–46 (especially No. 44, which the architectural historian Sir Nikolaus Pevsner thought London's finest terraced house) and Nos. 49–52 to get some idea of why it was once London's top address—not that it's in the least humble now. Snob nightclub Anabels is one current resident.

10 **Bond Street.** This world-class shopping haunt is divided into northern "New" (1710) and southern "Old" (1690) halves. New Bond Street boasts **Sotheby's,** the world-famous auction house, at No. 35, but there are other opportunities to flirt with financial ruin on Old Bond Street: the mirror-lined Chanel store, the vainglorious marble acres of Gianni Versace and the boutique of his more sophisticated compatriot Gucci, plus Tiffany's British outpost and art dealers Colnaghi, Léger, Thos. Agnew, and Marlborough Fine Arts. **Cork Street,** which parallels the top half of Old Bond Street, is where London's top dealers in contemporary art have their galleries—you're welcome to browse, but be dressed well.

British Telecom Tower. The unlovely 620-foot glass pencil was imposed on London by the Post Office in 1965 (everyone still calls it the Post Office Tower) to field satellite phone calls and beam radio and TV signals around. It has a habit of popping up on the skyline from the most surprising locations, though since a terrorist bomb went off upstairs in 1975, its great view from the top has been off-limits.

11 **Burlington Arcade.** Perhaps the finest of Mayfair's enchanting covered shopping alleys is the second-oldest in London, built in 1819. It's still patrolled by top-hatted beadles, who prevent you from singing, running, or carrying open umbrellas or large parcels (to say nothing of lifting English fancy goods from the mahogany-fronted shops).

Faraday Museum. In the basement of the Royal Institution is a reconstruction of the laboratory where the physicist Michael Faraday discovered electromagnetic induction in 1831—with echoes of Frankenstein. ✉ *21 Albermarle St.,* ☎ *0171/409–2992.* 🎫 *£1.* ⏲ *Weekdays 1–4; closed public holidays.*

Grosvenor Square. Pronounced "Grove-ṇa," this square was laid out in 1725–31 and is as desirable an address today as it was then. Americans certainly thought so—from John Adams, the second president, who as

St. James's and Mayfair

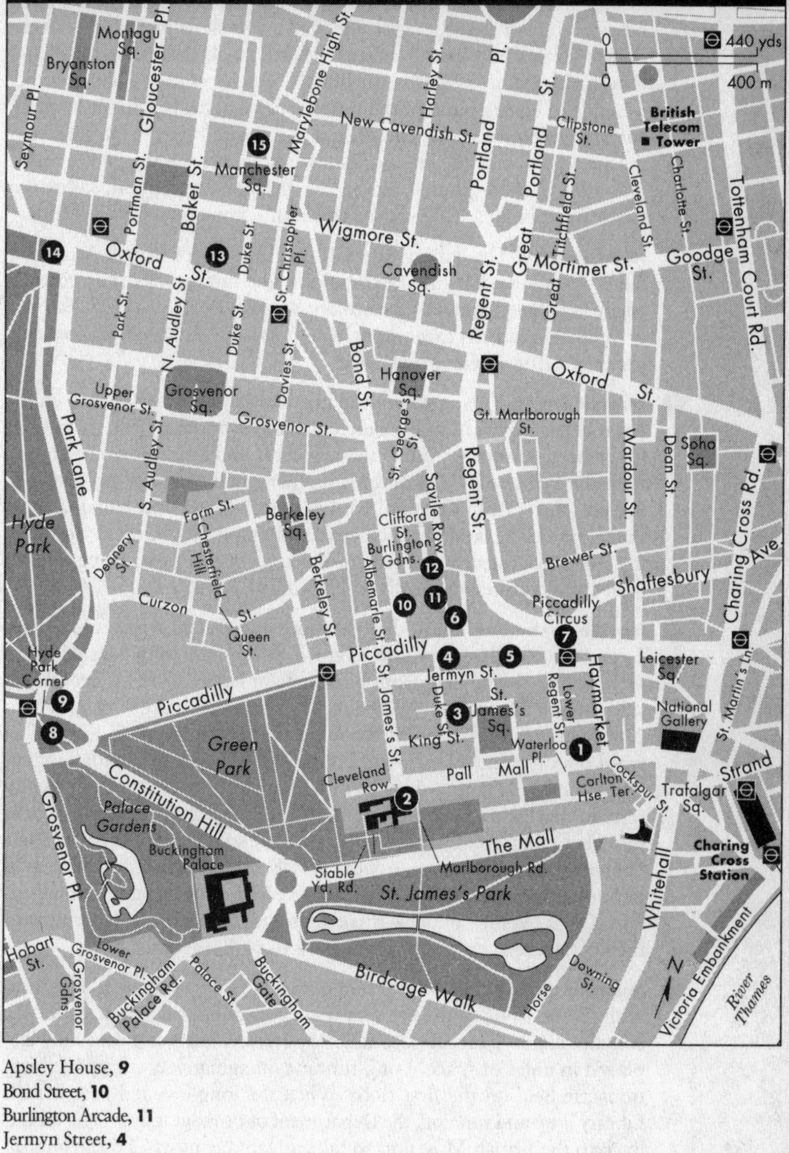

Apsley House, **9**
Bond Street, **10**
Burlington Arcade, **11**
Jermyn Street, **4**
Marble Arch, **14**
Museum of Mankind, **12**
Pall Mall, **1**
Piccadilly Circus, **7**
Royal Academy of Arts, **6**
St. James's Church, **5**
St. James's Palace, **2**
St. James's Square, **3**
Selfridges, **13**
Wallace Collection, **15**
Wellington Arch, **8**

ambassador lived at No. 38, to Dwight D. Eisenhower, whose wartime headquarters was at No. 20. Now the ugly '50s block of the U.S. Embassy occupies the entire west side, and a British memorial to Franklin D. Roosevelt stands in the center. The little brick chapel used by Eisenhower's men during World War II, the 1730 Grosvenor Chapel, stands a couple of blocks south of the square on South Audley Street, with the entrance to pretty St. George's Gardens to its left. Across the gardens is the headquarters of the English Jesuits, and society wedding favorite, the mid-19th-century Church of the Immaculate Conception, known as Farm Street because that is the name of the street on which it stands.

Heinz Gallery. The gallery of the Royal Institute of British Architects has a changing program of exhibitions, and interesting, often cutting-edge, evening lectures. ✉ *21 Portman Sq.,* ☎ *0171/580–5533.* 🎟 *Free.* ⏲ *Weekdays (during exhibitions) 11–5, Sat. 10–1; closed national holidays and Aug. Tube: Bond Street.*

❹ **Jermyn Street.** This is where the gentleman purchases his masculine paraphernalia. He buys his shaving sundries and hip flask from Geo. F. Trumper, briar pipe from Astley's, scent from Floris (for women too—both the Prince of Wales and his mother smell of Floris) or Czech & Speake, shirts from Turnbull & Asser, deerstalker and panama from Bates the Hatter, and his cheeses from Paxton & Whitfield (founded in 1740 and a legend among dairies). Shop your way east along Jermyn Street, and you're practically in Piccadilly Circus.

⓮ **Marble Arch.** The name denotes both the traffic whirlpool where Bayswater Road segues into Oxford Street and John Nash's 1827 arch, which moved here from Buckingham Palace in 1851. Search the sidewalk by the arch to find the stone plaque that marks (roughly) the place where the Tyburn Tree stood for four centuries, until 1783. This was London's central gallows, a huge wooden structure with hanging space for 21. Hanging days were holidays, the spectacle supposedly functioning as a crime deterrent to the hoi polloi. It didn't work, though. Oranges, gingerbread, and gin were sold, alongside ballads and "personal favors," to vast, rowdy crowds, and the condemned, dressed in finery for his special moment, was treated more as hero than as villain. Cross over (or under—there are signs to help in the labyrinth) to the northeastern corner of Hyde Park to ☞ Speakers' Corner.

⓬ **Museum of Mankind.** More than overspill from the British Museum, with the best bits of the ethnographic collection, this serene museum contains amazing artifacts from nonwestern civilizations beautifully displayed in miles of space. Long-running, imaginatively curated exhibitions are held on the first floor. When the long-awaited new British Library is up and running, the Department of Ethnography will be kicked back to the British Museum, so take advantage now. ✉ *6 Burlington Gardens,* ☎ *0171/437–2224.* 🎟 *Free.* ⏲ *Mon.–Sat. 10–5, Sun. 2:30–6; closed Good Friday, May Day, Dec. 23–26, Jan. 1.*

NEED A BREAK?

The suitably themed **Café de Colombia** is usually as peaceful as the Museum of Mankind it inhabits—unless you collide with a school visit. Salads and pastries, Colombian coffee, and wine and beer are on the lunch menu.

❶ **Pall Mall.** Like its near-namesake, *the* Mall, Pall Mall rhymes with "shall" and derives its name from the cross between croquet and golf that the Italians, who invented it, called *pallo a maglio,* and the French, who made it chic, called *palle-maille.* In England it was taken up with enthusiasm by James I, who called it "pell mell" and passed it down the royal line, until Charles II had a new road laid out for it in 1661. Needless to say, Catherine Street, as Pall Mall was officially named (after Charles's queen, Catherine of Braganza), was *very* fashionable. No. 79 must have been one of its livelier addresses, since Charles's gregarious mistress, Nell Gwyn, lived there. The king gave her the house when she complained about being a mere leaseholder, protesting that she had "always conveyed free under the Crown" (as it were); it remains, to this day, the only privately owned bit of Pall Mall's south side. Stroll slowly, the better to appreciate the creamy facades and perfect proportions along this showcase of 18th- and 19th-century British architecture.

Notable examples are two James Barry–designed buildings, the **Travellers' Club** and the **Reform Club,** both representatives of the upper class gentleman's retreat that made St. James's the clubland of London. The Reform is the most famous club of all, thanks partly to Jules Verne's Phineas Fogg, who accepted the around-the-world-in-80-days bet in its smoking room, and was thus soon qualified to join the Travellers'. And—hallelujah—women can join the Reform. The RAC Club (for Royal Automobile Club, but it's never known as that), with its marble swimming pool, and the Oxford and Cambridge Club complete the Pall Mall quota; there are other, even older, establishments—Brooks's, the Carlton, Boodles, and White's (founded in 1736, and the oldest of all)—in St. James's Street around the corner, alongside *the* gentlemen's bespoke (custom) shoemaker, Lobb's, and *the* hatter, James Lock.

7 **Piccadilly Circus.** The name got stuck during the early 17th century, when a humble tailor on the Strand called Robert Baker sold an awful lot of picadils—a collar ruff all the rage in courtly circles—and built a house with the proceeds. Snobs dubbed his new-money mansion Piccadilly Hall, and the name stuck. As for the "Circus," that refers not to the menagerie of backpackers and camera clickers clustered around the steps of **Eros,** but to the circular junction of five major roads.

Eros, London's favorite statue and symbol of the *Evening Standard* newspaper, is not in fact the Greek god of erotic love at all but the angel of Christian charity, commissioned in 1893 from the young sculptor Alfred Gilbert as a memorial to the philanthropic Earl of Shaftesbury. It cost Gilbert £7,000 to cast the statue he called his "missile of kindness" in the novel medium of aluminum, and since he was paid only £3,000, he promptly went bankrupt and fled the country. (Don't worry—he was knighted in the end.) Eros has lately done his best to bankrupt Westminster Council, too, owing to some urgent leg surgery and a new coat of protective microcrystalline synthetic wax. Outside of Eros, there's not much to see in this sometime hub of London beyond a bank of neon advertisements, a very large branch of Tower Records, the tawdry Trocadero Centre (video arcades, food courts, chain stores, the Guinness World of Records), and a perpetual traffic jam.

Portland Place. The elegant throughway to Regent's Park was London's widest street during the 1780s when the brothers Robert and James Adam designed it. The first sight to greet you there, drawing the eye around the awkward corner, is the curvaceous portico and pointy Gothic spire of **All Souls Church** one part of Nash's Regent Street plan that remains. It is now the venue for innumerable concerts and Anglican services broadcast to the nation by the British Broadcasting Corporation. The 1931 block of **Broadcasting House** next door is home to the BBC's five radio stations. It curves too, if less beautifully, and features an Eric Gill sculpture of Shakespeare's Ariel (aerial—get it?) over the entrance, from which the playful sculptor was obliged to excise a portion of phallus lest it offend public decency—which the modified model did in any case.

Queen's Chapel. Designed by Inigo Jones not for the queen of the realm, but for the Infanta of Castille when she was betrothed to Charles I in 1623. This was actually the first classical church in England, and attending a service is the only way you can get to delight in it. Behind it is **Marlborough House** designed by Wren in 1709 for the duchess of Marlborough, who asked for something "strong plain and convenient," and so it was—she remained there until she died in 1744.

Regent Street. This curvaceous thoroughfare was conceived by John Nash and his patron, the Prince Regent—the future George IV—as a kind of ultra-catwalk from the prince's palace, Carlton House, to Regent's Park (then called Marylebone Park). The section between Piccadilly and Oxford Street was to be called the Quadrant and lined with colonnaded purveyors of "articles of fashion and taste," in a big P.R. exercise to improve London's image as the provincial cousin of smarter European capitals. The scheme was never fully implemented, and what there was fell into such disrepair that, early this century, Aston Webb (of the Mall route) collaborated on the redesign you see today. It is still a major shopping street. Hamleys, the gigantic toy emporium, is fun; and since 1875 there has been Liberty, which originally imported silks from the East, then diversified to other Asian goods, and is now best for its "Liberty print" cottons, its jewelry department, and—still—its high-class Asian imports. The stained-glass–lighted mock-Tudor interior, with beams made from battleships, is worth a look.

6 **Royal Academy of Arts.** Burlington House was built in the Palladian style for the Earl of Burlington around 1720, and is one of the few surviving mansions from that period. Two sides of the courtyard are occupied by learned societies: the Geological Society, Chemistry Society, Society of Antiquaries, and the Royal Astronomical Society, but at the top is its chief occupant, the Royal Academy of Arts, which mounts major art exhibitions, usually years in the planning. The permanent collection (not all on show) includes at least one work by every academician past and present, including Gainsborough, Turner, and Constable, but its prize is, without doubt, a tondo (a sculpted disk) by Michelangelo of the Madonna and Child. It's up the glass staircase in the Sackler Galleries (opened in 1991 and designed by another academician, Sir Norman Foster), where temporary exhibitions are held. Every June, the RA mounts the **Summer Exhibition,** a mishmash of sculpture and painting, both amateur and professional, from abstract expressionist to photo-realist (bias is toward the latter), with about 1,000 things crammed into every cranny—it's an institution. Art-weary now? Try the shop; it's one of the best museum stores in town. ✉ *Burlington House, Piccadilly,* ☎ *0171/439–7438 or 0171/439–4996 (recorded information).* 🎫 *Admission varies according to exhibition. White Card accepted.* ⏲ *Daily 10–6; closed Good Friday, Dec. 24–26, Jan. 1.*

5 **St. James's Church.** Recessed from the street behind a courtyard filled, most days, with a crafts market, and completed in 1684, this was the last of Sir Christopher Wren's London churches, and his own favorite. It contains one of Grinling Gibbons's finest works, an ornate limewood reredos (the screen behind the altar). A 1940 bomb scored a direct hit here, but the church was completely restored, albeit with a fiberglass spire. It's a lively place, offering all manner of lecture series—many on incongruously New Age themes—and concerts, mostly Baroque, as well as a brass-rubbing center.

NEED A BREAK?

The Wren at St. James's, attached to the church, has not the faintest whiff of godliness, as the cake display proves. Hot dishes at lunchtime are vegetarian, very good, and very inexpensive. There are tables outside in spring and summer.

2 **St. James's Palace.** With its solitary sentry posted at the gate, this is a surprisingly small palace of Tudor brick. Matters to ponder as you look (you can't go in): It was named after a hospital for women lepers, which stood here during the 11th century; Henry VIII had it built; foreign ambassadors to Britain are still accredited to the Court of St. James's even though it has rarely been a primary royal residence; the present queen made her first speech here.

3 **St. James's Square.** One of London's oldest and leafiest squares was also the most snobbish address of all when it was laid out around 1670, with 14 resident dukes and earls installed by 1720. Since 1841, No. 14—one of the several 18th-century residences spared by World War II bombs—has housed the **London Library,** which with its million or so volumes is the best private humanities library in the land. You can go in and read the famous authors' complaints in the comments book—but not the famous authors' books, unless you join, for £100 a year.

13 **Selfridges.** With its row of massive Ionic columns, this huge store was opened three years after Harry Gordon Selfridge came to London from Chicago in 1906. Now British-run, Selfridges rivals Harrods (☞ Knightsbridge, Kensington, and Holland Park, *below*) in size and stock, and is finally rivaling its glamour too, since investing in major face-lift operations. It stands toward the Marble Arch end of Oxford street, close by the flagship branch of everyone's favorite chain store, **Marks and Spencer** (usually known by its pet names M&S or Marks & Sparks)—supplier of England's underwear, purveyor of woollies (sweaters, that is), producer of dishes passed off as homemade at dinner parties. This place has by far the highest turnover of any shop in the land, so expect crowds at all times.

Shepherd Market. Though it looks like a quaint and villagey tangle of streetlets, this was anything *but* quaint when Edward Shepherd laid it out in 1735 on the site of the orgiastic, fortnight-long May Fair (which gave the whole district its name). Now there are sandwich bars, pubs and restaurants, boutiques and nightclubs, and a (fading) red-light reputation in the narrow lanes.

Speakers' Corner. This corner harbors a late-20th-century public spectacle. Here, on Sunday afternoons, anyone is welcome to mount a soapbox and declaim upon any topic. It's an irresistible showcase of eccentricity, though sadly diminished since the death in 1994 of the "Protein Man," who thought meat, cheese, and peanuts led to uncontrollable acts of passion that would destroy Western civilization. The pamphlets he sold for four decades down Oxford Street are now collector's items.

15 **Wallace Collection.** Assembled by four generations of Marquesses of Hertford and given to the nation by the widow of Sir Richard Wallace, bastard son of the fourth, this collection of art and artifacts is important, exciting, undervisited—and free. As at the Frick Collection in New York, the setting here, Hertford House, is part of the show–a fine late-18th-century mansion, built for the Duke of Manchester, and completely renovated during the late 1970s.

The first marquess was a patron of Sir Joshua Reynolds, the second bought Hertford House, the third—a flamboyant socialite—favored Sèvres porcelain and 17th-century Dutch painting; but it was the eccentric fourth marquess who, from his self-imposed exile in Paris, really built the collection, snapping up Bouchers, Fragonards, Watteaus, and Lancrets for a song (the French Revolution having rendered them dangerously unfashionable), augmenting these with furniture and sculpture, and sending his son Richard out to do the deals. With 30 years of practice behind him, Richard Wallace continued acquiring treasures on his father's death, scouring Italy for majolica and Renaissance gold, then moving most of it to London. Look for Rembrandt's portrait of his son, the Rubens landscape, the Van Dycks, and Canalettos, the French rooms, and of course the porcelain, and don't forget to say hello to Frans Hals's *Laughing Cavalier* in the Big Gallery. ✉ *Hertford House, Manchester Sq.,* ☎ *0171/935–0687.* 🎫 *Free.* 🕓 *Mon.–Sat. 10–5, Sun. 2–5; closed Good Friday, May Day, Dec. 24–26, Jan. 1.*

Waterloo Place. This is a long rectangle off Pall Mall, punctuated by the Duke of York memorial column over the Duke of York Steps, and littered with statues, among them Florence Nightingale, the "Lady with the Lamp" nurse-heroine of the Crimean War; Captain R. F. Scott, who led a disastrous Antarctic expedition in 1911–12 and is here frozen in a bronze by his wife; Edward VII, mounted; George VI; and, as usual, Victoria, here in terra-cotta.

Flanking Waterloo Place looking onto Pall Mall are two of the gentlemen's clubs for which St. James's came to be known as Clubland: the **Athenaeum** and the former United Service Club, now the **Institute of Directors.** The latter was built by John Nash in 1827–8 but was given a face-lift by Decimus Burton 30 years later to match it up with the Athenaeum, which he had designed across the way. It's fitting that you gaze on the Athenaeum first, since it was—and is—the most elite of all the societies. (It called itself "The Society" until 1830 just to rub it in.) Most prime ministers and cabinet ministers, archbishops, and bishops have belonged; the founder, John Wilson Croker (the first to call the British right-wingers "Conservatives"), decreed it the club for artists and writers, and so literary types have graced its lists, too (Sir Arthur Conan Doyle, Rudyard Kipling, J. M. Barrie—the posh ones). Women are barred. Most clubs will tolerate female guests these days, but few admit women members, and anyway, even if your anatomy is correct it's almost impossible to become a member unless you have the connections—which, of course, is the whole point.

8 **Wellington Arch.** It is marooned on the central island of Hyde Park Corner—the cyclist's nightmare at the extreme west end of Piccadilly—so you need to descend the pedestrian underpasses, following the signs, to reach the arch itself. This 1828 Decimus Burton triumphal gateway almost wound up at the back door of Buckingham Palace, but here it stands instead, empty now of London's smallest police station, which occupied its cramped insides until 1992. A statue of Wellington also moved on, replaced by Adrian Jones's *Quadriga* in 1912.

SOHO AND COVENT GARDEN

A quadrilateral described by Regent Street, Coventry/Cranbourn streets, Charing Cross Road, and the eastern half of Oxford Street encloses Soho, the most fun part of the West End. This appellation, unlike the New York neighborhood's similar one, is not an elision of anything, but a blast from the past—derived (as far as we know) from the shouts of "So-ho!" that royal huntsmen in Whitehall Palace's parklands were once heard to cry. One of Charles II's illegitimate sons, the Duke of Monmouth, was an early resident, his dubious pedigree setting the tone for the future: For many years Soho was London's strip show/peep show/clip joint/sex shop/brothel center. The mid-'80s brought legislation that granted expensive licenses to a few such establishments and closed down the rest; most prostitution had already been ousted by the 1959 Street Offences Act. Only a cosmetic smear of red-light activity remains now, plus a shop called "Condomania" and one or two purveyors of couture fetishwear for outfitting trendy club goers.

These clubs, which cluster around the Soho grid, are the diametric opposite of the St. James's gentlemen's museums—they cater to youth, change soundtrack every month, and have tyrannical fashion police at the door. Another breed of Soho club is the strictly members-only media haunts (the Groucho, the Academy, the Soho House, Fred's, Brown's, Black's), salons for carefully segregated strata of high-income hipster. The same crowd populates the astonishing selection of restaurants, but then so does the rest of London and all its visitors—because Soho is gourmet country.

It was after the First World War, when London households relinquished their resident cooks en masse, that Soho's gastronomic reputation was established. It had been a cosmopolitan area since the first immigrant wave of French Huguenots arrived in the 1680s. More French came fleeing the revolution during the late 18th century, then the Paris Commune of 1870, followed by Germans, Russians, Poles, Greeks, and (especially) Italians and, much later, Chinese. Pedestrianized Gerrard Street, south of Shaftsbury Avenue, is the hub of London's compact Chinatown, which boasts restaurants, dim sum houses, Chinese supermarkets, and February New Year's celebrations, plus a brace of scarlet pagoda-style archways and a pair of phone booths with pictogram dialing instructions.

The former Covent Garden Market became the Piazza in 1980, and it still functions as the center of a neighborhood—one that has always been alluded to as "colorful." It was originally the "convent garden" belonging to the Abbey of St. Peter at Westminster (later Westminster Abbey). The land was given to the first Earl of Bedford by the Crown after the Dissolution of the Monasteries in 1536. The Earls—later promoted to Dukes—of Bedford held on to the place right up until 1918, when the eleventh Duke managed to offload what had by then become a liability. In between, the area enclosed by Long Acre, St. Martin's Lane, Drury Lane, and assorted streets north of the Strand had gone from the height of fashion (until the nobs moved west to brand-new St. James's) to a period of arty-literary bohemia during the 18th century, followed by an era of vice and mayhem, to become the vegetable supplier of London once more when the market building went up in the 1830s, followed by the Flower Market in 1870 (Eliza Dolittle's alma mater in Shaw's *Pygmalion* and Lerner and Loewe's musical version, *My Fair Lady*).

Still, it was no Mayfair, what with 1,000-odd market porters spending their 40-shillings-a-week in the alehouses, brothels, and gambling dens that had never quite disappeared. By the time the Covent Garden Estate Company took over the running of the market from the 11th Duke, it seemed as if seediness had set in for good, and when the fruit-and-veg trade moved out to the bigger, better Nine Elms Market in Vauxhall in 1974, it left a decrepit wasteland. But this is one of London's success stories: Now the (sadly defunct) Greater London Council stepped in with a dream of a rehabilitation scheme—not unlike the one that was tried, less successfully, in the Parisian equivalent, Les Halles. By 1980, the transformation was complete.

A Good Walk

Numbers in the text below correspond to numbers in the margin and on the Soho and Covent Garden map.

Soho, being small, is easy to explore, though it's also easy to mistake one narrow, crowded street for another, and even Londoners get lost here. Enter from the northwest corner, Oxford Circus, and head south about 200 yards down Regent Street, turn left into Great Marlborough Street, and head to the top of **Carnaby Street** ①. Turn right off Broadwick Street into Berwick (pronounced "Berrick") Street, famed as central London's best fruit and vegetable market. Then step through tiny Walker's Court (ignoring the notorious hookers' bulletin board), cross Brewer Street, named for two extinct 18th-century breweries, and you'll have arrived at Soho's hip hangout, Old Compton Street. From here, Wardour, Dean (home of the **French House** ② and St. Anne's Church), Frith, and Greek streets lead north, all of them bursting with restaurants and clubs. Either of the latter two lead north to **Soho Square** ③, but head one block south instead, to Shaftesbury Avenue, heart of theaterland, across which you'll find Chinatown's main drag, Gerrard Street. Below Gerrard Street is **Leicester Square** ④, and running along its west side is Charing Cross Road, the bibliophile's dream. You'll find some of the best of the specialist bookshops in little Cecil Court, running east just before Trafalgar Square.

The easiest way to find the **Covent Garden Piazza** ⑤ and market building is to walk down Cranbourn Street, next to Leicester Square tube, then down Long Acre, and turn right at James Street. Here, and around here, are **St. Pauls** ⑥—the actors' church—the **London Transport Museum** ⑦ and the **Theatre Museum** ⑧ as well as plenty of shops and cafés. (If your aim is to shop, **Neal Street,** Floral Street, the streets around Seven Dials, and the Thomas Neale's mall all repay exploration.) From Seven Dials, veer 45 degrees south into Mercer Street, turning right on Long Acre, then left into Garrick Street, past the **Garrick Club** ⑨, left into Rose Street, and right into Floral Street. At the other end you'll emerge onto Bow Street, right next to the **Royal Opera House** ⑩ and the **Magistrates' Court** ⑪. Continuing on, and turning left into Russell Street, you reach Drury Lane, and the **Theatre Royal** ⑫.

At the end of Drury Lane is the Aldwych, a great big croissant of a potential traffic accident, with a central island on which stand three hulking monoliths: India House, Melbourne House, and the handsome 1935 neo-classical Bush House, headquarters of the BBC World Service. Stranded (oops) on traffic islands to the west, are the 1717 St. Mary-le-Strand, James Gibbs's (of St.-Martin-in-the-Fields fame) first public building, inspired by the Baroque churches of Rome, and Wren's St. Clement Danes (with a tower appended by Gibbs), whose 10 bells peal the tune of the nursery rhyme "Oranges and lemons,/Say the bells of St. Clements . . ." even though the bells in the rhyme belong to St. Clements, Eastcheap. Inside is a book listing 1,900 American airmen who were killed during World War II. Heading west, perhaps stopping at the **Courtauld Institute Galleries** ⑬, walk the ¾-mile-long traffic-clogged **Strand** to the southern end, where you take Villiers Street down to the Thames. See the **York Watergate** ⑭ and **Cleopatra's Needle** ⑮ by Victoria Embankment Gardens, cross the gardens northwest to the **Adelphi** ⑯, circumnavigating the Strand by sticking to the embankment walk, and you'll soon reach Waterloo Bridge, where (weather permitting) you can catch some of London's most glamorous views, toward both the City and Westminster around the Thames bend.

TIMING

The distance covered here is around 8 kilometers (5 miles), if you include the lengthy walk down the Strand, and riverside stroll back. Skip that, and it's barely a couple of miles, but you will almost certainly get lost, because the streets in both Covent Garden and Soho are winding and chaotic, and not logically layed out. Although getting lost is half the fun, it does make it hard to predict how long this walk will take. You can whizz round both neighborhoods in an hour, but if the area appeals at all, you'll want all day–for shopping, lunch, the Theatre and Transport museums, and the Courtauld Galleries. One way to do it is to start at Leicester Square at 2 PM, when the Half Price Theatre Booth opens, pick up tickets for later, and walk, shop, and eat in between.

Sights To See

16 **Adelphi.** A regal riverfront row of houses that was the work of London's Scottish architects—all four of them. John, Robert, James, and William Adam, being brothers, gave rise to the name, from the Greek *adelphoi*, meaning brothers. All the late-18th-century design stars were roped in to beautify the interiors, but the grandeur gradually eroded, and today very few of the 24 houses remain; 7 Adam Street is the best.

11 **Bow Street Magistrates' Court.** This was where the prototype of the modern police force once operated. Known as the Bow Street Runners (because they chased thieves on foot), they were the brainchild of the second Bow Street magistrate—none other than Henry Fielding, the author of *Tom Jones* and *Joseph Andrews.* The late-19th-century edifice on the site went up during one of the market improvement drives. It now houses three courts, including that of the Metropolitan Chief Magistrate, who hears all extradition applications.

1 **Carnaby Street.** The '60s synonym for swinging London fell into a post-party depression, re-emerging sometime during the '80s as the main drag of a public-relations invention called West Soho. Blank stares would greet anyone asking directions to such a place, but it is geographically logical, and the tangle of streets—Foubert's Place, Broadwick Street, Marshall Street—do cohere, at least, in type of merchandise (youth accessories, mostly, with a smattering of designer boutiques). Broadwick Street is also notable as the birthplace, in 1758, of the great visionary poet and painter William Blake at No. 74. At age 26 he came back for a year to sell prints next door, at No. 72 (now an ugly tower block), and then remained a Soho resident in Poland Street.

15 **Cleopatra's Needle.** Off the triangular-handkerchief Victoria Embankment Gardens, where office sandwich-eaters and people who call it home coexist, is London's *very oldest thing,* predating its arbitrary namesake, and London itself, by centuries. The 60-foot pink granite obelisk was erected at Heliopolis, in Lower Egypt, in about 1475 BC, then moved to Alexandria, where in 1819 Mohammed Ali, the Turkish Viceroy of Egypt, rescued it from its fallen state and presented it to the British. The British, though grateful, had not the faintest idea how to get the 186-ton gift home, so they left it there for years until an expatriate English engineer contrived an iron pontoon to float it to London via Spain. Future archaeologists will find an 1878 "time capsule" underneath, containing the morning papers, several bibles, a railway timetable, some pins, a razor, and a dozen photos of Victorian pinup girls.

13 **Courtauld Institute Galleries.** The Galleries are found in grand 18th-century classical Somerset House, alongside a vast compilation of civil servants (conjure up the red-tape-bestrewn Circumlocution Offices in Dickens's *Little Dorrit*) who still lurk inside. Founded in 1931 by the textile maven Samuel Courtauld, this is London's finest Impressionist and post-Impressionist collection, with bonus post-Renaissance works thrown in. Botticelli, Breughel, Tiepolo, and Rubens are represented, but the younger French painters (plus Van Gogh) are the stars—here, for example, are Manet's *Bar at the Folies-Bergère* and *Déjeuner sur l'Herbe* (a companion to the bigger version at the Musée d'Orsay in

Soho and Covent Garden

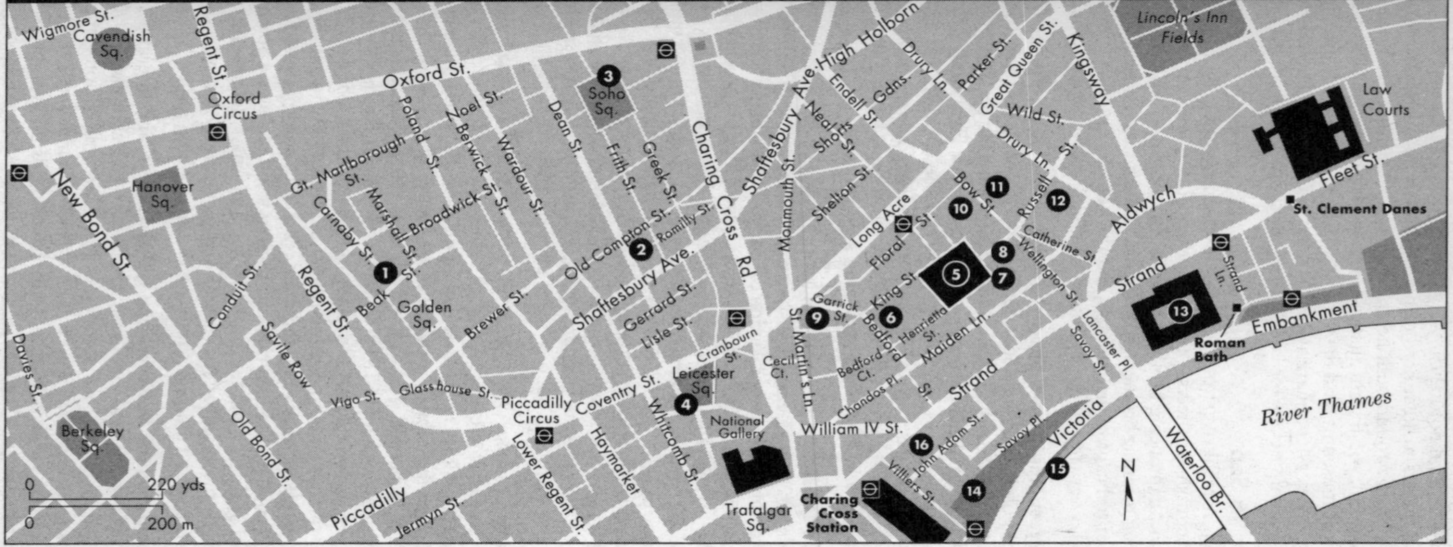

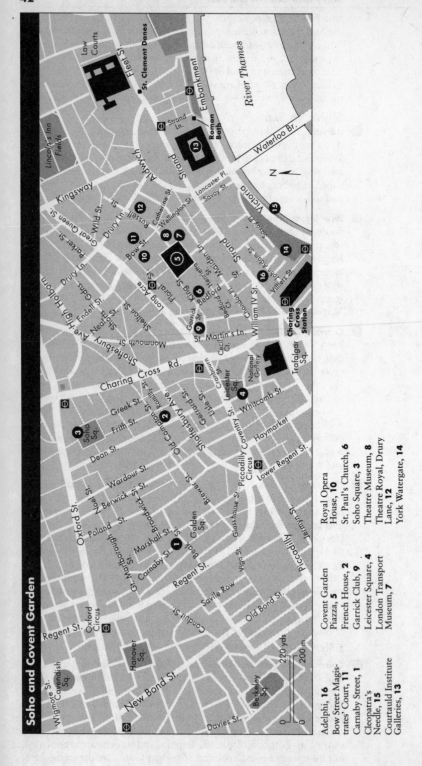

Adelphi, **16**
Bow Street Magistrates' Court, **11**
Carnaby Street, **1**
Cleopatra's Needle, **15**
Courtauld Institute Galleries, **13**
Covent Garden Piazza, **5**
French House, **2**
Garrick Club, **9**
Leicester Square, **4**
London Transport Museum, **7**
Royal Opera House, **10**
St. Paul's Church, **6**
Soho Square, **3**
Theatre Museum, **8**
Theatre Royal, Drury Lane, **12**
York Watergate, **14**

Paris). ✉ *The Strand,* ☎ *0171/873–2526.* *£3. White Card accepted.* *Mon.–Sat. 10–6, Sun. 2–6; closed public holidays. Tube: Temple, Embankment.*

5 **Covent Garden Piazza.** The Piazza is what the restored 1840 market building around which Covent Garden pivots is known as. Inside, the shops are mostly higher-class clothing chains, plus a couple of cafés and some knickknack stores that are good for gifts. There's a superior crafts market on most days, too. If you turn right, you'll reach the indoor **Jubilee Market**, with stalls selling clothing, army surplus gear, more crafts, and more knickknacks. At yet another market off to the left (on the way back to the tube), the leather goods, antiques, and secondhand clothing stalls are a little more exciting. In the summer it may seem that everyone you see around the Piazza (and the crowds are legion) is a fellow tourist, but there is still plenty of office life in the area, and Londoners continue to flock here.

2 **French House.** A longstanding Gallic outpost, recognizable by the *tricolor* fluttering outside on Dean Street, this pub has been crammed with people ever since de Gaulle's Free French Forces rendezvoused here during World War II. Nowadays the crowd isn't French—it's Soho trendies and peculiar bohemians, some heading for the trendy restaurant upstairs. No pints of beer here, but you can get a decent *vin ordinaire* or a glass of pastis beneath the signed photos of French boxers. Opposite the French House is all that remains of once-famous **St. Anne's Church**, probably the work of Wren. A German bomb in 1940 spared only the tower, and the graveyard behind it, on Wardour Street.

9 **Garrick Club.** Named for the 18th-century actor and theater manager David Garrick, this club is, because of its literary-theatrical bent, more louche than its St. James's brothers, and famous actors, from Sir Laurence Olivier down, have always been proud to join—along with Dickens, Thackeray, and Trollope, in their time. Find the **Lamb and Flag** down teeny Rose Street to the left. Dickens drank in this pub, better known in its 17th-century youth as the Bucket of Blood owing to the bare-knuckle boxing matches upstairs. (You'll find that many London pubs claim Dickens as an habitué, and it's unclear whether they lie or the author was the city's premier sot.)

4 **Leicester Square.** Pronounced "lester," not "lay-sess-ter," this square is showing no sign of its great age. Looking at the neon of the major movie houses, the fast-food outlets (plus a useful Häagen-Dazs café), and the disco entrances, you'd never guess it was laid out around 1630. By the 19th century it was already bustling and disreputable, and now it's usually one of the only places crowded after midnight—with suburban teenagers, Belgian backpackers, and London's swelling ranks of the homeless. That said, it is not a threatening place, and the liveliness can be quite cheering. In the middle are statues of Shakespeare, Hogarth, Reynolds, and Charlie Chaplin, and underneath is an invisible new £22-million electrical substation. One landmark certainly worth visiting is the **Society of London Theatre ticket kiosk,** on the southwest corner, which sells half-price tickets for many of that evening's performances (☞ Theater in Chapter 7, Nightlife and the Arts). On the northeast corner, in Leicester Place, stands **Notre Dame de France,** with a wonderful mural by Jean Cocteau in one of its side chapels.

7 **London Transport Museum.** Housed in the old Flower Market at the southeastern corner of the Covent Garden Piazza, this museum tells the story of mass transportation in the capital, and is much better than it sounds. It is particularly child-friendly, with lots of touch-screen interactive material, live actors in costume (including a Victorian horse-

dung collector), old rolling-stock, period smells and sounds, and best of all, a tube driving simulator. There's also a café, and a shop selling the wonderful old London Transport posters, plus mugs, socks, bow ties, and so on, printed with that elegant London tube map, designed by Harry Beck in 1933 and still in use today. ✉ *Piazza,* ☎ *0171/379–6344.* 🎫 *£3.95. White Card accepted.* ⏲ *Daily 10–6; closed Dec. 24–26. Tube: Covent Garden.*

Neal Street. One of Covent Garden's most intriguing shopping streets begins north of Long Acre catercorner to the tube station, and is closed to traffic halfway down. Here you can buy everything you never knew you needed—apricot tea, sitars, vintage flying jackets, silk kimonos, Alvar Aalto vases, halogen desk lamps, shoes with heel lower than toe, collapsible top hats, and so on. To the left off Neal Street, on Earlham Street, is Thomas Neal's—a new, upmarket, designerish clothing and housewares mall named after the founder (in 1693) of the star-shape cobbled junction of tiny streets just past there, called Seven Dials—a surprisingly residential enclave, with lots going on behind the tenement-style warehouse facades. Turning left into the next street off Neal Street, Shorts Gardens, you come to Neal's Yard (note the comical, water-operated wooden clock), originally just a whole-foods wholesaler, now an entire holistic village with therapy rooms, organic bakery and dairy, a great vegetarian café, and a medical herbalist's shop reminiscent of a medieval apothecary.

Rock Circus. This shamelessly touristique offshoot of Madame Tussaud's waxworks (☞ Regent's Park and Hampstead, *below*) features animatronic and wax pop stars miming to their hits, or frozen in time, chronologically displayed to give the impression of a museum of popular music. Strictly for young teens. ✉ *London Pavilion, Piccadilly Circus,* ☎ *0171/734–8025.* 🎫 *£7.50.* ⏲ *Sun., Mon., Wed., Thurs. 11–9, Tues. noon–9, Fri. and Sat. 11–10; closed Dec. 25. Tube: Piccadilly Circus.*

10 **Royal Opera House.** London's premier opera venue was designed in 1858 by E. M. Barry, son of Sir Charles, the House of Commons architect—except for the 1982 extension, which runs the entire length of the block between James and Bow streets, and added much-needed rehearsal and dressing-room space to the building. This one is the third theater on the site. The first opened in 1732 and burned down in 1808; the second opened a year later under the aegis of one John Anderson, only to succumb to fire in 1856. Anderson, who had lost two theaters already, had an appalling record when it came to keeping the limelights apart from the curtains. Despite government subsidies, tickets for the Royal Opera are pricey, though the expense is unlikely to lead to riots as it did in 1763, 1792, and for *61 days* of protest in the Old Price Riots of 1809, when the cost of rebuilding inflated the cost of seats. (The public won.) Many British and world premiers have been staged here (including the world's first public piano recital in 1767), and the Royal Opera attracts all the glittering divas on the international circuit. Nowadays you can see some of them for free, when selected summer performances are relayed live to a giant screen in the Piazza.

6 **St. Paul's Church.** Find this across the Covent Garden Piazza, punctuated with street entertainers—who have passed auditions for London's most coveted spot. This 1633 work of the great Inigo Jones has always been known as "the actors' church" thanks to the several theaters in its parish, and well-known actors often read the lessons at services. Its portico was the setting for *Pygmalion*'s opening scene. The matching tall, terraced houses Jones designed to form a quadrangle with the church are long since history.

❸ **Soho Square.** Laid out about 1680, this square was fashionable during the 18th century. Only two of the original houses still stand, plus the 19th-century central garden. It's now a place of peace and offices (among them Paul McCartney's music publishers, and Bloomsbury Publishing). That isn't a tudor landmark in the center, but a picturesque Victorian gardener's hut, recently renovated.

NEED A BREAK? Take any excuse you can think of to visit either of Soho's wonderful rival patisseries: **Maison Bertaux** (✉ 28 Greek St.) or **Pâtisserie Valerie** (✉ 44 Old Compton St.). Both serve divine gâteaux, milles-feuilles, croissants, éclairs, etc., the former in an upstairs salon, the latter in a dark room behind the cake counters.

Strand. Here is one of London's oldest streets. It was already lined with mansions seven centuries ago, when it was a mere Thames-side bridle path. In 1706 Thomas Twining, the tea tycoon, moved his shop into No. 216 (it's still there); it was closely followed by a slew of coffee houses, frequented by Boswell and Johnson, that persisted for most of that century. Remember Judy Garland doing Burlington Bertie in Chaplin drag, walking down the Strand with gloves in hand, in *A Star Is Born*? William Hargreaves's song was a popular number in the Strand music halls that put the street on the map afresh during the early 1900s. Now its presence on maps is about all that the characterless Strand has to recommend it.

❽ **Theatre Museum.** This mostly below-ground museum aims to re-create the excitement of theater itself. There are usually programs in progress allowing children to get in a mess with make-up or have a giant dressing-up session. Permanent exhibits paint a history of the English stage from the 16th century to Mick Jagger's jumpsuit, with tens of thousands of theater playbills, and sections on such topics as Hamlet-through-the-ages and pantomime—the peculiar British theatrical tradition whereby men dress as ugly women (as distinct from RuPaul), and girls wear tights and play princes. There's a little theater in the bowels of the museum and a ticket desk for "real" theaters around town, plus an archive holding video recordings of significant British theatrical productions. ✉ *7 Russell St.,* ☎ *0171/836–7891.* *£3.* *Tues.–Sun. 11–7; closed Good Friday, Dec. 24–26, Jan. 1. Tube: Covent Garden.*

⓬ **Theatre Royal, Drury Lane.** This is London's best-known auditorium and almost its largest. Since World War II, its forte has been musicals (*Miss Saigon* is the current resident; past ones have included *The King and I, My Fair Lady, South Pacific, Hello, Dolly!,* and *A Chorus Line*)—though David Garrick, who managed it from 1747 to 1776, made its name by reviving the works of the obscure William Shakespeare. It enjoys all the romantic accessories of a London theater—a history of fires (it burned down three times, once in a Wren-built incarnation), riots (in 1737, when a posse of footmen demanded free admission), attempted regicides (George II in 1716 and his grandson George III in 1800), and even sightings of the most famous phantom of theaterland, the Man in Grey (in the Circle, matinees). The entrance is on Catherine Street.

The Trocadero. The nearest thing to a US mall in London, this has shops and foodcourt eating places, but is best for the **Emaginators**—a pair of those pods that predated virtual reality, in which you are strapped in and flung about while visuals and soundtracks disorient you, and raise your heart rate. Where to go to placate kids who really wanted to go to Disneyworld. ✉ *13 Coventry St., tel. 0171/439–1791.* *Daily 10 AM–midnight.* *Trocadero free; Emaginator £3 per ride. Tube: Piccadilly Circus.*

⑭ **York Watergate.** Once the grand river entrance to York House, the Duke of Buckingham's mansion, this was built in 1625 and is about the oldest building extant around here, marking the place where the river used to flow before the road was built. A riverside road had seemed a good plan ever since Wren had come up with the idea after the Great Fire of 1666, but nobody got around to it until Sir Joseph Bazalgette set to work on the Victoria Embankment two centuries later. Bazalgette, incidentally, is better known for providing London with the sewer system still largely in use; he can be admired in effigy on the bronze bust right there by Hungerford Bridge.

Roman Bath. This curiosity is probably about a thousand years younger than Roman, but nobody is quite sure. To see it, you have to peer in the window at No. 5. Dickens may inadvertently have named it, in *David Copperfield,* though nobody seems quite sure of that, either.

BLOOMSBURY AND LEGAL LONDON

To the north and northeast of Soho and Covent Garden lie these two loosely delineated neighborhoods. The first is best known for its famous flowering of literary-arty bohemia during this century's first three decades, the Bloomsbury Group, and for the British Museum and the University of London, which dominate it now. The second sounds as exciting as, say, a center for accountancy or dentists, but don't be put off—it's more interesting than you might suppose.

Let's get the Bloomsbury Group out of the way, since you can't visit them, and nothing exists to mark their territory beyond a sprinkling of Blue Plaques. (London has about 400 of these government-sponsored tablets commemorating persons who enhanced "human welfare or happiness" and have been dead for at least 20 years.) There's also a plaque in Bloomsbury Square, saying nothing about this elite clique of writers and artists except that they lived around here.

The chief Bloomsburies were Virginia Woolf, T. S. Eliot, E. M. Forster, Vanessa and Clive Bell, Duncan Grant, Dora Carrington, Roger Fry, John Maynard Keynes, and Lytton Strachey, with satellites including Rupert Brooke and Christopher Isherwood. They agreed with G. E. Moore's philosophical notion that "the pleasures of human intercourse and the enjoyment of beautiful objects . . . form the rational ultimate end of social progress." True to their beliefs, when they weren't producing beautiful objects the friends enjoyed much human intercourse, as has been exhaustively documented, not least in Virginia's own diaries. All you need do to find out more about them is read the Review supplements of the Sunday broadsheets, which are forever running Bloomsbury exposés as if they were fresh gossip.

More clearly visible than those literary salons is the time-warp territory of interlocking alleys, gardens and cobbled courts, town houses and halls where London's legal profession grew up. The Great Fire of 1666 razed most of the city but spared the buildings of legal London, and the whole neighborhood oozes history. What is best about the area is that it lacks the commercial veneer of other historic sites, mostly because it still is very much the center of London's legal profession. Barristers, berobed and bewigged, may add an anachronistic frisson to your sightseeing, but they're only on their way to work.

They are headed for one of the four "Inns of Court": Gray's Inn, Lincoln's Inn, Middle Temple, and Inner Temple. Those arcane names are simply explained. The inns were just that: lodging houses for the lawyers who, back in the 14th century, clustered together here so everyone knew where to find them, and presently took over the running of the inns themselves. The temples were built on land owned by the Knights Templar, a chivalric order founded during the First Crusade during the 11th century; their 12th-century Temple Church still stands here. Few barristers (British for trial lawyers) still live in the inns, but nearly all keep chambers (British for barristers' offices) here, and all are still obliged to eat a requisite number of meals in the hall of "their" inn during training—no dinner, no career. They take exams, too.

A Good Walk

Numbers in the text correspond to numbers in the margin and on the Bloomsbury and Legal London map.

From Russell Square tube, walk south down Southampton Row, and west on Great Russell Street, passing **Bloomsbury Square** on the left, en route to London's biggest and most important collection of antiquities, the **British Museum** ①. Leaving this via the back exit leads you to Montague Place, which you should cross to Malet Street, straight ahead, to reach the **University of London** ②. On the left after you pass the university buildings is the back of the Royal Academy of Dramatic Art, or RADA (its entrance is on Gower Street), where at least half of the most stellar British thespians got their training, with **University College** ③ following at the top of Malet Place. Circumvent the university and head south down Gordon Street to reach Gordon Square. If you're interested in Asian art stop in at the **Percival David Foundation of Chinese Art** ④, otherwise contine south down busy Woburn Place, veering left down Guilford Street to reach Coram's Fields, home of the **Thomas Coram Foundation** ⑤, then turn left south of there on Guilford Place, then right to Doughty Street and the **Dickens House Museum** ⑥. Two streets west, parallel to Doughty Street, is pretty Lamb's Conduit Street (whose pretty pub, the Lamb, Dickens inevitably frequented), with Great Ormond Street, off it, where lies the **Hospital for Sick Children** ⑦.

At the bottom of Lamb's Conduit Street you reach Theobald's Road, where you enter the first of the Inns of Court, **Gray's Inn** ⑧, emerging from here onto High Holburn ("Hoe-bun"), heavy with traffic, as it (with the Strand) is the main route from the City to the West End and Westminster—and Hatton Garden, running north from Holburn Circus and still the center of London's diamond and jewelry trade, is a reminder of when it *was* the west end. Pass another ghost of former trading, **Staple Inn** ⑨, and turn left down tiny Great Turnstile Row to reach **Lincoln's Inn** ⑩, where you pass the Hall and continue around the west side of New Square to Carey Street, which leads you round into Portugal Street. Here you'll find The Old Curiosity Shop, probably one of the rare places in London Dickens did *not* frequent. Recross to the north side of Lincoln's Inn Fields to **Sir John Soane's Museum** ⑪, or walk the other way on Carey Street to reach the **Royal Courts of Justice** ⑫, which run through to the Strand. Off to the left is Fleet Street and the 1610 **Prince Henry's Room** ⑬. Cross the Strand to **Temple** ⑭, and pass through the elaborate stone arch to Middle Temple Lane, which you follow past **Temple Church** ⑮ to the Thames.

TIMING

This is a substantial walk of 4.8 to 6.4 kilometers (3 to 4 miles), and it has two distinct halves. The first half, around Bloomsbury is not so interesting on the surface, but features a major highlight of London, the British Museum, where you could easily add a 1½ kilometers (1 mile) to your total, and certainly at least two hours. The Dickens House is also worth a stop. The second half, legal London, is a real walker's walk, with most of the highlights in the architecture and atmosphere of the buildings and streets. The exception is Sir John Soane's

Museum, which will absorb an extra hour. The walk alone can be done comfortably in two hours, and is best on a sunny day.

Sights To See

Bloomsbury Square. This was laid out in 1660, making it the earliest of the Bloomsbury squares, although none of the original houses remain; what is most remarkable about it now is that you can always find a parking spot in the huge underground garage underneath. You'll find it by exiting the tube at Tottenham Court Road—a straight, very ugly street where London buys its electrical appliances, hi-fi equipment, and computer accessories—and taking Great Russell Street east.

❶ **British Museum.** Allow plenty of time here. There are 4 kilometers (2½ miles) of floor space inside, split into nearly 100 galleries of astonishing artifacts and treasures bought and donated, but mostly "discovered" and looted, from everywhere in the world, some as old as humankind itself. It started in 1753, when Sir Hans Sloane, physician to Queen Anne and George II, bequeathed his personal collection of curiosities and antiquities to the nation, and then quickly grew thanks to enthusiastic kleptomaniacs after the Napoleonic Wars—most notoriously the seventh Earl of Elgin, who lifted marbles from the Parthenon and Erechtheum while on a Greek vacation between 1801 and 1804. Although Lord Elgin did a great thing in saving the marbles for posterity, their continuing presence in the British Museum is a source of embarrassment to many British subjects, who believe the Greeks should now have their "Elgin Marbles" back, as, indeed, do the Greeks.

The enormous building, with its Classical Greek–style facade featuring figures representing the Progress of Civilization, was finished in 1847, the work of Sir Robert Smirke. Ascending the steps, you go straight into the main entrance hall, where you can pick up a floor plan. Wherever you go there are marvels, but certain objects and collections are more important, rarer, older, or downright unique, and since you may wish to include these in your wanderings, here follows a highly edited résumé (in order of encounter) of the BM's greatest hits:

Close to the entrance hall, in the south end of Room 25, is the **Rosetta Stone,** found in 1799, and carved in 196 BC with a decree of Ptolemy V in Egyptian hieroglyphics, demotic, and Greek. It was this multilingual inscription that provided the French Egyptologist Jean-François Champollion with the key to deciphering hieroglyphics.

Maybe the **Elgin Marbles** oughtn't to be here, but since they are—and they are, after all, among the most graceful and heartbreakingly beautiful sculptures on earth—you can find them in Room 8, west of the entrance. The best part is what remains of the Parthenon frieze that girdled the interior of Athena's temple on the Acropolis, carved around 440 BC. (The handless, footless Dionysus who used to recline along the east pediment is especially well-known.) While you're in the west wing, you can see one of the Seven Wonders of the Ancient World—in fragment form, unfortunately—in Room 12: the **Mausoleum of Halicarnassus.** This 4th-century tomb of Mausolus, king of Caria, was the original "mausoleum."

Also close to the entrance, but east, in Rooms 30 and 31 in the part of the British Library open to the public, are two of the four existing copies of that prototype census and manual of early British law, King John's 1215 charter, the **Magna Carta,** as well as the spectacularly illuminated 7th-century **Lindisfarne Gospels,** the work of a monk called Eadfrith. Also on display are handwritten manuscripts by, among others, Jane Austen, William Wordsworth, and John Lennon.

British Museum, **1**
Dickens House Museum, **6**
Gray's Inn, **8**
Hospital for Sick Children, **7**
Lincoln's Inn, **10**
Percival David Foundation of Chinese Art, **4**
Prince Henry's Room, **13**
Royal Courts of Justice, **12**
Sir John Soane's Museum, **11**
Staple Inn, **9**
Temple, **14**
Temple Church, **15**
Thomas Coram Foundation, **5**
University College, **3**
University of London, **2**

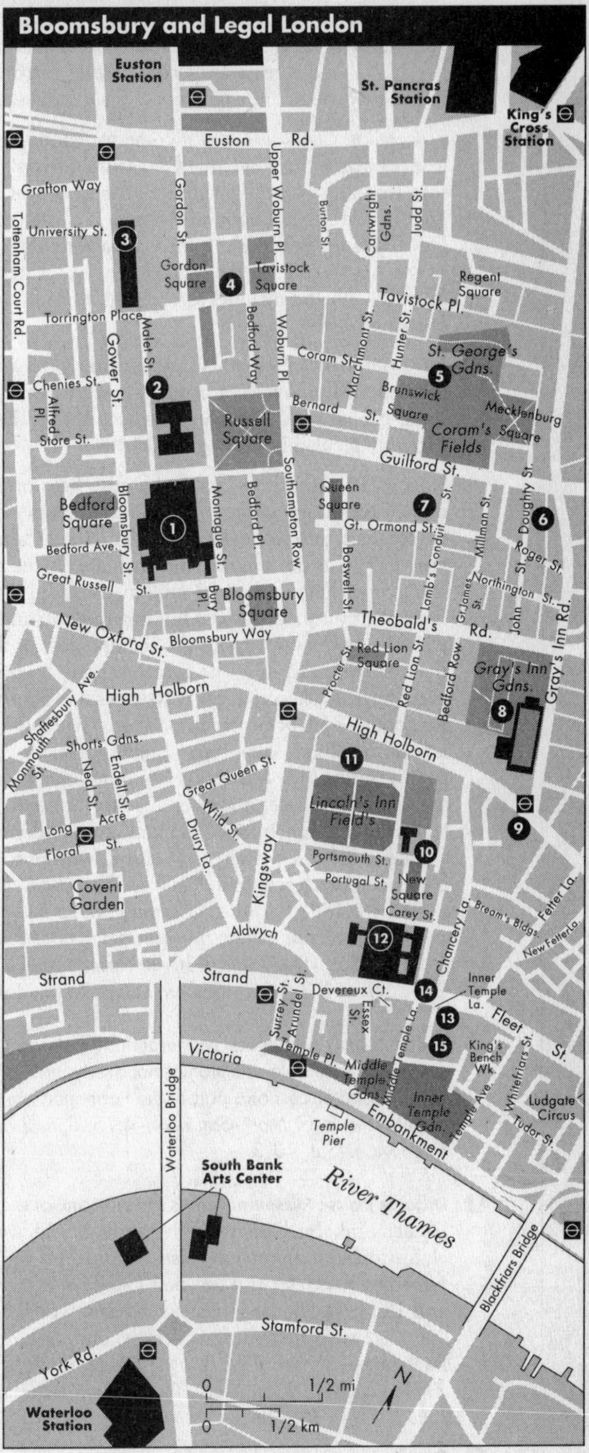

Upstairs are some of the most perennially popular galleries, especially beloved by children: Rooms 60 and 61, where the **Egyptian Mummies** live. You'll find here the preserved corpses not only of humans but also of a menagerie of animal companions discovered alongside them.

Proceeding clockwise, you'll come to Room 40, above the main entrance, where the **Mildenhall Treasure** glitters. This haul of 4th-century Roman silver tableware was found beneath the sod of a Suffolk field in 1942. Next door, in Room 41, is the equally splendid **Sutton Hoo Treasure,** which was buried at sea with (they think) Redwald, King of the Angles, during the 7th century, excavated from a Suffolk field in 1938–39, and includes swords and helmets, bowls and buckles, all encrusted with jewels.

In Room 37 lies Pete Marsh, so named by the archaeologists who unearthed the **Lindow Man** from a Cheshire peat marsh. He was ritually slain, probably as a human sacrifice, during the 1st century, and lay perfectly pickled in his bog until 1984.

Since 1759, the **British Library** has also been on this site, but in an imminent revolution in the world of English letters, the whole thing is to be decanted into its new home in St. Pancras after years of delay. The year 1991 was the intended moving date for the almost literally countless (somewhere around 18 million, actually) volumes, but the building wasn't finished, and the funding ran out, and there were problems with the new stacks, and, well, the operation will just have started by the time you read this. The British Library is entitled to a free copy of every single book, periodical, newspaper, and map published in the United Kingdom—a gift of George II, along with his Royal Library—which translates into 3.2 new kilometers (2 miles) of shelf space per year. Needless to say, room at the old library ran out long ago, and most of its books are not housed here. A Reader's Ticket for access to the library and entrance to the much-loved circular, copper-domed **Reading Room** is available only by written application, with proof of the serious intent of your research required. ✉ *Great Russell St.,* ☎ *0171/636–1555 or 0171/580–1788 (recorded information).* *Free. 1½-hour guided tours, £6; twice a day in winter, four times daily in summer. Phone for times.* ⏲ *Mon.–Sat. 10–5, Sun. 2:30–6; closed Good Friday, May Day, Dec. 23–26, Jan. 1. Tube: Tottenham Court Road, Holburn, Russell Square.*

NEED A BREAK? The museum's self-service restaurant and café gets very crowded but serves a reasonable selection of not overly mass-produced meals beneath a plaster cast of a part of the Parthenon frieze that Lord Elgin didn't remove. ⏲ *Mon.–Sat. noon–4:15, Sun. 2:45–5:15. Coffee shop open Mon.–Sat. 10–3.*

6 **Dickens House Museum.** This is the only one of the many London houses Dickens inhabited that's still standing, and would have had a real claim to his fame in any case, because he wrote *Oliver Twist* and *Nicholas Nickleby* and finished *Pickwick Papers* here between 1837 and 1839. The house looks exactly as it would have in Dickens's day, complete with first editions, letters, and desk, plus a treat for Lionel Bart fans—his score of *Oliver!* ✉ *48 Doughty St.,* ☎ *0171/405–2127.* *£3.* ⏲ *Mon.–Sat. 10–5; closed national holidays, Dec. 24–Jan. 1. Tube: Russell Square.*

8 **Gray's Inn.** Although the least architecturally interesting of the four Inns of Court and the one most damaged by German bombs during the '40s, this still has its romantic associations. In 1594, Shakespeare's *Comedy of Errors* was performed for the first time in its hall—which was lovingly restored after the World War II bombing and has a fine

Elizabethan screen of carved oak. You must make advance arrangements to view Gray's Inn's hall, but you can stroll around the secluded and spacious gardens, first planted by Francis Bacon in 1606. ✉ *Holborn,* ☎ *0171/405-8164. Visits only by advance written application to the librarian.* ⏲ *Chapel: weekdays 10-4; closed national holidays. Tube: Holburn, Temple.*

7 **Hospital for Sick Children.** The hospital was founded by Dr. Charles West, who, like Sir Thomas Coram a century before, was horrified at the inadequate provision made in London for the welfare of children–with some 21,000 dying every year. In 1929, Peter Pan gave the hospital a new lease of life—or rather his creator, Sir James Barrie, did, by donating the royalties from the play until 50 years after his death. (A special Act of Parliament enabled the gift to continue to this day.) Latterly, the hospital—like many in London—has been in financial difficulties again, but a new generation of benefactors has saved the day for now, and Princess Di came out of her self-imposed purdah early in 1994 to open a long-awaited new wing.

10 **Lincoln's Inn.** There's plenty to see at one of the oldest, best preserved, and most comely of the Inns of Court—from the Chancery Lane Tudor brick gatehouse to the wide-open, tree-lined, atmospheric Lincoln's Inn Fields and the 15th-century Chapel remodeled by Inigo Jones in 1620. The wisteria-clad New Square, London's only complete 17th-century square, is not the newest part of the complex; the oldest-looking buildings are—the 1845 Hall and Library, which you must obtain the porter's permission to enter. Pass the Hall and continue around the west side of New Square, and you'll see an archway leading to Carey Street. You have just headed "straight for Queer Street." Since the bankruptcy courts used to stand here, you can divine what the old expression means. ✉ *Chancery La.,* ☎ *0171/405-1393.* ⏲ *Gardens and chapel open weekdays 12:30-2:30 (the public may also attend Sun. service at 11:30 in the chapel during legal terms); guided tours available. Closed national holidays. Tube: Chancery Lane.*

4 **Percival David Foundation of Chinese Art.** This collection, belonging to the University of London, is dominated by ceramics from the Sung to Qing dynasties—10th to 19th century, in other words. It's on Gordon Square, which Virginia Woolf, the Bells, John Maynard Keynes (all, severally, at No. 46), and Lytton Strachey (at No. 51) called home for a while. ✉ *53 Gordon Sq.,* ☎ *0171/387-3909.* 🎫 *Free.* ⏲ *Weekdays 10:30-5 (sometimes closed 1-2 for lunch); closed weekends and bank holidays. Tube: Russell Square.*

Pollock's Toy Museum. This is a charming treasure trove of a small museum in a warren of rooms in this 18th-century town house. Most of the objects are dolls, dolls' houses, toy theaters, teddy bears, and folk toys. ✉ *1 Scala St.,* ☎ *0171/636-3452.* 🎫 *£2.* ⏲ *Mon.-Sat. 10-5. Check for national holiday opening. Tube: Goodge St.*

13 **Prince Henry's Room.** This is the Jacobean half-timbered house built in 1610 to celebrate the investiture of Henry, James I's eldest son, as Prince of Wales, and marked with his coat of arms and a "PH" on the ceiling. It's an entrance to the lawyers' sanctum, Temple, where the Strand becomes Fleet Street, and you can go in to visit the small Samuel Pepys exhibition. ✉ *17 Fleet St.,* ☎ *0171/936-2710.* ⏲ *Mon.-Sat. 11-2. Closed public holidays. Tube: Temple.*

12 **Royal Courts of Justice.** Here is the vast Victorian Gothic pile containing the nation's principal Law Courts, with 1,000-odd rooms running off 3½ miles of corridor. And here are heard the most important civil law cases—that's everything from divorce to fraud, with libel in between—

and you can sit in the viewing gallery to watch any trial you like, for a live version of *Court TV.* The more dramatic criminal cases are heard at the Old Bailey. Other sights to witness include the 238-foot-long main hall and the compact exhibition of judges' robes. ✉ *The Strand,* ☎ *0171/936–6000.* 🎫 *Free.* ⏲ *Weekdays 9–4:30; closed Aug.–Sept., national holidays. Tube: Temple.*

11 **Sir John Soane's Museum.** Guaranteed to raise a smile from the most blasé and footsore tourist, this museum hardly deserves the burden of its dry name. Sir John, architect of the Bank of England, bequeathed his house to the nation on condition that nothing be changed. We owe him our thanks, because he obviously had enormous fun with his home, having had the means to finance great experiments in perspective and scale and to fill the space with some wonderful pieces. In the Picture Room, for instance, two of Hogarth's *Rake's Progress* series are among the paintings on panels that swing away to reveal secret gallery pockets with more paintings. Everywhere mirrors and colors play tricks with light and space, and split-level floors worthy of a fairground fun house disorient you. In a basement chamber sits the vast 1300 BC Sarcophagus of Seti I, lighted by a domed skylight two stories up. When Sir John acquired this priceless object for £2,000, he celebrated with a three-day party. ✉ *13 Lincoln's Inn Fields,* ☎ *0171/405–2107.* 🎫 *Free.* ⏲ *Tues.–Sat. 10–5; closed national holidays. Tube: Holburn, Temple.*

9 **Staple Inn.** Despite its name, this is not an inn of court, but the former wool staple, where wool was weighed and traded and its merchants were lodged. It is central London's oldest surviving Elizabethan half-timbered building, and thanks to extensive restoration, with its overhanging upper stories, oriel windows, and black gables striping the white walls, looks the same as it must have in 1586 when it was brand-new.

14 **Temple.** The collective name for **Inner Temple** and **Middle Temple,** the entrance to Temple—the exact point of entry into the City—is marked by a young (1880) bronze griffin, the **Temple Bar Memorial.** He is the symbol of the City, having replaced (sadly) a Wren gateway. In the buildings opposite is an elaborate stone arch through which you pass into Middle Temple Lane, past a row of 17th-century timber-frame houses, and on into Fountain Court. This lane runs all the way to the Thames, more or less separating the two Temples, past the sloping lawns of Middle Temple Gardens, on the east border of which is the Elizabethan **Middle Temple Hall.** If it's open, don't miss that hammer-beam roof, among the finest in the land. ☎ *0171/353–4355.* ⏲ *Weekdays 10–noon and (when not in use) 3–4. Tube: Temple.*

15 **Temple Church.** Featuring "the Round"—a rare circular nave—this church was built by the Knights Templar during the 12th century. The Red Knights (so called after the red crosses they wore—you can see them in effigy around the nave) held their secret initiation rites in the crypt here. Having started poor, holy, and dedicated to the protection of pilgrims, they grew rich from showers of kingly gifts, until during the 14th century they were accused of heresy, blasphemy, and sodomy, thrown into the Tower, and stripped of their wealth. You might suppose the church to be thickly atmospheric, but Victorian and postwar restorers have tamed the antique mystery. Still, it's a very fine Gothic-Romanesque church, whose 1240 chancel ("the Oblong") has been accused of perfection. ✉ *The Temple,* ☎ *0171/353–8462.* ⏲ *Daily 10–4; closed national holidays. Tube: Temple.*

5 **Thomas Coram Foundation.** Captain Thomas Coram devoted half his life to setting up the sanctuary and hospital, which he named the

Foundling Hospital, for London's street orphans. He was a remarkable man, a master mariner and shipbuilder, who, having played a major role in the colonization of Massachusetts, returned to London in 1732 to sights he could not endure—abandoned babies and children "left to die on dung hills." Petitioning the lunching ladies of his day, and their lords, he raised the necessaries to set up what became the most celebrated Good Cause around, thanks partly to the sparkling benefactors he attracted. Handel gave an organ to the chapel, which he played himself in fundraising performances of his *Messiah,* and the chapel in turn became *the* place to be seen worshiping on a Sunday. Coram's great friend William Hogarth was one of several famous hospital governors, and his portrait of the founder hangs alongside other works of art (including paintings by Reynolds and Gainsborough) and mementos in the museum that now stands on the site of the hospital. The hospital was originally set in the 7-acre Coram's Fields, though it moved to Hertfordshire in 1926. Sadly, at press time, the museum was off-limits to the public, until the governors manage to find a fresh crop of volunteers to man the front of the house—an indefinite period, in other words. ✉ *40 Brunswick Sq.,* ☎ *0171/278–2424. Closed to visitors, but call for the latest information. Tube: Russell Square.*

❸ **University College.** Set in a satisfyingly classical edifice by the architect of the National Gallery, William Wilkins, within the college portals is the **Slade School of Fine Art,** which did for many of Britain's artists what the nearby (on Gower Street) Royal Academy of Dramatic Art did for its actors. There is a fine collection of sculpture by one of the alumni, John Flaxman, on view inside. You can also see more Egyptology, if you didn't get enough at the neighboring British Museum, in the **Petrie Museum** (accessed from Malet Place), which contains one of London's weirder treasures: the clothed skeleton of one of the university's founders, Jeremy Bentham, who bequeathed himself to the college.

❷ **University of London.** This relatively youthful institution grew out of the need for a nondenominational center for higher education (Oxford and Cambridge both demanded religious conformity to the Church of England). It was founded by Dissenters in 1826, with its first examinations held 12 years later. Jews and Roman Catholics were not the only people admitted for the first time to an English university—women were, too, though they had to wait 50 years (until 1878) to sit for a degree. The building you see here dates only from 1911. Previously this branch of academe had borrowed Somerset House (where the Courtauld Collection is now), Burlington House (now the Royal Academy), then Burlington House's extension (now the Museum of Mankind).

Wig and Pen Club. This—another of those St. James's–style affairs, this time for "men of justice, journalists, and businessmen of the City" (plus former presidents Nixon and Reagan)—has its home in the only Strand building to have survived the Great Fire of 1666. Its Legal Tours allow access to the gorgeous gardens of the Inner and Middle Temples, plus other secret sights, and include meals, refreshments, honorary membership for the day (even for women), and expert tour guides. ✉ *229 Strand, WC2,* ☎ *0171/583–7255. Legal Tours Cost: £50 (half-day) or £70.50 (full day).*

THE CITY

You may have assumed you had entered the City of London when your plane touched down at Heathrow, but note that capital letter: the City of London is not the same as the city of London. The capital-C City is an autonomous district, separately governed since William the Conqueror started building the Tower of London, and despite its compact size, it remains the financial engine of Britain and one of the world's leading centers of trade. Temple Bar marks the western edge of the Square Mile, which does cover 677 acres (a square mile is 640), though not in a remotely straight-sided fashion. The curvy shape described by its boundaries—Smithfield in the north, Aldgate and Tower Hill in the east, and the Thames on the south—resembles nothing so much as an armadillo, with Temple Bar at snout level.

The City is London's most ancient part, although there is little remaining to remind you of that fact beyond a scattering of Roman stones. It was Aulus Plautius, Roman ruler of Britain under Claudius, who established the Romans' first stronghold on the Thames halfway through the 1st century AD. The name "Londinium," though, probably derives from the Celtic *Lyn-dun,* meaning "fortified town on the lake," which suggests far earlier settlement. Not much is known about the period between AD 410, when the Roman legions left, and the 6th century, when the Saxons arrived, but it was really after Edward the Confessor moved his court to Westminster in 1060 that the City gathered momentum. As Westminster took over the administrative role, the City was free to develop the commercial heart that still beats strong.

The Romans had already found Londinium's position handy for trade—the river being navigable yet far enough inland to allow for its defense—but it was the establishment of crafts guilds in the Middle Ages, followed in Tudor and Stuart times by the proliferation of great trading companies (the Honourable East India Company, founded in 1600, was the star), that really started the cash flowing. King John had confirmed the City's autonomy by charter in 1215, and its commerce and government fed off each other, the leaders of the former electing the leaders of the latter. This is still largely the case: The Corporation of London has control over the Square Mile and elects a Lord Mayor just as it did in the Middle Ages, when the famous folk hero Richard Whittington was four times (not thrice, as in *Dick Whittington,* the pantomime) voted in.

Three times the City has faced devastation—and that's not counting the "Black Monday" of 1992, when sterling crashed. The Great Fire of 1666 spared practically none of the labyrinthine medieval streets—a blessing in disguise, actually, because the Great Plague of the year before had wiped (or driven) out most of the population and left a terrible mess in the cramped, downright sordid houses. With the wind in the west, they said, you could smell London from Tilbury. The fire necessitated a total reconstruction, in which Sir Christopher Wren had a big hand, contributing not only his masterpiece, St. Paul's Cathedral, but 49 other parish churches.

The third wave of destruction, after the plague and the fire, was, of course, dealt by the German bombers of the Second World War, who showered the City with 57 days and nights of special attention, wreaking as much havoc as the Great Fire had managed. The ruins were rebuilt, but slowly, and with no overall plan, leaving the City a patchwork of the old and the new, the interesting and the flagrantly awful. Since a mere 8,000 or so people call it home, the financial center of Britain is deserted outside the working week, with restaurants shuttered and streets forlorn and windswept.

A Good Walk

Numbers in the text correspond to numbers in the margin and on the City map.

Begin at the gateway to the City—and we mean that literally. Until the 18th century there were eight such gates, all but one of which survive in name only (Cripplegate, Ludgate, Bishopsgate, Moorgate, and so on). The surviving one is Temple Bar, a bronze griffin on the Strand opposite the Royal Courts of Justice, at which the sovereign has to ask the Lord Mayor's permission to enter the City. Walk east to **Fleet Street** and turn left on Bolt Court to Gough Square, and **Dr. Johnson's House** ①, passing **Ye Olde Cheshire Cheese** ② on Wine Office Courte en route back to Fleet Street and the journalists' church, **St. Bride's** ③. The end of Fleet Street is marked by the messy traffic intersection called Ludgate Circus, which you should cross to Ludgate Hill to reach **Old Bailey** ④, and the Central Criminal Courts.

Continuing along Ludgate Hill, you come to **St. Paul's** ⑤, Wren's masterpiece. There's not much else to see around here, though plans are pending for the re-installation of Sir Christopher Wren's 1672 Temple Bar gateway close to its original site, which will serve as the City's western gateway. Instead, retrace your steps to Newgate street, detouring up King Edward Street to the **National Postal Museum** ⑥, and to the road called Little Britain, where you'll see the archway to **St. Bartholomew's Church** ⑦ on the left, and will come to London's meat market, **Smithfield** ⑧ at the end. Cross Aldersgate Street and take the right fork to London Wall, named for the Roman rampart that stood along it. It's a dismal street, now dominated by post-modern architect Terry Farrell's late-'80s follies, but about halfway along you can see a section of 2nd- to 4th-century wall at St. Alphege Garden. There's another bit in an appropriate spot back at the start of London Wall, outside the **Museum of London** ⑨; and behind that is the important arts mecca of gray concrete, the **Barbican Centre** ⑩ and **St. Giles without Cripplegate** ⑪. You can walk all around there without touching the ground (well, ground level).

Back on London Wall, turn south into Coleman Street, then right onto Masons Avenue to reach Basinghall Street and the **Guildhall** ⑫, then follow Milk Street south to Cheapside (Chepe is Old English for "market", and on this street the bakers of Bread Street, the cobblers of Cordwainers Street, the goldsmiths of Goldsmith Street, and all their brothers gathered to sell their wares.) Here is another symbolic center of London, the church of **St. Mary-le-Bow** ⑬. Walk to the east end of Cheapside, where seven roads meet, and you will be facing the **Bank of England** ⑭, behind which is the **London Stock Exchange** ⑮. Turn your back on the Bank, and there's the Lord Mayor's abode, **Mansion House** ⑯, with Wren's **St. Stephen Walbrook Church** ⑰ behind it, and the **Royal Exchange** ⑱ in between Threadneedle Street and Cornhill. Further down Cornhill to Lime Street is **Lloyd's of London** ⑲.

Now head down Queen Victoria Street, where you'll pass the remains of the Roman **Temple of Mithras** ⑳, then, after a sharp left turn into Cannon Street, you'll come upon **Monument** ㉑, Wren's memorial to the Great Fire of London. Just south of there is **London Bridge** ㉒. Turn left onto Lower Thames Street, and it's just under a mile's walk—passing Billingsgate, London's principal fish market for 900 years, until 1982, and the Custom House, built early in the last century—to the **Tower of London** ㉓, which may be the single most unmissable of London's sights. **Tower Bridge** ㉔ just outside it isn't bad either.

TIMING

This is a marathon. Unless you want to be walking all day, without a chance to do justice to London's most famous sights, the Tower of London and St. Paul's Cathedral—not to mention the Museum of London, Tower Bridge, and the Barbican Centre—you should consider splitting the walk into sections. Conversely, if you're not planning to go inside, this walk is a great day out, with lots of surprising vistas, river views, and history. The City is a wasteland on weekends and after dark, so choose your time. There's a certain romantic charm to the streets when they're deserted, but it's hard to find lunch.

Sights To See

14 **Bank of England.** Known familiarly for the past couple of centuries as "The Old Lady of Threadneedle Street," after someone's parliamentary quip, the bank, which has been central to the British economy since 1694, manages the national debt and the foreign exchange reserves, issues banknotes, sets interest rates, looks after England's gold, and regulates its banking system. Sir John Soane designed the neo-classical hulk in 1788, wrapping it in windowless walls (which are all that survives of his building) to suggest a stability that the ailing economy of the post-Thatcher years tends to belie. The larger history of this economy, and the role that the Bank of England played in it, is traced in the Bank of England Museum. ✉ *Bartholomew La.,* ☎ *0171/601–5545.* 🎫 *Free.* ⏲ *Easter–Sept., weekdays 10–5, Sun. and public holidays 11–5; Oct.–Easter, weekdays 10–6; closed public holidays Oct.–Easter. Tube: Bank, Monument.*

10 **Barbican Centre.** Home to the Royal Shakespeare Company and its two theaters, the London Symphony Orchestra and its auditorium, the Guildhall School of Music and Drama, a major gallery for touring exhibitions, two cinemas, a convention center, and apartments for a hapless two-thirds of the City's residents (most part-time), the Barbican is an enormous concrete maze Londoners love to hate. The name comes from a defensive fortification of the City, and defensive is what Barbican apologists (including architects Chamberlain, Powell, and Bon) became when the complex was finally revealed in 1982, after 20 years as a building site. There ensued an epidemic of jokes about getting lost forever in the Barbican bowels. A hasty rethink of the contradictory signposts and nonsensical "levels" was performed, and navigatory yellow lines materialized, Oz-like, on the floors, but it didn't help much—the Barbican remains difficult to navigate. Time has mellowed the elephant-gray concrete into a darker blotchy brownish-gray, and Londoners have come to accept the place, if not exactly love it, because of its contents. Actors rate the theater acoustics especially high, and the steep bank of the seating makes for a good stage view. The visiting exhibitions are often worth a trek, as are the free ones in the foyer.

Negotiating the windy walkways of the deserted residential section, then descending in elusive elevators to the lower depths of the Centre (where the studio auditorium, the aptly named Pit, lives), spotting stray sculptures and water gardens, receiving electric shocks from the brass rails—all this has its perverse charm, but there is one unadulterated success in the Barbican, though unfortunately it's not often open to the public. Secreted on an upper floor is an enormous, lush conservatory in a towering glass palace, big enough for full-grown trees to flourish. ✉ *Silk St.,* ☎ *0171/638–4141.* 🎫 *Free.* ⏲ *Mon.–Sat. 9 AM–11 PM, Sun. noon–11 PM. Gallery:* 🎫 *£4.50. White Card accepted.* ⏲ *Mon.–Sat. 10–7:30, Sun. and national holidays noon–7:30. Conservatory:* 🎫 *80p.* ⏲ *Weekends noon–5:30 when not in use for private function (always call first). Tours (minimum 10 people; book in advance),* ☎ *0171/628–0183;* 🎫 *£3.50. RSC backstage tours,* ☎ *0171/628–3351. Tube: Moorgate, Barbican.*

NEED A BREAK? The Barbican Centre's **Waterside Café** has salads, sandwiches, and pastries; they're unremarkable but are served in a tranquil enclosed concrete (naturally) waterside terrace. Sometimes customers are serenaded

The City

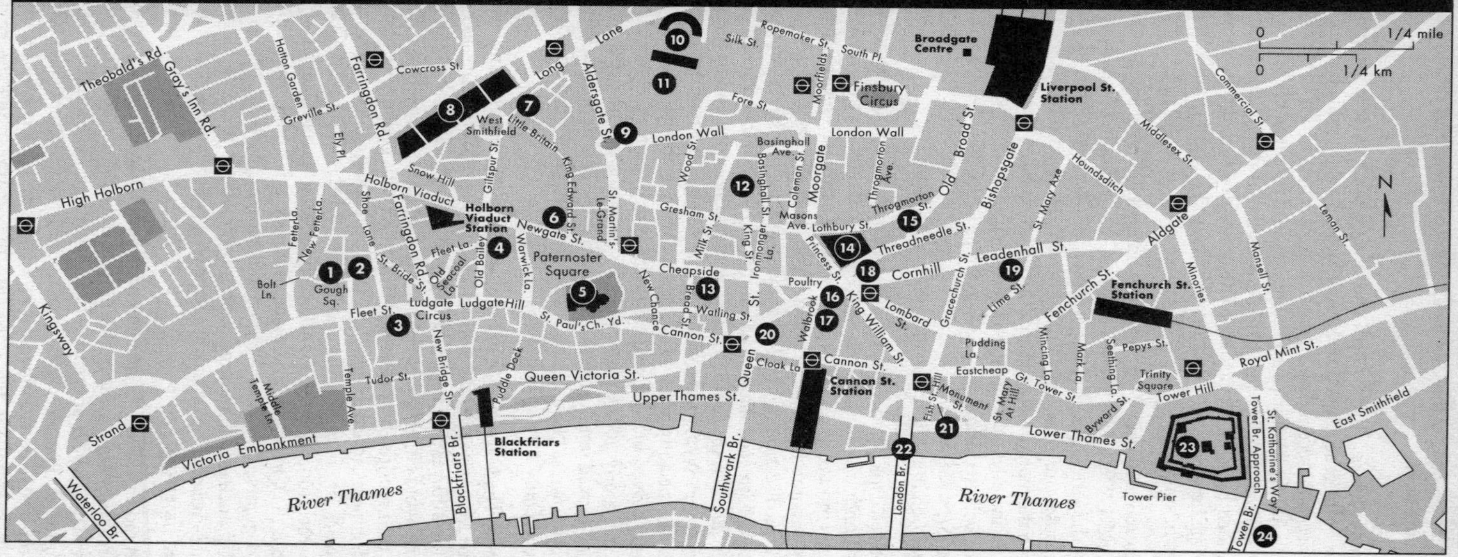

Bank of England, **14**
Barbican Centre, **10**
Dr. Johnson's House, **1**
Guildhall, **12**
Lloyd's of London, **19**
London Bridge, **22**
London Stock Exchange, **15**
Mansion House, **16**
Monument, **21**
Museum of London, **9**
National Postal Museum, **6**
Old Bailey (Central Criminal Court), **4**
Royal Exchange, **18**
St. Bartholomew the Great, **7**
St. Bride's, **3**
St. Giles without Cripplegate, **11**
St. Mary-le-Bow, **13**
St. Paul's Cathedral, **5**
St. Stephen Walbrook, **17**
Smithfield, **8**
Temple of Mithras, **20**
Tower Bridge, **24**
Tower of London, **23**
Ye Olde Cheshire Cheese, **2**

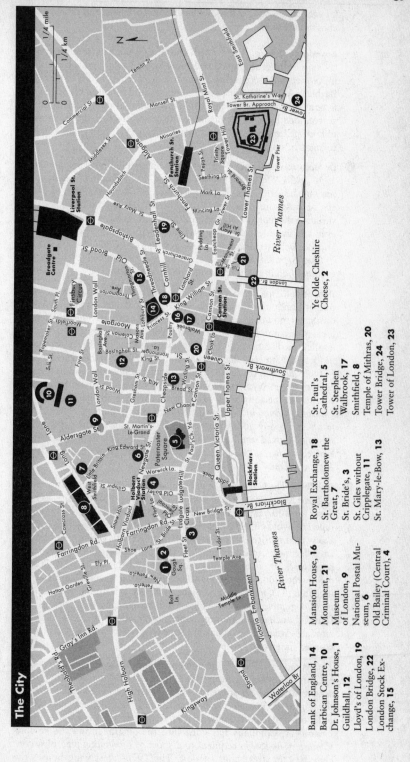

by practice sessions of the Guildhall School of Music and Drama's orchestra next door.

Broadgate Centre. At the north end of Old Broad Street, hanging on the tails of the redeveloped Liverpool Street Station is one of the City's more successful recent development schemes. In contrast to the nearby Barbican, this collection of offices, shops, and restaurants got good notices as soon as it opened in 1987, especially for its circular courtyard surrounded by hanging gardens. The courtyard is iced over in winter to become London's only outdoor skating rink; it hosts bands and performers in summer.

11 **Dr. Johnson's House.** This is where Samuel Johnson lived between 1746 and 1759, in the worst of health, compiling his famous dictionary in the attic. Like Dickens, he lived all over town, but, like Dickens's House, this is the only one of his abodes remaining today. It is a shrine to the man possibly more attached to London than anyone else, ever, and includes a first edition of his dictionary among the Johnson-and-Boswell mementos. ✉ *17 Gough Sq.,* ☎ *0171/353–3745.* 💷 *£3.* ⌚ *May–Sept., Mon.–Sat. 11–5:30; Oct.–Apr., Mon.–Sat. 11–5; closed national holidays. Tube: Chancery Lane, Temple.*

Fleet Street. This famous street follows the course of, and is named after, one of London's ghost rivers. The Fleet, so called by the Anglo-Saxons, spent most of its centuries above ground as an open sewer, offending local noses until banished below in 1766. It still flows underfoot, now a sanctioned section of London's sewer system. The street's sometime nickname, "Street of Shame," has nothing to do with the stench. It refers to the trade that made it famous: the press. Since the end of the 15th century, when Wynkyn de Worde set up England's first printing press here, and especially after 1702, when the first newspaper, the *Daily Courant,* moved in, followed by (literally) all the rest, "Fleet Street" has been synonymous with newspaper journalism. The papers themselves all moved out during the 1980s, but the British press is still collectively known as "Fleet Street." (Don't miss the black-glass-and-chrome Art Deco *Daily Mirror* building.)

12 **Guildhall.** The Corporation of London ceremonially elects and installs its Lord Mayor here in the symbolic nerve center of the City, as it has done for 800 years. The Guildhall was built in 1411, and though it failed to avoid either the 1666 or 1940 flames, its core survived, with a new roof sensitively appended during the 1950s and further cosmetic embellishments added during the '70s. The fabulous hall is a psychedelic patchwork of coats of arms and banners of the City Livery Companies, which inherited the mantle of the medieval trade guilds, which invented the City in the first place. Actually, this honor really belongs to two giants, Gog and Magog, the pair of mythical beings who founded ancient Albion, and who glower upon the prime minister's annual November banquet from their west gallery grandstand in 9-foot painted limewood form.

The 94 modern Livery Companies are more than symbolic banner-bearers, since they fund education and research in the trades they represent, and many offer apprenticeships. Most are modern and useful, like the Vintners', Plaisterers', Grocers', and Insurers' companies. Other, older ones have had to move with the times and diversify—the Tallow Chandlers' Company has gone into the oil trade, and the Paviors' Company, no longer required to dispose of scavenging pigs, now concentrates on street construction. The 1970s west wing houses the **Guildhall Library**—mainly City-related books and documents, plus a collection belonging to one of the Livery Companies, the Worshipful

Company of Clockmakers, with more than 600 timepieces on show, including a skull-faced watch that belonged to Mary, Queen of Scots. ✉ *Gresham St.,* ☎ *0171/606–3030.* 🎫 *Free.* ⏲ *Mon.–Sat. 10–5 (library closed Sat.); closed national holidays. Tube: St. Paul's, Moorgate, Bank, Mansion House.*

19 **Lloyd's of London.** Richard Rogers's (of Paris Pompidou Centre fame) fantastical steel-and-glass medium-rise of six towers around a vast atrium, with his trademark inside-out ventilation shafts, stairwells and gantries, may be the most exciting recent structure in London. The building is best seen at night, when cobalt and lime spotlights make it leap out of the deeply boring gray skyline like Carmen Miranda at a funeral.

The institution that commissioned this fabulous £163-million fun house has been trading in insurance for two centuries and is famous the world over for several reasons: (1) having started in a coffee house; (2) insuring Marilyn Monroe's legs; (3) accepting no corporate responsibility for losses, which are carried by its investors; (4) having its "Names"—the rich people who underwrite Lloyd's losses; (5) seeming unassailable for a very long time . . .; (6) until 1990 when it lost £2.9 billion; (7) which caused the financial ruination of many Names, and worse: According to reports (possibly hyperbolic), more than 30 of the unfortunates were so devastated by the loss of an apparently safe investment that they committed suicide.

Lloyd's has been allowed to continue trading, however, and claims that good times are coming "in the not too distant future." Meanwhile, the viewing galleries over the trading floor and the museum of Lloyd's history, containing the Lutine Bell, which heralds important announcements (one ring for bad news), have all been closed to the public. ✉ *1 Lime St.,* ☎ *0171/623–7100.*

22 **London Bridge.** Dating from only 1972, this bridge replaced the 1831 Sir John Rennie number that now graces Lake Havasu City, Arizona, the impulse purchase of someone at the McCulloch Oil Corporation, who (rumor has it) was under the impression that he'd bought the far more picturesque Tower Bridge. The version before that one, the first in stone and the most renowned of all, stood for 600 years after it was built in 1176, the focus of many a gathering thanks to the shops and houses crammed along its length, not to mention the boiled and tar-dipped heads of traitors that decorated its gatehouse after they were removed at the Tower of London. Before *that* the Saxons had put up a wooden bridge; it collapsed in 1014, which was probably the origin of "London bridge is falling down." Nobody is sure of the exact location of the very earliest London Bridge—the Roman version around which focus London grew—but it was certainly very close to the 100-foot-wide, three-span, prestressed concrete cantilever one that you see today.

15 **London Stock Exchange.** This institution was rendered practically useless a mere 14 years after this building opened (the third on its site), when the "Big Bang," the stock market crash of late 1986, put a stop to trading in equities on the floor. The London Traded Options Market persisted in one corner, which visitors could spy on from the Viewing Gallery, until security-consciousness following an IRA bomb in July 1990 closed *that* down. It was due to close anyway, because in February 1992 that last bastion of the jobbers and brokers of the stock exchange floor merged with the London International Financial Futures Exchange (LIFFE, pronounced "life"). Everyone packed their phones, and they all decamped to deal at **Cannon Bridge Station** (☎ 0171/623–0444; tours available by arrangement) in nearby Cousin's Lane, leaving the dealing floor at the Stock Exchange echoing with red-suspender,

stripe-shirt '80s phantoms. All you can visit here now is the reception desk, where a long-suffering security guard says you can't go in and somewhat tetchily hands over an information booklet.

16 **Mansion House.** With its mid-18th-century Palladian facade, this is the Lord Mayor's abode. Unfortunately, you won't see the colonnaded Egyptian Hall, or the cell where the suffragette Emmeline Pankhurst was held early in this century, or any of the state rooms where the mayor entertains his fellow dignitaries, because the building is closed to public scrutiny.

21 **Monument.** Commemorating the "dreadful visitation" of the Great Fire of 1666, this is the world's tallest isolated stone column. It is the work of Wren, who was asked to erect it "On or as neere unto the place where the said Fire soe unhappily began as conveniently may be." And so here it is—at 202 feet, exactly as tall as the distance it stands from Farriner's baking house in Pudding Lane, where the fire started. Above the viewing gallery (311 steps up—better than any StairMaster) is a flaming bronze urn, and around it a cage for the prevention of suicide, which was a trend for a while during the 19th century. ✉ *Monument St.,* ☎ *0171/626–2717.* 🎫 *£1.* ⏲ *Apr.–Sept., weekdays 9–5:30, weekends 2–5:30; Oct.–Mar., Mon.–Sat. 9–3:30. Tube: Monument.*

9 **Museum of London.** This museum, with its self-explanatory title, appropriately shelters a section of the 2nd- to 4th-century London wall, which you can view from a window inside, near to the Roman monumental arch the museum's archaeologists reconstructed a mere two decades ago. Anyone with the least interest in how this city evolved will adore this museum, especially said reconstructions and the dioramas—like one of the Great Fire (flickering flames! sound effects!), a 1940s air-raid shelter, a Georgian prison cell, and a Victorian street complete with fully stocked shops. There are plenty of treasures (the Cheapside Hoard of Jacobean jewelry shouldn't be missed), costumes, furniture, and domestic paraphernalia to flesh it all out, and galleries proceed chronologically for easy comprehension. ✉ *London Wall,* ☎ *0171/600–3699.* 🎫 *£3.50; free 4:30–6. All tickets allow unlimited return visits for three months. White Card accepted.* ⏲ *Tues.–Sat. 10–6, Sun. noon–6; closed Good Friday, Dec. 24–25.*

6 **National Postal Museum.** An important landmark for philatelists, this was founded in 1965, but the collection is as old as the postal service itself, and is one of the world's best. ✉ *King Edward Bldg., King Edward St.,* ☎ *0171/239–5420.* 🎫 *Free.* ⏲ *Mon.–Thurs. 9:30–4:30, Fri. 9:30–4; closed national holidays. Tube: St. Paul's.*

4 **Old Bailey.** This, the present-day **Central Criminal Court,** is where Newgate Prison stood from the 12th century right until the beginning of this one. Few survived for long in the version pulled down in 1770. Those who didn't starve were hanged, or pressed to death in the Press Yard, or they succumbed to the virulent gaol (the archaic British spelling of "jail") fever—any of which must have been preferable to a life in the stinking, subterranean, lightless Stone Hold, or to suffering the robberies, beatings, and general victimization endemic in what Henry Fielding called the "prototype of hell." The next model lasted only a couple of years before being torn down by insane mobs during the anti-Catholic Gordon Riots of 1780, to be replaced by the Newgate that Dickens visited several times (in between pubs) and used in several novels—Fagin ended up in the Condemned Hold here in *Oliver Twist,* from which he would have been taken to the public scaffold which replaced the Tyburn Tree (see Marble Arch) and stood outside the prison until 1868. The Central Criminal Court replaced Newgate in 1907. The most

famous, and most interesting, feature of the solid Edwardian building is the gilded statue of blind Justice perched on top, scales in her left hand, sword in her right. Ask the doorman which current trial is likely to prove juicy, if you're that kind of ghoul—you may catch the conviction of the next Crippen or Christie (England's most notorious wife-murderers, both tried here). ⏲ *Public Gallery open weekdays 10–1 and 2–4; queue forms at the Newgate St. entrance. No cameras allowed. Check the day's hearings on the sign outside. Tube: Blackfriars.*

18 **Royal Exchange.** Inhabiting the isosceles triangle between Threadneedle Street and Cornhill, this is the third version to have stood here, but the first to have been blessed by Queen Victoria—at its 1844 opening. Sir William Tite designed the massive templelike building, its pediment featuring 17 limestone figures (Commerce, plus merchants) supported by eight sizable Corinthian columns, to house the then thriving futures market. This has now moved on, leaving the Royal Exchange, which you may no longer enter, as a monument to money.

7 **St. Bartholomew the Great.** Reached via a perfect half-timbered gatehouse atop a 13th-century stone archway, this is one of London's oldest churches. Along with its namesake on the other side of the road, St. Bartholomew's Hospital, the Norman church was founded by Rahere, Henry I's court jester. At the Dissolution of the Monasteries, Henry VIII had most of it torn down, so that the Romanesque choir is all that survives from the 12th century. The former hospital across the street, although one of London's most famous, and despite protests, has been closed down as part of a government reorganization of the British Health Service.

3 **St. Bride's.** This, the first of Wren's city churches, did not escape wartime bomb damage, and was reconsecrated only in 1960 after a 17-year restoration. As St. Paul's, Covent Garden is the actor's church, so St. Bride's belongs to journalists, many of whom have been buried or memorialized here, as reading the wall plaques will tell you. Even before the press moved in, it was a popular place to take the final rest. By 1664 the crypts were so crowded that Samuel Pepys had to bribe the grave digger to "justle together" some bodies to make room for his deceased brother. Now the crypts house a museum of the church's rich history, and a bit of Roman sidewalk. ✉ *Fleet St.,* ☎ *0171/353–1301.* 🎫 *Free.* ⏲ *Mon.–Sat. 9–5, Sun. between the services at 11 and 6:30. Tube: Chancery Lane.*

11 **St. Giles without Cripplegate.** Standing south of the Barbican complex, this is one of the only City churches to have withstood the Great Fire, only to succumb to the Blitz bombs three centuries later. The tower and a few walls survived; the rest was rebuilt to the 16th-century plan during the 1950s, and now the little church struggles hopelessly for attention among the Barbican towers, whose parishioners it tends. Past parishioners include Oliver Cromwell, married here in 1620, and John Milton, buried here in 1674.

13 **St. Mary-le-Bow.** Wren's 1673 church has one of the most famous sets of bells around–a Londoner must be born within the sound of Bow bells to be a true cockney. The origin of that idea was probably the curfew rung on the Bow Bells during the 14th century, even though "cockney" only came to mean Londoner three centuries later, and then it was an insult.

NEED A BREAK? The **Place Below** is literally below the church, in St. Mary-le-Bow's crypt, and gets packed with City workers weekday lunchtime—the self-service soup and quiche are particularly good. It's also open for breakfast, and

Thursday and Friday evenings it features a posh and sophisticated vegetarian set dinner.

5 **St. Paul's Cathedral.** This will take your breath away. In fact, the dome—the world's third largest—will already be familiar, since you see it peeping through on the skyline from many an angle. The cathedral is, of course, Sir Christopher Wren's masterpiece, completed in 1710 after 35 years of building and much argument with the royal commission, then, much later, miraculously (mostly) spared by the World War II bombs. Wren had originally been commissioned to restore Old St. Paul's, the Norman cathedral that had replaced, in its turn, three earlier versions, but the Great Fire left so little of it behind that a new cathedral was deemed necessary.

Wren's first plan, known as the New Model, did not make it past the drawing board, while the second, known as the Great Model, got as far as the 20-foot oak rendering you can see here today before being rejected, too, whereupon Wren is said to have burst into tears. The third, however, known as the Warrant Design (because it received the royal warrant), was accepted, with the fortunate coda that the architect be allowed to make changes as he saw fit. Without that, there would be no dome, because the approved design had featured a steeple. Parliament felt that building was proceeding too slowly (in fact, 35 years is lightning speed, as cathedrals go) and withheld half of Wren's pay for the last 13 years of work. He was pushing 80 when Queen Anne finally coughed up the arrears.

When you enter and see the dome from the inside, you may find that it seems smaller than you expected. You aren't imagining things; it *is* smaller, and 60 feet lower, than the lead-covered outer dome. Between the inner and outer domes is a brick cone, which supports the familiar 850-ton lantern, surmounted by its golden ball and cross. Nobody can resist making a beeline for the dome, so we'll start beneath it, standing dead center, on top of Wren's memorial, which his son composed and had set into the pavement, and which reads succinctly: *Lector, si monumentum requiris, circumspice*—"Reader, if you seek his monument, look around you."

Now climb the 259 spiral steps to the **Whispering Gallery.** This is the part of the cathedral with which you bribe children, who are fascinated by the acoustic phenomenon: Whisper something to the wall on one side, and a second later it transmits clearly to the other side, 107 feet away. The only problem is identifying "your" whisper from the cacophony of everyone else's, since this is a popular game. Look down onto the Nave from here, and up to the frescoes of St. Paul by Sir James Thornhill (who nearly fell off while painting them), before ascending farther to the Stone Gallery, which encircles the outside of the dome and affords a spectacular panorama of London. Up again (careful—you will have tackled 627 steps altogether) and you reach the Golden Gallery, from which you can view the lantern through a circular opening called the oculus.

Back downstairs there are the inevitable monuments and memorials to see, though fewer than one might expect, because Wren didn't want his masterpiece cluttered up. The poet John Donne, who had been Dean of St. Paul's for his final 10 years (he died in 1631), lies in the south choir aisle, his the only monument remaining from Old St. Paul's. The vivacious choir stall carvings nearby are the work of Grinling Gibbons, as is the organ, which Wren designed and Handel played. The painters Sir Joshua Reynolds and J. M. W. Turner are commemorated, as is George Washington. The American connection continues behind the high altar

Adm. Collingwood, **21**
Adm. Howe, **20**
The American Chapel, **13**
All Souls' Chapel, **1**
Bishop's Throne, **18**
Chapel of Modern Martyrs, **11**
Chapel of St. Michael and St. George, **27**
Crypt Entrance, **19**
Dean's Vestry, **16**
The Donne Effigy, **15**
Dr. Johnson, **8**
Duke of Wellington, **5**
General Gordon Monument, **4**
Geometric Staircase, **28**
High Altar, **12**
J.M.W. Turner, **22**
The Lady Chapel, **14**
Lord Leighton Monument, **3**
Lord Mayor's Stall, **17**
Lord Mayor's Vestry, **6**
Minor Canons' Vestry, **9**
Nelson, **23**
St. Dunstan's Chapel, **2**
St. Paul's Watch Memorial Stone, **26**
Sanctuary Screens, **10**
Sir John Moore, **24**
Sir Joshua Reynolds, **7**
Staircase to Whispering Gallery, Dome, and Golden Gallery, **25**

St. Paul's Cathedral

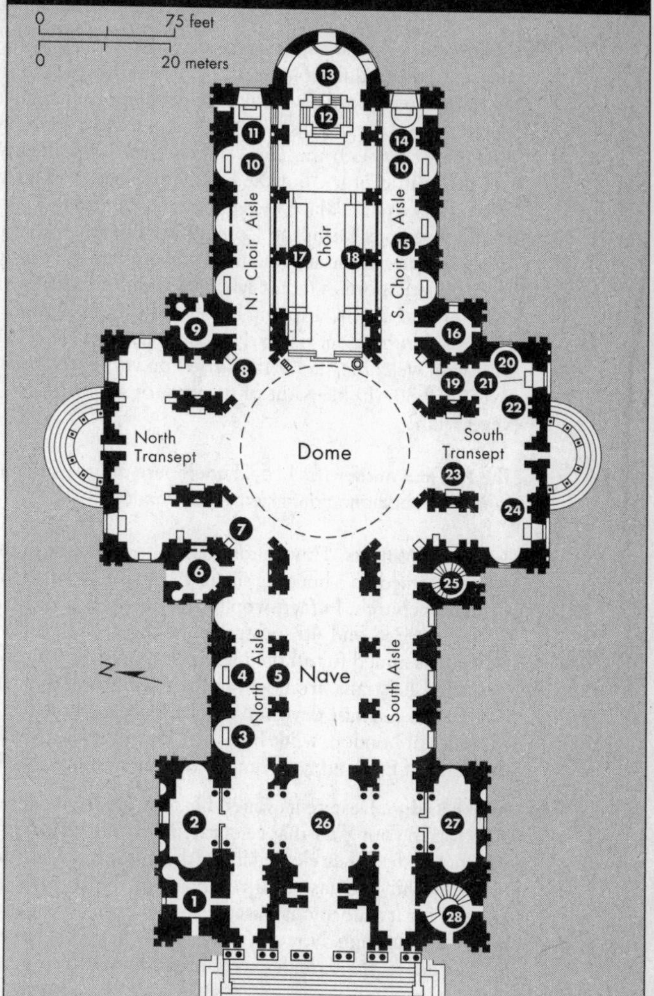

in the **American Memorial Chapel,** dedicated in 1958 to the 28,000 GIs stationed here who lost their lives in World War II.

A visit to the **crypt** brings you to Wren's tomb, the black marble sarcophagus containing Admiral Nelson (who was pickled in alcohol for his final voyage here from Trafalgar), and an equestrian statue of the Duke of Wellington on top of his grandiose tomb. ☎ *0171/248–2705.* *Cathedral, ambulatory (American Chapel), crypt, and treasury: £3; galleries: £2.50; combined ticket: £5.* *Cathedral open for sightseeing Mon.–Sat. 8:30–4:30 (closed occasionally for special services); ambulatory, crypt, and galleries open Mon.–Sat. 9:30–4:15. Tube: St. Paul's.*

17 **St. Stephen Walbrook.** This is the parish church many think is Wren's best, by virtue of its practice dome, which predates the Big One at St. Paul's by some 30 years. Two inside sights warrant investigation: Henry Moore's 1987 central stone altar, which sits beneath the dome ("like a lump of Camembert," say critics), and, well, a telephone—an eloquent

tribute to that genuine savior of souls, Rector Chad Varah, who founded the Samaritans, givers of phone help to the suicidal, here in 1953.

8 **Smithfield.** London's main meat market. Nowadays the meat is dead, but up to the middle of last century, it was livestock that was sold here, by human meatheads, who liked to get blind drunk and stampede their herds around the houses—"like a bull in a china shop," which is where that phrase comes from. This "smooth field" was already a market during the 12th century, but the building you see today, modeled on the Victorian Crystal Palace, was not opened until 1868. Although threatened by various European Community directives, not to mention the disappearance of the artisan butcher, Smithfield still bustles like nowhere else, frenetic porters (actor Michael Caine's father was one) slinging sides of beef about, dripping blood down their aprons, then repairing to pubs that have special early alcohol licenses for breakfast. Visitors, although welcome, had better (a) get up very early, because the show's over by 9:30, (b) keep out of the way, or get sworn at, and (c) not be vegetarian.

NEED A BREAK? The **Fox and Anchor** (⊠ 115 Charterhouse St.) serves beer alongside its famous Brobdingnagian mixed grills, from 6:30 AM.

20 **Temple of Mithras.** This minor place of pilgrimage in the Roman City was unearthed on a building site in 1954 and taken, at first, for an early Christian church. In fact, worshipers here favored Christ's chief rival during the 3rd and 4th centuries, Mithras, the Persian god of light. Mithraists aimed for all the big virtues, but still were not appreciated by early Christians, from whom their sculptures and treasures had to be concealed. These devotional objects are now on display back at the Museum of London, while here, on Queen Victoria Street, not far from the Bank of England, you can see the foundations of the temple itself.

24 **Tower Bridge.** Despite its venerable, nay medieval, appearance, this is a Victorian youngster that celebrated its centenary in June 1994. Constructed of steel, then clothed in Portland stone, it was deliberately styled in the Gothic persuasion to complement the Tower next door, and is famous for its enormous bascules—the "arms," which open to allow large ships through. Nowadays this rarely happens, but when river traffic was dense, the bascules were raised about five times a day.

The bridge's 100th-birthday gift was a new exhibition, one of London's most imaginative and fun. You are conducted in the company of "Harry Stoner," an animatronic bridge construction worker worthy of Disneyland, back in time to witness the birth of the Thames's last downstream bridge. History and engineering lessons are painlessly absorbed as you meet the ghost of the bridge's architect, Sir Horace Jones, see the bascules work, and wander the walkways with their grand upstream–downstream views annotated by interactive video displays. Be sure to hang on to your ticket and follow the signs to the Engine Rooms for part two, where the original steam-driven hydraulic engines gleam, and a cute rococo theater is the setting for an Edwardian music-hall production of the bridge's story. ☎ *0171/403–3761.* *£5.* *Apr.–Oct., daily 10–6:30; Nov.–Mar., daily 10–5:15 (last entry 1¼ hrs before closing); closed Good Friday, Dec. 24–25, Jan. 1. Tube: Tower Hill.*

Tower Hill Pageant. London's first "dark-ride" museum, where automated cars take you past mock-ups of scenes from most periods of London's past, complete with "people," sound effects, and even smells. There's also an archaeological museum with finds from the Thames, set up by the Museum of London. ⊠ *Tower Hill Terrace,* ☎ *0171/709–*

0081. 🖃 *£5.95.* ⏲ *Apr.–Oct., daily 9:30–5:30; Nov.–Mar., daily 9:30–4:30; closed Dec. 25. Tube: Tower Hill.*

👆 ㉓ **Tower of London.** This has top billing on every tourist itinerary for good reason. Nowhere else does London's history come to life so vividly as in this mini-city of melodramatic towers stuffed to bursting with heraldry and treasure, the intimate details of lords and dukes and princes and sovereigns etched in the walls (literally in some places, as you'll see), and quite a few pints of royal blue blood spilled on the stones. Be warned that visitor traffic at the sight of sights is copious, meaning not only lines for the best bits, but a certain dilution of atmosphere, which can be disappointing if you've been fantasizing scenes from *Elizabeth and Essex.* At least you need no longer spend all day in line for the prize exhibit, the Crown Jewels, since they have been transplanted to a new home where moving walkways hasten progress at the busiest times.

The reason the Tower holds the royal gems is that it is still one of the royal palaces, although no monarch since Henry VIII has called it home. It has also housed the Royal Mint, the Public Records, the Royal Menagerie, and the Royal Observatory, although its most renowned and titillating function has been, of course, as a jail and place of torture and execution.

A person was mighty privileged to be beheaded in the peace and seclusion of **Tower Green** instead of before the mob at Tower Hill. In fact, only seven people were ever important enough—among them Anne Boleyn and Catherine Howard, wives two and five of Henry VIII's six; Elizabeth I's friend Robert Devereux, Earl of Essex; and the nine-days queen, Lady Jane Grey, aged 17. Tower Green's other function was as a corpse dumping ground when the chapel just got too full. You can see the executioner's block, with its charming forehead-sized dent, and his axe—along with the equally famous rack, where victims were stretched, and the more obscure scavenger's daughter, which pressed a body nearly to death, plus assorted thumbscrews, iron maidens, etc.—in the **Martin Tower,** which stands in the northeast corner.

Before we go any farther, you should know about the excellent free and fact-packed tours that depart every half hour or so from the Middle Tower. They are conducted by the 42 Yeoman Warders, better known as "Beefeaters"—ex-servicemen dressed in resplendent navy-and-red (scarlet-and-gold on special occasions) Tudor outfits. Beefeaters have been guarding the Tower since Henry VII appointed them in 1485. One of them, the Yeoman Ravenmaster, is responsible for making life comfortable for the eight ravens who live in the Tower—an important duty, since if they were to desert the Tower (goes the legend), the kingdom would fall.

In prime position stands the oldest part of the Tower and the most conspicuous of its buildings, the **White Tower.** This central keep was begun in 1078 by William the Conqueror; by the time it was completed, in 1097, it was the tallest building in London, underlining the might of those victorious Normans. Henry III (1207–1272) had it whitewashed, which is where the name comes from, then used it to house his menagerie, including the polar bear the King of Norway had given him.

The spiral staircase—winding clockwise to help the right-handed swordsman defend it—is the only way up, and here you'll find the **Royal Armouries,** Britain's national museum of arms and armor, with about 40,000 pieces on display. One of the Tower's original functions was as arsenal, supplying armor and weapons to the kings and their armies. Henry VIII started the collection in earnest, founding a workshop at Greenwich as a kind of bespoke tailor of armor to the gentry, but the

Beauchamp Tower, **10**
Bloody Tower, **12**
Byward Tower, **15**
Chapel of St. John, **2**
Hospital Block, **5**
Jewel House, **8**
Martin Tower, **7**
Middle Tower, **16**
New Armouries, **4**
Queen's House, **11**
Royal Fuseliers' Museum, **6**
St. Peter ad Vincula, **9**
Traitors' Gate, **14**
Wakefield Tower, **13**
Wardrobe Tower, **3**
White Tower, **1**

The Tower

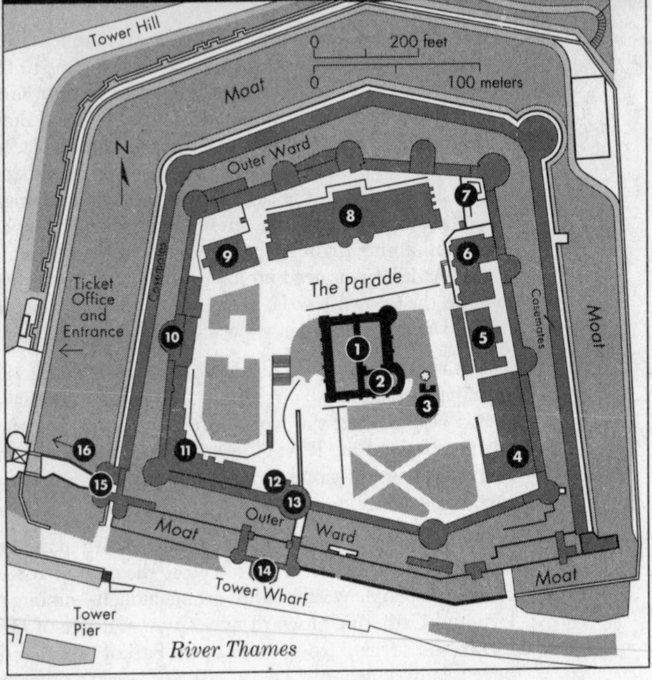

public didn't get to see it until the second half of the 17th century, during Charles II's reign—which makes the Tower Armouries Britain's oldest public museum.

Here you can see weapons and armor from Britain and the Continent, dating from Saxon and Viking times right up to our own. Among the highlights are four of those armors Henry VIII commissioned to fit his ever-increasing bulk, plus one for his horse. The medieval war horse was nothing without his *shaffron,* or head protector, and here you'll find a 500-year-old example, one of the oldest pieces of horse armor in the world. Don't miss the tiny armors on the third floor—one belonging to Henry's son (who survived in it to become Edward VI), and another just a bit more than 3 feet tall. In the **New Armouries,** added during the 17th century, are examples of almost every weapon made for the British soldier from the 17th to the 19th century.

Most of the interior of the White Tower has been much altered over the centuries, but the **Chapel of St. John,** downstairs from the armouries, is unadulterated 11th-century Norman—very rare, very simple, and very beautiful. Underneath it is "Little Ease," the cell where Guy Fawkes (☞ The Houses of Parliament in Westminster and Royal London, *above*) was held, chained to a ring in the floor.

The other fortifications and buildings surrounding the White Tower date from the 11th to the 19th century. Starting from the main entrance, you can't miss the **moat.** Until the Duke of Wellington had it drained in 1843, this was a stinking, stagnant mush, obstinately resisting all attempts to flush it with water from the Thames. Now there's a little raven graveyard in the grassed-over channel, with touching memorials to some of the old birds (who are not known for their kind natures, by the way, and you risk a savage pecking if you try to befriend them).

Across the moat, the **Middle Tower** and the **Byward Tower** form the principal landward entrance, with **Traitors' Gate** a little farther on to the right. This London equivalent of Venice's Bridge of Sighs was where the boats delivered prisoners to their cells, and so it was where those condemned to death got their last look at the outside world. During the period when the Thames was London's chief thoroughfare, this was the main entrance to the Tower.

Immediately opposite Traitors' Gate is the former Garden Tower, better known since about 1570 as the **Bloody Tower.** Its name comes from one of the most famous unsolved murders in history, the saga of the "little princes in the Tower." In 1483 the boy king, Edward V, and his brother Richard were left here by their uncle, Richard of Gloucester, after the death of their father, Edward I. They were never seen again, Gloucester was crowned Richard III, and in 1674 two little skeletons were found under the stairs to St. John's Chapel. The obvious conclusions have always been drawn—and were, in fact, even before the skeletons were discovered.

Another famous inmate was Sir Walter Raleigh, who was kept here from 1603 to 1616. It wasn't such an ordeal, as you'll see when you visit his spacious rooms, where he kept two servants, had his wife and two sons live with him (the younger boy was christened in the Tower chapel), and amused himself by writing his *History of the World*. Unfortunately, he was less lucky on his second visit in 1618, which terminated in his execution at Whitehall.

Next to the Bloody Tower is the circular **Wakefield Tower,** which dates from the 13th century and once contained the king's private apartments. It was the scene of another royal murder in 1471, when Henry VI was killed in mid-prayer. Henry founded Eton College and King's College, Cambridge, and they haven't forgotten: Every May 21, envoys from both institutions mark the anniversary of his murder by laying white lilies on the site.

The shiniest, the most expensive, and absolutely the most famous exhibits here are, of course, the **Crown Jewels,** now housed in the **Duke of Wellington's Barracks.** In their new setting you get so close that you could lick the gems (if it weren't for the wafers of bulletproof glass), and they are enhanced by new laser lighting, which almost hurts the eyes with sparkle. Before you meet them in person, you are given a high-definition-film preview along with a few scenes from Elizabeth's 1953 coronation.

It's a commonplace to call these baubles priceless, but it's impossible not to drop your jaw at the notion of their worth. They were, in fact, lifted once—by Colonel Thomas Blood, in 1671—though only as far as a nearby wharf. The colonel was given a royal pension instead of a beating, fueling speculation that Charles II, short of ready cash as usual, had his hand in the escapade somewhere. These days security is as fiendish as you'd expect, since the jewels—even though they would be literally impossible for thieves to sell—are *so* priceless that they're not insured.

A brief résumé of the top jewels: Finest of all is the **Royal Sceptre,** containing the earth's largest cut diamond, the 530-carat Star of Africa. This is also known as Cullinan I, having been cut from the South African Cullinan, which weighed 20 ounces when dug up from a De Beers mine at the beginning of the century. Another chip off the block, Cullinan II, lives on the **Imperial Crown of State** that Prince Charles is due to wear at his coronation—the same one that Elizabeth II wore in her coronation procession; it had been made for Victoria's in 1838. Aside from its 2,800 diamonds, it features the Black Prince's ruby, which Henry

V was supposed to have worn at Agincourt, and is actually an imposter—it's no ruby, it's a semiprecious spinel. The other most famous gem is the Koh-i-noor, or "Mountain of Light," which adorns the **Queen Mother's crown.** When Victoria was presented with this gift horse in 1850, she looked it in the mouth, found it lacking in glitteriness, and had it chopped down to almost half its weight.

The little chapel of **St. Peter ad Vincula** can be visited only as part of a Yeoman Warder tour. The third church on the site, it conceals the remains of some 2,000 people executed at the Tower, Anne Boleyn and Catherine Howard among them. Being traitors, they were not so much buried as dumped under the flagstones, but the genteel Victorians had the courtesy to rebury their bones during renovations.

One of the more evocative towers is **Beauchamp Tower,** built west of Tower Green by Edward I (1272–1307). It was soon designated as a jail for the higher class of miscreant, including Lady Jane Grey, who is thought to have added her Latin graffiti to the many inscriptions carved by prisoners that you can see here.

Just south of the Beauchamp Tower is an L-shape row of half-timbered Tudor houses, with the **Queen's House** at the center. Built for the governor of the Tower in 1530, this place saw the interrogation or incarceration of several of the more celebrated prisoners, including Anne Boleyn and the Gunpowder Plot conspirators. The Queen's House also played host to the Tower's last-ever prisoner, Rudolph Hess, the Nazi who parachuted into London in 1941 to seek asylum.

Don't forget to stroll along the battlements before you leave; from them, you get a wonderful overview of the whole Tower of London. ✉ *H. M. Tower of London,* ☎ *0171/709–0765.* 💷 *£8.30. Small additional admission charge to the Fusiliers Museum.* ⏲ *Mar.–Oct., Mon.–Sat. 9:30–6:30, Sun. 2–6; Nov.–Feb., Mon.–Sat. 9:30–5; closed Good Friday, Dec. 24–26, Jan. 1. For tickets to Ceremony of the Keys (the locking of the main gates, nightly at 10), write well in advance to The Resident Governor and Keeper of the Jewel House, Queen's House, H. M. Tower of London, EC3. Give your name, the dates you wish to attend (including alternate dates), and number of people (up to 7), and enclose a self-addressed stamped envelope. Yeoman Warder guides leave daily from Middle Tower, subject to weather and availability, at no charge (but a tip is always appreciated), about every 30 min until 3:30 in summer, 2:30 in winter. Tube: Tower Hill.*

❷ **Ye Olde Cheshire Cheese.** One of the many places in which that acerbic compiler of the first dictionary, Dr. Johnson drank (like Dickens, he is claimed by many a pub). This was, in fact, his "local" around the corner from his house. It retains a venerable open-fires-in-tiny-rooms charm when not too packed with tourists. Among 19th-century writers who followed Johnson's footsteps to the bar here were Mark Twain and, yes, Charles Dickens.

THE EAST END

Whitechapel and Spitalfields, Shoreditch, Mile End, and Bethnal Green began as separate villages, melding together during the population boom of the 19th century—a boom that was shaped by French Huguenot and Jewish refugees, by poverty, and, in the past several decades, by a growing Bengali community. Whitechapel is where the Salvation Army was founded and the original Liberty Bell was forged, but what everyone remembers about it is that its Victorian slum streets were stalked by the most infamous serial killer of all, Jack the Ripper. Two centuries earlier, neighboring Spitalfields provided sanctuary for the French Huguenots. They had fled here after the Edict of Nantes (which had allowed them religious freedom in Catholic France) was revoked in 1685, and had found work in the nascent silk industry, many of them becoming prosperous master weavers.

Prosperous is not really the word for the East End of today, but what the area lacks in tourist attractions it makes up for in history, and urban romance. There's a good argument for calling this the real London, since Eastenders are born "within the sound of Bow Bells," and are therefore cockneys through and through–not to mention models for the characters of England's favorite soap opera, *Eastenders.*

A Good Walk

Numbers in the text correspond to numbers in the margin and on the East End map.

The easiest way to reach Whitechapel High Street is via the District Line to Aldgate East tube. Turn left out of the tube station, and you'll see **Bloom's** ①, behind which once stood George Yard Buildings, where Jack the Ripper's first victim, Martha Turner, was discovered in August 1888. Almost next door is the **Whitechapel Gallery** ②. Continue east until you reach Fieldgate Street on the right, where you'll find the **Whitechapel Bell Foundry** ③, then, retracing your steps, turn right into Osborn Street, which soon becomes **Brick Lane** ④.

Brick Lane itself and the narrow streets running off it offer a paradigm of the East End's development. Its population has always been in flux, with some moving in to find refuge here as others were escaping its poverty. Just before the start of Brick Lane you can take a short detour (turn left, then right) to see the birthplace of one who did just that. Flower and Dean Street, past the ugly 1970s housing project on Thrawl Street and once the most disreputable street in London, was where Abe Saperstein, founder of the *Harlem Globetrotters,* was born in 1908. On the west end of **Fournier Street** ⑤, see Nicholas Hawkesmoor's masterpiece, **Christ Church, Spitalfields** ⑥, and some fine early Georgian houses, then follow Wilkes Street north of the church, where you'll find more 1720s Huguenot houses (one has been turned into the **Spitalfields Heritage Centre** ⑦), and turn right into Princelet Street, once important to the Jewish settlers. Where No. 6 stands now, the first of several thriving Yiddish theaters opened in 1886, playing to packed houses until the following year, when a false fire alarm during a January performance ended with 17 people being crushed to death, and so demoralized the theater's actor-founder, Jacob Adler, that he moved his troupe to New York. Adler played a major role in founding that city's great Yiddish theater tradition—which, in turn, had a significant effect on Hollywood.

Now you reach Brick Lane again and the **Black Eagle Brewery** ⑧. Turn left at Hanbury Street, where, in 1888, behind a seedy lodging house at No. 29, Jack the Ripper left his third mutilated murderee, "Dark" Annie Chapman. A double murder followed, and then, after a month's lull, came the death on this street of Marie Kelly, the Ripper's last victim and his most revolting murder of all. He had been able to work indoors this time, and Kelly, a young widow, was found strewn all over the room, charred remains of her clothing in the fire grate. (Of course, Jack the Ripper's identity never has been discovered, although to this day theories are still bandied about.)

Now turn onto Lamb Street, and the two northern entrances to **Spitalfields Market** ⑨, or turn left on Commercial Street to Folgate Street, and **Dennis Sever's House** ⑩. (If you have kids, they might have fun—and learn something too—going to **Spitalfields City Farm** ⑪ a few blocks away.) Go back west through Folgate Street, to reach Shoreditch High Street, where you can catch Bus 22a, 22b, or 149 north to Kingsland Road, or get there across Bethnal Green Road, left, then right onto Club Row, **Arnold Circus** ⑫ and two streets north, **Columbia Road** ⑬. Cross Hackney Road and slip up Waterson Street—that's about a half-mile's walk. On Kingsland Road, you'll come to the row of early 18th-century almshouses which is the **Geffrye Museum** ⑭. Head east about 500 yards on Hackney Road (Cremer Street, south of the museum, gets you there) and you come to the **Hackney City Farm** ⑮. Going south down Warner Place (across Hackney Road opposite the farm entrance) you come to Old Bethnal Green Road, at the end of which a right turn brings you to the **Bethnal Green Museum of Childhood** ⑯.

Now you can either catch Bus 106 or 253 or walk south about half a mile down Cambridge Heath Road as far as the Mile End Road. Turning left, you'll pass four historical landmarks, which provide, let's be honest, more food for thought than thrills for the senses. On the north side of the street, are the former **Trinity Almshouses** ⑰, with the statue of William Booth on the very spot where the first Salvation Army meetings were held. Behind you, on the northwest corner of Cambridge Heath Road is **The Blind Beggar** ⑱ pub, with the **Royal London Hospital** ⑲ a few yards to the left, and its Archives behind.

TIMING

This is a long walk, and not for everyone. The East End isn't picturesque, and the sights are anything but world famous. However, those who get pleasure from discovery and an adventurous route will enjoy these hidden corners. If you visit on a Sunday morning, the East End has a festive air: About half the neighborhood sprouts hundreds of market stalls (especially in and around Middlesex Street, Brick Lane, and Columbia Road). After shopping, you could go on to take brunch among cows and sheep on a farm, then play at being Georgians in a restored, candlelighted 18th-century town house. You would miss out on a few weekday-only sights, but—as a Victorian peep-show barker might say—you pays yer money and you takes yer choice. A weekday focus for your jaunt might well be the excellent Whitechapel Gallery, the Geffrye Museum, or the Bethnal Green Museum of Childhood, any of which will take an hour or two. Aside from visits, the walk alone is a three-hour marathon, at a brisk pace. The suggested bus links might appeal, since the in-between parts aren't going to win tourism awards.

Sights To See

⓬ **Arnold Circus.** A perfect circle of arts-and-crafts–style houses around a central raised bandstand, this is the core of the Boundary Estate—"model" housing built by Victorian philanthropists and do-gooders for the slum-dwelling locals, and completed as the century began. It's of especial interest for architecture buffs.

⓰ **Bethnal Green Museum of Childhood.** This is the East End outpost of the Victoria and Albert museum–in fact this entire iron, glass, and brown-brick building was transported here from South Kensington in 1875. Since then, believe it or not, its contents have grown into the biggest toy collection in the world. The central hall is a bit like the Geffrye Museum zapped into miniature: Here are doll's houses (some royal) of every period. Each genre of plaything has its own enclosure, so if teddy bears are your weakness, you need waste no time with the train sets. The museum's title is justified upstairs, in the recently opened, fascinating—and possibly unique—social-history-of-childhood galleries. ✉ *Cambridge Heath Rd.,* ☎ *0181/980–4315.* *Free.* *Mon.–Thurs. and Sat. 10–5:50, Sun. 2:30–5:50. Free art workshops for children* *over 3: Sat. 11 and 2. Closed May Day holiday, Dec. 24–26, Jan. 1. Tube: Bethnal Green.*

8 **Black Eagle Brewery.** This is the only one of the several East End breweries still standing. And a very handsome example of Georgian and 19th-century industrial architecture it is, too, along with its mirrored 1977 extension. It belonged to Truman, Hanbury, Buxton & Co., which in 1873 was the largest brewery in the world (the English always did like their bitter). The building now houses the East End Tourism Trust offices and the modern Truman brewery's administration. You can't go in except to look at the old stables and vat house on the east side. Opposite, however, the old brewery canteen has been turned into the little **Brick Lane Music Hall,** a cute and shabby theater serving up an *echt* East End dinner (latkes feature on most menus) and an old-fashioned laugh-a-minute cabaret show. *Brewery:* ✉ *91 Brick La. Music Hall:* ✉ *152 Brick La.,* ☎ *0171/377–8787.* 💳 *Dinner and show £15–£20.* ⏲ *Wed.–Sat. 7:30* PM. *Tube: Aldgate East, Shoreditch.*

18 **The Blind Beggar.** The Victorian den of iniquity where Salvation Army founder, William Booth preached his first sermon. Also, on the south side of the street stands a stone inscribed "Here William Booth commenced the work of the Salvation Army, July 1865, marking the position of the first Sally Army platform, while back by the pub, a statue of William Booth stands where the first meetings were held. Booth didn't supply the pub's main claim to fame, though. The Blind Beggar's real notoriety dates only from March 1966, when Ronnie Kray—one of the Kray twins, the former gangster kings of London's East End underworld—shot dead rival "godfather" George Cornell in the saloon bar.

1 **Bloom's.** The United Kingdom's most famous kosher restaurant has been run by the same family for more than 70 years. You can clog your arteries here with *heimische* latkes, gefilte fish, and Bloom's famous salt beef, all at bargain rates. Sephardic Jews settled around here during the late 17th century, but the biggest wave of Jewish refugees were those fleeing the pogroms of Eastern Europe between the 1880s and the outbreak of World War I. Though most of London's Jews have now moved out of the East End, they have a sort of potted history written into the walls around here. It was behind Bloom's that Jack the Ripper's first victim was discovered. ✉ *90 Whitechapel High St.,* ☎ *0171/247–6001; meals served Sun.–Thurs. 11–9:30, Fri. 11–2.*

4 **Brick Lane.** This street has, in its time, seen the manufacture of bricks (during the 16th century, when it was named), beer, and bagels, but nowadays it is the center of the East End's Bengali community. (You can still get the bagels, though, at No. 159, the 24-hour **Beigel Bake.**) All along here you'll see shops selling psychedelic saris and stacks of sticky Indian sweets, video stores renting Indian movies, and Bengali, Bangladeshi, and Pakistani restaurants, well known among Londoners for the most authentic and least expensive curries in town. On Sunday morning the entire street is packed with stalls in a companion market to the nearby Petticoat Lane.

6 **Christ Church, Spitalfields.** This is Wren's associate Nicholas Hawksmoor's 1729 masterpiece. Hawksmoor built only six London churches; this one was commissioned as part of Parliament's 1711 "Fifty New Churches Act." The idea was to score points for the Church of England against such Nonconformists as the Protestant Huguenots. (It must have worked; in the churchyard, you can still see some of their gravestones, with epitaphs in French.) The silk industry declined as 19th-century machinery made hand weaving redundant, and the church fell into disrepair, its gardens acquiring a reputation as a tramps' ground (and the sobriquet

The East End

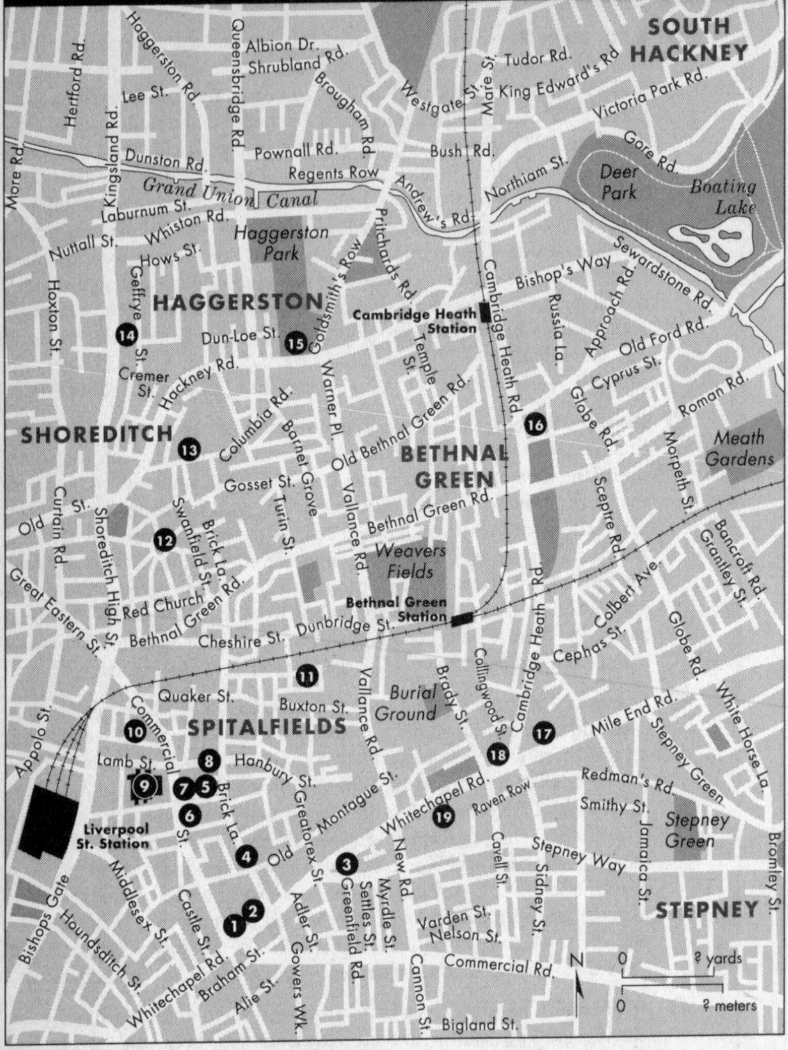

Arnold Circus, **12**
Bethnal Green Museum of Childhood, **16**
Black Eagle Brewery, **8**
The Blind Beggar, **18**
Bloom's, **1**
Brick Lane, **4**
Christ Church, Spitalfields, **6**
Columbia Road, **13**
Dennis Sever's House, **10**
Fournier Street, **5**
Geffrye Museum, **14**
Hackney City Farm, **15**
Royal London Hospital, **19**
Spitalfields City Farm, **11**
Spitalfields Heritage Centre, **7**
Spitalfields Market, **9**
Trinity Almshouses, **17**
Whitechapel Bell Foundry, **3**
Whitechapel Gallery, **2**

"Itchy Park"). By 1958 the structure was crumbling to bits and had to be closed. It was saved from demolition—but only just—and reopened in 1987, though restoration work won't be complete until 1998 or so. Until then, opening hours are restricted, but there are occasional evening concerts (and a music festival in June), and always a fine view of the colonnaded portico and tall spire from Brushfield Street to the west. ✉ *Commercial St.,* ☎ *0171/377–0287.* 🎫 *Free (charge for concerts).* ⏲ *Weekdays noon–2:30; Sun. services. Tube: Aldgate East.*

⓭ **Columbia Road.** On Sundays, this narrow street gets buried under forests of potted palms, azaleas, ivy, ficuses, and freesias, tiger lilies, carnations, roses, and hosts of daffodils in London's main plant and flower market. Prices are ultra-low, and lots of the Victorian shop windows around the stalls are filled with wares—terra-cotta pots, vases, gardening tools, hats, and antiques. ⏲ *Sun. 7 AM–2 PM. Tube: Old Street.*

❿ **Dennis Sever's House.** A Georgian terrace belonging to the eponymous performer/designer/scholar from Escondido, California, who has dedicated his life not only to the restoration of his house but also to raising the ghosts of a fictitious Jervis family who might have inhabited it over two centuries. Sever himself lives a replica of Georgian life, without electricity but with a butler in full 18th-century livery to light the candles and lay the fires—for the Jervises. Three evenings a week he stages a performance, or a "time travel experience," of philosophical bent, trailing the Jervises through 10 rooms and five generations (from 1724 to 1919, to be precise), always missing them by moments. Sever's stunning house, sans Jervises, is also open one Sunday afternoon a month. ✉ *18 Folgate St.,* ☎ *0171/247–4013.* 🎫 *£5 Sun., £30 evenings. Reservations essential. No children.* ⏲ *First Sun. of the month 2–5; 3 performances per wk (days vary) 7:30–10:20 PM. Tube: Liverpool Street.*

❺ **Fournier Street.** This contains fine examples of the neighborhood's characteristic Georgian terraced houses, many of them built by the richest of the early 18th-century Huguenot silk weavers (see the enlarged windows on the upper floors). Most of those along the north side of Fournier Street have now been restored by conservationists, others still contain textile sweatshops—only now the workers are Bengali. On the Brick Lane corner is the **Jamme Masjid,** where local Muslims worship. *Umbra summus* ("We are shadows"), announces the inscription above the entrance, an apt epitaph for the successive communities that have had temporary claim on the building. Built in 1742 as a Huguenot chapel, it converted to Methodism in 1809, only to become the Spitalfields Great Synagogue when the Orthodox Machzikei Hadath sect bought it in 1897.

⓮ **Geffrye Museum.** A small and perfectly formed museum that re-creates domestic English interiors of every period from Elizabethan through postwar '50s utility, all in sequence, so that you walk through time. The best thing about the Geffrye (named after the 17th-century Lord Mayor of London whose land this was) is that its rooms are not the grand parlors of the gentry one normally sees in historic houses but copies of real family homes, as if talented movie set designers had been let loose instead of academic museum curators. There's also a walled, scented herb garden and a full program of accessible lectures, including regular "bring a room to life" talks, and a new set of 20th-century rooms is in the offing. ✉ *Kingsland Rd.,* ☎ *0171/739–9893.* 🎫 *Free.* ⏲ *Tues.–Sat. 10–5, Sun. and bank holiday Mon. 2–5. Period Room Talks: Sat. 2 and 3:30. Closed Good Friday, Dec. 24–26, Jan. 1. Tube: Liverpool Street, then bus 2A, 22B, 67, 149, or 243.*

⓯ **Hackney City Farm.** This one is smaller than the city farm at Spitalfields (☞ *below*), and so are its animals. Bees and butterflies are the stars here, along with the kinds of wildflowers they like, as well as an ecologically sound pond. If you're walking this route, drop in and buy a pot of London honey. ✉ *1A Goldsmiths Row,* ☎ *0171/729–6381.* *Free.* ⏲ *Tues.–Sun. 10–4:30.*

OFF THE BEATEN PATH

London Docklands Visitors Centre. This is the place to jump off for exploring London's most rapidly changing neighborhood. Docklands has emerged from what only a decade ago was a wasteland—partly low-cost residential, partly working docks, partly nothing. Now it houses national newspaper offices, a brand-new riverside business community containing Britain's tallest building, sports facilities, and even a farm. Its boundaries are roughly defined by **Tower Bridge** and the **Design Museum** to the west and **London City Airport** and the **Royal Docks** to the east, though the area inside a loop of the Thames called the **Isle of Dogs** is of most interest. Here is **Canary Wharf,** which, with its 50-story Cesar Pelli **Tower** (✉ 1 Canada Sq.), is the most notorious development project Britain has seen in years. Olympia & York, the Canadian developers, went bust; bomb scares closed the observation deck; the arts funding ran out; shops stayed unlet; jokes were made. But here are waterfront promenades and pubs, a new London piazza called **Cabot Square,** a large shopping mall, and even a concert hall. Take the high-tech **Docklands Light Railway** (DLR) to Crossharbour (change at Bank) and pick up a free map. An exhibition, information desk, and film introduce the area. ✉ *3 Limeharbour, Isle of Dogs, E14,* ☎ *0171/512–1111.* ⏲ *Weekdays 9–6, weekends and holidays 10–4:30. Bus tours of the area depart Tues. at 2, Thurs. at 10:30, Sun. at 11:30.*

19 **Royal London Hospital.** Founded in 1740, the early days of the Royal London were as nasty as its then-neighborhood near the Tower of London. Waste was carried out in buckets and dumped in the street; bedbugs and alcoholic nurses were problems, but according to hospital records, nobody died—they were "relieved." Anyone who lived but refused to give thanks to both the hospital committee and God went on a blacklist, banned from further treatment. In 1759, the hospital moved to a new building, the core of the one you see today. By then it had become the best hospital in London, and it was enhanced further by the addition of a small medical school in 1785, and then, 70 years later, an entire state-of-the-art medical college. Thomas John Barnado, who went on to found the famous Dr. Barnado's Homes for orphans, came to train here in 1866. Ten years later, with the opening of a new wing, the hospital became the largest in the United Kingdom, and now, though mostly rebuilt since World War II, it remains one of London's most capacious. Behind it, the **Royal London Hospital Archives** have displays of medical paraphernalia, objects, and documentation to illustrate the 250-year history of this East London institution. ✉ *Crypt of St. Augustine with St. Philip's Church, Newark St.,* ☎ *0171/377–7000, ext. 3364.* *Free.* ⏲ *Weekdays 10–4:30; closed Dec. 24–26, Jan. 1. Tube: Whitechapel.*

11 **Spitalfields City Farm.** This is just what it sounds like—a sliver of rural England squashed between housing projects. It's one of about a dozen such places in London, which exist to educate city kids in country matters. Available are pony rides, local history tours by horse and cart, a Sunday brunch, summer barbecues, and an altogether surreal experience. ✉ *Pedley St.,* ☎ *0171/247–8762.* *Free.* ⏲ *Tues.–Sun. 9:30–5:30. Sun. brunch 11–3; barbecue June–Sept., Wed. 7 PM (call to confirm). Horse and cart tours, Sun. 11 and 2:30 (weather permitting), start at £3. Tube: Shoreditch, Liverpool Street.*

❼ **Spitalfields Heritage Centre.** This modest institution is dedicated to research into local immigrant communities and the preservation of the neighborhood's historic buildings. Huguenots rented the 1720 house—it still has their silk weaving attic—but in 1870 the little **United Friends Synagogue** was grafted onto the back. You can still see its wooden ark, pulpit, seats, and boards listing benefactors, complete with Hebrew errors. London's third-oldest (purpose-built) synagogue sometimes houses exhibitions and presents videos about the Jewish East End; otherwise, the Heritage Centre remains rather erratic as a museum, since it is in the process of (underfunded) restoration. ✉ *19 Princelet St.,* ☎ *0171/377–6901.* 🎫 *Free.* ⏲ *Normally open weekdays 10–5, but phone first. Tube: Aldgate East.*

❾ **Spitalfields Market.** There's been a market here since the mid-17th century, but the current version is overflowing with crafts and design shops and stalls, a sports hall, restaurants and bars, and different markets every day of the week. The nearer the weekend, the busier it all gets, culminating in the Sunday arts-and-crafts and greenmarket. The latest additions are an opera house and a swimming pool, and events are staged all the time. ✉ *65 Brushfield St.,* ☎ *0171/247–6590.* 🎫 *Free.* ⏲ *Daily 10–7; market stalls weekdays 11–2, weekends 9–4. Tube: Liverpool Street.*

⓱ **Trinity Almshouses.** This is just a redbrick student hostel, but has interesting origins, having been built (possibly with Wren's help) in 1695 for "28 decayed Masters and Commanders of Ships or ye widows of such," bombed during World War II, and restored thus by London County Council. Behind, even better concealed, is the oldest Jewish cemetery in Britain, founded by the Sephardic community in 1657 after Cromwell allowed them back into the country. (If you would like to view the cemetery, call the United Synagogues Cemetery Maintenance Department, ☎ 0171/790–1445.)

❸ **Whitechapel Bell Foundry.** It may be off the beaten track, but this working foundry was responsible for some of the world's better-known chimes. Before moving to this site in 1738, the foundry cast Westminster Abbey's bells (in the 1580s), but its biggest work, in every sense, was the 13-ton Big Ben, cast in 1858 by George Mears, and requiring 16 horses to transport from here to Westminster. Its other important work was casting the original Liberty Bell (now in Philadelphia) in 1752, and both it and Big Ben can be seen in pictures, along with exhibits about bell making, in a little museum in the shop. You can even buy a small table bell (for about £36) if they have them in stock, though the actual foundry is off-limits. ✉ *34 Whitechapel Rd.,* ☎ *0171/247–2599.* 🎫 *Free.* ⏲ *Weekdays 8:30–5:30; closed public holidays. Tube: Aldgate East.*

❷ **Whitechapel Gallery.** Housed in a spacious 1901 Art Nouveau building, this has an international reputation for its shows, which are often on the cutting edge of contemporary art. The American "action painter" Jackson Pollock showed here in the '50s, the pop artist Robert Rauschenberg in the '60s, and David Hockney had his first solo show here in the '70s. More recently the Tate Gallery visited the Whitechapel and bought the American Bill Viola's powerful video installation, the *Nantes Triptych,* which shows Viola submerged underwater, his wife giving birth on one side, his mother dying in a hospital on the other. Other exhibitions highlight the local community and culture, and there are programs of lectures, too. ✉ *Whitechapel High St.,* ☎ *0171/377–0107.* 🎫 *Free (fee for some exhibitions).* ⏲ *Tues.–Sun. 11–5, Wed. 11–8. Closed Dec. 25–26, Jan. 1, and for exhibition installation. Tube: Aldgate East.*

NEED A BREAK? The **Whitechapel Café** in the gallery serves remarkably inexpensive home-cooked whole-food hot meals, soups, and cakes.

OFF THE BEATEN PATH **William Morris Gallery.** An 18th-century house in northeast London where the artistic polymath William Morris (craftsman, painter, and writer) lived for eight years, containing many examples of his work and that of his fellows in the Arts and Crafts Movement. ✉ *Water House, Lloyd Park, Forest Rd.,* ☎ *0181/527–3782.* ⏲ *Tues.–Sat. 10–1 and 2–5, first Sun. each month 10–noon and 2–5; closed national holidays. Tube: Walthamstow Central, then 15 min walk down Hoe St., left at Forest Rd.*

THE SOUTH BANK

London's oldest "suburb," **Southwark,** though just across the river from London Bridge, was conveniently outside the City walls and laws, and therefore was the ideal location for the taverns and cock-fighting arenas that served as after-hours entertainment in the Middle Ages. By Shakespeare's time it had become a veritable den of iniquity, famous above all for the "Southwark stews," or brothels, and for being very rough. The Globe Theatre, in which Shakespeare acted and held shares, was one of several established here after theaters were banished from the City in 1574 for encouraging truancy in young apprentices and being generally rowdy and insubordinate. The Globe was as likely to stage a few bouts of bear-baiting as the latest Shakespeare.

Southwark was heavily bombed during World War II, then neglected for a few decades while more central parts of London were repaired. The active ports had moved downstream by then anyway, so Southwark's 19th-century warehouses and winding alleys had little to recommend them to developers. This circumstance began to change when theater returned to the Bankside environs (Bankside being the street along the South Bank from Southwark to Blackfriars Bridges) in the form of the national arts complex that opened downstream in 1976, but it took another decade or so for developers and local authorities to catch on to the potential farther east. Now the pockets of the new and the renovated—Gabriel's Wharf, London Bridge City, Hay's Galleria, Butler's Wharf—have practically connected to form a South Bank that even Londoners, who have an attitude problem about crossing the river, have been known to admire and even frequent.

A Good Walk

Numbers in the text correspond to numbers in the margin and on the South Bank map.

Start scenically at the south end of Tower Bridge, finding the steps on the east (left) side, which descend to the start of a pedestrians-only street, Shad Thames. Now turn your back on the bridge and follow this quaint path between cliffs of the good-as-new warehouses, which are now **Butler's Wharf** ①, but were once the seedy, dingy, dangerous shadowlands where Dickens killed off evil Bill Sikes in *Oliver Twist.* See the foodies' center, the Gastrodrome, and the **Design Museum** ②, then just before you get back to Tower Bridge, turn away from the river, along Horsleydown Lane, follow Tooley Street, take the right turn at Morgan Lane to **HMS *Belfast*** ③, or continue to **Hay's Galleria** ④ with **St. Olave's House** ⑤, London Bridge, and the **London Dungeon** ⑥ beyond. Next, turn left into Joiner Street underneath the arches of London's first (1836) railway, then right onto St. Thomas Street, where you'll find the **Old St. Thomas's Operating Theatre** ⑦ and Herb Garret, with **Southwark Cathedral** ⑧ just across Borough High Street, and another of the South Bank's recent office developments, St. Mary Overie Dock down Cathedral Street. See the west wall, with rose window outline, of Winchester House, palace of the Bishops of Winchester until 1626 built into it, and **the Clink** ⑨ next door. Continue to the end of Clink Street onto Bankside, detouring left up Rose Alley, where in 1989 the remains of a famous Jacobean theater, the Rose Theatre, were unearthed, though the office development surrounding the preserved foundations means there's not much to see. The next little alley is New Globe Walk, where there is much to see: the reconstruction of that most famous of Jacobean theaters, **Shakespeare's Globe** ⑩. Next along Bankside is the 17th-century Cardinal's Wharf, where, as a plaque explains, Wren lived while St. Paul's Cathedral was being built, then Bankside Power Station, which is to become the new Tate Gallery by the year 2000, and **Bankside Gallery** ⑪.

Now you reach your fourth bridge on this walk, Blackfriars Bridge, which you pass beneath to join the street called Upper Ground, passing the Coin Street Community Builders' embryo neighborhood, including **Gabriel's Wharf** ⑫. Further along Upper Ground, you reach the South Bank Centre, with the **Royal National Theatre** ⑬ first, followed by the **Museum of the Moving Image (MOMI)** ⑭, the **Royal Festival Hall** ⑮, and the **Hayward Gallery** ⑯. You'll find distractions all over here, especially in summer—secondhand bookstalls, entertainers, and a series of plaques annotating the buildings opposite. Look to the opposite bank for the quintessential postcard vista of the Houses of Parliament—it's good from Jubilee Gardens, past **County Hall** ⑰ and Westminster Bridge to St. Thomas's Hospital. Further along the river, beyond the **Florence Nightingale Museum** ⑱, **Lambeth Palace** ⑲ stands by Lambeth Bridge, with the **Museum of Garden History** ⑳ in St. Mary's next door. Now if you take a detour to the right off Lambeth Road, you could be "doing the Lambeth Walk" down the street of the same name. A cockney tradition ever since the 17th century, when there was a spa here, the Sunday stroll was immortalized in a song from the 1937 musical *Me and My Gal,* which recently proved a hit all over again in the West End and on Broadway. A little farther east along Lambeth Road you reach the **Imperial War Museum** ㉑.

TIMING

On a fine day, this 3- to 5-kilometer walk (2 to 3 miles) makes a very scenic wander, since you're following the south bank of the great Thames nearly all the way. Fabulous views across to the north bank take you past St. Paul's and the Houses of Parliament, and you pass—under, over, or around—no fewer than seven bridges. It's bound to take far longer than a couple of hours, because the sightseeing is heavy. The Imperial War Museum, MOMI, Shakespeare's Globe, the Hayward Gallery, and the Design Museum are major events, needing much more than an hour apiece (depending on your interests), while the London Dungeon doesn't take long, unless you have kids in tow–which is why you'd go in at all. The other museums on this route—the Clink, Garden History, Old Operating Theatre, Florence Nightingale, the South Bank Centre foyers, and the Bankside Gallery—are compact enough to squeeze together en route to your main event. And that's the nicest thing to do with this walk; have tickets waiting at the end. The National Theatres, the NFT, or Shakespeare's Globe can all oblige, but remember the theaters are dark on Sundays. Dinner or a riverside drink at the Gastrodrome restaurants or the People's Palace are another idea for a big finish. Public transportation is thin on the ground around this way, so pick a day when you're feeling energetic; there are no short cuts once you're under way.

The South Bank

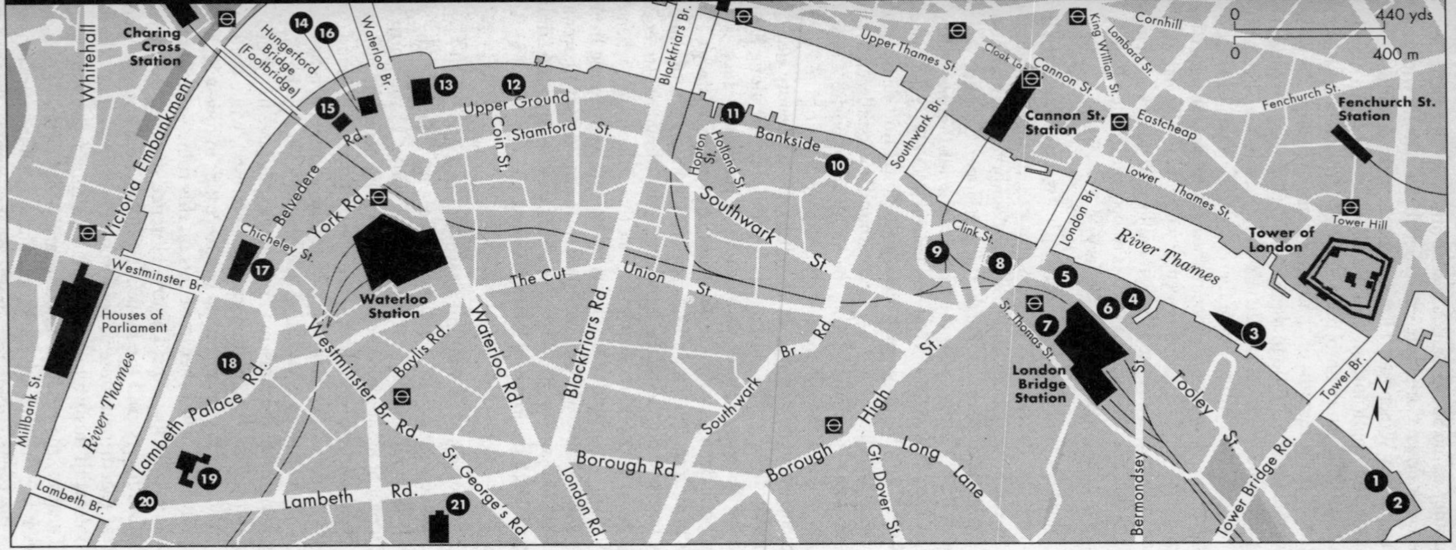

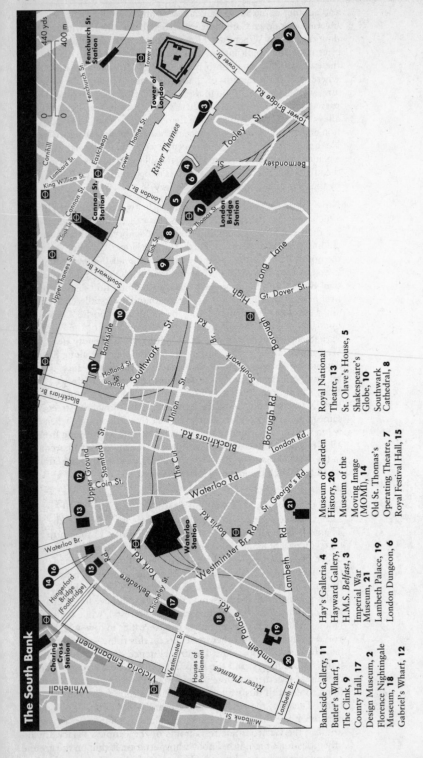

Bankside Gallery, **11**
Butler's Wharf, **1**
The Clink, **9**
County Hall, **17**
Design Museum, **2**
Florence Nightingale Museum, **18**
Gabriel's Wharf, **12**
Hay's Galleria, **4**
Hayward Gallery, **16**
H.M.S. *Belfast*, **3**
Imperial War Museum, **21**
Lambeth Palace, **19**
London Dungeon, **6**
Museum of Garden History, **20**
Museum of the Moving Image (MOMI), **14**
Old St. Thomas's Operating Theatre, **7**
Royal Festival Hall, **15**
Royal National Theatre, **13**
St. Olave's House, **5**
Shakespeare's Globe, **10**
Southwark Cathedral, **8**

Sights To See

⓫ **Bankside Gallery.** In this modern building, two artistic societies—the Royal Society of Painter-Printmakers and the Royal Watercolour Society—have their headquarters. Together they mount exhibitions of current members' work, usually for sale, alongside artists' materials and books. Next door is **Bankside Power Station, which is to become the new Tate Gallery by the year 2000.** ✉ *48 Hopton St.,* ☎ *0171/928–7521.* 🎫 *£3.50.* ⏲ *Tues.–Sat. 10–5, Sun. 1–5; closed Dec. 24–Jan. 2, Easter. Tube: Blackfriars, then walk across bridge.*

❶ **Butler's Wharf.** An '80s development that is maturing gracefully. Many apartments in its deluxe loft-style warehouse conversions and swanky new blocks still lack inhabitants, but there *is* life here, thanks partly to London's saint of the stomach, Sir Terence Conran (also responsible for high-profile central London restaurants Bibendum, Mezzo, and Quaglino's). He gave it his "Gastrodrome" of four restaurants, a vintner's, a deli, a bakery, and who knows what else by now.

❾ **The Clink.** Originally the prison attached to Winchester House, palace of the Bishops of Winchester until 1626, the name "the clink" still serves as a general term for jail. One of five Southwark prisons, it was the first to detain women, most of whom were "Winchester Geese"—another euphemism the bishops donated to the language, meaning prostitutes. The oldest profession was endemic in Southwark, especially around the bishops' area of jurisdiction, known as "The Liberty of the Clink." Their graces' sensible solution was to license prostitution rather than ban it, but a Winchester goose who flouted the rules ended up, of course, in the Clink. Now there is a museum tracing the history of prostitution in "the Liberty"—complete with an "R"-rated section—and showing what the Clink was like during its 16th-century prime. ✉ *1 Clink St.,* ☎ *0171/403–6515.* 🎫 *£2.50.* ⏲ *Daily 10–6. Closed Dec. 25–26. Tube: London Bridge.*

⓱ **County Hall.** This curved, colonnaded neo-classical hulk, which took 46 years (1912–1958; two world wars interfered) to build, was home to London's local government, the Greater London Council (or GLC, which mutated out of the London County Council in 1965) until it disbanded in 1986. Since then the question of whether a new citywide governing body would enhance London has been a contentious issue. (It is politicians who wrangle; most Londoners would like to have one.) At press time, the future of the building was still in doubt, though a plan to convert it into a hotel looked to have been resurrected, and there was talk of a giant aquarium being founded in the basement. Between here and the South Bank Centre is **Jubilee Gardens,** the rectangle of grass planted in 1977 to mark the queen's 50th year on the throne; it is the site of arts festivals and often, during summer, a visiting circus. The views of the Houses of Parliament and Westminster Bridge are fine from both these sights.

❷ **Design Museum.** The first museum in the world to elevate the everyday design we take for granted to the status of exhibit, slotting it into its social and cultural context, opened in 1989. On the top floor, the Collection traces the evolution of mass-produced goods, with cases full of telephones and washing machines, plates and hi-fi equipment, computers and Coke bottles, and plenty of back-up material from ads to films. Alongside the Collection, the regularly revamped Review looks deeply into a particular aspect of the consumer durable. Special exhibitions are held downstairs on the first floor, and there's also a program of lectures and events, as well as the very good Blueprint Café with its own river terrace. ✉ *Butler's Wharf,* ☎ *0171/403–6933.* 🎫

£4.50. ⏲ Daily 10:30–5:30; closed Dec. 24–26, Jan. 1. Tube: Tower Hill, then walk across river.

OFF THE BEATEN PATH

Dulwich Picture Gallery. A really distinguished and loveable small gallery with important works by Rembrandt, Van Dyck, Rubens, Poussin, and Gainsborough, among others. Anyone who fell in love with Sir John Soane's house (☞ Bloomsbury and Legal London, *above*) may wish to make the trek out here, since this gallery was designed by the same architect. If you do come all this way, you'll be happy to know that Dulwich Village itself is pleasant for wandering in, and has handsome 18th-century houses strung out along its main street. Most of the land around here belongs to the local, famous school, the Dulwich College Estate, founded during the early 17th century by the actor Edward Alleyn, and this keeps strict control of modern development. This corner of southeast London's most famous resident, you might say, also kept strict control of modern development during the Eighties: it was Baroness Thatcher. Opposite the Gallery, Dulwich Park is a well-kept municipal park with a particularly fine display of rhododendrons in late May. ✉ *College Rd.,* ☎ *0181/693–8000.* 🎫 *£2. Fri. Free* ⏲ *Tues.–Fri. 10–1 and 2–5, Sat. 11–5, Sun. 2–5; closed national holidays. British Rail: Dulwich (from Victoria or London Bridge).*

18 **Florence Nightingale Museum.** Here you can learn all about the founder of the first school of nursing, that most famous of nursing reformers, "The Lady with the Lamp." See the reconstruction of the barracks ward at Scutari (Turkey), where she tended soldiers during the Crimean War (1854–56) and earned her nickname; here is also a Victorian East End slum cottage showing what she did to improve living conditions among the poor; and here is The Lamp. The museum is in **St. Thomas's Hospital,** which was built in 1868, to the specifications of Florence Nightingale. Most of it was bombed to death in the Blitz, then rebuilt to become one of London's teaching hospitals. ✉ *2 Lambeth Palace Rd.,* ☎ *0171/620–0374.* 🎫 *£2.50.* ⏲ *Tues.–Sun. and public holidays 10–4; closed Good Friday, Easter, Dec. 25–26, Jan. 1. Tube: Waterloo, or Westminster and walk over the bridge.*

12 **Gabriel's Wharf.** A dinky marketplace of shops and cafés, where about 15 designers sell jewelry, ceramics, toys, etc., and music is staged in summer. It's part of a (fairly) new development of an entirely different character from the surrounding business behemoths. Coin Street Community Builders, as their name suggests, is a nonprofit action group formed by local residents in the mid-'70s to create family housing and public spaces out of land that would otherwise have gone to commercial developers. You can see the human-scale homes and gardens they've already built since 1984, and adjacent Stamford Wharf, which is being converted into housing, performance spaces, crafts workshops, and restaurants. The nearby OXO building has recently been renovated, featuring a restaurant-with-a-view, among other things.

NEED A BREAK?

In Gabriel's Wharf, a goat's cheese and sun-dried tomato pizza from **The Gourmet Pizza Company** or a burger and cocktail from **Studio Six** (both open daily) may hit the spot after so many bridges have been crossed.

4 **Hay's Galleria.** Hay's Wharf was built by Thomas Cubitt in 1857 on the spot where the port of London's oldest wharf had stood since 1651. It was known as "London's larder" on account of the edibles landed here until it wound down gradually, then closed in 1970. In 1987 it was reborn as this Covent Gardenesque parade of bars and restaurants, offices, and shops, all weatherproofed by an arched glass atrium roof

supported by tall iron columns. The centerpiece is a fanciful kinetic sculpture by David Kemp, *The Navigators,* which looks like the skeleton of a pirate schooner crossed with a dragon and spouts water from various orifices. Inevitably, jugglers, string quartets, and crafts stalls abound. This courtyard hub of the developing London Bridge City needed all the help it could get in its early days, but it has settled in nicely now with its captive crowd of office workers from the adjacent new developments.

16 **Hayward Gallery.** This is one of the city's major art-exhibition spaces, its bias fixed firmly in this century. This stained and windowless bunker tucked behind the South Bank Centre concert halls has come in for the most flak of all the Thames-side buildings, enduring constant threats to flatten it and start again, but it's still here, topped by its multicolored neon tube sculpture, the most familiar feature on the South Bank skyline. ✉ *South Bank Complex,* ☎ *0171/928–3144. Admission varies according to exhibition.* ⏲ *Daily 10–6, Tues. and Wed. until 8; closed Good Friday, May Day, Dec. 25–26, Jan. 1. Tube: Waterloo.*

3 **HMS *Belfast.*** At 656 feet, this is one of the largest and most powerful cruisers the Royal Navy ever had. It played a role in the D-day landings off Normandy, left for the Far East after the war, and has been becalmed here since 1971. On board there's an outpost of the Imperial War Museum, which tells the Royal Navy's story from 1914 to the present and shows you what life on board a World War II battleship was like, from mess decks and bakery, punishment cells, and operations room to engine room and armaments. ✉ *Morgan's La., Tooley St.,* ☎ *0171/407–6434.* *£4.* ⏲ *Mid-Mar.–Oct., daily 10–5:30; Nov.–mid-Mar., daily 10–4; closed Dec. 24–26, Jan. 1. Tube: London Bridge.*

OFF THE BEATEN PATH

Horniman Museum. An educational museum of anthropology that manages to be fun too, set in 16 acres of gardens in south London with well-displayed ethnographic and natural history collections, a Music Gallery, and a colony of honey bees visibly at work in their glass-fronted hive. Another highlight is the aquarium stocked with endangered species. ✉ *100 London Rd., Forest Hill,* ☎ *0181/699–1872/2339.* *Free.* ⏲ *Mon.–Sat. 10:30–6, Sun. 2–6. British Rail: Forest Hill.*

21 **Imperial War Museum.** This national museum is housed in an elegant domed and colonnaded building, erected during the early 19th century to house the Bethlehem Hospital for the Insane, better known as the infamous Bedlam. By 1816, when the patients were moved here, they were no longer kept in cages to be taunted by tourists (see the final scene of Hogarth's *Rake's Progress* at Sir John Soane's Museum for an idea of how horrific it was), since reformers—and George III's madness—had effected more humane confinement. Bedlam moved to Surrey in 1930.

Despite its title, this museum of 20th-century warfare does not glorify bloodshed but attempts to evoke what it was like to live through the two world wars. Of course, there is hardware for martial children—a Battle of Britain Spitfire, a German V2 rocket, tanks, guns, submarines—but there is an equal amount of war art (David Bomberg, Henry Moore, John Singer Sargent, Graham Sutherland, to name a few), poetry, photography, and documentary film footage. One very affecting exhibit is *The Blitz Experience,* which is what it sounds like—a 10-minute taste of an air raid in a street of acrid smoke with sirens blaring and searchlights glaring. More recent wars attended by British forces are thoughtfully commemorated, too, right up to the Gulf War of 1991. ✉ *Lambeth Rd.,* ☎ *0171/416–5000.* *£4.10.* ⏲ *Daily 10–6; closed Dec. 24–26, Jan. 1. Tube: Lambeth North.*

19 **Lambeth Palace.** This has, for 800 years, been the London base of the Archbishop of Canterbury, top man in the Church of England. Much of the palace is hidden behind great walls, and even the Tudor gatehouse, visible from the street, is closed to the public, but you can stand here and absorb the historical vibrations echoing from such momentous events as the 1381 storming of the palace during the Peasants' Revolt against the poll tax (a modern version of which Thatcher recently reinstated, whereupon modern riots ensued, and the tax was sheepishly repealed), and the 1534 clash of wills when Thomas More refused to sign the Oath of Supremacy claiming Henry VIII (and not the pope) as leader of the English Church, was sent to the Tower, and executed for treason the following year.

6 **The London Dungeon.** Here's the most gory, grisly, gruesome museum in town, where realistic waxwork people are subjected in graphic detail to all the historical horrors the Tower of London merely suggests. Tableaux depict famous bloody moments—like Anne Boleyn's decapitation, or the martyrdom of St. George—alongside the torture, murder, and ritual slaughter of more anonymous victims, all to a soundtrack of screaming, wailing, and agonized moaning. London's times of deepest terror—the Great Fire and the Great Plague—are brought to life, too, and so are its public hangings. And did you ever wonder what a disembowelment actually looks like? See it here. Children absolutely adore this place, which is among London's top tourist attractions and usually features long lines. ✉ *28–34 Tooley St.,* ☎ *0171/403–0606.* *£7.50.* ⊙ *Apr.–Sept., daily 10–5:30; Oct.–Mar., daily 10–4:30; closed Dec. 24–26. Tube: London Bridge.*

20 **Museum of Garden History.** Housed in St. Mary's Church, next to Lambeth Palace, this museum was founded in 1977 (when the church was deconsecrated), by the Tradescant Trust. The Trust is named after John Tradescant (c. 1575–1638), botanist extraordinaire, who brought to these shores the lilac, larch, jasmine, and spiderwort, named Tradescantia in his honor. In the nave are changing horticulturally themed exhibitions, supplemented by a reconstructed—or regrown—17th-century knot garden. Tradescant's tomb in the graveyard is carved with scenes from his worldwide plant-discovery tours and surrounded with the plants he discovered. Near it, William Bligh, captain of the *Bounty,* is buried, which suits the theme—the *Bounty* was on a breadfruit-gathering mission in 1787 when the crew mutinied. ✉ *Lambeth Palace Rd.,* ☎ *0171/261–1891.* *Free; donations welcome.* ⊙ *Weekdays 11–3, Sun. 10:30–5; closed mid-Dec.–early Mar. Tube: Waterloo.*

14 **Museum of the Moving Image (MOMI).** This popular museum is attached to the National Film Theatre (or NFT) underneath Waterloo Bridge, whose two movie theaters boast easily the best repertory programming in London, favoring rare, obscure, foreign, silent, forgotten, classic, noir, or short films over blockbusters. There's a third theater in MOMI, but if you reckon you'll just have a quick look around before you catch a movie here, think again. MOMI may be the most fun of all London's museums, and you will get stuck for a couple of hours minimum. The main feature is a history of cinema from 4,000-year-old Javanese shadow puppets to Spielbergian special effects, and very good the displays are, too, but the supporting program is even better, and it stars *you.* Actors dressed as John Wayne or Mae West, or usherettes, or chorus girls pluck you out of obscurity to read the TV news or audition for the chorus line or fly like Superman over the Thames. They also perform, mime, improvise, and generally bring celluloid to life, while all around, various screens show clips from such epoch-making giants as Hitchcock and Eisenstein, plus newsreels and ads. Techies can learn focus-pulling and satellite beaming; artists can try animation; eggheads can explore such ethical issues as censorship and documentary objectivity. Needless to say, this is always a big hit with kids. ✉ *South Bank Centre,* ☎ *0171/401–2636.* 🎫 *£5.95. White Card accepted.* ⏲ *Daily 10–6, last admission 5 PM; closed Dec. 24–26. Tube: Waterloo.*

NEED A BREAK? The NFT restaurant and cafeteria—especially the big wooden tables outside—are popular for lunch or supper. You don't have to buy a membership.

7 **Old St. Thomas's Operating Theatre.** All that remains of one of England's oldest hospitals, which stood here from the 12th century until the railway forced it to move in 1862, this was where women went under the knife. The theater was bricked up and forgotten for a century but has now been restored into an exhibition of early 19th-century medical practices: the operating table onto which the gagged and blindfolded patients were roped, the box of sawdust underneath for catching their blood, the knives, pliers, and handsaws the surgeons wielded, and—this was a theater in the round—the spectators' seats. Next door is a sweeter show: the **Herb Garret,** with displays of medicinal herbs used during the same period. ✉ *9A St. Thomas St.,* ☎ *0171/955–4791.* 🎫 *£2.* ⏲ *Tues.–Sun. 10–4; closed Dec. 15–Jan. 5. Tube: London Bridge.*

15 **Royal Festival Hall.** This is the largest auditorium of the South Bank Centre, with superb acoustics and a 3,000-plus capacity. It is the oldest of the riverside blocks, raised as the centerpiece of the 1951 Festival of Britain, a postwar morale-boosting exercise. The London Philharmonic resides here, symphony orchestras from the world over like to visit, and choral works, ballet, serious jazz and pop, and even film with live accompaniment are also staged. There is a multiplicity of foyers, with free rotating exhibitions, a good, independently run restaurant, the People's Palace, and a very good bookstore. The next building you come to also contains one medium and one small concert hall, the **Queen Elizabeth Hall** and the **Purcell Room,** respectively. Both offer predominantly classical recitals of international caliber, with due respect paid to 20th-century composers and the more established jazz and vocal artists.

13 **Royal National Theatre.** Londoners generally felt the same way about this low-slung, multilayered block the color of heavy storm clouds, designed by Sir Denys Lasdun, when it opened in 1976, that they would feel a decade later about the far nastier Barbican. But whatever its merits or demerits as a landscape feature (and architects have subsequently given it an overall thumbs up, while rejecting the derogatory-sounding term "Brutalist"), the Royal National Theatre—still abbreviated colloquially to the preroyal warrant "NT"—has wonderful insides.

There are three auditoriums in the complex. The biggest one, the **Olivier,** is named after Sir Laurence, chairman of the first building commission and first artistic director of the National Theatre Company, formed in 1962. (In between the first proposal of a national theater for Britain and the 1949 formation of that building commission, an entire century passed.) The **Lyttleton** theater, unlike the Olivier, has a traditional proscenium arch, while the little **Cottesloe** mounts studio productions and new work in the round. Interspersed with the theaters are various levels of foyer, where exhibitions are shown, bars and restaurants are frequented, and free entertainment is provided, and the whole place is lively six days a week. The Royal National Theatre Company does not rest on its laurels. It attracts many of the nation's top actors (Anthony Hopkins, for one, does time here) in addition to launching future stars. Since it's a repertory company, you'll have several plays to choose from even if your London sojourn is short, but, tickets or not, have a wander round, and catch the buzz. ✉ *South Bank,* ☎ *0171/928–2252 (box office);* ☎ *0171/633–0880 (tours). Hour-long tours of the theater backstage: Mon.–Sat. at 10:15, 12:30, and 5:30;* *£3.50.* ⏲ *Foyers open Mon.–Sat. 10 AM–11 PM; closed Dec. 24–25. Tube: Waterloo.*

❺ **St. Olave's House.** In the former Hay's Wharf offices, this is an exciting black-and-white-and-gold-striped Art Deco block built in 1931 by H. S. Goodhart-Rendel and named after the church it replaced. The shiny square edifice has far more style than the newer buildings around it, and quite puts them to shame. At the end of Tooley Street (difficult to see how, but the name is a corruption of St. Olave's) stands the 1972 version of **London Bridge.**

❿ **Shakespeare's Globe.** The fruit largely of the American actor and film director Sam Wanamaker's last two decades. Until he died in 1993, he worked ceaselessly to raise funds for this ambitious project, so appalled had he been that England lacked a center for the study and worship of the Bard of Bards. In addition to an exact replica of Shakespeare's open-roofed Globe Playhouse (built in 1599; incinerated in 1613), using authentic Elizabethan materials and craft techniques—green oak timbers joined only with wooden pegs and mortise and tendon joints; plaster made of lime, sand, and goat's hair; and the first thatched roof in London since the Great Fire—he planned a second, indoor theater, which is being built to a design of the 17th-century architect Inigo Jones. The whole thing stands 100 yards from the original Globe on the appropriate site of the 17th century Davies Amphitheatre, admittedly more a bull-baiting, prize-fighting sort of venue than a temple to the legitimate stage, but at least Samuel Pepys immortalized it in his diaries. The Globe is a celebration of the great bard's life and work, an actual rebirth of his "Great Wooden O" (see *Henry V*), where his plays are presented in natural light (and sometimes rain), to 1,000 people on wooden benches in the "bays," plus 500 "groundlings," standing on a carpet of filbert shells and clinker, just as they did nearly four centuries ago. For any theater buff, this stunning project is unmissable. ✉ *New Globe Walk, Bankside,* ☎ *0171/928–6406.* *Exhibition: £4.* ⏲ *Daily. 10–5. Call for performance schedule. Closed Dec. 24–25. Tube: Mansion House, then walk across Southwark Bridge.*

❽ **Southwark Cathedral.** Pronounced "*suth*-uck," this is the second-oldest Gothic church in London, next to Westminster Abbey, with parts dating from the 12th century. Although it houses some remarkable memorials, not to mention a program of lunchtime concerts, it is little visited. It was promoted to cathedral status only in 1905, before that having been the priory church of **St. Mary Overie** (as in "over the water"—on the South Bank). Look for the gaudily renovated 1408 tomb of the poet John Gower, friend of Chaucer, and for the Harvard Chapel, named after John Harvard, founder of the college, who was baptized here in 1608. Another notable buried here is Edmund Shakespeare, brother of William.

CHELSEA AND BELGRAVIA

Albert Bridge marks the edge of Chelsea. It is a hybrid cantilever-suspension model that went up in 1873 and is probably London's favorite (except to those trapped on it daily by rush-hour traffic) on account of its prettiness, especially when fairy-lighted by night. Chelsea starts to its north, a neighborhood as handsome as its real estate is costly.

Strolling its streets you will often notice gigantic windows adorning otherwise ordinary houses. They are now mostly used to hike property values a few notches higher, but these remnants of Chelsea's 19th-century bohemian days once lighted artists' studios; many famous artists and writers have lived here. Latterly Chelsea—especially the King's Road—gave birth to Swinging '60s London, then to '70s punk youth culture. The '90s version is not really the center of anything, but it's hard not to like walking it.

Its next-door neighborhood is aristocratic Belgravia, with King's Road and Knightsbridge its southern and northern borders, Sloane Street and Grosvenor Place its western and eastern ones, and vast Belgrave Square, home to many embassies, in the middle. Belgravia is relatively young: It was built between the 1820s and the 1850s by the builder-developer-entrepreneur Thomas Cubitt (who had as great an influence on the look of London in his day as Wren and Nash had in theirs), under the patronage of Lord Grosvenor, and was intended to rival Mayfair for spacious snob value and expense. Today it still does.

A Good Walk

Numbers in the text correspond to numbers in the margin and on the Chelsea and Belgravia map.

Start at **Cheyne Walk** ①, stretching in both directions from Albert Bridge, going all the way west to see the statue of Thomas More, then doubling back for a left turn into Cheyne Row to reach **Carlyle's House** ②. Where the east end of Cheyne Walk runs into Royal Hospital Road, you'll find the **Chelsea Physic Garden** ③, while a right after the garden on Royal Hospital Road brings you to the **National Army Museum** ④. Royal Hospital Road takes its name from the institution next door to the museum, the magnificent **Royal Hospital** ⑤. A left turn from here up Franklin's Row and Cheltenham Terrace brings you to famous **King's Road** ⑥, which you could follow east until you reach the beginning of Belgravia: Sloane Square, named after Sir Hans Sloane, whose collection founded the British Museum (☞ Bloomsbury and Legal London, *above*), and who bought the manor of Chelsea in 1712. Cross the square more or less in a straight line, and follow Cliveden Place for a taste of Belgravia. The grand, white-stucco houses have changed not at all since the mid-19th century, and Eaton Square which you'll soon come upon, remains such a desirable address that the rare event of one of its houses coming on the market makes all the property pages. Its most famous residents were fictional: The enduringly popular period soap, *Upstairs Downstairs,* was set here. A left turn on Belgrave Place brings you to Belgrave Square, dense with embassies, but the best thing to do around here is follow your nose. There are no particular Belgravia sights.

TIMING

This may read like a short hop, but the walk above covers a good 3 to 5 kilometers (2 to 3 miles). If you explore side streets, you could double the figure—and if you don't explore side streets, you'll be missing the best aspect of these neighborhoods, which are primarily, expensively, residential. The sights along the way will probably detain you less than the shops, even though King's Road ain't what it used to be, it's still fruitful. In summer you'll want to spend time in the Physic Garden or around the Royal Hospital, so make sure you're heading out on one of the opening days. If you're dead set on the Physic Garden, that means Wednesday or Sunday afternoon, April to October.

Sights To See

❷ **Carlyle's House.** Carlyle's house was a thriving salon of 19th-century authors attracted by the fame of Thomas Carlyle (who wrote a then-blockbuster, since all-but-forgotten history of the French Revolution, and founded the London Library), and by the wit of his wife, the poet Jane Carlyle. Dickens, Thackeray, Tennyson, and Browning were regular visitors, and you can see the second-floor drawing room where they met just as they saw it, complete with leather armchair, decoupage screen, fireplace, and oil lamps, all in ruddy Victorian hues. ✉ *24 Cheyne Row,* ☎ *0171/352–7087.* 🎟 *£2.90.* ⏲ *Apr.–Oct., Wed.–Sun. and public holidays 11–5 (last admission 4:30); closed Good Friday, Dec. 24–26, Jan. 1. Tube: Sloane Square, then walk down King's Rd., or take bus 11, 19, 22, 49, 219, or 249.*

❸ **Chelsea Physic Garden.** First planted by the Society of Apothecaries in 1673 for the study of medicinal plants, these gardens are still in use for the same purpose today. The herbs and shrubs and flowers, planted to a strict plan but tumbling rurally over the paths nevertheless, are interspersed with woodland areas, England's first rock garden, and ancient trees, some of which were tragically uprooted in a 1987 hurricane. In the middle stands a statue of Sir Hans Sloane, Queen Anne and George II's physician, whose collection formed the basis of the British Museum, and who saved the garden from closure in 1722, making sure nobody would ever be allowed to build over it. ✉ *Swan Walk, 66 Royal Hospital Rd.,* ☎ *0171/352–5646.* 🎟 *£3.50.* ⏲ *Apr.–Oct., Sun. and Wed. 2–5; daily noon–5 during the Chelsea Flower Show in the 3rd wk of May. Tube: Sloane Square, then walk down King's Rd., or take bus 11, 19, 22, 49, 219, or 249.*

❶ **Cheyne Walk.** Rhyming with "rainy," this street features some beautiful Queen Anne houses (particularly Norman Shaw's ornamental 1876 Cheyne House, to the right off Albert Bridge) and a storm of Blue Plaques marking famous ex-residents' abodes. George Eliot died at No. 4 in 1880; Dante Gabriel Rossetti annoyed the neighbors of No. 16 with his peacock collection (there's still a clause in the lease banning the birds); at Carlyle Mansions (after the King's Head and Eight Bells pub), Henry James died, and T. S. Eliot and Ian Fleming lived. The western reaches was painters' territory, most notably James McNeill Whistler, who lived at No. 96 and then No. 101, and J. M. W. Turner, who used No. 119 as a retreat, shielding his identity behind the name Admiral "Puggy" Booth. Also toward the western end, outside the church of All Saints, is a golden-faced statue of **Thomas More** (who wouldn't sign the Oath of Supremacy at Lambeth Palace in 1534 and was executed as a traitor), looking pensive and beatific on a throne facing the river, in a 1969 addition to the Walk.

❻ **King's Road.** This was where the miniskirt strutted its stuff in the '60s and where Vivienne Westwood and Malcolm McLaren clothed the Sex Pistols in bondage trousers from their shop, Sex, in 1975, thus spawning punk rock. Westwood, one of Britain's most innovative fashion stars, still has her shop at No. 430, where the road kinks. Both boutique and neighborhood are called **World's End,** possibly because Chelsea-ites believe that's what it does here—the less-fancy Fulham begins around this stretch. The other end of King's Road, leading into Sloane Square, has various fashion stores (no longer style-setters, on the whole) and some rather good antiques shops and markets along the way. The **Pheasantry** at No. 152 is recognizable by some over-the-top Grecian statuary in a fancy portico. Named in its mid-19th-century pheasant-breeding days, it had a phase from 1916 to 1934 as a ballet school where Margot Fonteyn and Alicia Markova learned first position. Now it's a club-restaurant haunted by the braying breed of Chelsea yuppie, dubbed "Sloane Rangers" by '80s style-watchers. Peter Jones department store

Chelsea and Belgravia

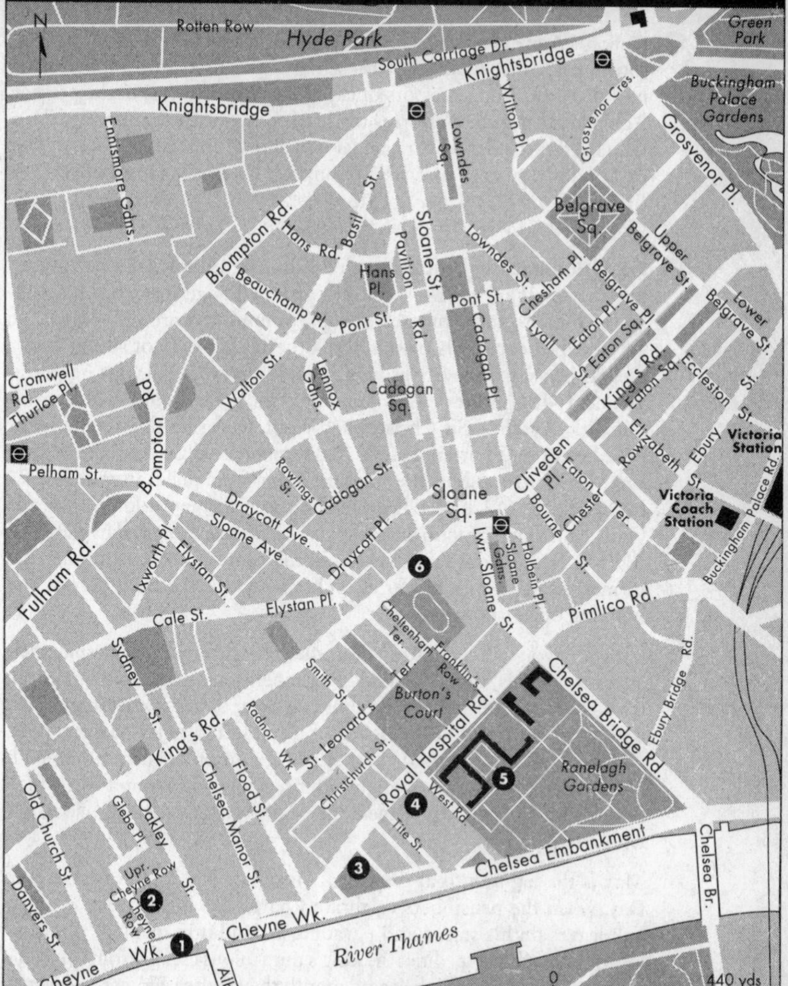

Carlyle's House, **2**
Chelsea Physic Garden, **3**
Cheyne Walk, **1**
King's Road, **6**
National Army Museum, **4**
Royal Hospital, **5**

marks the exit from the north of Chelsea and the beginning of Belgravia: Sloane Square.

4 **National Army Museum.** This museum covers the history of British land forces from the Yeoman of the Guard (the first professional army, founded 1485 and ancestors of the Tower's Beefeaters) to the present. Again, a great deal of effort is made to convey the experience of those who lived through the wars, and a visit should enhance anyone's grasp of London's history and its personages. ✉ *Royal Hospital Rd.,* ☎ *0171/730–0717.* *Free.* *Mon.–Sat. 10–5:30, Sun. 2–5:30; closed Good Friday, May Day, Dec. 24–26, Jan. 1. Tube: Sloane Square.*

5 **Royal Hospital.** The hospice for elderly and infirm soldiers was founded by Charles II in 1682—some say after a badgering from his soft-hearted, high-profile mistress, Nell Gwynn, but more probably as an act of expedience—his troops had hitherto enjoyed not so much as a meager pension and were growing restive after the civil wars of 1642–46 and 1648. Charles wisely appointed the great architect of burned-out City churches, Sir Christopher Wren, to design this small village of red brick and Portland stone, set in manicured gardens (which you can visit) surrounding the "Figure Court"—named after the 1692 bronze figure of Charles II dressed up as a Roman soldier—and the Great Hall (dining room) and chapel. The latter is enhanced by the choir stalls of Grinling Gibbons (who did the bronze of Charles, too), the former by a vast oil of Charles on horseback by Antonio Verrio, and both are open to inspection.

No doubt you will run into some of the 400-odd residents. Despite their advancing years, these "Chelsea Pensioners" are no shrinking violets. In summer and for special occasions they wear dandy scarlet frock coats with gold buttons and breastfuls of medals, and natty tricorne hats, and, being of proven good character (a condition of entry, along with old age and loyal service), might offer to show you around—in which case you may wish to supplement their daily beer and tobacco allowance with a tip.

May is the big month at the Royal Hospital. The 29th is Oak Apple Day, when the pensioners celebrate Charles II's birthday by draping oak leaves on his statue and parading around it in memory of a hollow oak tree that expedited the king's miraculous escape from the 1651 Battle of Worcester. In the same month the Chelsea Flower Show, the year's highlight for thousands of garden-obsessed Brits, is also held here. ✉ *Royal Hospital Rd.,* ☎ *0171/730–0161.* *Free.* *Mon.–Sat. 10–noon and 2–4, Sun. 2–4; closed national holidays and Sun. Oct.–Mar. Tube: Sloane Square.*

KNIGHTSBRIDGE, KENSINGTON, AND HOLLAND PARK

Salubrious Knightsbridge, east of Belgravia and north of Chelsea, offers about equal doses of elite residential streets and ultra-shopping opportunities. To *its* east is one of the highest concentrations of important artifacts anywhere, the "museum mile" of South Kensington, with the rest of Kensington offering peaceful strolls, a noisy main street, and another palace. The Holland Park neighborhood is worth visiting for its big, fancy, tree-shaded houses and its exquisite and surprising park.

Kensington first became the *Royal* Borough of Kensington (and Chelsea) by virtue of a king's asthma. William III, who suffered terribly from the Thames mists over Whitehall, decided in 1689 to buy Nottingham House in the rural village of Kensington so that he could breathe more easily; besides, his wife and co-monarch, Mary II, felt confined by water and wall at Whitehall. Courtiers and functionaries and society folk soon followed where the crowns led, and by the time Queen Anne was on the throne (1702–14), Kensington was overflowing. In a way, it still is, because most of its grand houses, and the later, Victorian ones of Holland Park, have been divided into apartments, or else are serving as foreign embassies.

A Good Walk

Numbers in the text correspond to numbers in the margin and on the Knightsbridge, Kensington, and Holland Park map.

This is an all-weather walk—museums and shops for rainy days, grass and strolls for sunshine. When you surface from the Knightsbridge tube station—one of London's deepest—you are immediately engulfed among the angry drivers, professional shoppers, and ladies-who-lunch who comprise the local population. If you're in a shopping mood, Harvey Nichols—right at the tube—has six floors of total fashion, Sloane Street, leading south, is strung with the boutiques of big French and English designers, while **Harrods** ① is found to the west down Brompton Road—continue west down Brompton Road, pausing at Beauchamp ("Bee-chum") Place and Walton Street if shopping is your intention. Presently, at the junction of Brompton and Cromwell roads, you come to the pale, Italianate **Brompton Oratory** ②, which marks the beginning of museum territory, with the **Victoria and Albert** ③ first, at the start of Cromwell Road, the **Natural History Museum** ④ next, and the **Science Museum** ⑤ behind it. (The neighborhood's three large museums, incidentally, can be reached via a long underground passage from the South Kensington tube.) Turn left to continue north up Exhibition Road, a kind of unfinished cultural main drag that was Prince Albert's conception (the **National Sound Archive** ⑥ is here, among others), toward the road after which British moviemakers named their fake blood, Kensington Gore, to reach the giant round Wedgewood china box of the **Royal Albert Hall** ⑦ the scaffolding-shrouded **Albert Memorial** ⑧ opposite, and the **Royal College of Art** ⑨ next door.

Now follow **Kensington Gardens** (which is what this western neighbor of Hyde Park is called) west to its end, and a little further, perhaps detouring into the Park to see **Kensington Palace** ⑩ and, behind it, one of London's rare private roads, "Millionaire's Row," **Kensington Palace Gardens** ⑪. Turn off Kensington High Street down little Derry Street, with the offices of London's local paper, the *Evening Standard,* on the left, and what was once Derry and Tom's department store—it closed down in the '70s—on the right. (The best feature of the store was its magical roof garden, complete with palm trees, ponds, and flamingos; it's still there, now part of a nightclub owned by Richard Branson, the high-profile London figure who also owns Virgin Atlantic Airways.) Take a turn around peaceful **Kensington Square** ⑫, then, returning to the High Street, either follow Kensington Church Street up to Notting Hill Gate—with the little 1870 St. Mary Abbots Church on its southwest corner and a cornucopia of expensive antiques in its shops all along the way—or take the longer, scenic route.

Turn left off Kensington Church Street into Holland Street, admiring the sweet 18th-century houses (Nos. 10, 12–13, and 18–26 remain). As you cross Hornton Street you'll see to your left an orange-brick 1970s building, the Kensington Civic Centre (donor of parking permits, home of the local council), and Holland Street becomes the leafy Duchess of Bedford's Walk, with Queen Elizabeth College, part of London University, on the right. Turn left before Holland Park into Phillimore Gardens (perhaps detouring east into Phillimore Place to see No. 44, where

Kenneth Grahame, author of *The Wind in the Willows,* lived from 1901 to 1908), then left again into Stafford Terrace to reach **Linley Sambourne House** ⑬. Step back to the High Street, and turn right. Past the gates of the park is the **Commonwealth Institute** ⑭, which you could explore before entering **Holland Park** ⑮. Exit the park at the gate by the tennis courts (near the Orangery) onto Ilchester Place, follow Melbury Road a few yards, and turn right onto Holland Park Road to reach **Leighton House** ⑯. Late last century, Melbury Road was a veritable colony of artists, though the Victorian muse they followed failed to appeal to later sensibilities, and they're now an obscure bunch—excepting Dickens's illustrator, Marcus Stone, who had No. 8 built in 1876. From here you could turn right onto Addison Road to see the Technicolor tiles rioting over Sir Ernest Debenham's "Peacock House" at No. 8 (he founded the eponymous Oxford Street department store). If you continue north, you reach the plane tree-lined Holland Park Avenue, main thoroughfare of an expensive residential neighborhood which provides more pleasant strolling territory, if you haven't walked enough.

TIMING

This walk is at least 6.4 kilometers (4 miles) long, and is almost impossible to achieve without going inside somewhere. The best way to approach these neighborhoods is to treat Knightsbridge shopping and the South Kensington museums as separate days out—though you may find all three of the museums too much to take in at once. The rest of the tour works as a scenic walk on a fine day, because the places to see—Leighton and Linley Sambourne Houses, the Commonwealth Institute, and Kensington Palace—are less time consuming than the V&A, Natural History and Science Museums. During "term time," those are populated by more or less orderly school parties during the week, while weekends and school vacations see them fill up with more random arrangements of children. The parks are best in the growing seasons—from the crocuses and daffodils of early spring through the tulips to the roses—and during fall, when the foliage show easily rivals New England's. Kensington Gardens closes its gates at sundown, though you can get into Holland Park later during the summer, thanks to the restaurant, and the Open Air Theatre.

Sights To See

❽ **Albert Memorial.** Permanently shrouded in the world's tallest freestanding piece of scaffolding, the intricate structure housing this 14-foot bronze statue of Albert is undergoing a £14-million renovation (including a pure gold-leaf coat donated by an anonymous benefactor). The work is not due to be finished until the year 2000. Albert's grieving widow, Queen Victoria, had this elaborate confection erected on the spot where his Great Exhibition had stood a mere decade before his early death from typhoid in 1861.

❷ **Brompton Oratory.** This is a product of the English Roman Catholic revival of the late 19th century led by John Henry Cardinal Newman (1801–1890), who established this oratory in 1884 and whose statue you see outside. A then-unknown 29-year-old architect, Herbert Gribble, won the competition to design the place, an honor that you may assume went to his head when you see the vast, incredibly ornate interior. It is punctuated by treasures far older than the church itself, like the giant Twelve Apostles in the nave, carved from Carrara marble by Giuseppe Mazzuoli during the 1680s and brought here from Siena's cathedral. New and dastardly treasure was also found here, in the side altar, when the second pillar to the left of the pietà was unmasked as a "dead letter box"—a hot line from secret agent to KGB.

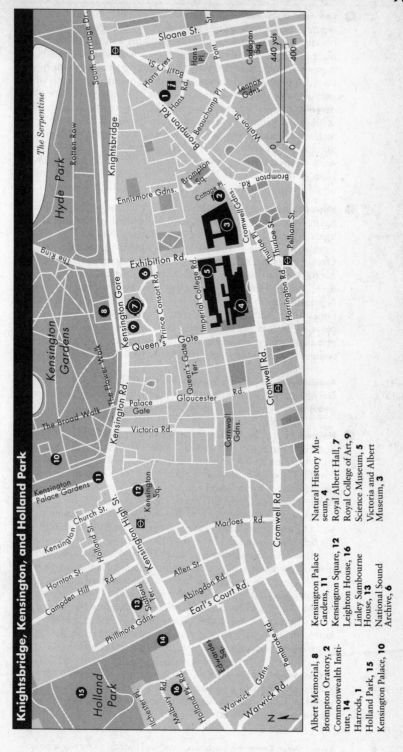

Knightsbridge, Kensington, and Holland Park

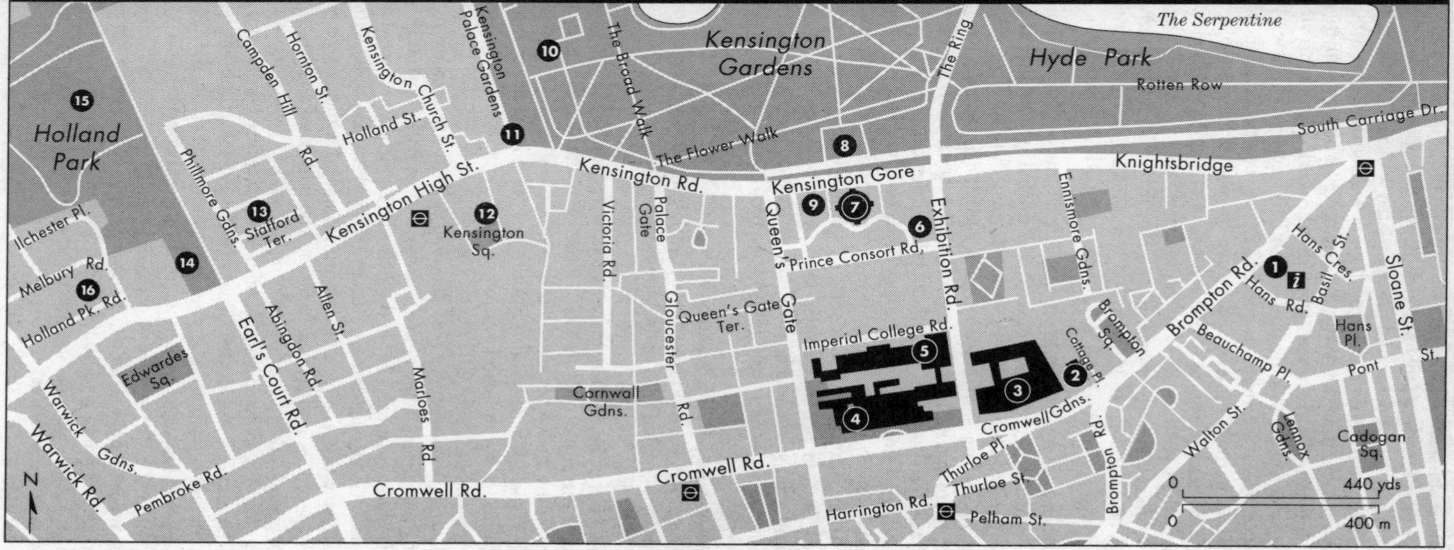

Albert Memorial, **8**
Brompton Oratory, **2**
Commonwealth Institute, **14**
Harrods, **1**
Holland Park, **15**
Kensington Palace, **10**
Kensington Palace Gardens, **11**
Kensington Square, **12**
Leighton House, **16**
Linley Sambourne House, **13**
National Sound Archive, **6**
Natural History Museum, **4**
Royal Albert Hall, **7**
Royal College of Art, **9**
Science Museum, **5**
Victoria and Albert Museum, **3**

14 **Commonwealth Institute.** With its swimming-pool-blue walls and asymmetric copper tent roof, this museum is one of London's more eccentric structures. A wander round the open-plan walkways of this lovable place is like a trip around the world, or at least around the 50 Commonwealth nations, with lifestyles and histories of other continents displayed. Education is an important part of the work done at this vibrant institute, which hosts a lot of music, art, and film events. The new "Wonders of the World" exhibit owes more to Disneyworld than to the world of museum curators—passenger cars travel through simulations of a coral reef, a Caribbean storm, an African safari, underground volcanic eruptions, and the like. If it's early in the year, call ahead to check the museum has reopened after its complete renovations. ✉ *230 Kensington High St.,* ☎ *0171/603–4535.* *£1.* *Mon.–Sat. 10–5, Sun. 2–5; closed Good Friday, Dec. 24–26, Jan. 1. Tube: High Street Kensington.*

1 **Harrods.** In case you didn't notice it, this well-known shopping mecca has its domed terra-cotta Edwardian bulk outlined in thousands of white lights by night. The 15-acre Egyptian-owned store's sales weeks are world-class, and the store is as frenetic as a stock market floor; its motto, *Omnia, omnibus, ubique* ("everything, for everyone, everywhere") is not too far from the truth. Visit the pet department, a highlight for children, and don't miss the extravagant Food Hall, with its stunning Art Nouveau tiling in the neighborhood of meat and poultry, which continues in the fishmonger's territory, where its glory is rivaled by displays of the sea produce itself. This is the place to acquire your green-and-gold souvenir Harrods bag, as food prices are surprisingly competitive. Go as early as you can to avoid the worst of the crowds.

NEED A BREAK?

Patisserie Valerie (✉ 215 Brompton Rd., ☎ 0171/832–9971; open daily), just down the road from Harrods, offers light meals and a gorgeous array of pastries. It's perfect for breakfast, lunch, or tea.

15 **Holland Park.** The former grounds of the Jacobean Holland House opened to the public only in 1952. Since then, many treats have been laid on within its 22 hectares. Holland House itself was nearly flattened by World War II bombs, but the east wing remains, now incorporated into a youth hostel and providing a fantastical stage for the April–September Open Air Theatre (box office, ☎ 0171/602–7856). The glass-walled Orangery also survived to host art exhibitions and wedding receptions, while next door, the Garden Ballroom has become the Belvedere restaurant. From the Belvedere's terrace you see the formal Dutch Garden, planted by Lady Holland in the 1790s with the first English dahlias. North of that are woodland walks, lawns populated by peacocks and guinea fowl and the odd emu, a fragrant rose garden, great banks of rhododendrons and azaleas (which bloom profusely in May), a well-supervised children's Adventure Playground, and even a Japanese water garden, legacy of the 1991 London Festival of Japan. If that's not enough, you can watch cricket on the Cricket Lawn on the south side, or tennis on the several courts.

NEED A BREAK?

The **Holland Park Café** is run by an Italian family who serves a homemade risotto or pasta, and good cappuccino, alongside the sandwiches, cakes, and tea you'd expect. There are lots of bucolically tree-shaded outside tables.

OFF THE BEATEN PATH

Kensal Green Cemetery. Heralding itself as "London's first Necropolis," this west London cemetery was established in 1832 and beats the more famous Highgate for atmosphere, if only because it is less populated with live people. Within its 77 acres are more freestanding mausolea than in any other cemetery in Britain, some of them almost the size of small churches, and most of them constructed while their future occupants were still alive. Those who balked at burial but couldn't afford a mausoleum of their own could opt for a position in the catacombs, and these, with their stacks of moldering caskets, are a definite highlight for seekers of the macabre, though they can only be seen as part of a tour. In the cemetery you will find the final resting places of the novelists Trollope, Thackeray, and Wilkie Collins; of the great engineer Isambard Kingdom Brunel (1806–1859); and of Decimus Burton, Victorian architect of the Athenaeum Club, the Wellington Arch, the Kew Gardens greenhouses, and many other bits of London you'll have just seen. ✉ *Harrow Rd. W10,* ☎ *0181/969–0152. Suggested donation: £2.* ⏲ *Mon.–Sat. 9–5:30, Sun. 10–5:30 (times may vary Nov.–Feb., so call first). 2-hr guided tours (including catacombs) Mar.–Oct., weekends 2:30; Oct.–Feb., Sun. 2. Catacomb tours first Sun. of the month; phone for times. Tube: Kensal Green.*

---

10 **Kensington Palace.** This royal palace stands close to the western edge of Kensington Gardens. It did not enjoy a smooth passage as royal residence. Twelve years of renovation were needed before William and Mary could move in; it continued to undergo all manner of refurbishment during the next three monarchs' times. By coincidence, these monarchs happened to suffer rather ignominious deaths. First, William III fell off his horse when it stumbled on a molehill, and succumbed to pleurisy in 1702. Then, in 1714, Queen Anne (who, you may recall, was fond of brandy) suffered an apoplectic fit brought on by overeating. Next, George I, the first of the Hanoverian Georges, had a stroke as a result of "a surfeit of melons"—admittedly not at Kensington, but in a coach to Hanover, in 1727. Worst of all, in 1760, poor George II burst a blood vessel while on the toilet (the official line was, presumably, that he was on the throne).

The best-known royal Kensington story, though, concerns the 18-year-old Princess Victoria of Kent, who was called from her bed in June 1837, by the Archbishop of Canterbury and the Lord Chamberlain. Her uncle, William IV, was dead, they told her, and she was to be queen. The state rooms where Victoria had her ultrastrict upbringing have recently been completely renovated, and depict the life of the royal family through the past century. ✉ *Kensington Gardens,* ☎ *0171/937–9561.* 🎫 *£4.50. Tube: High Street Kensington.*

11 **Kensington Palace Gardens.** Starting behind Kensington Palace, this is one of London's rare private roads, guarded and gated both here and at the Notting Hill Gate end. If you walk it, you will see why it earned the nickname "Millionaires' Row"—it is lined with palatial white-stucco houses designed by a selection of the best architects of the mid-19th century. The novelist William Makepeace Thackeray, author of *Vanity Fair,* died in 1863 at No. 2—a building that now houses an embassy (Israeli), as do most of the others.

12 **Kensington Square.** Having been laid out around the time William moved to Kensington palace up the road, this is therefore one of London's oldest squares. A few early 18th-century houses remain, with Nos. 11 and 12 the oldest.

NEED A BREAK? In Wright's Lane you'll find **The Muffin Man,** a cozy anachronism of a tea shop. Here floral-aproned waitresses serve toasted sandwiches, cream teas, and, yes, English muffins.

---

16 **Leighton House.** This was the home of Frederic Leighton—painter, sculptor, president of the Royal Academy—who was endowed with a peerage by Queen Victoria, unfortunately expiring a month later. The prize room here is the incredible Arab Hall. George Aitchison designed this Moorish fantasy in 1879 to show off Leighton's valuable 13th- to 17th-century Islamic tile collection, and, adorned with marble columns, dome, and fountain, it is exotic beyond belief. The rest of the rooms are more conventionally, stuffily Victorian, but they do feature many paintings by Leighton, plus Edward Burne-Jones, John Millais, and other leading Pre-Raphaelites. ✉ *12 Holland Park Rd.,* ☎ *0171/602–3316.* *Free.* *Mon.–Sat. 11–5; closed national holidays. Tube: Holland Park.*

13 **Linley Sambourne House.** During the 1870s, this was home to the political cartoonist Edward Linley Sambourne. It has been renovated by the Victorian Society to look as it did then, complete with William Morris wallpapers and illustrations from the (recently deceased) satirical magazine *Punch,* including many of Sambourne's own, adorning the walls. ✉ *18 Stafford Terr.,* ☎ *0181/994–1019.* *£3.* *Mar.–Oct., Wed. 10–4, Sun. 2–5. Tube: High Street Kensington.*

London Toy & Model Museum. Here are five floors of—yes—toys and models of all vintages from practically prehistoric (OK, Year One AD) to not yet born, in the case of the Whatever Next? gallery's displays. Two highlights are the minutely detailed working coal mine and cityscape with moving parts. All was extensively renovated by its Japanese owners not long ago. ✉ *21–23 Craven Hill,* ☎ *0171/262–9450.* *£4.95.* *Tues.–Sat. 10–5:30, Sun. 11–5:30; closed all Mons. (except national holidays), Good Friday, Dec. 24–25, Jan. 1.*

6 **National Sound Archive.** In this aural outpost of the British Library, you may listen to the queen who made this neighborhood possible: The million recordings held here include one of Victoria speaking sometime in the 1880s, but you have to book in advance to hear her or anyone else. There's a small exhibit of early recording equipment and ephemera, too. ✉ *29 Exhibition Rd.,* ☎ *0171/589–6603.* *Free.* *Weekdays 10–5 (Thurs. 10–9); closed public holidays, Dec. 24–26, Jan. 1. Tube: South Kensington.*

4 **Natural History Museum.** Architect Alfred Waterhouse had relief panels scattered across the outrageously ornate French Romanesque–style terra-cotta facade of this museum, depicting living creatures to the left of the entrance, extinct ones to the right. Inside, that categorization is sort of continued in reverse, with Dinosaurs on the left and the Ecology Gallery on the right. Both these newly renovated exhibits (the former with life-size moving dinosaurs, the latter complete with moonlit "rain forest") make essential viewing in a museum that realized it was getting crusty and has consequently invested millions overhauling itself in recent years.

The Creepy Crawlies Gallery features a nightmarish superenlarged scorpion, yet ends up making tarantulas cute (8 out of 10 animal species, one learns here, are arthropods). Other wonderful bits include the Human Biology Hall, which you arrive at through a birth-simulation chamber; the full-size blue whale; and in the east wing, once the separate Geological Museum, an earthquake machine in the Earth Galleries. Understandably, this place usually resembles grade-school recess. ✉ *Cromwell Rd.,* ☎ *0171/938–9123.* *£5.50. Free weekdays 4:30–5:50, weekends 5–5:50. White Card accepted.* *Mon.–Sat. 10–5:50, Sun. 11–5:50; closed Dec. 24–26, Jan. 1. Tube: South Kensington.*

7 **Royal Albert Hall.** This domed, circular 8,000-seat auditorium (as well as the Albert Memorial, opposite) was made possible by the Victo-

rian public, who donated funds for it. More money was raised, however, by selling 1,300 future seats at £100 apiece—not for the first night, but for every night for 999 years. (Some descendants of purchasers still use the seats.) The Albert Hall is best-known and best-loved for its annual July–September Henry Wood Promenade Concerts (the "Proms"), with bargain standing (or promenading, or sitting-on-the-floor) tickets sold on the night of the world-class classical concerts. London also enjoys the "Erics," when the rock guitarist Eric Clapton services adoring fans for 10 days there every February. ✉ *Kensington Gore,* ☎ *0171/589–3203. Admission varies according to event. Tube: South Kensington.*

❾ **Royal College of Art.** Housed in a glass-dominated building designed by Sir Hugh Casson in 1973, this provides great contrast with the Victoriana which surrounds it, including the Albert Hall next door. Famous in the '50s and '60s for processing David Hockney, Peter Blake, and Eduardo Paolozzi, the RCA is still one of the country's foremost art schools, and there's usually an exhibition, lecture, or event here open to the public. ✉ *Kensington Gore,* ☎ *0171/584–5020.* *Free.* *Weekdays 10–6; phone first to check exhibition details. Tube: South Kensington.*

❺ **Science Museum.** This, the third of the great South Kensington museums stands behind the Natural History Museum in a far plainer building. It features loads of hands-on exhibits, with entire schools of children apparently decanted inside to play with them; but it is, after all, painlessly educational. Highlights include the Launch Pad gallery, which demonstrates basic scientific principles (try the beautiful plasma ball, where your hands attract "lightning"—if you can get them on it); the Computing Then and Now show, which gets the most crowded of all; ***Puffing Billy,*** the oldest train in the world; and the actual ***Apollo 10*** capsule, which took U.S. astronauts around the moon in 1969 and now sits beside a mock-up moon-base in the space exploration segment. Food technology, medical history, flight, navigation, transport, meteorology—all these topics are explored, and the entire height of the museum is used for a Foucault's Pendulum that has been there, in perpetual motion thanks to the movement of the earth, from the start. ✉ *Exhibition Rd.,* ☎ *0171/938–8000.* *£5. White Card accepted.* *Mon.–Sat. 10–6, Sun. 11–6; closed Dec. 24–26, Jan. 1. Tube: South Kensington.*

❸ **Victoria and Albert Museum.** Recognizable by the copy of Victoria's Imperial Crown it wears on the lantern above the central cupola, this institution is always referred to as the V&A. It is a huge museum, showcasing the applied arts of all disciplines, all periods, all nationalities, and all tastes, and is a wonderful, generous place to get lost in, full of innovation and completely devoid of pretension. The collections are *so* catholic that confusion is a hazard—one minute you're gazing on the Jacobean oak 12-foot-square four-poster Great Bed of Ware (one of the V&A's most prized possessions, given that Shakespeare immortalized it in *Twelfth Night*); the next, you're in the 20th-century end of the equally celebrated Dress Collection, coveting a Jean Muir frock you could actually buy at nearby Harrods.

Prince Albert, Victoria's adored consort, was responsible for the genesis of this permanent version of the 1851 Great Exhibition, and his queen laid its foundation stone in her final public London appearance in 1899. From the start, the V&A had an important role as a research institution, and that role continues today, with many resources available to scholars, designers, artists, and conservators. Two of the latest are the Textiles and Dress 20th Century Reference Centre, with ingenious space-saving storage systems for thousands of bolts of cloth, and the Textile Study Galleries, which perform the same function for 2,000 years' worth of the past.

Follow your own whims around the 7 miles of gallery space, but try to reach the new and spectacular Glass Gallery, where a collection spanning four millennia is reflected between room-size mirrors, under young designer Danny Lane's breathtaking glass balustrade. ✉ *Cromwell Rd.,* ☎ *0171/938–8500.* 💳 *Suggested contribution: £4.50. White Card accepted.* ⏲ *Mon. noon–5:50, Tues.–Sun. 10–5:50; closed Good Friday, May Day, Dec. 24–26, Jan. 1. Tube: South Kensington.*

NEED A BREAK? Rest your overstimulated eyes in the brick-walled V&A café, where full meals and small snacks are available, and where the Sunday Jazz Brunch (11–5), accompanied by live music and Sunday papers, is fast becoming a London institution.

HYDE PARK, KENSINGTON GARDENS, BAYSWATER, AND NOTTING HILL

Many Londoners, not to mention visitors, love the city above all for its huge chunks of green, which cut right through the middle of town. Hyde Park and Kensington Gardens together form by far the biggest of central London's royal parks (Richmond Park, in the far west, is larger). It's probably been centuries since any major royal had a casual stroll here, but the parks remain the property of the Crown, and it was the Crown that saved them from being devoured by the city's late-18th-century growth spurt. North of the parks—which are separate, although the boundary is virtually invisible—lies Bayswater. The main drag, Queensway, expresses Bayswater's nature quite aptly: This is a neighborhood that looks fancy, with its grand white-stucco terraced houses and leafy squares, but is somewhat disreputable, as demonstrated by the 1963 Profumo sex scandal—involving a government minister, a teenage showgirl, and a Soviet naval attaché—which unfurled behind closed Bayswater doors and toppled a government (see the movie *Scandal* for the whole story). You'll notice dozens of identical medium-priced hotels along the streets east of Queensway, but probably won't notice the prostitution, of which there's a certain amount still going on around here. Further north west lies Notting Hill, a trendsetting square mile of multi-ethnicity, music, and markets, with lots of see-and-be-seen-in restaurants and the younger, more egalitarian and adventurous versions of the Cork Street commercial modern-art galleries. The style-watching media dub the musician/novelist/filmbiz/drug-dealer/fashion-victim local residents and hangers-out Notting Hillbillies. The whole thing has mushroomed around one of the world's great antiques markets, the Portobello Road.

A Good Walk

Sights below correspond to the Hyde Park, Kensington Gardens, and Notting Hill map.

Where else would you enter Hyde Park but at **Hyde Park Corner**? The most impressive of the many entrances is the Hyde Park Screen by Apsley House, usually called **Decimus Burton's Gateway** because it was he who designed this triple-arched monument in 1828. The next gate along to the north, a gaudy unicorns-and-lions-rampant number wrought in scarlet-, cobalt-white-, and gold-painted metal was a 90th-birthday gift to Queen Elizabeth the Queen Mother (who is as old as the century), and is therefore the **Queen Mother's Gate.** Follow the southern perimeter along the sand track called **Rotten Row.** It was Henry

VIII's royal path to the hunt—hence the name, a corruption of *route du roi*. It's still used by the Household Cavalry, who live at the **Knightsbridge Barracks**—a high-rise and a long, low, ugly red block—to the left. This is the brigade that mounts the guard at the palace, and you can see them leave to perform this duty, in full regalia, plumed helmet and all, at around 10:30, or await the return of the exhausted ex-guard about noon.

Follow Rotten Row west to the **Serpentine.** When you pass its **Bridge,** you leave Hyde Park, enter **Kensington Gardens,** and come to the **Serpentine Gallery.** En route to the formal garden at the end of the Long Water, **The Fountains,** you pass the statues of **Peter Pan,** and the horse and rider called **Physical Energy,** then continuing westward you reach the **Round Pond,** and **Kensington Palace.** Follow the Broad Walk north past the playground on the left, to the Bayswater Road leaving the park by Black Lion Gate, and you are almost opposite Queensway, a rather peculiar, cosmopolitan street of ethnic confusion, late-night cafés and restaurants, a skating rink, and the Whiteleys shopping-and-movie mall. Turn left at the end into Westbourne Grove, however, and you've entered Notting Hill, and will reach the famous **Portobello Road** after a few blocks. Turn left for the Saturday antiques market and shops; right to reach the Westway, and the flea market.

TIMING

This is a route that changes vastly on weekends. Saturday is Portobello Road's most fun day, so you may prefer to start at the end and work backwards, using the parks as r&r from your shopping exertions. Ditto Fridays, if you're a fleamarket fan. Sundays, the Hyde Park and Kensington Gardens railings all along the Bayswater Road are hung with very bad art, which may slow your progress; also this is prime perambulation day for locals. Whatever your priorities, this is a long walk if you explore every corner, with the perimeter of the two parks alone covering a good 6½ kilometers (4 miles), and about half as far again around the remainder of the route. You could cut out a lot of park without missing out on essential sights, and walk the whole thing in a brisk three hours.

Sights To See

Hyde Park. Along with the smaller St. James's and Green Parks to the east, Hyde Park started as Henry VIII's hunting grounds. He had no altruistic intent but more or less stole the land for his pleasure, from the monks at Westminster at the 1536 Dissolution of the Monasteries. James I was more generous and allowed the public in at the beginning of the 17th century, as long as they were "respectably dressed." Nowadays, as summer visitors can see, you may wear whatever you like—a bathing suit will do. Along its south side runs **Rotten Row.** It was Henry VIII's royal path to the hunt—hence the name, a corruption of *route du roi*. It's still used by the Household Cavalry, who live at the **Knightsbridge Barracks**—a high rise and a long, low, ugly red block—to the left. This is the brigade that mounts the guard at the palace, and you can see them leave to perform this duty, in full regalia, plumed helmet and all, at around 10:30, or await the return of the exhausted ex-guard about noon.

Kensington Gardens. More formal than neighboring Hyde Park, Kensington Gardens was first laid out as palace grounds. The paved Italian garden at the top of the Long Water, **The Fountains** is a reminder of this, though, of course **Kensington Palace** itself is the main clue to its royal status, with its early 19th-century Sunken Garden north of it, complete with a living tunnel of lime trees and golden laburnum. Several statues are worth looking out for: George Frampton's 1912 ***Peter***

Hyde Park, Kensington Gardens, and Notting Hill

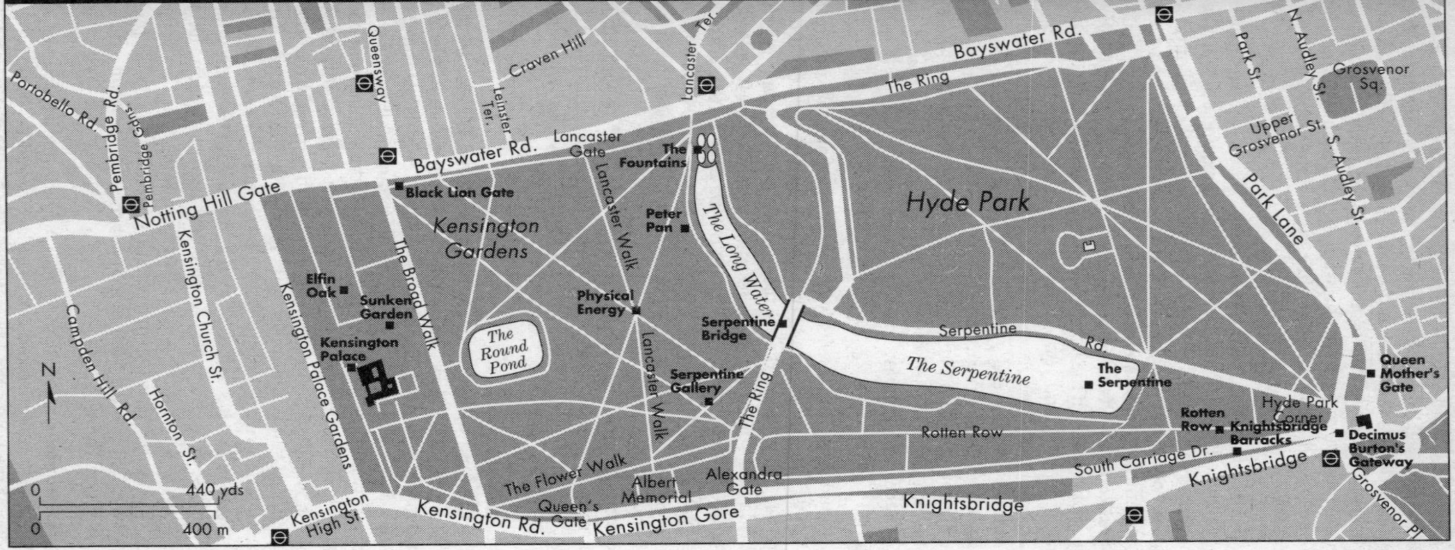
Hyde Park
Kensington Gardens
Bayswater Rd.
Notting Hill Gate
Portobello Rd.
Pembridge Rd.
Pembridge Gdns.
Queensway
Craven Hill
Leinster Ter.
Lancaster Ter.
Lancaster Gate
Black Lion Gate
The Fountains
Peter Pan
The Long Water
Lancaster Walk
Physical Energy
Serpentine Bridge
Serpentine Gallery
The Ring
Serpentine Rd.
The Serpentine
Rotten Row
Kensington Church St.
Campden Hill Rd.
Hornton St.
Kensington Palace Gardens
The Broad Walk
Elfin Oak
Sunken Garden
Kensington Palace
The Round Pond
The Flower Walk
Albert Memorial
Alexandra Gate
Queen's Gate
Kensington High St.
Kensington Rd.
Kensington Gore
Knightsbridge
South Carriage Dr.
Knightsbridge Barracks
Hyde Park Corner
Decimus Burton's Gateway
Queen Mother's Gate
Grosvenor Pl.
Park Lane
Park St.
N. Audley St.
S. Audley St.
Upper Grosvenor St.
Grosvenor Sq.
N
0
440 yds
400 m

Pan is a bronze of the boy who lived on an island in the Serpentine and never grew up, and whose creator, J. M. Barrie, lived at 100 Bayswater Road, not 500 yards from here. Southwest of Peter at the intersection of several paths is George Frederick Watts's 1904 bronze of a muscle-bound horse and rider, entitled ***Physical Energy.*** By the playground close to the Round Pond is the remains of a tree carved with scores of tiny woodland creatures, Ivor Innes's ***Elfin Oak.*** The **Round Pond,** is a magnet for model-boat enthusiasts and duck feeders.

NEED A BREAK? About halfway down Queensway (No. 127), **Maison Pechon** is a patisserie, but one that serves full English breakfasts, omelets, jacket potatoes, and salads alongside its French tarts, brioches, cream cakes, and cookies.

Portobello Road. Famous for its Saturday antiques market, this street begins at Notting Hill Gate, though the stalls start a couple of blocks north, around Chepstow Villas. They continue for about three blocks before giving way to fruit and vegetable stalls. Lining the sloping street are also dozens of antiques shops and indoor markets, open most days. Where the road levels off, around Elgin Crescent, youth culture and a vibrant neighborhood life kicks in, with all manner of interesting small stores and restaurants interspersed with the fruit and vegetable market. This continues to the Westway overpass ("flyover" in British), where London's best flea market (high-class, vintage, antique, and second-hand clothing, jewelry, and junk) happens Friday and Saturday, then on up to Goldbourne Road. There's a strong West Indian flavor to Notting Hill, with a Trinidad-style Carnival centered along Portobello Road on the August bank-holiday weekend. *Tube: Notting Hill Gate, Ladbroke Grove.*

Serpentine Gallery. A gallery influential on the trendy artist circuit, this hangs several exhibitions of modern work a year, often very avant-garde indeed, and always worth a look. It overlooks the west bank of the **Serpentine,** a beloved lake, much frequented in summer, when the south shore Lido resembles a beach and the water is dotted with hired rowboats. The long, narrow, stretch of water was first filled in 1730, though not by the Serpentine Swimming Club—a band of eccentrics guaranteed to appear on TV at the first hard frost each winter, since they dive in here at 6 AM every single day of the year, breaking the ice first if necessary. Walk the bank and you will soon reach the picturesque stone **Serpentine Bridge** built in 1826 by George Rennie, which marks the boundary between Hyde Park and Kensington Gardens. ✉ *Kensington Gardens,* ☎ *0171/402–6075.* 🎫 *Free.* ⏲ *Daily 10–6; closed Christmas wk. Tube: Lancaster Gate.*

NEED A BREAK? The tearoom on the Serpentine is constantly changing hands, and always seems rather overpriced, but it does offer tea, coffee, and snacks in an overwhelming green setting.

REGENT'S PARK AND HAMPSTEAD

This section covers a large area. It starts from the Georgian houses superimposed on medieval Maryburne, continues around John Nash's Regency facades, and his park, stretches on into North London's canal-side youth center, climbs up the hill to the city's prettiest, most expensive "village," and finishes, fittingly, at its most famous cemetery.

Marylebone Road (pronounced "Marra-le-bun") these days is remarkable mostly for its permanent traffic jam, some of it heading to

Madame Tussaud's. At the east end is the first part of John Nash's impressive Regent's Park scheme, the elegantly curvaceous Park Crescent (1812–1818), which Nash planned as a full circus at the northern end of his ceremonial route from St. James's. Like most of the Nash houses around the park, it was wrecked during World War II, reconstructed, and rebuilt behind the repaired facade in the 1960s. Northeast of the park, Camden Town is the neighborhood that houses London's highest concentration of single people in their twenties. Gentrification has been layered over a once overwhelmingly Irish neighborhood, vestiges of which coexist with the youth culture: Inverness Street fruit-and-vegetable market alongside the Arlington House homeless shelter, architects' offices, and antiques stores.

The cliché about Hampstead is that it is just like a pretty little village—albeit one with designer shops, expensive French delicatessens, restaurants, cafés, cinemas, and so on. In fact, like so many London neighborhoods, Hampstead did start as a separate village, when plague-bedeviled medieval Londoners fled the city to this clean hilltop 6½ kilometers (4 miles) away. By the 18th century its reputation for cleanliness had spread so far that its water was being bottled and sold to the hoi polloi down the hill as the Perrier of its day. That was the beginning of Hampstead's heyday as an artistic and literary retreat attracting many famous writers, painters, and musicians to its leafy lanes—as it still does today. Just strolling around here is rewarding: Not only are the streets incredibly picturesque, they also harbor some of London's best Georgian buildings.

A Good Walk

Numbers in the text correspond to numbers in the margin and on the Regent's Park and Hampstead map.

Begin at the tube station whose name will thrill the Sherlock Holmes fan: Baker Street. (The **Sherlock Holmes Museum** is at 221B, of course.) Turn left and follow the line of tour buses past **Madame Tussaud's** ① and the **London Planetarium,** then the end of Harley Street—an English synonym for private (as opposed to state-funded) medicine, because it is lined with the consulting rooms of the country's top specialist doctors—to Park Crescent and, across the street, **Regent's Park** ②. Enter along the Outer Circle, and turn left on Chester Road. Straight ahead are Queen Mary's Gardens, the Lake, and the **Open-Air Theatre** ③. Turn left onto the Broad Walk from Chester Road, look west past the mock-Tudor prefab tearoom for one of London's rare uninterrupted open vistas toward the London Central Mosque, then continue on to the **London Zoo** ④. From here, you can take a round-trip detour on the water bus and spy on the back gardens along the **Grand Union Canal** (which everyone calls the Regent's Canal) to Little Venice. Don't get *too* excited—the canal you're on (constructed 1812–1820) is the only one there is, but this peaceful little bit of London does have an atmosphere unique to it, with enormous white wedding-cake houses set back from the banks, and it's a good strolling location.

North of the zoo, cross Prince Albert Road to Primrose Hill, a high point (literally, at 206 feet), and the best place to be on the night of November 5, when London's biggest bonfire burns a Guy Fawkes effigy, and there's a spectacular fireworks display. Heading east from here (the easiest route is Regent's Park Rd., then left down Parkway, past the **Jewish Museum** ⑤) brings you to the center of Camden Town. Turn left at the foot of Parkway, and battle north along Camden High Street (actually, the crowds are unbearably dense only on the weekend), to **Camden Lock** ⑥. From here you can keep going east, although it's less scenic, to King's Cross, site of one of London's main train stations, of the new British Library building, of the city's highest concentration of streetwalkers, and the **London Canal Museum** ⑦.

Back at the Lock, you could walk up Haverstock Hill, or travel three stops on the Northern Line from Camden Town tube (make sure you take the Edgware branch) to Hampstead (or 181 feet below it, in London's deepest tube station). Cross the High Street to Heath Street and turn right to Church Row, said to be London's most complete Georgian street. At the west end is the 1745 "village" church of St. John's, where the painter John Constable is buried. Just south of the tube, Flask Walk is another pretty street, narrow and shop-lined at the High Street end, then widening after you pass The Flask—the pub it is named for, which in turn is named for the flasks that contained that therapeutically clean Hampstead spa water. The pub has a pretty courtyard, by the way. Nearby Well Walk was where the spring surfaced, its place now marked by a dried-up fountain. John Constable lived here, as well as John Keats (in, of course, **Keats House** ⑧) and, later, D. H. Lawrence. you now have two choices: If you've had enough fresh air, walk down Fitzjohn's Avenue and visit the **Freud Museum** ⑨ and then continue down Finchley Road to the impressive **Saatchi Collection** ⑩. If you've been blessed by a clear London day, take advantage and take the long walk northeast up Spaniards Road, traversing **Hampstead Heath,** to Hampstead lane to the bucolic oasis of **Kenwood House** ⑪, well worth a visit for its setting alone. To the east of Hampstead, and also topping a hill, is the former village of Highgate, which has some fine houses, especially along its Georgian High Street, and retains a peaceful period atmosphere. But it is most famous for **Highgate Cemetery** ⑫.

TIMING

You may well want to divide this tour into segments, using the (notoriously inefficient) Northern Line of the tube to jump between the Regent's Park and Hampstead neighborhoods. It will take you at least three hours to walk the full length of this walk.

There are several approaches, of course. In summer, with children you might center a north London jaunt around Regent's Park, the Zoo, Camden Lock and a canal trip, a day's worth of sightseeing. If you wanted to add Madame Tussaud's and the Planetarium, you'd have a frenetic day, especially in summer, because you may be in line for an hour. A summer's day without children might start the other end, with Hampstead Heath, Kenwood House, a stroll around Hampstead and a pub or two on the agenda—plenty for one day. Teenagers and youth will spend all day and night in Camden Town, and may as well admit it. They, and anyone else who wants the whole Camden Lock spectacle, should go north on a weekend; those who prefer quiet should do the opposite. Neither Camden nor Hampstead are completely dead during the week, though, because both have residents who tend to go out a lot. Bear in mind that much of this itinerary is washed out by rain, not only because there's a lot of ground to cover, but because many of the pleasures are to be had from strolling.

Sights To See

❻ **Camden Lock.** What was once just a pair of locks on the Grand Union Canal, has now developed into London's third most visited tourist attraction. It's a vast honeycomb of markets that sell just about everything, but mostly crafts, clothing (vintage, ethnic, and young designer), and antiques, and is a virtual caricature of its neighborhood, Camden Town. Here, especially on a weekend, the crowds are dense, young and relentless, and you may tire of the identical T-shirts, pants, boots, vintage wear, and cheap leathers on their backs and in the shops. Camden definitely has its charms, though. Gentrification has been layered

Camden Lock, **6**
Freud Museum, **9**
Highgate Cemetery, **12**
Jewish Museum, **5**
Keats House, **8**
Kenwood House, **11**
London Canal Museum, **7**
London Zoo, **4**
Madame Tussaud's, **1**
Open-Air Theatre, **3**
Regent's Park, **2**
Saatchi Collection, **10**

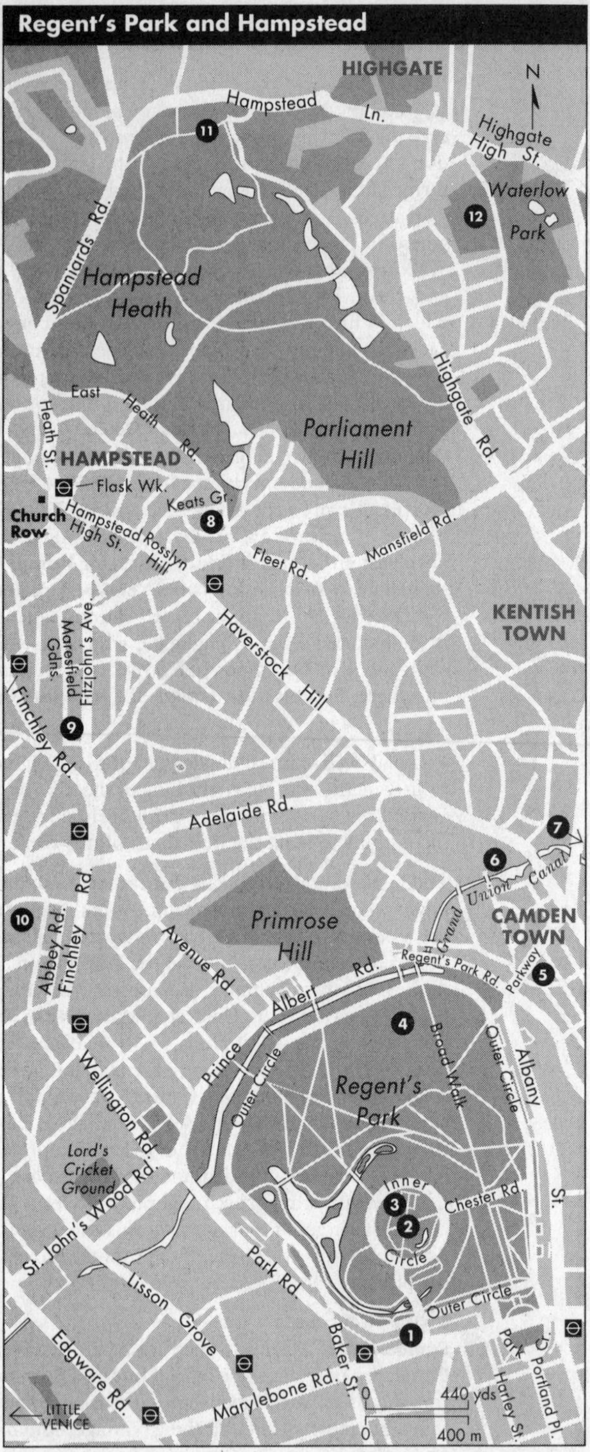

over a once overwhelmingly Irish neighborhood, vestiges of which co-exist with the youth culture: Inverness Street fruit-and-vegetable market alongside the Arlington House homeless shelter, architects' offices, and antiques stores. ✉ *Camden Lock, Camden High Street NW1. No phone. Markets open weekends. Tube: Camden Town or Chalk Farm.*

NEED A BREAK? You will not go hungry in Camden Town. Among the countless cafés, bars, pubs, and restaurants, the following stand out for good value and good food: **Marine Ices** (✉ 8 Haverstock Hill, past the lock) has a window dispensing ice cream to strollers, or pasta, pizza, and sundaes inside. **Bar Gansa** (✉ 2 Inverness St., near the tube) offers Spanish tapas—small dishes for sharing. **Cottons Rhum Shop, Bar and Restaurant** (✉ 55 Chalk Farm Rd., past the lock) is a Caribbean island in miniature, with great rum cocktails and jerk chicken.

9 **Freud Museum.** The father of psychoanalysis lived here for only a few months, between his escape from Nazi persecution in his native Vienna in 1938 and his death in 1939. Many of his possessions emigrated with him and were set up by his daughter, Anna (herself a pioneer of child psychoanalysis), as a shrine to her father's life and work. Four years after Anna's death in 1982, the house was opened as a museum. It replicates the atmosphere of Freud's famous consulting rooms, particularly through the presence of The Couch. You'll find Freud-related books, lectures, and study groups here, too. ✉ *20 Maresfield Gardens,* ☎ *0171/435–2002.* *£2.50.* *Wed.–Sun. noon–5; closed Easter, Dec. 24–26, Jan. 1. Tube: Swiss Cottage, Finchley Road.*

Hampstead Heath. However pretty the houses may be, this wild park, which spreads for miles to the north, is quite the nicest thing about Hampstead. On the southwest corner stands the rebuilt version of a famous inn **Jack Straw's Castle.** It is named after the Peasant Revolt leader who hid out and was captured here in 1381 after destroying Sir Robert Hales's residence and Priory, the Prior of St. John. Hales was hated for enforcing the poll tax, which led to the uprising—and which, when reintroduced in 1990, proved as unpopular the second time around. Another historic pub stands off the northwest edge, on Hampstead Lane. The **Spaniard's Inn,** in contrast to the above, is little changed since the early 18th century, when (they say) the notorious highwayman Dick Turpin hung out here. Keats also drank here, as did Shelley and Byron—but not Dickens. When his eternal pub crawl brought him up to Hampstead, he preferred Jack Straw's Castle. ✉ *Jack Straw's Castle, North End Way NW3,* ☎ *0171/435–8885.* ✉ *Spaniard's Inn, Spaniard's Rd., NW3,* ☎ *0181/455–3276. Tube: Hampstead.*

12 **Highgate Cemetery.** The older, west side of this sprawling early Victorian graveyard, featuring many an overwrought stone memorial, can be visited only by a tour given by the Friends of Highgate Cemetery—a group of volunteers who virtually saved the place from ruin. The shady streets of the dead, Egyptian Avenue and the Circle of Lebanon, are particularly Poe-like, but the famous graves are mostly on the newer, less atmospheric east side, which is still in use and may be wandered freely. Karl Marx's enormous black bust is probably the most visited place, but George Eliot is also buried here. This is not London's oldest cemetery—that distinction belongs to Kensal Green, with its spine-chilling catacombs and Gothic mausolea. ✉ *Swains La., Highgate,* ☎ *0181/340–1834.* *East side, £1; west side tour, £2. East side open Apr.–Oct., daily 10–4:45; Oct.–Mar., daily 10–3:45. West side tours: Apr.–Oct., weekdays 2 and 4 PM, weekends periodically 11–*

4; Nov.–Mar., weekdays noon, 2, and 3; weekends periodically 11–3. Closed Dec. 25 and for funerals. Tube: Archway.

NEED A BREAK? Lauderdale House in Waterlow Park, across Swain's Lane from Highgate cemetery, was built during the 16th century by a master of the Royal Mint and is now a community and arts center, with a great café serving homemade hot meals as well as snacks.

5 **Jewish Museum.** This newly located museum tells a potted history of the Jews in London from Norman times, though the bulk of the exhibits date from the end of the 17th century (when Cromwell repealed the laws against Jewish settlement) and later. ✉ *Raymond Burton House, 129 Albert St., NW1,* ☎ *0171/284–1997.* *£3.* *Sun.–Thurs. 10–4; closed national and Jewish holidays.*

8 **Keats House.** Here you can see the plum tree under which the young Romantic poet composed "Ode to a Nightingale," many of his original manuscripts, his library, and other possessions he managed to acquire in his short life. He died in Rome of consumption, aged 25, two years after taking up residence here, in 1818. ✉ *Keats House, Wentworth Pl., Keats Grove,* ☎ *0171/435–2062.* *Free.* *Apr.–Oct., weekdays 10–6, Sat. 10–5, Sun. and national holidays 2–5; Nov.–Mar., weekdays 1–5, Sat. 10–5, Sun. 2–5; closed 1 hr at lunch and Easter, May Day, Dec. 24–26, Jan. 1. Tube: Hampstead.*

NEED A BREAK? Hampstead is full of eating places, including a few that have been here forever. Try **The Coffee Cup** (✉ 74 Hampstead High St.), serving all-day English breakfasts, pastries, and things-on-toast; or the **Hampstead Tea Rooms** (✉ 9 South End Rd.) for its sandwiches, pies, and its great windowful of pastries and cream cakes.

11 **Kenwood House.** This magnificent mansion was first built in 1616 and remodeled by Robert Adam in 1764. Adam refaced most of the exterior and added the glorious library, which, with its curved, painted ceiling and gilded detailing, is the highlight of the house. The other unmissable part is the **Iveagh Bequest**—a collection of paintings the Earl of Iveagh gave the nation in 1927, starring a Rembrandt self-portrait and works by Reynolds, Van Dyck, Hals, Gainsborough, Vermeer, and Turner. In front of the house, a graceful lawn slopes down to a little lake crossed by a dinky bridge—all in perfect 18th-century upper-class taste. Nowadays the lake is dominated by its concert bowl, which stages a popular summer series of orchestral concerts, including at least one performance of Handel's *Music for the Royal Fireworks,* complete with fireworks. ✉ *Hampstead La.,* ☎ *0181/348–1286.* *Free.* *Easter–Sept., 10–6, Oct.–Easter, 10–4; closed Christmas. Tube: Golder's Green, then bus 210.*

NEED A BREAK? The café in the former stables at Kenwood serves sandwiches, salads, light lunches, and pastries, and has many outside tables in its sheltered courtyard.

7 **London Canal Museum.** Here, in a former ice storage house, you can learn about the rise and fall of London's once extensive canal network: the trade, the vessels, and the way of life. Outside, on the Battlebridge Basin, float the gaily painted narrow boats of modern canal dwellers—a few steps and a world away from King's Cross, which remains one of London's least salubrious neighborhoods, despite recent police action to clean up street activities like drug dealing and prostitution. The quirky little museum is accessible from Camden Lock if you take the

towpath. ✉ *12–13 New Wharf Rd., N1,* ☎ *0171/713–0836.* 🎟 *£2.50.* ⏲ *Apr.–Sept., Tues.–Sun. 10–4; call for winter hours; closed national holidays. Tube: King's Cross.*

London Planetarium. This domed building stands right next to Madame Tussaud's, but could hardly provide greater contrast with the waxworks (though you can save a bit of cash by combining them in a single visit). Inside the dome, exact simulations of the night sky are projected by the Digistar Mark 2 projector and accompanied by gosh-wow-fancy-that narration. The shows, which change daily, are good enough to leave children addicted to astronomy. The "Space Trail" of interactive planet and spacecraft models is also worth seeing, and there are occasional laser shows and rock music extravaganzas. ✉ *Marylebone Rd.,* ☎ *0171/935–6861.* 🎟 *£5.45. Joint ticket with Madame Tussaud's (☞ below): £10.95. Shows every 40 min, weekdays 12:20–5, weekends 10:20–5; extra shows during school vacations. Tube: Baker Street.*

❹ **London Zoo.** The Zoo opened in 1828, peaked in popularity during the 1950s (when more than 3 million visitors passed through its turnstiles every year), but recently faced the prospect of closing its gates forever. Its problems started when animal-crazy Brits, apparently anxious about the morality of caging wild beasts, simply stopped visiting. But the zoo fought back, pulling heartstrings with a *Save Our Zoo* campaign and tragic predictions of mass euthanasia for homeless polar bears, and, at the 11th hour, found commercial sponsorship that was generous enough not only to keep the wolves from the door (or the wolves indoors) but also to fund a great big modernization program.

Zoo highlights that will not change include the Elephant and Rhino Pavilion, which closely resembles the South Bank Arts Complex; the graceful Snowdon Aviary, spacious enough to allow its tenants free flight; and the 1936 Penguin Pool, where feeding time sends small children into raptures. New thrills will include the construction of a desert swarming with locusts; a rain forest alive with butterflies, bats, and hummingbirds; and a cave lighted by fireflies. This being the headquarters of the Zoological Society of London, much work is done here in wildlife conservation, education, and the breeding of endangered species, and emphasis is being shifted onto these aspects in the exhibits, with more displays to help explain them to visitors. The first step along this road was the Children's Zoo, which shows how people and animals live together, and features domestic animals from around the world. ✉ *Regent's Park,* ☎ *0171/722–3333.* 🎟 *£7. Penguin feed, 2:30; aquarium feed, 2:30; reptile feed, 2:30 Fri. only; elephant bath, 3:45.* ⏲ *Summer, daily 9–6; winter, daily 10–4; closed Dec. 25. Tube: Camden Town, and bus 74.*

❶ **Madame Tussaud's.** This—one of London's busiest sights—is nothing more, nothing less, than the world's premier exhibition of lifelike waxwork models of celebrities. Madame T. learned her craft while making death masks of French Revolutionary victims and in 1835 set up her first show of the famous ones near this spot. Nowadays, "Super Stars" of entertainment, in their own hall of the same name, outrank any aristo in popularity, along with the newest segment, "The Spirit of London," a "time taxi ride" that visits every notable Londoner from Shakespeare to Benny Hill. But top billing still goes to the murderers in the Chamber of Horrors, who stare glassy-eyed at you—this one from the electric chair, that one next to the tin bath where he dissolved several wives in quicklime. What, aside from ghoulish prurience, makes people stand in line to invest in London's most expensive museum ticket? It must be the thrill of rubbing shoulders with Shakespeare, Martin Luther King, Jr., the queen, and the Beatles—most of them dressed in their own clothes—in a single day. ✉ *Marylebone Rd.,* ☎ *0171/935–6861.* 🎟 *£8.75. Joint ticket with planetarium* (☞ above) *£10.95, adults, £8.50 senior citizens, £6.95 children.* ⏲ *Sept.–June, weekdays 10–5:30, weekends 9:30–5:30; July–Aug., daily 9:30–5:30; closed Dec. 25. Tube: Baker Street.*

❷ **Regent's Park.** This, the youngest of London's great parks, was laid out in 1812 by John Nash, working, as ever, for his patron, the Prince Regent (hence the name), who was crowned George IV in 1820. The idea was to re-create the feel of a grand country residence close to the center of town, with all those magnificent white-stucco terraces facing in on the park. As you walk the Outer Circle, you'll see how successfully Nash's plans were carried out, although the center of it all, a palace for the prince, was never built—George was too busy fiddling with the one he already had, Buckingham Palace. The most famous and impressive of Nash's terraces would have been in the prince's line of vision from the planned palace, so was extra ornamental. **Cumberland Terrace** has a central block of Ionic columns surmounted by a triangular Wedgwood-blue pediment that is like a giant cameo. Snow-white statuary personifying Britannia and her empire (the work of the onsite architect, James Thomson) further single it out from the pack.

As in all London parks, planting here is planned with the aim of having something in bloom in all seasons, but if you hit the park in May, June, or July, head first to the Inner Circle. Your nostrils should lead you to **Queen Mary's Gardens,** a fragrant 17-acre circle that riots with roses in summer, and heather, azaleas, and evergreens in other seasons. The **Broad Walk** is a good vantage point to glimpse the minaret and golden dome of the **London Central Mosque** on the far west side of the park, or—if it's a summer evening or a Sunday afternoon—witness a remarkable recent phenomenon. Wherever you look, the sport being enthusiastically played (subject to the ritual annual banning by the park authorities) is not cricket but softball, now Britain's fastest-growing participant sport (bring your mitt). Actually, you're likely to see cricket, too.

❸ **Regent's Park Open-Air Theatre.** This has been mounting mostly Shakespeare productions every summer since 1932. *A Midsummer Night's Dream* is the one to catch—never is that enchanted Greek wood more lifelike than it is here, augmented by genuine bird squawks and a rising moon. The park can get chilly, so bring a blanket—and rain stops the play only when heavy, so an umbrella may be wise, too. ✉ *Open-Air Theatre, Regent's Park,* ☎ *0171/486–2431.* ⏲ *June–Aug. Tube: Baker Street, Regent's Park.*

❿ **Saatchi Collection.** This blinding white space is all crisp lines and quietness the better to contemplate the front lines of contemporary paintings, installations and sculpture—by the likes of Lucian Freud, Paula Rego, Damian Hirst, Rachel Whiteread, Janine Antoni—collected by the advertising mogul. It's hard to find, but worth the visit. ✉ *98a Boundary Rd., NW8,* ☎ *0171/624–8299.* 🎟 *Free.* ⏲ *Fri.–Sat. noon–6. Tube: Swiss Cottage.*

Sherlock Holmes Museum. You can tell you've reached this museum when you see the actor dressed as a Victorian policeman outside, and the sign that claims this as 221B Baker Street, the address of Conan Doyle's fictional detective. Inside, "Holmes's housekeeper" conducts you into a series of Victorian rooms, full of Sherlockabilia. The 221B, if it existed, would be down the block in the Abbey National Building Society's head office at Abbey House, 215–229 Baker Street, by the way. ✉ *"221B" Baker St.,* ☎ *0171/935–8866.* 🎟 *£5.* ⏲ *Daily 10–6; closed Dec. 25, Jan. 1. Tube: you guessed it.*

Wellcome Building. Various medicine-based science exhibitions are housed here, featuring interactive technology. "Science for Life" about biomedicine, and the History of Medicine Gallery are permanent fixtures. ✉ *183 Euston Rd.,* ☎ *0171/611–8727.* 🎟 *Free.* ⏲ *Weekdays 9:45–5, Sat. 9:45–1; closed national holidays. Tube: Euston.*

GREENWICH

About 13 kilometers (8 miles) downstream—which means seaward, to the east—from central London lies a neighborhood you'd think had been designed to provide the perfect day out. Greenwich is another of London's self-contained "villages," only one with unique and splendid sights surrounding the residential portion. Sir Christopher Wren's Royal Naval College and Inigo Jones's Queen's House reach architectural heights; the Old Royal Observatory measures time for our entire planet; and the Greenwich Meridian divides the world in two—you can stand astride it with one foot in either hemisphere. The National Maritime Museum and the proud clipper ship *Cutty Sark* are thrilling to seafaring types, and landlubbers can stroll the green acres of parkland that surround the buildings, the quaint 19th-century houses, and the weekend crafts and antiques markets.

A Good Walk

Numbers in the text correspond to numbers in the margin and on the Greenwich map.

Before you start to walk, bear in mind that the journey to Greenwich is fun in itself, especially if you approach by river, arriving at the best possible vista of the **Royal Naval College,** with the **Queen's House** behind. On the way, the boat glides past famous sights on the London skyline (there's a guaranteed spine chill on passing the Tower) and ever-changing docklands, and there's always a cockney navigator enhancing the views with wiseguy commentary. You could also take the Docklands Light Railway (DLR), a high-speed elevated track, which opened in 1987. It connects with the tube network at Bank, and brings you to Island Gardens, exactly opposite the Royal Naval College, with the finest possible view, of course. You can't miss the squat little circular brick building with its glass-domed roof. This is the entrance to the Greenwich Foot Tunnel, where an ancient elevator takes you down to a walkway under the Thames that brings you up very close to the ***Cutty Sark***① and the ***Gipsy Moth IV***②.

By continuing along King William Walk, you come to the wrought-iron gates of the **Royal Naval College** ③, from the south end of which you approach the building that Wren's majestic quadrangles frame, the **Queen's House** ④ followed by the **National Maritime Museum** ⑤. Now head up the hill in Greenwich Park overlooking the Naval College and Maritime Museum to the **Old Royal Observatory** ⑥ and the **Ranger's House** ⑦. Walking back through the park toward the river, you'll enter the pretty streets of Greenwich Village to the west. There are plenty of bookstores and antiques shops for browsing, and, at the foot of Crooms Hill, the modern **Greenwich Theatre** ⑧—a West End theater, despite its location, which mounts well-regarded, often star-spangled productions—and the **Fan Museum** ⑨ opposite. Finish up at the excellent **Greenwich Antique Market** ⑩ (on Burney St. near the museum and theater), and the Victorian **Covered Crafts Market** ⑪ by the *Cutty Sark,* on College Approach. An addition 25-minute boat ride away is the **Thames Barrier** ⑫, which helps keep London dry—at least from the ground up.

TIMING

First of all, the boat trip takes about an hour from Westminster Pier (next to Big Ben), or 25 minutes from the Tower of London, so figure in enough time for the round-trip, unless the weather's really awful, or it's winter and the boats have stopped. Aim for an early start. Although the distance covered in this walk is barely a mile, Greenwich can't be "done" in a day. There are such riches here, especially if the maritime theme is your thing, that whatever time you allow will seem halved. If the weather's good, you'll be tempted to stroll aimlessly around the quaint village-like streets too, and maybe take a turn in the park. If you want to take in the markets, you'll need to come on a weekend. The antique market is open 8–4; the crafts market, 9–5.

Sights To See

⓫ **Covered Crafts Market.** You'll find this Victorian market by the *Cutty Sark,* on College Approach. As you'd expect, this one features crafts, but there are more of the sort of ceramics, jewelry, knitwear, and leather goods that you might actually want to own than is common in such places, and you get to buy them from the people who made them. ⏲ *Weekends 9–5.*

❶ **Cutty Sark.** This romantic tea clipper was built in 1869, one of fleets and fleets of similar wooden tall-masted clippers, which during the 19th century plied the seven seas trading in exotic commodities—tea, in this case. The *Cutty Sark,* the last to survive, was also the fastest, sailing the China–London route in 1871 in only 107 days. Now the photogenic vessel lies in dry dock, a museum of one kind of seafaring life—and not a comfortable kind for the 28-strong crew, as you'll see. The collection of figureheads is amusing, too. ✉ *King William Walk,* ☎ *0181/858–3445.* 🎫 *£3.25.* ⏲ *Apr.–Sept., Mon.–Sat. 10–6, Sun. and public holidays noon–6; Oct.–Mar., Mon.–Sat. 10–5, Sun. and public holidays noon–5. Last admission 30 min before closing. Closed Dec. 24–26.*

❾ **Fan Museum.** In two newly restored houses dating from the 1820s opposite the Greenwich Theatre is this highly unusual museum. The 2,000 fans here, which date from the 17th century onward, comprise the world's only such collection, and the history and purpose of these often exquisitely crafted objects are explained satisfyingly. It was the personal vision—and fan collection—of Helene Alexander that brought it into being in 1991, and the workshop and conservation and study center that she has also set up ensure that this anachronistic art has a future. ✉ *10–12 Croom's Hill,* ☎ *0181/858–7879.* 🎫 *£3.* ⏲ *Tues.–Sat. 11–4:30, Sun. noon–4:30; closed Dec. 24–26, Jan. 1.*

❷ ***Gipsy Moth IV***. The boat in which Sir Francis Chichester achieved the first single-handed circumnavigation of the globe in 1966 is dry-docked beside the Cutty Sark. Inside you'll see the tiny space the sailor endured for 226 days, and the ingenious way everything he needed was installed. The queen knighted him on board here, using the same sword with which the previous Elizabeth had knighted that other seagoing Francis, Sir Francis Drake, three centuries before. ✉ *King William Walk,* ☎ *0181/858–3445.* 🎫 *50p.* ⏲ *Apr.–Oct., Mon.–Sat. 10–6, Sun. noon–6; closed Nov.–Mar.*

❿ **Greenwich Antique Market.** If you're visiting on the weekend, this market on Burney Street near the Fan Museum and Greenwich Theatre has a lot of bric-a-brac and books, too, and is well-known among the cognoscenti as a good source for vintage clothes.

Greenwich

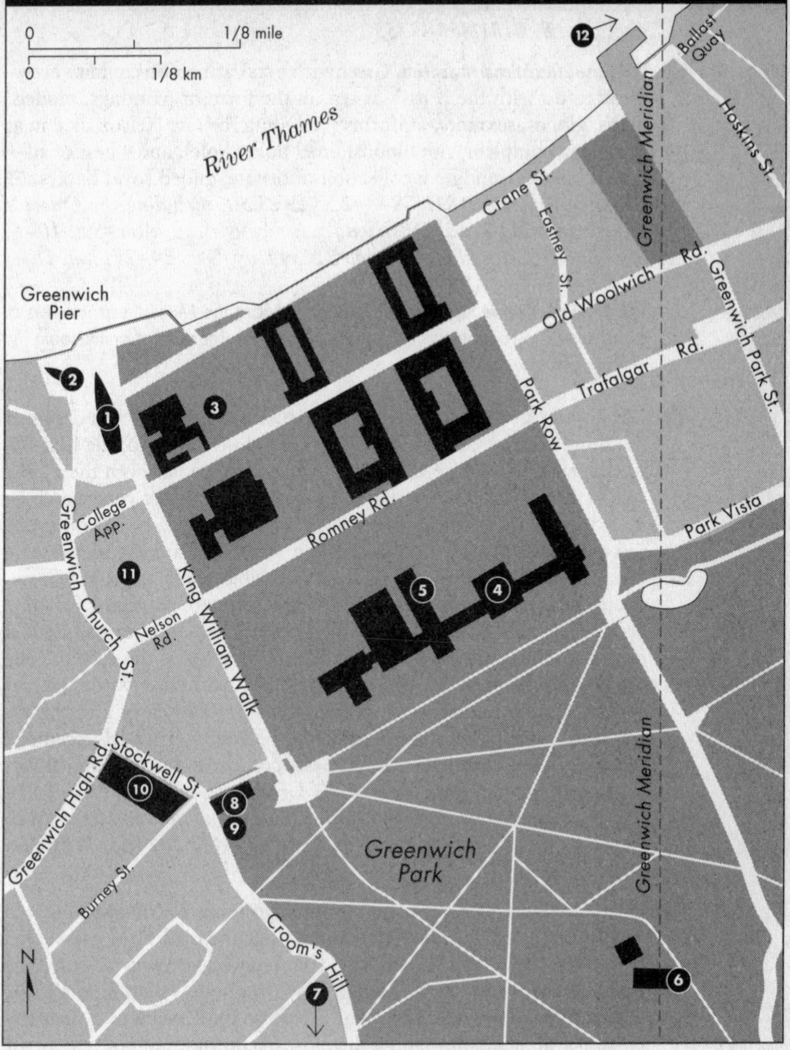

Covered Crafts Market, **11**
Cutty Sark, **1**
Fan Museum, **9**
Gipsy Moth IV, **2**
Greenwich Antique Market, **10**
Greenwich Theatre, **8**
National Maritime Museum, **5**
Old Royal Observatory, **6**
Queen's House, **4**
Ranger's House, **7**
Royal Naval College, **3**
Thames Barrier, **12**

8 **Greenwich Theatre.** Officially a West End theater, despite its location, this modern venue mounts well-regarded, often star-spangled productions. ☎ *0181/858–7755.*

5 **National Maritime Museum.** Greenwich's star attraction contains everything to do with the British at sea, in the form of paintings, models, maps, globes, sextants, uniforms (including the one Nelson died in at Trafalgar, complete with bloodstained bullet hole), and—best of all—actual boats, including a collection of ornate, gilded royal barges. ✉ *Romney Rd.,* ☎ *0181/858–4422.* *£5.50, including the Queen's House and Old Royal Observatory (☞ below).* ⏲ *Mon.–Sat. 10–6, Sun. noon–6; closed Good Friday, May Day, Dec. 24–27, Jan. 1.*

NEED A BREAK? The **Dolphin Coffee Shop** on the National Maritime Museum grounds is a good place to recuperate after the rigors of the museum; non-museum visitors are also welcome.

6 **Old Royal Observatory.** Founded in 1675 by Charles II and designed the same year by Christopher Wren for John Flamsteed, the first Astronomer Royal. The red ball you see on its roof has been there only since 1833. It drops every day at 1 PM, and you can set your watch by it, as the sailors on the Thames always have. In fact, nearly everyone sets their watch by it: This "Greenwich Timeball," along with the Gate Clock inside the observatory, are the most visible manifestations of Greenwich Mean Time, and since 1884, the ultimate standard for time around the world. Also here is the **Prime Meridian,** a brass line laid on the cobblestones at 0° longitude, one side being the eastern, one the western hemisphere. In 1948, the Old Royal Observatory lost its official status: London's glow had grown too intense, and the astronomers moved to Sussex, while the Astronomer Royal decamped to Cambridge. They left various telescopes, chronometers, and clocks for you to view in their absence. ✉ *Greenwich Park,* ☎ *0181/858–4422.* *Joint admission with National Maritime Museum (☞ above).* ⏲ *Mon.–Sat. 10–6, Sun. noon–6; closed Good Friday, May Day, Dec. 24–27, Jan. 1.*

4 **Queen's House.** The queen for whom Inigo Jones began designing it in 1616 was James I's Anne of Denmark, but she died three years later, and it was Charles I's French wife, Henrietta Maria, who inherited the building when it was completed in 1635. It is no less than Britain's first Classical building—the first, that is, to use the lessons of Italian Renaissance architecture—and is therefore of enormous importance in the history of English architecture. Inside, the Tulip Stair, named for the fleur-de-lys–style pattern on the balustrade, is especially fine, spiraling up, without a central support, to the Great Hall. The Great Hall itself is a perfect cube, exactly 40 feet in all three directions, and decorated with paintings of the Muses, the Virtues, and the Liberal Arts. ☎ *0181/858–4422. £5.50, including National Maritime Museum and Old Royal Observatory (☞ above). White Card accepted.* ⏲ *Mon.–Sat. 10–6, Sun. noon–6; closed Good Friday, May Day, Dec. 24–27, Jan. 1.*

7 **Ranger's House.** This handsome early 18th-century mansion, which was the Greenwich Park Ranger's official residence during the 19th century, now houses collections of Jacobean portraits and early musical instruments. Concerts are regularly given here too. It stands just outside the park boundaries, on the southwest side of **Greenwich Park,** which is one of London's oldest royal parks. It had been in existence for more than 200 years before Charles II commissioned the French landscape artist Le Nôtre (who was responsible for Versailles and for St. James's Park) to redesign it in what was, in the 1660s, the latest

French fashion. The Flower Garden on the southeast side and the deer enclosure nearby are particularly pleasant. Look also for Queen Elizabeth's Oak on the east side, around which Henry VIII and his second queen, Anne Boleyn, Elizabeth I's mother, are said to have danced. ✉ *Chesterfield Walk, Blackheath,* ☎ *0181/853–0035.* 🎟 *Free.* ⏲ *Daily Apr.–Sept. 10–6, Oct.–Mar. 10–4 except for 1 hr at lunch; closed Good Friday, Dec. 24–26, Jan. 1.*

❸ **Royal Naval College.** Begun by Christopher Wren in 1694 as a home, or hospital (as in the Chelsea Royal Hospital; not Charing Cross Hospital), for ancient mariners, it became instead a school for young ones in 1873. You'll notice how the blocks part to reveal the Queen's House across the central lawns. Wren, with the help of his assistant, Hawksmoor, was at pains to preserve the river vista from the house, and there are few more majestic views in London than the awe-inspiring symmetry he achieved. Behind the college are two buildings you can visit. The **Painted Hall,** the college's dining hall, derives its name from the baroque murals of William and Mary (reigned 1689–95; William alone 1695–1702) and assorted allegorical figures, the whole supported by trompe l'oeil pillars that Sir James Thornhill (who decorated the inside of St. Paul's dome, too) painted between 1707 and 1717. In the opposite block stands the **College Chapel,** which was rebuilt after a fire in 1779 and is altogether lighter, in a more restrained, neo-Grecian style. At Christmas 1805, Admiral Nelson's body was brought from the battle of Trafalgar to lie in state here. ✉ *Royal Naval College, King William Walk,* ☎ *0181/858–2154.*

⓬ **Thames Barrier.** This mammoth piece of civil engineering will come in handy if the water table ever again rises as high as it did in 1928 and 1953 and London is threatened with another flood. This curiously haunting ¼-mile-long barrier, with its 10 upstanding steel gates, contains enough concrete to build 10 miles of six-lane freeway, and looks like a cross between the Sydney Opera House and a line of submerged alien beings. You can't visit the control room, but there's an exhibition, with videos explaining why it's necessary and how it works, and you can walk along the riverbank close to it, though the best view is from out on the river. Also here is **Hallett's Panorama,** an incongruous re-creation, with oils and sculpture, of the city of Bath. The 1967-vintage ***U-475 Foxtrot*** was the Soviet navy's largest submarine, and is now moored at nearby Long's Wharf, where visitors can clamber around its cramped and spooky decks, and peer up the periscope at the Barrier. Everything lies a few miles farther downstream from Greenwich—another 25-minute boat ride away (though you can also get here by Network SouthEast trains from Greenwich or Charing Cross to Charlton). ✉ *Unity Way, off Woolwich Rd.,* ☎ *0181/854–1373.* 🎟 *(including Hallett's Panorama): £2.50.* ⏲ *Weekdays 10:30–5, weekends 10:30–5:30; closed Dec. 25–26, Jan. 1.* U-475 Foxtrot ☎ *0181/855–7560.* 🎟 *£3.95.* ⏲ *Daily 10–6; closed Dec. 25–26, Jan. 1.*

THE THAMES UPSTREAM

The Thames is Britain's longest river. It winds its way through the Cotswolds, beyond the "dreaming spires" of Oxford and past majestic Windsor Castle—far more the lazy, leafy country river than the dark gray urban waterway you see in London. Once you leave the city center, going west, or upstream, you reach a series of former villages—Chiswick, Kew, Richmond, Putney—that, apart from the roar of aircraft coming in to land at Heathrow a few miles farther west, still retain a peaceful, almost rural atmosphere, especially in places where parkland rolls down to the riverbank. In fact, it was really only at the beginning of this century that these villages expanded into London proper. The royal palaces and grand houses that dot the area were built not as town houses but as country residences with easy access to London by river.

TIMING

Each of the places we list here could easily absorb a whole day of your time, and Hampton Court is especially huge. Access is fairly easy: The District Line of the Underground runs out to Kew and Richmond, as does Network SouthEast from Waterloo, which also serves Twickenham and Hampton Court. Chiswick House can be reached by tube to Turnham Green, then the E3 bus; or by tube to Hammersmith and Bus 290. A pleasant, if slow, way to go is by river. Boats depart Westminster Pier (just by Big Ben) for Kew (1½ hours), Richmond (2–3 hours), and Hampton Court (4 hours) several times a day in summer, less frequently from October through March. As you can tell from those sailing times, the boat trip is worth taking only if you make it an integral part of your day out, and even then, be aware that it can get very breezy on the water and that the scenery going upstream is by no means constantly fascinating. ✉ *Westminster Pier,* ☏ *0171/930–4097.*

Chiswick and Kew

Chiswick is the nearest Thames-side destination to London, with Kew just a mile or so beyond it. Much of Chiswick today is a nondescript suburb developed at the beginning of this century. But, incongruously stranded among the terraced houses, a number of fine 18th-century houses and a charming little village survive. The village atmosphere of Kew is still distinct, making this one of the most desirable areas of outer London. What makes Kew famous, though, are the Royal Botanic Gardens.

A Good Walk

Chiswick's **Church Street** (reached by an underpass from Hogarth's House) is the nearest thing to a sleepy country village street in all of London, despite its proximity to the Great West Road. Follow it down to the Thames and turn left at its foot to reach the sturdy 18th-century riverfront houses of **Chiswick Mall.** The half-mile walk along here takes you far away from London and into a world of elegance and calm. You will pass several riverside pubs as you head along this stretch of the Thames toward Hammersmith Bridge. The **Dove** is the prettiest, if the most crowded, with its terrace hanging over the water, though the food is better at the **Blue Anchor,** which you reach first.

There's a similarly peaceful walk to be had about a mile to the west, along the 18th-century river frontage of **Strand-on-the-Green,** whose houses look over the narrow towpath to the river, their tidy brick facades covered with wisteria and roses in summer. Strand-on-the-Green ends at Kew Bridge, opposite which is **Kew Green,** where local teams play cricket on summer Sundays. All around it are fine 18th-century houses, and, in the center, a church in which the painters Gainsborough and John Zoffany (1733–1810) are buried.

Sights To See

Chiswick House. Built circa 1725 by the Earl of Burlington as a country residence in which to entertain friends, and as a kind of temple to the arts, this is the very model of a Palladian villa, inspired by the Villa Capra near Vicenza in northeastern Italy. The house fans out from a central octagonal room in perfect symmetry, guarded by statues of Burlington's heroes, Palladio himself and his disciple Inigo Jones. Burlington's friends—Pope, Swift, Gay, and Handel among them—were well qualified to adorn a temple to the arts. This is the Lord Burlington of Burlington House, Piccadilly, home of the Royal Academy and, of course, Burlington Arcade. It goes without saying that he was a great connoisseur, and an important patron, of the arts, but he was also an accomplished architect in his own right, fascinated—obsessed even—by the architecture and art of the Italian Renaissance and ancient Rome, with which he'd fallen in love during his Italian grand tour (every well-bred boy's rite of passage). Along with William Kent (1685–1748), who designed the interiors and the rambling gardens here, Burlington did an awful lot to disseminate the Palladian ideals around Britain: Chiswick House sparked enormous interest, and you'll see these forms reflected in hundreds of subsequent English stately homes both small and large. ✉ *Burlington La.,* ☎ *0181/995–0508.* 🎟 *£2.50.* ⏲ *Apr.–Sept., daily 10–6; Oct.–Mar., daily 10–4; closed 1 hr at lunch and Dec. 25–26, Jan. 1. Tube: Turnham Green.*

Hogarth's House. This is where the painter lived from 1749 until his death in 1764. Unprotected from the six-lane Great West Road, which remains a main route to the West Country, the poor house is besieged by the surrounding traffic, but is worth visiting for its little museum consisting mostly of the amusingly moralistic engravings for which Hogarth is best known, including the most famous one of all, *The Rake's Progress* series of 1735. ✉ *Hogarth La.,* ☎ *0181/994–6757.* 🎟 *Free.* ⏲ *Apr.–Sept., Mon.–Sat. 11–6, Sun. 2–6; Oct.–Mar., Mon.–Sat. 11–4, Sun. 2–4; closed Good Friday, first 3 wks of Sept., last 3 wks of Dec., Jan. 1. Tube: Turnham Green.*

Kew Gardens. The Royal Botanic Gardens at Kew are a spectacular 300 acres of public gardens, containing more than 60,000 species of plants. In addition, this is the country's leading botanical institute, with strong royal associations. Until 1840, when Kew Gardens was handed over to the nation, it had been the grounds of two royal residences: the White House (formerly Kew House), and Richmond Lodge, or the Dutch House. George II and Queen Caroline lived at Richmond Lodge in the 1720s, while their eldest son, Frederick, Prince of Wales, and his wife, Princess Augusta, came to the White House during the 1730s. The royal wives were keen gardeners. Queen Caroline got to work on her grounds, while next door Frederick's pleasure garden was developed as a botanic garden by his widow after his death. She introduced all kinds of "exotics," foreign plants brought back to England by botanists. Caroline was aided by a skilled head gardener and by the architect Sir William Chambers, who built a series of temples and follies, of which the crazy 10-story **Pagoda** (1762), visible for miles around, is the star turn. The celebrated botanist Sir Joseph Banks (1743–1820) then took charge of Kew, which developed rapidly in both its roles—as a beautiful landscaped garden, and as a center of study and research.

The highlights of a visit to Kew are the two great 19th-century greenhouses filled with tropical plants, many of which have been there as long as their housing. Both the **Palm House** and the **Temperate House** were designed by Sir Decimus Burton, the first opening in 1848, the second in 1899 (though it had been begun 40 years earlier). The older Palm House, with its ornate cast-iron supports and curvaceous glass walls, is generally more celebrated than the later building, although on its completion the latter was the biggest greenhouse in the world and today contains the biggest greenhouse plant in the world, a Chilean wine palm rooted in 1846. You can climb the spiral staircase almost to the roof and look down on this and the dense tropical profusion from the walkway. The **Princess of Wales Conservatory,** the latest and the largest plant house at Kew, was opened in 1987 by Princess Diana. Under its bold glass roofs, designed to maximize energy conservation, there are no less than 10 climatic zones, their temperatures all precisely controlled by computer. Within a few minutes you can move from the humid pool-and-swamp habitats, where the Amazon water lily flourishes, to the cloud-forest zone, which reproduces the conditions on the upper reaches of tropical mountains, through to the savanna of eastern Africa.

The **Centre for Economic Botany** is housed in the newly constructed Joseph Banks Building, the majority of which is devoted to Kew's research collection on economic botany and to its library. But the public can enjoy exhibitions here on the theme of plants in everyday life. (*Free. Mon.–Sat. 9:10–4:30, Sun. 9:30–5:30.*) The plant houses make Kew worth visiting even in the depths of winter, but in spring and summer the gardens come into their own. In late spring, the woodland nature reserve of Queen Charlotte's Cottage Gardens is carpeted in bluebells; a little later, the Rhododendron Dell and the Azalea Garden become swathed in brilliant color. High summer features glorious displays of roses and water lilies, while fall is the time to see the heather garden, near the pagoda. Whatever time of year you visit, something is in bloom, and your journey is never wasted. ✉ *Royal Botanic Gardens,* ☎ *0181/940–1171. £4. Gardens open at 9:30 daily, glasshouses at 10; closing time varies according to sunset, usually 4PM in winter, later in summer. Tube: Kew Gardens.*

Kew Palace. In 1802, George III, who had been brought up largely at Kew, united what were formerly two estates, knocking down the White House, which he intended to rebuild on a more lavish scale, and living in the Dutch House meanwhile. But George was, famously, losing his reason, and the new palace never got built. The Dutch House became known as Kew Palace and remains to this day quietly domestic. The little formal gardens to its rear were redeveloped in 1969 as a 17th-century garden. These, too, are a pleasure to see, with their trim hedges, statuary, and carefully laid-out plants and flowers. ✉ *Kew Gardens.* ☎ *0181/940–3321. £1. Apr.–Sept., daily 11–5:30.*

NEED A BREAK?

Maids of Honour (✉ 288 Kew Rd.), the most traditional of Olde Worlde English tearooms, is named for the famous tarts invented here and still baked by hand on the premises. It's only open for tea from Tuesday through Saturday, 2:45–5:30.

Osterley Park

You reach Osterly Park by getting off the Piccadilly Line five stops before Heathrow Airport, then making a 15-minute walk from the station. A unique hybrid of Tudor and 18th-century architecture, Osterley was built in the 1560s, then tinkered with extensively by Robert Adam two centuries later. The result is a Tudor brick mansion with a pepper-pot tower at each corner and a sweeping central staircase leading to an incongruous Doric-columned doorway with a carved pediment. The inside is maximum Adam, down to much of the furniture. The architect himself described it as being all "delicacy, gaiety, grace, and beauty," with "fanciful figures and winding foliage." Sir Horace Walpole, on the other hand, found much of it "too theatric"—an attribute rather in its favor if you don't have to live in it but are just visiting. The outrageously elaborate neo-Gothic blue, green, and gold ceiling (with matching frilly window blinds and handloomed carpet) in the Drawing Room, and the all-over fresco work of the Etruscan Room ("like Wedgwood's vase," said Walpole) are nothing if not arresting. When it all gets to be too much, you can retire to the gardens, designed by William Chambers (who was responsible for much of Kew Gardens, too), with an Adam greenhouse. ✉ *Isleworth,* ☎ *0181/560–3918.* 🎟 *£3.65.* ⏲ *Apr.–Oct., Wed.–Sat. 1–5, Sun. 11–5; closed Nov.–Mar. Tube: Osterley.*

Richmond

Named after the palace Henry VII built here in 1500, Richmond is still a welcoming and extremely pretty riverside "village" with many handsome (and mountainously expensive) houses, many antiques shops, a Victorian theater, and, best of all, the biggest of London's royal parks.

Sights to See

Ham House. Ham House stands to the west of Richmond Park, overlooking the Thames and nearly opposite the oddly named Eel Pie Island. The house was built in 1610 by Sir Thomas Vavasour, knight marshal to James I, then refurbished later the same century by the Duke and Duchess of Lauderdale, who, although not particularly nice (a contemporary called the duchess "the coldest friend and the most violent enemy that ever was known"), managed to produce one of the finest houses in Britain at the time. Now that £2 million has been sunk into restoring Ham House—a project overseen by the National Trust—its splendor can be appreciated afresh. The formerly empty library has been filled with 17th- and 18th-century volumes; the original decorations in the Great Hall, Round Gallery, and Great Staircase have been replicated; and all the furniture and fittings, on permanent loan from the V&A, have been cleaned and restored. The 17th-century gardens, too, merit a visit in their own right. You can reach Ham from Richmond on Bus 65 or 371, or by one of Greater London's most pleasant rural walks, along the eastern riverbank south from Richmond Bridge, of half an hour or so. ✉ *Ham St., Richmond,* ☎ *0181/940–1950.* 🎟 *£4; admission to gardens free.* ⏲ *Mar.–Oct., Sat.–Wed. 1–5; Nov.–Dec., weekends 1–5. Closed Jan.–Feb. Tube: Richmond.*

Marble Hill House. On the northern bank of the Thames, almost opposite Ham House, stands another mansion, this one a near-perfect example of a Palladian villa. Marble Hill House was built during the 1720s by George II for his mistress, the "exceedingly respectable and respected" Henrietta Howard. Later the house was occupied by Mrs. Fitzherbert, who was secretly married to the Prince Regent (later George IV) in 1785. Marble Hill House was restored in 1901 and opened to the public two years later, looking very much like it did in Georgian times. A ferry service operates during the summer from Ham House across the river; access by foot is via a half-hour walk south along the west bank from Richmond Bridge. ✉ *Richmond Rd., Twickenham,* ☎ *0181/892–5115.* 🎟 *Free.* ⏲ *Easter–Sept., daily 10–6; Oct.–Easter, daily 10–4; closed Dec. 24–25, Jan. 1. Tube: Richmond.*

Richmond Park. Charles I enclosed this one in 1637 for hunting purposes, as with practically all the parks. Unlike the others, however, Richmond Park still has wild red and fallow deer roaming its 2,470 acres of grassland and heath, among the oldest oaks you're likely to see—vestiges of the medieval forests that once encroached on London from all sides. White Lodge, inside the park, was built for George II in 1729. Edward VIII was born here; now it houses the Royal Ballet School. You can walk from the park past the fine 18th-century houses in and around Richmond Hill to the river, admiring first the view from the top. At the Thames, you may notice Quinlan Terry's recent Richmond Riverside development, which met with the approval of England's architectural advisor, Prince Charles, for its classical facades, and was vilified by many others for playing it safe. *Tube: Richmond.*

Anne Boleyn's Gateway, **3**
Banqueting House, **26**
Cartoon Gallery, **13**
Chapel Royal, **18**
Communication Gallery, **14**
Flowerpot Garden, **30**
George II Gateway, **4**
Great Fountain Garden, **23**
Great Gatehouse, **2**
Great Hall, **20**
Haunted Gallery, **17**
Henry VII's Great Watching Chamber, **19**
King's Rooms, **8**
King's Staircase, **6**
Knot & Pond Gardens, **27**
Lion Gates, **33**
Lower Orangery, **28**
Main Entrance, **1**
The Maze, **32**
Prince of Wales' Staircase, **12**
Prince of Wales' Suite, **11**
Privy Garden, **24**
Public Dining Room, **10**
Queen's Rooms, **9**
Queen's Staircase, **16**
Renaissance Picture Gallery, **22**
State Apartments Entrance, **5**
State Apartments Exit, **21**
Tennis Court, **29**
Tijou Ironwork Screen, **25**
Tiltyard Gardens, **34**
Wilderness, **31**
Wolsey Rooms, **7**

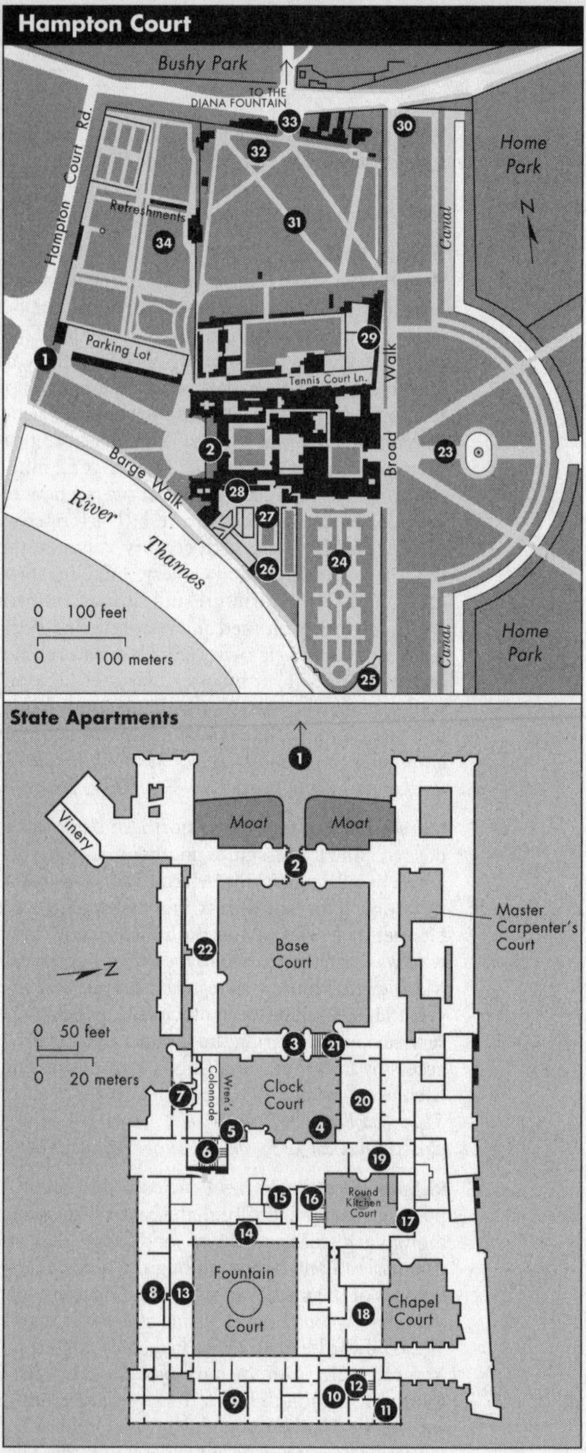

NEED A BREAK? The **Cricketers** on Richmond Green serves a good pub lunch. The modern, partially glass-roofed **Caffé Mamma,** on Hill Street, serves inexpensive Italian food. **Beeton's,** on Hill Rise, offers a good, traditional English breakfast, lunch, and afternoon tea, as well as proper dinners.

Hampton Court Palace

Hampton Court. Some 20 miles from central London, on a loop of the Thames upstream from Richmond, lies one of London's oldest royal palaces, more like a small town in size, and requiring a day of your time to do it justice. The magnificent Tudor brick house was begun in 1514 by Cardinal Wolsey, the ambitious and worldly lord chancellor (roughly, prime minister) of England and archbishop of York. He wanted it to be the absolute best palace in the land, and in this he succeeded so effectively that Henry VIII grew deeply envious, whereupon Wolsey felt obliged to give Hampton Court to the king. Henry moved in in 1525, adding a great hall and chapel, and proceeded to live much of his rumbustious life here. James I made further improvements at the beginning of the 17th century, but by the end of the century the palace was getting rather run-down. Plans were drawn up by the joint monarchs William III and Mary II to demolish the building and replace it with a still larger and more splendid structure in conscious emulation of the great palace of Versailles outside of Paris. However, the royal purse wouldn't stretch quite that far. It was decided to keep the original buildings but add a new complex adjoining them at the rear, for which Wren was commissioned, and his graceful South Wing is one of the highlights of the whole palace. (A serious fire badly damaged some of Wren's chambers in 1986, but they were restored and opened again in 1992, with some of the Tudor features he had covered up uncovered again.) William and, especially, Mary loved Hampton Court and left their mark on the place—see their fine collections of Delftware and other porcelain.

The site beside the slow-moving Thames is perfect. The palace itself, steeped in history, hung with priceless paintings, full of echoing cobbled courtyards and cavernous Tudor kitchens, complete with deer pies and cooking pots—not to mention the ghost of Catherine Howard, who is still abroad, screaming her innocence (of adultery) to an unheeding Henry VIII—is set in a fantastic array of ornamental gardens, lakes, and ponds. Among the horticultural highlights are an Elizabethan Knot Garden, Henry VIII's Pond Garden, the enormous conical yews around the Fountain Garden, and the Great Vine near the Banqueting House, planted in 1768 and still producing Black Hamburg grapes, which you can buy in season. Best of all is the celebrated maze, which you enter to the north of the palace. It was planted in 1714 and is truly fiendish.

Royalty ceased living here with George III; poor George preferred the seclusion of Kew, where he was finally confined in his madness. The private apartments that range down one side of the palace are now occupied by pensioners of the Crown. Known as "grace and favor" apartments, they are among the most coveted homes in the country, with a surfeit of peace and history on their doorsteps. ✉ *East Molesey,* ☎ *0181/977–8441.* 🎟 *Apartments and maze: £7.50; maze only: £1.75; grounds free.* ⏲ *State apartments: Apr.–Oct., Tues.–Sun. 9:30–6, Mon. 10:15–6; Nov.–Mar., Tues.–Sun. 9:30–4:30, Mon. 10:15–4:30; grounds: daily 8–dusk. Closed Good Friday, Dec. 24–25, Jan. 1.*

3 Lodging

MAKE NO MISTAKE, London hotels are expensive. The city has a peculiar dearth of the pleasant, medium-priced hotels that other European capitals have no difficulty supplying. Grand hotels London has got (and, at the other end of the scale, seedy lodging houses that you will not find in these pages), but modest, family-run hotels tend to inflate their rates a few notches above what one would expect in, say, Paris or Madrid. There's nothing for it but to resign yourself to spending the greater part of your budget on a bed—or investigate the B&Bs at the end of this chapter.

Our rating system is based simply on price, and does not itself indicate the quality of the hotel, although we have been at pains to select ones whose caliber is tried and tested. Our price categories are based on the average room cost, and you should note that in some establishments, especially those in the $$$$ category, you could pay considerably more—well past the £200 mark in some cases. Like hotels in most other European countries, British hotels are obliged by law to display a tariff at the reception desk. If you have not booked ahead, you are strongly advised to study this carefully.

The general custom these days in all but the bottom end of the scale is for rates to be quoted for the room alone (which unless otherwise noted is with bath); breakfast, whether Continental or "Full English," comes at extra cost. VAT is usually included, and service, too, in nearly all cases. All the hotels listed here are graded according to their spring 1996 rates, so check for the latest figures, remembering, of course, that there can be a significant difference off-season.

Be sure to make reservations well in advance, as seasonal events, trade shows, or royal occasions can fill hotel rooms for sudden brief periods, and, of course, during highly touristed July and August, too. Thinking ahead also allows you to investigate the various U.S.-based membership programs that offer discount travel in Europe, including on London hotel rooms at a savings of up to 50%. Try **Privilege Card International** (☎ 800/236–9732), Entertainment Publications' **Europe Hotel Directory** (☎ 800/445–4137), or **RMC Travel Centre** (☎ 800/782–2674). If you do manage to arrive in the capital without a room, the **London Tourist Board Information Centres** at Heathrow and Victoria Station Forecourt can help; or call the **LTB Accommodation Sales Service** (☎ 0171/824–8844, weekdays 9:30–5:30) for prepaid credit-card bookings (MC, V).

CATEGORY	COST*
$$$$	over £180
$$$	£120–£180
$$	£70–£120
$	under £70

**All prices are for a double room; VAT included.*

Mayfair to Regent's Park

$$$$ ▣ **Athenaeum.** This well-loved baby grand opposite Green Park received a new lease on life when it was sold to independent owners about four years ago. The welcome here is in the details: from Donald, the super-concierge at his doorside desk, to the disposable camera, Japanese rice crackers, and teddy bear (twee, but they get away with it) in the minibar, to the compact Health Spa with whirlpool, steam room and sauna, cardio and freeweight equipment, and masseuse. Rooms retain the distinctive custom-made leather-topped mahogany and yew furniture, now set against navy-and-cream checkered drapes, Wedgwood green walls, and thick, thick cream carpets. Without getting out of bed, you can control lighting and temperature, order free videos and CDs, and listen to your voice mail from your two phone lines. Also—hallelujah—there's a *real* hair dryer, and an outlet by the mirror (there's also a U.S. voltage outlet). In glittering gray marble bathrooms are power showers, mirrors angled to get the back of your head, and old-fashioned Bronnley toiletries; downstairs, there's the cozy Whisky Bar, famed for its 70 single malts, and the not too formal Bullochs restaurant (☞ Chapter 5, Restaurants and Pubs). Rooms 201–205 face Green Park; others have a bay that affords a partial, angled view. ✉ *116 Piccadilly, W1V 0BJ, ☎ 0171/499–3464, FAX 0171/493–1860. 123 rooms. Restaurant, bar, in-room VCR and CD players, health club (no pool). AE, DC, MC, V. Tube: Green Park.*

$$$$ **Brown's.** Founded in 1837 by Lord Byron's "gentleman's gentleman," James Brown, this Victorian country house in central Mayfair comprises 11 Georgian houses and is occupied by many Anglophile Americans—a habit that was established by the two Roosevelts (Teddy while on honeymoon). Bedrooms feature thick carpets, soft armchairs, sweeping drapes, brass chandeliers, and moiré or brocade wallpapers, as well as, in the newly refitted ones, air-conditioning, while the public rooms retain their cozy oak-paneled, chintz-laden, grandfather-clock-ticking-in-the-parlor ambience. Right outside the door are the boutiques and art galleries of Bond and Cork streets, while in the lounge, one of London's best-known afternoon teas is served from 3 to 6. This, plus several more of London's top hotels, belonged to the Forte group, which had just been bought out by catering giant, Granada, at press time. ✉ *34 Albemarle St., W1A 4SW, ☎ 0171/493–6020, FAX 0171/493–9381. 132 rooms. Restaurant, bar. AE, DC, MC, V. Tube: Green Park.*

$$$$ ★ **Claridges.** Stay here, and you're staying at a hotel legend, with one of the world's classiest guest lists. The liveried staff are friendly and not in the least condescending, and the rooms are never less than luxurious. It was founded in 1812, but present decor is either 1930s Art Deco or country-house traditional. Have a drink in the Foyer lounge (24 hours a day) with its Hungarian mini-orchestra, or retreat to the reading room for perfect quiet, interrupted only by the sound of pages turning. The bedrooms are spacious, as are the bathrooms, with their enormous shower heads and bells (which still work) to summon either "maid" or "valet" from their station on each floor. Beds are handmade and supremely comfortable—the King of Morocco once brought his own, couldn't sleep, and ended up ordering 30 from Claridges to take home. The grand staircase and magnificent elevator are equally impressive. ✉ *Brook St., W1A 2JQ, ☎ 0171/629–8860 or 800/223–6800, FAX 0171/499–2210. 200 rooms. 2 restaurants, beauty salon. AE, DC, MC, V. Tube: Bond Street.*

$$$$ ★ **Connaught.** Make reservations well in advance for this *very* exclusive, small hotel just off Grosvenor Square. The bar and lounges have the air of an ambassadorial residence, an impression reinforced by the imposing oak staircase and dignified staff. Each bedroom has a foyer, antique furniture (if you don't like the desk, they'll change it), and fresh flowers, and the management is above such vulgarities as brochure and tariff—which would be extraneous for guests who inherited the Connaught from their great-grandfathers, anyway. If you value privacy, discretion, and the kind of luxury that eschews labels, then you have met your match here. For a preview of the hotel's style, lunch at its famous Grill or Restaurant (book well ahead), where waiters speak only when spoken to (☞ Chapter 5, Restaurants and Pubs). ✉ *Carlos Pl., W1Y*

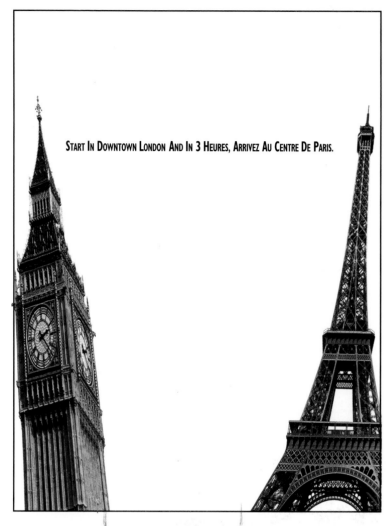

6AL, ☎ 0171/499–7070, FAX 0171/495–3262. 90 rooms. Restaurant, bar. MC. Tube: Bond Street.

$$$$ ★ **The Dorchester.** A London institution since its 1931 inception (apart from a break in continuity for its complete refurbishment in 1990), the Dorchester appears on every "World's Best" list. The glamour level is off the scale: 1,500 square meters of gold leaf, 1,100 of marble, and 2,300 of hand-tufted carpet gild this lily, and bedrooms (some not as spacious as you might imagine) feature Irish linen sheets on canopied beds, brocades and velvets, Italian marble and etched glass bathrooms with Floris goodies, individual climate control, dual voltage outlets, and cable TV. There's a beauty spa, run by Elizabeth Arden, a nightclub, the Oriental and Terrace restaurants, plus the well-known power-dining Grill Room. Afternoon tea, drinking, lounging, and posing are all accomplished in the catwalk-shape Promenade lounge, where you may spot one of the film-star types who will stay nowhere else. Probably no other hotel this opulent manages to be this charming. ✉ *Park La., W1A 2HJ, ☎ 0171/629–8888, FAX 0171/409–0114. 197 rooms, 55 suites. 3 restaurants, bar, health club (no pool), nightclub, business services, meeting rooms, ballroom, theater ticket desk. AE, DC, MC, V. Tube: Marble Arch.*

$$$$ ★ **47 Park Street.** Secreted back to back with the grand hotels of Park Lane, this dear (in every sense) little all-suite hotel has the best room service in town, with 24-hour food direct from the kitchen of Le Gavroche (☞ Chapter 5, Restaurants and Pubs). The hotel shares its bar with that poshest of posh dining establishments, too, which means there's a jacket-and-tie requirement for your quiet nightcap. Bathrooms are on the small side, but no other drawbacks are apparent in this fabulously discreet, exquisitely decorated, quiet, relaxed, and homey haven, as long as you can afford it. One woman who could afford it liked it so much that she's still there—five years later. ✉ *47 Park St., W1Y 4EB, ☎ 0171/491–7282, FAX 0171/491–7281. 52 suites with kitchen. Private dining room, bar (jacket and tie required), baby-sitting. AE, DC, MC, V. Tube: Marble Arch.*

$$$$ **Four Seasons.** The discretion of this beautifully situated (opposite Hyde Park, off the end of Piccadilly, but tucked away), understated hotel inspires more-than-average loyalty in its guests, which have included Howard Hughes, but most of whom, these days, are business travelers. Like some others in this ever-expanding upper class chain, it's particularly child-friendly too, supplying a "VIK" (Very Important Kid) package of games, videos, books, and baby-sitting. The bedrooms are extremely comfortable, with gigantic beds; the bathrooms have plenty of extras. One extra nonguests can also enjoy is the Four Seasons restaurant, which has lost one star chef, Bruno Loubet, only to gain another, Jean-Christophe Novelli—even younger, and just as bright (☞ Chapter 5, Restaurants and Pubs). There's also a less formal restaurant, Lane's, open from early till late. ✉ *Hamilton Pl., Park La., W1A 1AZ, ☎ 0171/499–0888 or 800/223–6800, FAX 0171/493–6629. 228 rooms. 2 restaurants, health club. AE, DC, MC, V. Tube: Hyde Park Corner.*

$$$$ **Grosvenor House.** "The old lady of Park Lane" had settled happily back into top-dowager position, having thrown off her creeping frumpiness during a complete overhaul, only to have her future thrown into doubt once more by the selling of parent company, Forte (☞ Brown's, *above*). It's still not the kind of place that encourages hushed whispers or that frowns on jeans, despite the marble floors and wood-paneled "library," open fires, oils, and fine antiques, all inspired by the Earl of Grosvenor's residence, which occupied the site during the 18th century. The hotel health club is just about the best around, especially since the gym part was completely redone in 1995 (the pool didn't need any

London Lodging *(Boxes Refer to Detail Maps)*

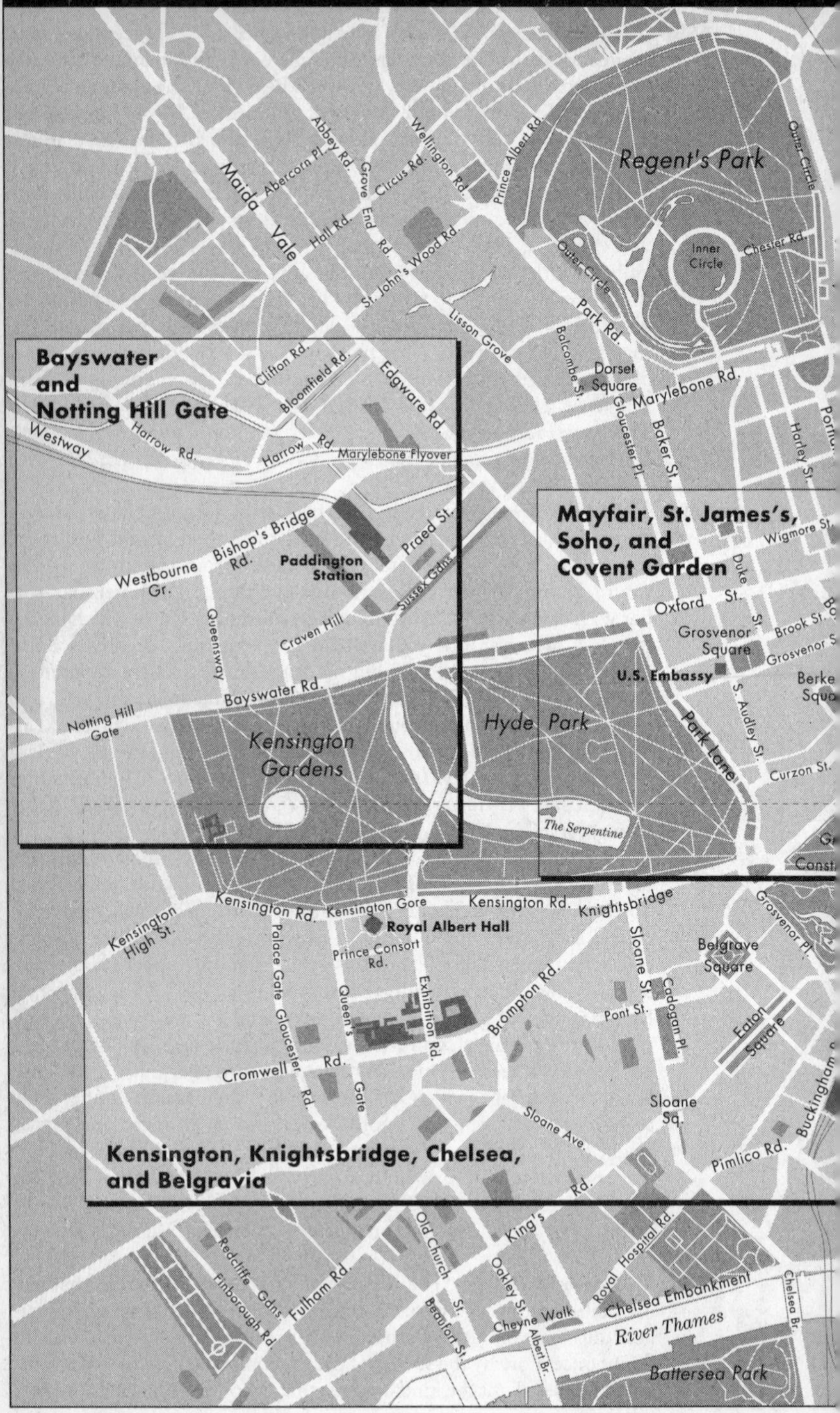
Regent's Park
Inner Circle
Outer Circle
Chester Rd.
Park Rd.
Maida Vale
Abercorn Pl.
Abbey Rd.
Grove End Rd.
Circus Rd.
Wellington Rd.
Prince Albert Rd.
Hall Rd.
St. John's Wood Rd.
Lisson Grove
Balcombe St.
Dorset Square
Gloucester Pl.
Baker St.
Marylebone Rd.
Harley St.
Bayswater and Notting Hill Gate
Clifton Rd.
Bloomfield Rd.
Edgware Rd.
Westway
Harrow Rd.
Marylebone Flyover
Bishop's Bridge Rd.
Westbourne Gr.
Paddington Station
Praed St.
Sussex Gdns.
Queensway
Craven Hill
Bayswater Rd.
Notting Hill Gate
Kensington Gardens
Hyde Park
The Serpentine
Mayfair, St. James's, Soho, and Covent Garden
Wigmore St.
Duke St.
Oxford St.
Grosvenor Square
Brook St.
Grosvenor St.
U.S. Embassy
S. Audley St.
Park Lane
Curzon St.
Kensington Rd.
Kensington Gore
Royal Albert Hall
Knightsbridge
Kensington High St.
Palace Gate
Gloucester Rd.
Prince Consort Rd.
Queen's Gate
Exhibition Rd.
Cromwell Rd.
Brompton Rd.
Sloane St.
Cadogan Pl.
Pont St.
Belgrave Square
Grosvenor Pl.
Eaton Square
Sloane Sq.
Sloane Ave.
Pimlico Rd.
Buckingham
Kensington, Knightsbridge, Chelsea, and Belgravia
King's Rd.
Redcliffe Gdns.
Finborough Rd.
Fulham Rd.
Old Church St.
Beaufort St.
Oakley St.
Cheyne Walk
Albert Br.
Royal Hospital Rd.
Chelsea Embankment
Chelsea Br.
River Thames
Battersea Park

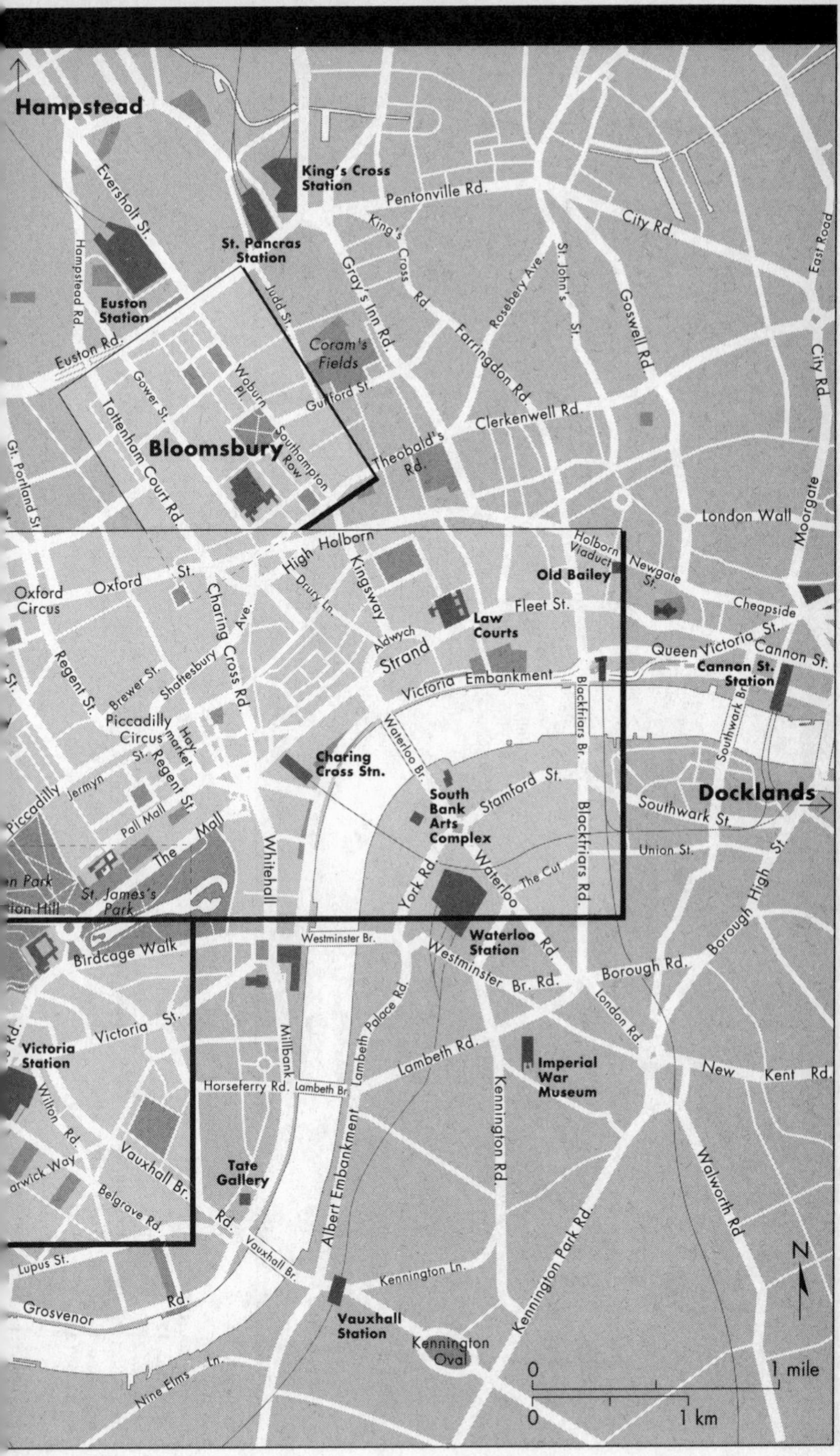
Hampstead
King's Cross Station
Pentonville Rd.
City Rd.
East Road
St. Pancras Station
Eversholt St.
Hampstead Rd.
Euston Station
Euston Rd.
Judd St.
Gray's Inn Rd.
King's Cross Rd.
Rosebery Ave.
St. John's St.
Goswell Rd.
City Rd.
Coram's Fields
Farringdon Rd.
Gower St.
Woburn Pl.
Guilford St.
Clerkenwell Rd.
Tottenham Court Rd.
Bloomsbury
Southampton Row
Theobald's Rd.
Gt. Portland St.
London Wall
Moorgate
High Holborn
Holborn Viaduct
Newgate St.
Old Bailey
Oxford Circus
Oxford St.
Charing Cross Rd.
Drury Ln.
Kingsway
Fleet St.
Cheapside
Law Courts
Aldwych
Strand
Queen Victoria St.
Cannon St.
Cannon St. Station
Regent St.
Brewer St.
Shaftesbury Ave.
Victoria Embankment
Blackfriars Br.
Southwark Br.
Piccadilly Circus
Haymarket
Regent St.
Waterloo Br.
Charing Cross Stn.
Piccadilly
Jermyn St.
South Bank Arts Complex
Stamford St.
Docklands
Pall Mall
The Mall
Southwark St.
Blackfriars Rd.
Union St.
Whitehall
Waterloo Rd.
The Cut
York Rd.
St. James's Park
Westminster Br.
Waterloo Station
Borough High St.
Birdcage Walk
Westminster Br. Rd.
Borough Rd.
London Rd.
Victoria St.
Victoria Station
Millbank
Lambeth Palace Rd.
Lambeth Rd.
Imperial War Museum
New Kent Rd.
Horseferry Rd.
Lambeth Br.
Wilton Rd.
Kennington Rd.
Warwick Way
Vauxhall Br. Rd.
Albert Embankment
Tate Gallery
Walworth Rd.
Belgrave Rd.
Kennington Park Rd.
Vauxhall Br.
N
Lupus St.
Kennington Ln.
Grosvenor Rd.
Vauxhall Station
Kennington Oval
Nine Elms Ln.
0
1 mile
0
1 km

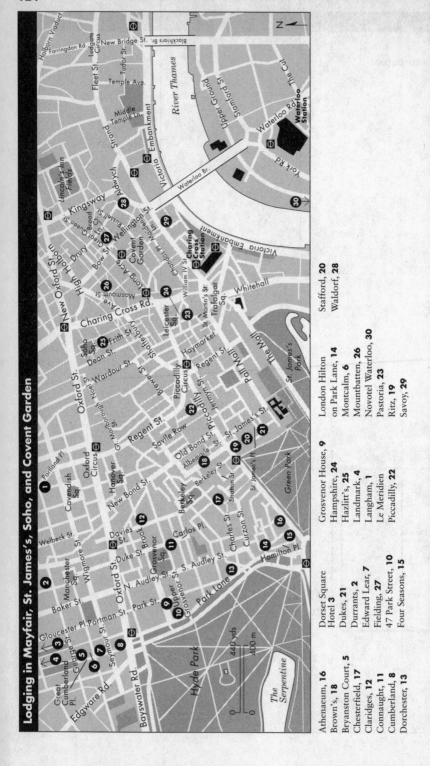

Lodging in Mayfair, St. James's, Soho, and Covent Garden

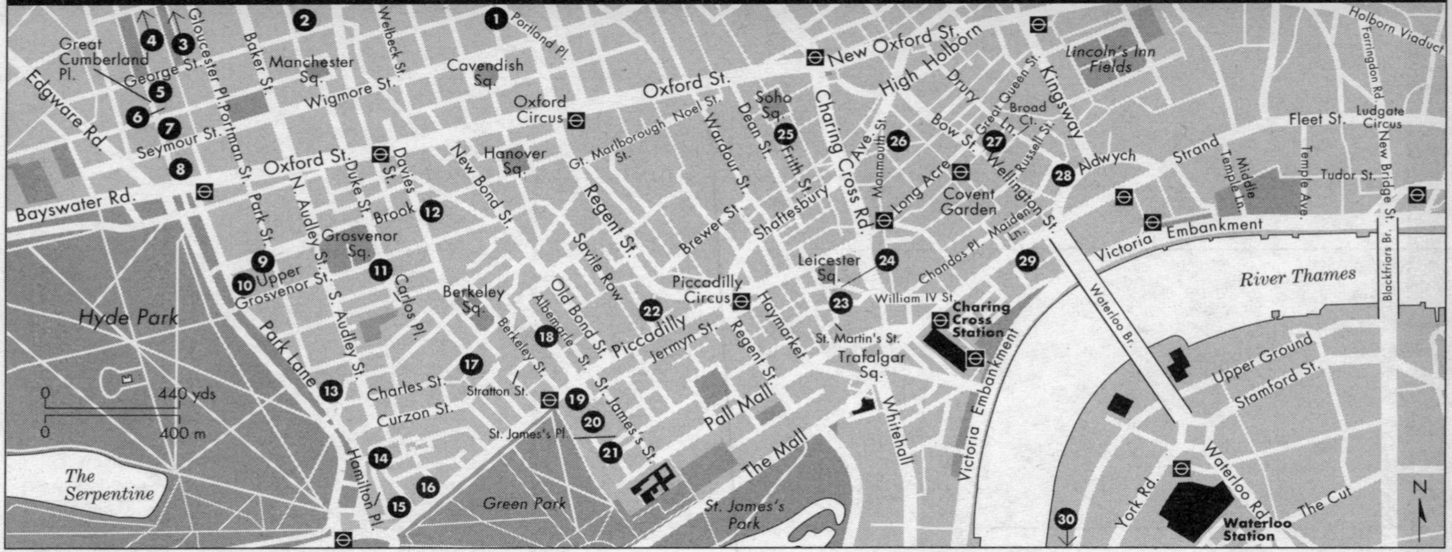

Athenaeum, **16**	Dorset Square Hotel **3**	Grosvenor House, **9**	London Hilton on Park Lane, **14**	Stafford, **20**
Brown's, **18**	Dukes, **21**	Hampshire, **24**	Montcalm, **6**	Waldorf, **28**
Bryanston Court, **5**	Durrants, **2**	Hazlitt's, **25**	Mountbatten, **26**	
Chesterfield, **17**	Edward Lear, **7**	Landmark, **4**	Novotel Waterloo, **30**	
Claridges, **12**	Fielding, **27**	Langham, **1**	Pastoria, **23**	
Connaught, **11**	47 Park Street, **10**	Le Meridien Piccadilly, **22**	Ritz, **19**	
Cumberland, **8**	Four Seasons, **15**		Savoy, **29**	
Dorchester, **13**				

help). Bedrooms are spacious, and most of the freshly glamorized big marble bathrooms have natural light. ✉ *Park La., W1A 3AA,* ☎ *0171/499–6363,* FAX *0171/493–3341. 360 rooms, 70 suites. 3 restaurants, bar, indoor pool, health club, banquet suites, ballroom, theater ticket desk. AE, DC, MC, V. Tube: Marble Arch.*

$$$$ **Hampshire.** Leicester Square is next to all the theaters, big movie houses, and clubs—and so, therefore, is the Hampshire. Though built in 1899 to house the Royal Dental Hospital, virtually all that's left of the original structure is the elegant Edwardian facade. But a very reliable small chain called Edwardian Hotels was responsible for fixing the interior, and the place is done out in their trademark "gracious country house" style, with open fires, dark wood, and, in this one, a fair bit of Chinoiserie. There are six rooms and two suites with four-poster beds, and 42 studios with seating areas and huge, magnificently equipped bathrooms. Try for one of the rooms in the front of the hotel, overlooking the square, as they are the largest. This location would suit a shopping spree or theater crawl. ✉ *31 Leicester Sq., WC2H 7LH,* ☎ *0171/839–9399,* FAX *0171/930–8122. 124 rooms. Restaurant, bar. AE, DC, MC, V. Tube: Leicester Square.*

$$$$ **The Landmark.** A year older than the century, the onetime Great Central Hotel and former BritRail HQ is London's newest luxury hotel—and a most elegantly understated place it is, too. A palm-filled, eight-story glazed atrium "Winter Garden" forms the core, and odd-numbered rooms overlook this. If size matters to you, note that even standard rooms here are among the largest in London and with their glamorous bathrooms in marble and chrome, complete with robe and hair dryer. Despite appearances, this is the only London grand hotel that doesn't force you to dress up—even jeans are okay. The Landmark is very near Regent's Park; the West End is a 15-minute walk away. ✉ *222 Marylebone Rd., NW1 6JQ,* ☎ *0171/631–8000,* FAX *0171/631–8080. 309 rooms. Restaurant, 2 bars, indoor pool, health club, business center. AE, DC, MC, V. Tube: Marylebone.*

$$$$ **Langham.** A historic hotel reconstructed, renovated, and reopened by Hilton Hotels in 1991 (though up for sale at press time), the Langham is certainly an impressive landmark from the outside, especially at night with its fairy-tale floodlighting. Inside, the lobby has varnished white marble floors and sandblasted stone walls, and there are two theme restaurants (one Raj, one Czarist Russia), a Chukka Bar (polo is in this year), and a Palm Court serving tea with a little piano tinkling. Proportions are grand, but you could be in Disney's London; the only clues to the past are in the punctuation: a preserved ironwork "LH" motif and assembly-line prints of the old city. Standard bedrooms are generic deluxe, medium-size, and very pale peach; only the more expensive, larger front ones have the good view over Portland Place to the park, as well as a snazzier decor, wishfully referred to as French provincial. Marble bathroom, robe, trouser press, and hair dryer are standard issue. ✉ *1C Portland Pl., W1N 3AA,* ☎ *0171/636–1000,* FAX *0171/323–2340. 410 rooms. 2 restaurants, bar. AE, DC, MC, V. Tube: Oxford Circus.*

$$$$ **London Hilton on Park Lane.** London's only major high-rise hotel offers fine views over Hyde Park—when you can see through the mist—and an impressive array of facilities, including the Fitness on Five center, with personal trainers at your beck and call. Public areas are glitzy in white marble, topped off by an oblong of crystal chandelier; suites have been recently redecorated to bring them out of *Dynasty* territory and into the '90s. Bedrooms, too have been renovated. They're a fair size, but you may forget which city they're in—decor is uniform corporate Hiltonese. This is hardly surprising in a hostelry whose guest list is 70% business travelers, for whom there is a Clubroom on the designated Executive Floor. The top-floor Windows Roof Restaurant, known for the view, is making a culinary effort with a new French chef, but hokey old Trader Vic's on the ground floor is still cranking out those lurid, soup tureen–size cocktails. ✉ *22 Park La., W1A 2HH,* ☎ *0171/493–8000,* FAX *0171/493–4957. 448 rooms. Restaurant, beauty salon, health club, baby-sitting, laundry service, business services, travel services, theater ticket desk. AE, DC, MC, V. Tube: Hyde Park Corner.*

$$$$ **Le Meridien Piccadilly.** The massive, turn-of-the-century building is fin de siècle elegant, if slightly antiseptic in its white marble and plush carpet public areas. The vast Oak Room restaurant, however, is exquisite in limed oak paneling and gilt, and it is (yes, another) one of the best hotel restaurants in London. The hotel's second restaurant, far less formal, is a miniature Kew Gardens of arched glass, ferns, and palms. Bedrooms vary ridiculously in size, though most are on the small side; others are very large indeed, and a few seventh-floor ones have balconies overlooking Piccadilly. Decor is Edwardian gent's club with frills. The health club is the most luxurious and exclusive in London and boasts squash courts, saunas, and billiard tables, as well as a swimming pool. You can't be more central than here. ✉ *Piccadilly, W1V 0BH,* ☎ *0171/734–8000,* FAX *0171/437–3574. 284 rooms. 3 restaurants, bar, indoor pool, health club, library, business services. AE, DC, MC, V. Tube: Piccadilly Circus.*

$$$$ **The Montcalm.** Secreted behind Marble Arch in a peaceful Georgian crescent, the Montcalm has kept a low profile since its rock star days (when the Jackson 5, Stevie Wonder, and Elton John favored it above all other London grands), but it is now back up there with the best of them, after a major, and ongoing, refurbishment by the Japanese owners, Nikko, who have made it an especially efficient, spotless and calm hotel, with some unusual features. Here is London's only low-allergen bedroom, its only canopied waterbed (not in the same room), and one of its few Japanese breakfasts; here are toilets with electronic air dryers and bidets in the bathrooms, and, by the conservatory-like Crescent restaurant, a CD-operated player piano serenading lunchers with a little Brahms. The duplex suites, with their cast iron spiral staircases, are especially winning. ✉ *Great Cumberland Pl., W1A 2LF,* ☎ *0171/402–4288,* FAX *0171/724–9180. 116 rooms. Restaurant, bar, meeting rooms. AE, DC, MC, V. Tube: Marble Arch.*

$$$ **Chesterfield.** This former town house of the Earl of Chesterfield is popular with American visitors, many of whom are repeat guests or have links with the English Speaking Union, which has its headquarters next door. It is deep in the heart of Mayfair and has welcoming, wood-and-leather public rooms and spacious bedrooms. The staff is outstandingly pleasant and helpful. ✉ *35 Charles St., W1X 8LX,* ☎ *0171/491–2622,* FAX *0171/491–4793. 113 rooms. Restaurant. AE, DC, MC, V. Tube: Green Park.*

$$$ **Cumberland.** This huge, busy hotel (built in 1933, with some Art Deco features on the facade and in the public areas) is double-glazed to counter the traffic noise of Oxford Street, and boasts every modern convenience, though it lacks character of any sort. Impersonal bedrooms are comfortable and well fitted, with adequate bathrooms. The hotel's restaurants—a carvery, a café, a Japanese restaurant, and a fourth, Austen's—serve plastic food, but there's little need to eat here when you're this centrally based. Although there are no fitness facilities in the hotel, a pool and a health club are nearby. ✉ *Marble Arch, W1A 4RF,* ☎ *0171/262–1234,* FAX *0171/724–4621. 905 rooms. 4 restaurants, 3 bars, coffee shop, beauty salon. AE, DC, MC, V. Tube: Marble Arch.*

$$$ ★ **Dorset Square Hotel.** A little more than a decade old, this special small hotel off Baker Street was the first of three London addresses for husband and wife Tim and Kit Kemp, an architect and an interior designer. What they did was decant the English country look into a fine pair of Regency town houses, then turn up the volume. Everywhere you look are covetable antiques, rich colors, and ideas *House Beautiful* subscribers will steal. Naturally, every room is different: The first-floor balconied "Coronet" ones are the largest (two have grand pianos), and a virtue is made of the smallness of the small ones. The marble and mahogany bathrooms have power showers; glossy magazines, a half-bottle of claret, and boxes of vitamin C are complimentary. Instead of minibars guests will find an "honesty bar" in the small front parlor. There's a reason for the ubiquitous cricket memorabilia: Dorset Square was the first Lord's ground. (Nowadays you can have your drinks served in the garden that still remains.) The basement bar/restaurant has cheerful frescoes, chess, and backgammon boards. ✉ *39–40 Dorset Sq., NW1 6QN,* ☎ *0171/723–7874,* FAX *0171/724–3328. 37 rooms. Bar/restaurant, car rental (vintage Bentley limousine). AE, MC, V. Tube: Baker Street.*

$$ **Bryanston Court.** Three Georgian houses have been converted into a hotel in an historic conservation area, a couple of blocks north of Hyde Park and Park Lane. The style is traditional English—open fireplaces, comfortable leather armchairs, oil portraits—though the bedrooms are small and modern, with pink furnishings, creaky floors, and minute bathrooms. Rooms at the back are quieter and face east, so they're bright in the mornings; room 77 is as big as a suite, but being on the lower ground floor typical of London houses, it's dark. This family-run hotel is excellent value for the area. ✉ *56–60 Great Cumberland Pl., W1H 7FD,* ☎ *0171/262–3141,* FAX *0171/262–7248. 56 rooms. Restaurant, bar. AE, DC, MC, V. Tube: Marble Arch.*

$$ **Durrants.** A hotel since the late 18th century, Durrants occupies a quiet corner almost next to the Wallace Collection, a stone's throw from Oxford Street and the smaller, posher shops of Marylebone High Street. It's good value for the area, and if you like ye wood-paneled, leather-armchaired, dark-red-patterned-carpeted style of olde Englishness, this will suit you. Bedrooms, by way of contrast, are wan and motel-like but perfectly adequate—a few have no bathrooms, though this disadvantage has the advantage of saving you £10 a night. Each landing harbors a communal minibar (a maxibar?) and ice machine. Best give the baron of beef-type restaurant a miss. ✉ *George St., W1H 6BH,* ☎ *0171/935–8131,* FAX *0171/487–3510. 96 rooms, 85 with bath. Restaurant, bar, dining rooms. AE, MC, V. Tube: Bond Street.*

$$ **Novotel Waterloo.** One thing often asked about London hotels is: "Where's the room with a view of the Houses of Parliament?" Well—until the former County Hall becomes a hotel next to Westminster Bridge—the answer has been: Nowhere. Not from the exorbitant Conrad in Chelsea Harbour, nor the Savoy's river rooms. . . until now. Sort of. Looking otherwise precisely like 280 other hotels in 44 countries, this French-owned, inexpensive, reliable chain hotel offers a fitness center and brasserie, conference facilities, in-room satellite TV, tea/coffee maker, direct dial phone and hair dryer in very compact rooms, plus—in 40 of them—*that* view. Actually, the view is more a flagrant grandstand spying over Lambeth Palace than a river vista, though you can see from Big Ben to St Paul's for the £5 supplement the higher rooms command. Mind you, the romance rating does plummet rather when you can't fling open the window and breathe the Thames breeze on account of the guest room climate control. ✉ *113–127 Lambeth Rd., SE1 7JL,* ☎ *0181/748–3433 (central reservations). 189 rooms. Restaurant, bar, health club, meeting rooms. AE, DC, MC, V. Tube: Waterloo.*

$ 🏨 **Edward Lear.** This is a good-value, family-run hotel in a Georgian town house, a minute's walk from Oxford Street, that used to be home to writer/artist Edward Lear (famous for his nonsense verse). Rooms vary enormously in size, with some family rooms very spacious indeed and others barely big enough to get out of bed (avoid Room 14); rooms at the back are quieter. It's a friendly place with a lot of repeat customers, but there are no hotel-type facilities (although if you want a jacket pressed you're welcome to borrow the iron), except for a lounge and the light and pleasant brick-walled breakfast room. The management is very proud of the English breakfasts—they use the same butcher as the queen. ✉ *28–30 Seymour St., W1H 5WD,* ☎ *0171/402–5401,* FAX *0171/706–3766. 31 rooms, 15 with shower (no WC), 4 with full bath. Breakfast room. MC, V. Tube: Marble Arch.*

St. James's

$$$$ 🏨 **The Ritz.** Management of the Ritz was assumed in 1994 by the enormously respected Mandarin Oriental Group, which had yet to break into Europe. Mandarin has not altered the palatial (as in Versailles) Belle Epoque decor: Not in the Palm Court, with its cranberry velvet chairs, statuary, fluted columns, and greenery, nor in the resplendent dining room which, with its frescoes, gilding, and Italian Garden, is generally thought the prettiest in town. Bedrooms, too, remain as César Ritz prescribed—white pilasters and moldings on sorbet paintwork; antique bureaus; specially commissioned brass beds (17 of these remain); reproduction bronze figurines on the mantle, huge mirrors above it; heavy brocades, and linens embroidered with "R"—but they are getting rigorous refreshment, and (especially where the original marble baths were tragically ripped out) new bathrooms. Big work started early in 1996, including the addition of a much-needed health club. Don't forget to check out the cozy, tiny, secret Rivoli Lounge up the curved staircase off Reception. ✉ *Piccadilly, W1V 9DG,* ☎ *0171/493–8181,* FAX *0171/493–2687. 129 rooms. Restaurant, bar, baby-sitting. AE, DC, MC, V. Tube: Green Park.*

$$$$ 🏨 **The Stafford.** The unique features here in ascending order of importance: The American Bar, where a million ties, baseball caps, and toy planes depend from a ceiling modeled, presumably, on New York's "21" Club, and where Charles (who claims the first dry martini: see the Savoy) has been mixing for 35 years; and the 12 Carriage House rooms, installed in the 18th-century stable block, with their own cobbled mews entrances. Although these feel fake-18th century inside, with gas log fires, peculiar windowpane check carpets, mahogany repro cabinets, black-stained exposed beams, and floral-sprigged drapes, they are very cute and private, and have extra 20th-century features, such as CD players, CNN, and safes. In the main hotel, labyrinthine corridors lead to widely varying rooms, with the same repro mahogany and some over-colorization (green, gray, cream, *and* pink? Navy and mulberry?). They're OK, and the blue-and-lemon lobby bustles, but the mews is the Stafford's best profile. ✉ *St. James's Place, SW1A 1NJ,* ☎ *0171/493–0111,* FAX *0171/493–7121. 74 rooms. Restaurant, bar, dining rooms. AE, DC, MC, V. Tube: Green Park.*

$$$ 🏨 **Dukes.** This small, exclusive, Edwardian-style hotel, with its lantern-lighted entrance, is central but still quiet as it is set in its own silent cul-de-sac behind the Ritz, and close to the Stafford, too. Though all three were once stablemates, this one is now run by the same upmarket management as the Franklin and Egerton House (☞ *below*), and has transformed itself completely into a small hotel of character, suitably filled with squashy sofas, oil paintings of assorted dukes, and muted, rich colors. Its trump cards are that, for such a central location, it offers immense peace and quiet and very reasonable rates, plus personal service (they greet you by name every time), and an especially sweet suite or two, on the top floor, with views over St. James's Park. ✉ *35 St. James's Pl., SW1A 1NY,* ☎ *0171/491–4840,* FAX *0171/493–1264. 62 rooms. Restaurant, dining room. AE, DC, MC, V. Tube: Green Park.*

Soho and Covent Garden

$$$$ ★ **The Savoy.** This historic, grand, late-Victorian hotel is beloved by the international influential, now as ever. Like the other Savoy Group hotels, it boasts handmade beds and staff who are often graduates of its exclusive training school. Its celebrated Grill (☞ Chapter 5, Restaurants and Pubs) has the premier power lunch tables; it hosted Elizabeth Taylor's first honeymoon in one of its famous river-view rooms; and it poured the world's first martini in its equally famous American Bar—haunted by Hemingway, Fitzgerald, Gershwin, et al. And does it measure up to this high profile? Absolutely. The impeccably maintained, spacious, elegant, bright, and comfortable rooms are furnished with antiques and serviced by valets. A room facing the Thames costs an arm and a leg and requires an early booking, but there are few better views in London. Bathrooms have original fittings, with the same sunflower-size shower heads as at Claridges, and there's a compact "Fitness Gallery" (with pool) secreted above the entrance. Though the Savoy is as grand as they come, the air is tinged with a certain naughtiness, which goes down well with Hollywood types. ✉ *Strand, WC2R 0EU,* ☎ *0171/836–4343,* FAX *0171/240–6040. 202 rooms. 3 restaurants, 2 bars, indoor pool, beauty salon, theater ticket desk. AE, DC, MC, V. Tube: Aldwych.*

$$$$ **Waldorf.** Close to the Aldwych theaters and Covent Garden, the Waldorf emerged from a total refit a few years ago, gleaming in luscious Edwardiana, and very pretty it is, with polished marble floors, chandeliers, and cozily comfortable period bedrooms. This is another one that was formerly a flagship in the Forte fleet, and whose future was therefore undecided at press time, though whether it goes to sensitive new owners, or back to Forte, it will no doubt continue providing a booking challenge for the wealthy theatergoer (Waldorf or Savoy?) and a suitably glamorous setting for the famous Palm Court tea dances, still going strong every weekend after nearly 90 years. ✉ *Aldwych, WC2B 4DD,* ☎ *0171/836–2400,* FAX *0171/836–7244. 292 rooms. Restaurant, brasserie, beauty salon. AE, DC, MC, V. Tube: Aldwych.*

$$$ ★ **Hazlitt's.** The solo Soho hotel is in three connected early 18th-century houses, one of which was the last home of essayist William Hazlitt (1778–1830). It's a disarmingly friendly place, full of personality, but devoid of such hotel features as elevators, room service (though if the staff isn't too busy, you can get ad-hoc take-outs), and porterage. Robust antiques are everywhere, assorted prints crowd every wall, plants and stone sculptures (by a father-in-law of one of the owners) appear in odd corners, and every room has a Victorian claw-foot tub in its bathroom. There are tiny sitting rooms, wooden staircases, and more restaurants within strolling distance than you could patronize in a year. Book way ahead—this is the London address of media people, literary types, and antiques dealers everywhere. ✉ *6 Frith St., W1V 5TZ,* ☎ *0171/434–1771,* FAX *0171/439–1524. 23 rooms. AE, DC, MC, V. Tube: Tottenham Court Road.*

$$$ **Mountbatten.** It may seem rather odd for one of London's newer hotels to be named after the late Lord Mountbatten, last viceroy of India and favorite uncle of Prince Charles. But the name is probably just an excuse to go overboard with the old British Raj theme. The decor reflects Mountbatten's life: photos of the estate where he lived, Indian

furnishings, silks, inlaid tables, and screens. It is another Edwardian Hotels property, with a good standard of service, bedrooms in various shades of red, with chintz drapes, and bathrooms of Italian marble. A harpist plays in the lounge and a pianist in the comfortable bar, and there are post-theater cabarets in the Centre Stage restaurant three times a week, featuring the very actors you may have just left in the West End theaters. A minute's walk brings you to the Royal Opera House or the Covent Garden Piazza. ✉ *Seven Dials, Covent Garden. WC2H 9HD,* ☎ *0171/836–4300,* FAX *0171/340–3540. 127 rooms. Restaurant, bar. AE, DC, MC, V. Tube: Covent Garden.*

$$ **Fielding.** Tucked away in a quiet alley by the world's first police station (now Bow St. Magistrates' Court), and feeling far from the madding crowds of Covent Garden, this very small and pretty hotel is so adored by its regulars that you'd be wise to book well ahead. Cameron Mackintosh, the Broadway musical producer (who could no doubt afford Claridges), stays here—presumably for the homey atmosphere; the old London Town character; the continuity of a loyal, friendly staff which maintains the place as the two founders, now retired, kept it for more than two decades; and, of course, for the convenience of having the Royal Opera House, every theater, and half of London's restaurants within spitting distance. It is not uneccentric. The bedrooms are all different, shabby-homey rather than chic, and cozy rather than spacious, though you can have a suite here for the price of a chain-hotel double. There's no elevator; only one room comes with bath (most have showers); and only breakfast is served in the restaurant. Cute. ✉ *4 Broad Ct., Bow St., WC2B 5QZ,* ☎ *0171/836–8305,* FAX *0171/497–0064. 26 rooms, 1 with bath, 23 with shower. Bar, breakfast room. AE, DC, MC, V. Tube: Covent Garden.*

$$ **Pastoria.** A less exorbitant choice for the theatergoer than the Waldorf (although rates are at the very top of this category), handily situated just off Leicester Square. The building is about 70 years old, with a suitably modern decor, the bedrooms done in limed oak with light pink walls and navy blue carpets. There's a brasserie-style restaurant to dine in, but Soho, which is restaurant central, is only a few hundred yards away. ✉ *3–6 St. Martin's St., WC2H 7HL,* ☎ *0171/930–8641,* FAX *0171/925–0551. 58 rooms. Restaurant, bar, coffee shop. AE, DC, MC, V. Tube: Leicester Square.*

Kensington

$$$$ ★ **Blakes.** Blakes is another world—some would say a '70s rock-star era time-warp. It was designed by owner Anouska Hempel (aka Lady Weinberg), and each room is a fantasy packed with precious Biedermeier, Murano glass, and modern pieces inside walls of red lacquer and black, or dove-gray moiré, or perhaps—like 007, the movie stars' favorite suite—pink. Cinematic mood lighting, featuring recessed halogen spots, compounds the impression that you, too, are a movie star living in a big-budget biopic. The foyer sets the tone with its piles of cushions, Phileas Fogg valises and trunks, black walls, rattan and bamboo, and a noisy parakeet under a gigantic Asian parasol. Downstairs, an equally dramatic, exorbitant black-and-white restaurant displays Thai warriors' costumes in glass cases. Stay away if you don't like Hollywood or the music biz; look out for The Hempel, Lady W's sister hotel, if you do. ✉ *33 Roland Gardens, SW7 3PF,* ☎ *0171/370–6701,* FAX *0171/373–0442. 52 rooms. Restaurant. AE, DC, MC, V. Tube: Gloucester Road.*

$$$ **The Cranley.** The pedigree of this small young Georgian town-house hotel is Ann Arbor, Michigan (where the owners hail from), out of South Ken (where it stands, near the big museums), and it looks the part. Anglo

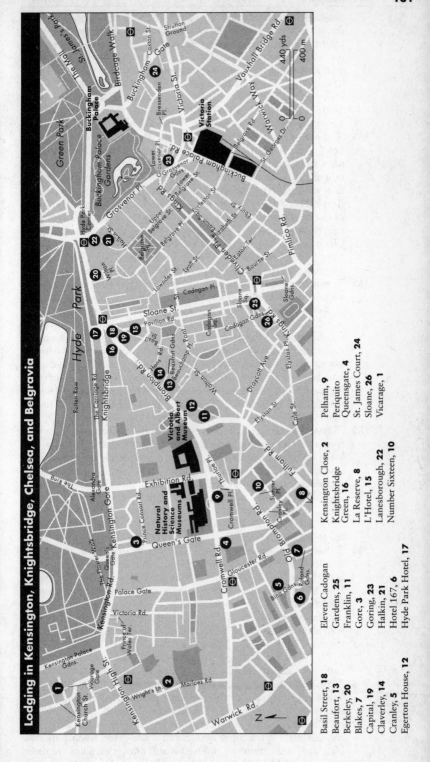

Lodging in Kensington, Knightsbridge, Chelsea, and Belgravia

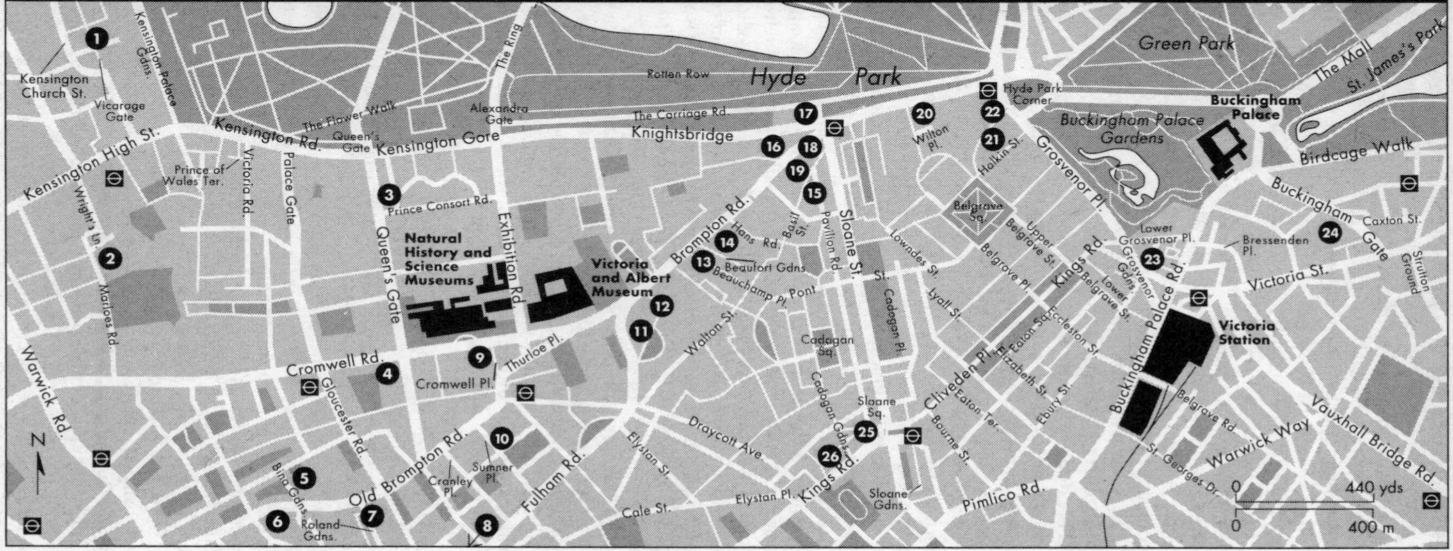

Basil Street, **18**
Beaufort, **13**
Berkeley, **20**
Blakes, **7**
Capital, **19**
Claverley, **14**
Cranley, **5**
Egerton House, **12**
Eleven Cadogan Gardens, **25**
Franklin, **11**
Gore, **3**
Goring, **23**
Halkin, **21**
Hotel 167, **6**
Hyde Park Hotel, **17**
Kensington Close, **2**
Knightsbridge Green, **16**
La Reserve, **8**
L'Hotel, **15**
Lanesborough, **22**
Number Sixteen, **10**
Pelham, **9**
Periquito Queensgate, **4**
St. James Court, **24**
Sloane, **26**
Vicarage, **1**

antiques, oils, and etchings are mixed with a lot of U.S.-style swagged drapery in assorted florals and vivid color schemes. Bedrooms have kitchenettes, and many are high-ceilinged and huge-windowed, while two of the apartments have Jacuzzis and patio gardens. The cheaper rooms here and at their nearby 10-room **One Cranley Place** (SW7 3AB, ☎ 0171/589–7944, FAX 0171/225–3931), which operates March to October, belong in the **$$** category. ✉ *10–12 Bina Gardens, SW5 0LA, ☎ 0171/373–0123, FAX 0171/373–9497. 26 rooms, 10 apartments. Breakfast room. AE, DC, MC, V. Tube: Gloucester Road.*

$$$ ★ **The Gore.** Just down the road from the Albert Hall, this very friendly hotel is run by the same people who run Hazlitt's (☞ *above*) and features a similar eclectic selection of prints, etchings, and antiques. Here, though, are spectacular folly-like rooms—Room 101 is a Tudor fantasy with minstrel gallery, stained glass, and four-poster bed, and Room 211, done in over-the-top Hollywood style, has a tiled mural of Greek goddesses in the bathroom. Despite all that, the Gore manages to remain most elegant. Bistrot 190 and Downstairs at 190 (☞ Chapter 5, Restaurants and Pubs) serve as dining rooms and bar. ✉ *189 Queen's Gate, SW7 5EX, ☎ 0171/584–6601, FAX 0171/589–8127. 54 rooms. Brasserie. AE, DC, MC, V. Tube: Gloucester Road.*

$$$ **Number Sixteen.** A luxury bed-and-breakfast close to South Kensington tube and three blocks or so from the great museums, Number Sixteen stands in a white-porticoed row of Victorian houses, many of which are fellow B&Bs, with not a sign outside to indicate it. There's no uniformity to the bedrooms except for their spaciousness and recently refitted bathrooms, but the decor overall is not so much interior-designed as understated, with new furniture and antiques, yellowed oils and modern prints juxtaposed. There's an elevator, and an enticing garden complete with conservatory and fountain-ette. ✉ *16 Sumner Pl., SW7 3EG, ☎ 0171/589–5232, FAX 0171/584–8615. 36 rooms. Bar. AE, DC, MC, V. Tube: South Kensington.*

$$ **Hotel 167.** This friendly little bed-and-breakfast is a two-minute walk from the V&A, in a grand white-stucco Victorian corner house. The lobby is immediately cheering, with its round marble tables, wrought-iron chairs, palms, and modern paintings; it also does duty as lounge and breakfast room. Bedrooms have a hybrid, with Venetian blinds over double-glazed windows (which you need on this noisy road), plus cable TV and minibars. ✉ *167 Old Brompton Rd., SW5 0AN, ☎ 0171/373–0672, FAX 0171/373–3360. 19 rooms with bath or shower. Breakfast room. AE, DC, MC, V. Tube: Gloucester Road.*

$$ **Kensington Close.** This large, fairly utilitarian hotel feels like a smaller one and boasts a few extras you wouldn't expect for the reasonable rate and convenient location (in a quiet lane off Kensington High Street). The main attraction is the health club, with an 18-meter pool, two squash courts, a steam room, and a beauty salon; there's also a secluded little water garden. Standard rooms are on the small side, with plain chain-hotel built-in furniture. Some Executive rooms are twice the size. Good value. ✉ *Wrights La., W8 5SP, ☎ 0171/937–8170, FAX 0171/937–8289. 530 rooms. 2 restaurants, 2 bars, indoor pool, health club, baby-sitting. AE, DC, MC, V. Tube: High Street Kensington.*

$ **Periquito Queensgate.** When a hotel calls its own rooms "compact," you should imagine a double bed, then add a foot all round, and, yes, that is about the measure of a room here. However, like a cruise ship state room, all you need is creatively secreted—there's a closet, mirror, satellite TV, tea/coffee maker, and a hair dryer. Rooms are double-glazed against noisy Cromwell Road, though earplugs are useful on account of LOUD color schemes, like purple, kingfisher, and canary, caused by this small chain's tropical parrot logo. If you want a divorce, the kids can share free, or else they get their own room at half price. The Natural History Museum is just across the street. ✉ *68–69 Queensgate, London SW7 5JT,* ☎ *0171/370–6111,* FAX *0171/370–0932. 61 rooms. Bar. AE, MC, V. Tube: Gloucester Road.*

$ ★ **Vicarage.** A great deal of care goes into the running of this family-owned hotel in a leaf-shaded big white Victorian house just off Kensington Church Street (spend the cash you save here in its antiques shops). The decor is sweetly anachronistic, full of heavy, dark-stained wood furniture, patterned carpets, and brass pendant lights, and there's a little conservatory. Many of the spotless bedrooms now have TVs. ✉ *10 Vicarage Gate, W8 4AG,* ☎ *0171/229–4030. 19 rooms. No credit cards. Tube: High Street Kensington.*

Knightsbridge, Chelsea, and Belgravia

$$$$ ★ **Berkeley.** The Berkeley is a remarkably successful mixture of the old and the new. It is a luxurious, air-conditioned, double-glazed modern building with a splendid penthouse swimming pool that opens to the sky when the weather's good. The bedrooms are decorated by various designers, but tend to be serious and opulent, some with swags of William Morris prints, others plain and masculine with little balconies overlooking the street. All have sitting areas and big, tiled bathrooms with bidets. For the ridiculously rich, there are spectacular suites, one with its own conservatory terrace, another with a sauna, but—such is the elegance of this place—you'd feel almost as spoiled in a normal room. Its restaurant is Vong, the Thai/French hybrid cloned from New York; though in London, its expensive decor, work-of-art dishes, and exorbitant prices come across as pretentious, and attract casino types. The hotel is conveniently placed for Knightsbridge shopping. ✉ *Wilton Pl., SW1X 7RL,* ☎ *0171/235–6000,* FAX *0171/235–4330. 160 rooms. 2 restaurants, indoor and outdoor pool, health club, beauty salon, cinema. AE, DC, MC, V. Tube: Knightsbridge.*

$$$$ **Capital.** Reserve well ahead if you want a room here—as you must for a table in the hotel's superb restaurant (☞ Chapter 5, Restaurants and Pubs). This grand hotel decanted into a private house is the work of David and Margaret Levin, who also own L'Hôtel (☞ *below*), and it exudes their irreproachable taste, with French floral fabrics, fine-grained woods, sober prints, and shelves of books. The 10 rooms of the Edwardian Wing, with its carved wooden staircase, enjoyed the attentions of superstar designer Nina Campbell (who did some of Claridges' suites), and were already the height of fashion in the 1920s, when this was the Squires Hotel. ✉ *22–24 Basil St., SW3 1AT,* ☎ *0171/589–5171,* FAX *0171/225–0011. 48 rooms. Bar. AE, DC, MC, V. Tube: Knightsbridge.*

$$$$ ★ **The Halkin.** If you can't take any more Regency stripes, English-country florals, or Louis XV chaises, this luxurious little place is the antidote. You could say its slickness doesn't belong in the '90s, or you could just enjoy the Milanese design: the clean-cut white marble lobby with its royal-blue leather bucket chairs, the arresting curved charcoal-gray corridors, the "diseased mahogany" veneers that darken as you climb, and the gray-on-gray bedrooms that light up when you insert your electronic key. Wealthy business and media types frequent the Halkin, and they can't breathe easy without a fax, Reuters, and two phone lines with conference-call. These are provided, along with two touch-control pads for all the gadgets, cable TV and video (library downstairs), room safe, and minibar. The bathrooms are palaces of shiny chrome, anti-mist mirrors, and marble that changes color according to which floor you're on. It might be like living in the Design Museum, except that this place employs some of the friendliest staff around—and they look pretty good in their white Armani uniforms, too. ✉ *Halkin St., SW1X 7DJ,* ☎

0171/333–1000, FAX *0171/333–1100. 41 rooms. Restaurant, business services. AE, DC, MC, V. Tube: Hyde Park Corner.*

$$$$ ★ **Hyde Park Hotel.** For more than 100 years, the Hyde Park has entertained lavishly, its banqueting rooms and ballroom regularly hosting royalty—including the current batch, who still have a designated Royal Entrance—its bedrooms comforting assorted stars from Rudolph Valentino to Winston Churchill. Forte Hotels did a grand job restoring its eight-kinds-of-marble halls and strewing fine antiques and paintings throughout, only to lose the hotel in its 1996 buyout (☞ Brown's, *above*). Bedrooms are large and hushed. Some have gentle windowfuls of treetop; from others, you can preview your Harvey Nichols purchases, as the building stands on the cusp of Knightsbridge shops and Hyde Park itself. The 1993 opening of Marco Pierre White: The Restaurant (☞ Chapter 5, Restaurants and Pubs) did no harm to the Hyde Park's image, though there was doubt, at press time, as to whether Marco would stay in a non-Forte Hyde Park. The blinding white basement gym is a plus. ✉ *66 Knightsbridge, SW1Y 7LA,* ☎ *0171/235–2000,* FAX *0171/235–2000. 160 rooms. 2 restaurants, bar, beauty salon, health club, theater ticket desk. AE, DC, MC, V. Tube: Knightsbridge.*

$$$$ **The Lanesborough.** This very grand hotel acts for all the world as though the Prince Regent took a ride through time and is about to resume residence. Royally proportioned public rooms (not lounges but "The Library" and "The Withdrawing Room") lead one off the other like an exquisite giant Chinese box in this multimillion-pound American-run conversion of the old St. George's Hospital opposite Wellington's house. Everything undulates with richness—brocades and Regency stripes, moiré silks and fleurs-de-lys in the colors of precious stones, magnificent antiques and oil paintings, reproductions of more gilded splendor than the originals, handwoven £250-per-square-yard carpet, as if Liberace and Laura Ashley had collaborated on the design. All you do to register is sign the visitors book, then retire to your room, where you are waited on by a personal butler. Full-size Lanesborough toiletries, umbrellas (take them home), robes (don't), a drinks tray (pay by the inch), and even business cards with your temporary fax (in every room) and phone numbers (two lines) are waiting. If you yearn for a bygone age and are very rich, this is certainly for you. Nonresidents can have lunch in the slightly self-conscious conservatory, invest £500 in a shot of "liquid history," or a sip of 1812 cognac from bar manager Salvatore Calabrese's eccentric collection. ✉ *1 Lanesborough Pl., SW1X 7TA,* ☎ *0171/259–5599,* FAX *0171/259–5606. 95 rooms. 2 restaurants, bar. AE, DC, MC, V. Tube: Hyde Park Corner.*

$$$$ **St. James Court.** You enter this Edwardian pile through a pair of enormous wrought-iron gates, which used to admit carriages into what is now the towering Reception. From here, you pass ranks of green leather sofas to reach the pièce de résistance, the landscaped courtyard with its fountain and ceramic frieze of scenes from Shakespeare. Some bedrooms are disproportionately large but cost the same as standards—the reverse is also true, so beware the expensive shoeboxes—and all are plainly decorated in pallid shades with a smattering of antiques and the odd (and some *are* very odd) painting. There's a health club, well-equipped except for the lack of a pool, and an extensive business center, scoring big points. The two restaurants aren't at all bad either, especially the Sichuan Inn of Happiness, and the many apartments offer good deals for weekly and longer stays, but, unless you have business at Buckingham Palace or around Victoria, the location is a fraction uncentral for the rates. ✉ *Buckingham Gate, SW1E 6AF,* ☎ *0171/834–6655,* FAX *0171/630–7587. 400 rooms. 2 restaurants, coffee shop, health club, business services. AE, DC, MC, V. Tube: St. James's Park.*

$$$ **Basil Street.** This gracious Edwardian hotel is on a quiet street behind busy Brompton Road and off (rich) shoppers heaven, Sloane Street. It's been family-run for three quarters of a century, and has always been popular with lone women travelers, who get automatic membership at the Parrot Club—an enormous lounge, with copies of *The Lady* and *Country Life* among the coffee cups. All the bedrooms are different; many are like grandma's guest room, with overstuffed counterpanes and a random selection of furniture—some good pieces, some utilitarian. You can write letters home in the peaceful gallery, which has polished wooden floors and fine Turkish carpets underneath a higgledy-piggledy wealth of antiques. Americans with a taste for period charm like this place; some come back often enough to merit the title "Basilite"—a privileged regular offered a 15% discount. ✉ *Basil St., SW3 1AH,* ☎ *0171/581–3311,* FAX *0171/581–3693. 92 rooms, 72 with bath. Restaurant, wine bar. AE, DC, MC, V. Tube: Knightsbridge.*

$$$ ★ **Beaufort.** You can practically hear the jingle of Harrods's cash registers from a room at the Beaufort, the brainchild of ex–TV announcer Diana Wallis, who employs an all-woman team to run the hotel. Actually, "hotel" is a misnomer for this elegant pair of Victorian houses. There's a sitting room instead of Reception; guests have a front door key and the run of the drinks cabinet, and even their own phone number, with the customary astronomical hotel surcharges waived. The high-ceilinged, generously proportioned rooms are decorated in muted, sophisticated shades to suit the muted, sophisticated atmosphere—but don't worry, you're encouraged by the incredibly sweet staff to feel at home. The rates are higher than the top range for this category but include unlimited drinks, breakfast, plus membership at a local health club. ✉ *33 Beaufort Gardens, SW3 1PP,* ☎ *0171/584–5252,* FAX *0171/589–2834. 29 rooms. Air-conditioning. AE, DC, MC, V. Tube: Knightsbridge.*

$$$ **Egerton House.** This absolutely peaceful, private house-style small hotel was the first in the stable that includes the Franklin and Dukes, and remains many people's favorite, appealing especially to bankers, for some reason. Many chintzy, floral, or regency stripe bedrooms overlook the gorgeous gardens in back; some have quirky shapes, others have four-poster beds, still others are extra-well endowed with closet space—in other words, all are different. The staff here is especially personable—and the manager would love to know what you thought of the selections in his hand-written local restaurant guide. ✉ *Egerton Terrace, SW3 2BX,* ☎ *0171/589–2412,* FAX *0171/584–6540. 30 rooms. AE, DC, MC, V. Tube: Knightsbridge.*

$$$ **Eleven Cadogan Gardens.** This aristocratic, late-Victorian gabled town house is the perfect spot for a pampered honeymoon, but very difficult to get into—and we're not referring to the lack of a sign or a reception desk. Fine period furniture and antiques, books, and magazines on the tables, landscape paintings and portraits, coupled with some of that solid, no-nonsense furniture that *real* English country houses have in unaesthetic abundance make for a family-home ambience; you might be borrowing the house and servants of some wealthy friends while they're away. Take the elevator or walk up the fine oak staircase to your room, which will have mahogany furniture, a restful color scheme, and pretty bedspreads and drapes. The best rooms are at the back. There's a private garden for summertime. ✉ *11 Cadogan Gardens, Sloane Sq., SW3 2RJ,* ☎ *0171/730–3426,* FAX *0171/730–5217. 62 rooms. Chauffeur-driven car. AE, MC, V. Tube: Sloane Square.*

$$$ **The Franklin.** It's hard to imagine, while taking tea in this pretty hotel overlooking a quiet, grassy square, that you're an amble away from busy Brompton and Cromwell roads and the splendors of the V&A. A few of the rooms are small, but the marble bathrooms—in which

Floris toiletries and heated towel racks are standard issue—are not; the large garden rooms and suites (which fall into the **$$$$** category) are romantic indeed. Tea is served daily in the lounge, and there's also a self-service bar. The staff is friendly and accommodating. ✉ *28 Egerton Gardens, SW3 2DB,* ☎ *0171/584–5533,* FAX *0171/584–5449. 40 rooms. Bar, parking (fee). AE, DC, MC, V. Tube: South Kensington.*

$$$ **Goring.** Useful if you have to drop in at Buckingham Palace, just around the corner. In fact, visiting VIPs use it regularly as a conveniently close, and suitably dignified, base for royal occasions. The hotel was built by Mr. Goring in 1910 and is now run by third-generation Gorings. The atmosphere remains Edwardian: Bathrooms are marble-fitted, and some of the bedrooms have brass bedsteads and the original built-in closets; many have been opulently redecorated. The bar/lounge looks onto a well-tended garden. ✉ *15 Beeston Pl., Grosvenor Gardens, SW1W 0JW,* ☎ *0171/834–8211,* FAX *0171/834–8211. 87 rooms. Restaurant, bar. AE, DC, MC, V. Tube: Victoria.*

$$$ ★ **L'Hotel.** An upscale bed-and-breakfast run by the same Levins who own the Capital next door (and run the People's Palace on the South Bank; ☞ Chapter 5: Restaurants and Pubs). This is a plainer alternative—less pampering, unfussy decor. There's an air of provincial France around, with the white wrought-iron bedsteads, pine furniture, and delicious breakfast croissants and baguettes (included in the room rate) served on chunky dark green and gold Parisian café china in Le Metro cellar wine bar (also open to nonguests). This really is like a house—you're given your own front door key, there's no elevator, and the staff leaves in the evening. Reserve ahead—it's very popular. ✉ *28 Basil St., SW3 1AT,* ☎ *0171/589–6286,* FAX *0171/225–0011. 12 rooms. Restaurant, wine bar. AE, V. Tube: Knightsbridge.*

$$$ **The Pelham.** The second of Tim and Kit Kemp's gorgeous hotels; they opened it in 1989 and run it along exactly the same lines as the Dorset Square (☞ Mayfair to Regent's Park, *above*), except that this one looks more the country house. There's 18th-century pine paneling in the drawing room, flowers galore, quite a bit of glazed chintz and antique lace bed linen, and the odd four-poster and bedroom fireplace. The first floor (American second floor) suites are extra-spacious with their high ceilings and chandeliers, while some of the top floor rooms under the eaves have adorable sloping ceilings and casement windows. The Pelham stands opposite the South Kensington tube stop, by the big museums, and close to the shops of Brompton Cross and Knightsbridge, with Kemps restaurant supplying an on-site trendy menu of "food that most people like to eat." Lauren Bacall deserted the Athenaeum for this hotel. ✉ *15 Cromwell Pl., SW7 2LA,* ☎ *0171/589–8288,* FAX *0171/584–8444. 37 rooms. Restaurant, air-conditioning, outdoor pool. AE, MC, V. Tube: South Kensington.*

$$–$$$ **The Sloane.** Many hotels abuse the word "unique" to describe their identical canopied beds or garden views, but the tiny Sloane really *is* unique. It is the only hotel we know in which you can lie in your canopied bed, pick up the phone, and buy the bed. You could buy the phone too, but it's the covetable, tasty antiques that you might actually be tempted to take home, and these are also for sale. Nothing so tacky as a price tag besmirches the gorgeous decor—which doesn't stint on strong hues to show off the ever-changing collection of Regency armoires and occasional tables, Victorian desk lamps and crystal decanters, Japanese screens and Edwardian oils, all collected by the antique-addicted owner—instead the sweet, young Euro staff harbor a book of price lists at the desk. Room service is not 24-hour, but there's an aerie of a secret roof terrace, with upholstered garden furniture and a panorama over Chelsea, where lunch and dinner is served to guests.

✉ *29 Draycott Pl., SW3 2SH,* ☎ *0171/581–5757,* FAX *0171/584–1348. 12 rooms. AE, DC, MC, V. Tube: Sloane Square.*

$$ **Claverley.** Can't afford the Beaufort, but like the area? This B&B is on the same quiet street a moment from Harrods and makes a good alternative. The less expensive rooms have either bath or shower (not both); as you go up the scale, rooms get larger, decor (homey florals, either Victorian- or Edwardian-style) newer, and bathrooms better equipped; some top-rate rooms have four-poster beds. The service is friendly, everything's spotless, and breakfast is included. ✉ *13–14 Beaufort Gardens, SW3 1PS,* ☎ *0171/589–8541,* FAX *0171/584–3410. 36 rooms. AE, V. Tube: Knightsbridge.*

$$ **Knightsbridge Green.** There are more suites than bedrooms at this Georgian hotel that's a two-minute walk from Harrods. One floor is French-style, with white furniture, another English, in beech. Costing only £15 more than a double room, the suites are not overpriced, and all the rooms have trouser presses and tea/coffee makers. There's no restaurant, but there are plenty in the area; or if you ask they'll send the porter out to find you a sandwich. There's also coffee and cake left out in the lounge—a detail that exemplifies the friendliness of this place. ✉ *159 Knightsbridge, SW1X 7PD,* ☎ *0171/584–6274,* FAX *0171/225–1635. 13 rooms, 12 suites. AE, MC, V. Closed 5 days over Christmas. Tube: Knightsbridge.*

$$ **La Reserve.** You'll find this unusual small hotel in the lively, classy residential neighborhood of Fulham. The varnished floorboards, black Venetian blinds, works of art (for sale), and primary-color upholstery in the public areas are contemporary and sophisticated. Bedrooms are cluttered only with the minibars, hair dryers, trouser presses, and tea/coffee makers of more expensive places. Fulham is not within walking distance of central London, but this is two minutes from Fulham Broadway tube, near Chelsea Football (soccer) Grounds and plenty of restaurants; there's also a brasserie in-house. ✉ *422–428 Fulham Rd., SW6 1DU,* ☎ *0171/385–8561,* FAX *0171/385–7662. 37 rooms. Restaurant, bar. AE, DC, MC, V. Tube: Fulham Broadway.*

Bayswater and Notting Hill Gate

$$$$ ★ **Halcyon.** Discretion, decadent decor, and disco divas (everyone from RuPaul and Simple Minds to Snoop Doggy Dogg) make this expensive, enormous, wedding cake Edwardian on Holland Park Avenue desperately desirable. You want film stars? They got Johnny Depp and William Hurt and Julia Roberts, and there are usually local residents like Sting, John Cleese, and *Absolutely Fabulous* Joanna Lumley haunting the absolutely excellent restaurant. But that's all by the by, because it's for perfect service and gorgeous rooms you'd follow them here. Many hotels lie when they claim "individual" room decor; not this one. The Blue Room has moons and stars, the famous Egyptian Suite is canopied like a bedouin tent; one room has a Jacuzzi and mint green stripes, another has heraldic motifs, black and red walls, a four-poster, and creaky floorboards; the Halcyon Suite has its own conservatory. All rooms are very large, with the high ceilings and big windows typical of the grand houses here—here being a 10-minute tube ride to the West End, and steps from London's most exquisite park. ✉ *81 Holland Park, W11 3RZ,* ☎ *0171/727–7288,* FAX *0171/229–8516. 44 rooms. Restaurant. AE, DC, MC, V. Tube: Holland Park.*

$$$$ **Whites.** Ease into this cream-facaded Victorian "country mansion" with a white wrought-iron portico and a view of Kensington Gardens. Thick carpets, gilded glass, marble balustrades, swagged silk drapes, and Louis XV–style furniture all make this the most luxurious hotel in the area. Some of the bedrooms have balconies (one also has a four-

Abbey Court, **3**
Camelot, **10**
Columbia, **7**
Commodore, **6**
The Gate, **3**
Halcyon, **1**
Lancaster Hall Hotel, **9**
London Elizabeth, **8**
Pembridge Court, **4**
Portobello, **2**
Whites, **5**

Lodging in Bayswater and Notting Hill Gate

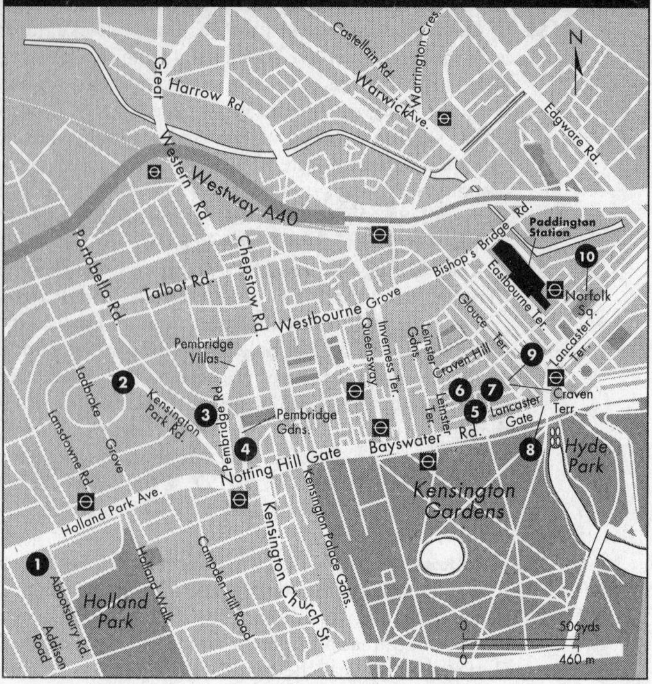

poster bed), and the colors are muted—powder blue, old rose, and lemon yellow—and prettiest when softly illuminated by the crystal wall-lights. The bathrooms are splendid. ✉ *Lancaster Gate, W2 3NR,* ☎ *0171/262–2711,* FAX *0171/262–2147. 55 rooms. Restaurant. AE, DC, MC, V. Tube: Lancaster Gate.*

$$$ **Abbey Court.** This is a very elegant little hotel that is more like a private home—albeit one with a resident designer. It's in a gracious white Victorian mansion in a quiet streetlet off Notting Hill Gate, which gives easy access to most of London. Inside, the era of Victoria is reflected in deep-red wallpapers (downstairs), Murano glass and gilt-framed mirrors, framed prints, mahogany, and plenty of antiques. Bathrooms look the part but are entirely modern in gray Italian marble, with brass fittings and whirlpool baths. There's 24-hour room service instead of a restaurant (there are plenty around here, though), and guests can relax in the lounge or the pretty conservatory. ✉ *20 Pembridge Gardens, W2 4DU,* ☎ *0171/221–7518,* FAX *0171/792–0858. 22 rooms. AE, DC, MC, V. Tube: Notting Hill.*

$$ **London Elizabeth.** Steps from Hyde Park, Lancaster Gate tube, and from rows of depressing cheap hotels, is this family-owned gem. Foyer and lounge are crammed with coffee tables and chintz drapery, lace antimacassars, and little chandeliers, and this country sensibility persists through the bedrooms. All have been redone—in palest blue-striped walls, wooden picture rails and Welsh wool bedspreads, or in pink cabbage rose prints and mahogany furniture—and although they do vary in size, there's a thoughtful tendency here to make sure that what you lose on the swings (small wedge-shaped room), you gain on the roundabouts (bigger, brand new bathroom, or a small balcony). You wouldn't expect 24-hour room service in a little place like this, but Chez Joseph, the "Continental" restaurant provides. Some rooms lack a full-length mirror, but they do have TV, direct-dial phone, and hair dryer, and they're serviced by an exceptionally charming Anglo-Irish staff. ✉ *Lancaster Terrace, W2 3PF,* ☎ *0171/402–6641,* FAX *0171/224–8900. 55 rooms. Restaurant, bar. AE, DC, MC, V. Tube: Lancaster Gate.*

$$–$$$ **Portobello.** This small, eccentric hotel consists of two adjoining Victorian houses that (as is common around here) back onto a beautiful large garden that is shared with the neighbors. It has long been the favorite of the arty end of the music biz and other media types, and it must be said a tinge of the groovy early '70s still adheres to the corners—and also to the slightly shabby Victorian/Chinoiserie decor—though this enhances the overall effect for those who prefer somewhere louche and laid back. "Cabin Rooms" are minute, but have made a virtue of this fact, with everything you need accessible by reaching out your hand from bed, just like on board ship. Many bigger rooms have free-standing Victorian claw-foot bathtubs, though the famous round-bedded suite has the *pièce de résistance* of the bath world—an Edwardian "bathing machine," all knobs and shiny brass pipes. Rates include breakfast, and there's a 24-hour bar/restaurant in the basement, though there are a hundred other options in this very happening area. ✉ *22 Stanley Gardens, W11 2NG,* ☎ *0171/727–2777,* FAX *0171/792–9641. 25 rooms. Restaurant, bar. AE, DC, MC, V. Closed 10 days over Christmas. Tube: Ladbroke Grove.*

$$ **Pembridge Court.** A few doors down from the Abbey Court (☞ *above*), in a similar colonnaded white-stucco Victorian row house, is this sweet home-away-from-home of a hotel, cozy with scatter cushions and books, quirky Victoriana, and framed fans from the neighboring Portobello Market—around which Merete gives private insider tours. Bedrooms have a great deal of swagged floral drapery, direct-dial phones, and satellite TV, and there's an elevator to the upper floors. Rates include English breakfast (brought to your room if you prefer)—take that into account when doing your sums, since only the half-size small twin rooms fall into the **$$** category; larger ones are £10–£30 more. ✉ *34 Pembridge Gardens, W2 4DX,* ☎ *0171/229–9977,* FAX *0171/727–4982. 25 rooms. Restaurant. AE, DC, MC, V. Tube: Notting Hill.*

$ **Camelot.** This is an affordable hotel, just around the corner from Paddington Station, with bedrooms featuring utility pine furniture, TVs, tea/coffee makers, and attractive bathrooms. There's a lounge, and a very pretty breakfast room complete with exposed brick wall, large open fireplace, wooden farmhouse tables and floorboards, and a gallery of child guests' works of art. Everyone here is friendly beyond the call of duty. The few bathless single rooms are great bargains; the normal rate just busts the top of this category, but includes a breakfast of anything you want—full English or organic muesli, fruit, and herb tea. ✉ *45–47 Norfolk Sq., W2 1RX,* ☎ *0171/723–9118,* FAX *0171/402–3412. 44 rooms, 36 with bath. MC, V. Tube: Paddington.*

$ **Columbia.** If you're a sucker for '70s kitsch and like to stay out late, or alternatively, if you're a family on a tight budget, this unique paradox of a bargain hotel is worth a try. The public rooms in these five joined-up Victorians are as big as museum halls, painted in icy hues of powder blue and buttermilk, or paneled in dark wood. During the day, at one end they contain the most hip band du jour drinking alcohol; at the other, there are sightseers sipping coffee. However, the place is big enough and the walls thick enough that you'd not even know they were shooting sleazy clubwear for *The Face* magazine in room 100 while you use the hair dryer (provided) sip tea (provided), and watch TV in room 101 (there's a direct-dial phone and a safe, too). Rooms are clean and ceilings high, and some are very large (especially those with three or four beds), with park views and balconies. It's just a shame that teak veneer, khaki-beige-brown color schemes, and avocado bathroom suites haven't made it back into the style bible yet. ✉ *95–99 Lancaster Gate, W2 3NS,* ☎ *0171/402–0021,* FAX *0171/706–4691. 103 rooms. Restaurant, bar, meeting rooms. AE, MC, V. Tube: Lancaster Gate.*

$ ★ **Commodore.** This peaceful hotel of three converted Victorians is close to the Columbia, deeper in the big leafy square known as Lancaster Gate. It's another independent, and another find, of a very different stripe, as you'd notice on entering the cozy, carpeted lounge with its muted colors and little fireplace. Try your best to get one of the amazing rooms—as superior to the regular ones (which usually go to package tour groups) as Harrods is to Woolworths, but priced the same. Twenty of these are split-level rooms, with sleeping gallery, all large, all different, all with something special—like a walk-in closet with its own stained-glass window—and all with the full deck of tea/coffee makers, hair dryers, and TV with pay movies. One (No. 11) is a duplex, entered through a secret mirrored door off a lemon-yellow hallway with palms and Greek statuary, with thick-carpeted *very* quiet bedroom upstairs and its toilet below. It's getting very popular here, so book ahead. ✉ *50 Lancaster Gate, W2 3NA,* ☎ *0171/402–5291,* FAX *0171/262–1088. 90 rooms. Bar, business services. AE, MC, V. Tube: Lancaster Gate.*

$ **The Gate.** It's absolutely teeny, the Gate, just a normal house at the very top of Portobello Road, off Notting Hill Gate. The plain bedrooms have fridges, TVs, direct-dial phones, and tea/coffee facilities, plus bath (unless you opt for a smaller, £10 cheaper, shower-only room), and you can have the inclusive Continental breakfast brought up to you, or take it in the first-floor lounge. ✉ *6 Portobello Rd., W11 3DG,* ☎ *0171/221–2403,* FAX *0171/221–9128. 6 rooms. AE, MC, V. Tube: Notting Hill.*

$ **Lancaster Hall Hotel.** This modest hotel is owned by the German YMCA, which guarantees efficiency and spotlessness. There's a bargain 20-room "youth annex" offering basic rooms with shared baths. ✉ *35 Craven Terr., W2 3EL,* ☎ *0171/723–9276,* FAX *0171/224–8343. 100 rooms, 80 with bath or shower. Restaurant, bar. MC, V. Tube: Lancaster Gate.*

Bloomsbury

$$–$$$ **The Kingsley.** On the main street, steps from the British Museum, this is one Edwardian-style hotel that really does feel sweetly old-fashioned, while avoiding shabbiness or stuffiness. Flouncy, English country house–decor has the strong color schemes currently favored in hotel land, and has been recently refreshed, with tea/coffee makers and free in-house movies among the facilities. The rooms in the turret on the southwest corner with their curved, six-window wall are worth asking for, being brighter than most, while executive suites have four posters and Jacuzzis at a rate falling about halfway down the **$$$** category. ✉ *Bloomsbury Way, WC1A 2SD,* ☎ *0171/242–5881,* FAX *0171/831–0225. 145 rooms. Restaurant, bar, meeting rooms. AE, DC, MC, V. Tube: Holborn.*

$$ **Academy.** These three joined-up Georgian houses, boasting a little patio garden and a fashion-conscious wood-floored, mirrored basement bar/brasserie, supply the most sophisticated and hotel-like facilities in the Gower Street "hotel row." The comfortable bedrooms have TV (with no extra channels), direct-dial phones, and tea/coffee makers, and the two without ensuite bathrooms are an entire £30/night cheaper. Like all the hotels in this section, the Academy neighbors the British Museum and University of London, a circumstance that appeals to culture vultures on a budget and the more affluent students. ✉ *17–21 Gower St., WC1E 6HG,* ☎ *0171/631–4115,* FAX *0171/636–3442. 33 rooms, 25 with bath/shower. Restaurant/bar. AE, DC, MC, V. Tube: Russell Square.*

Academy, **2**
Kingsley, **4**
Morgan, **3**
Ridgemount, **1**
Ruskin, **5**
St. Margaret's, **6**

Lodging in Bloomsbury

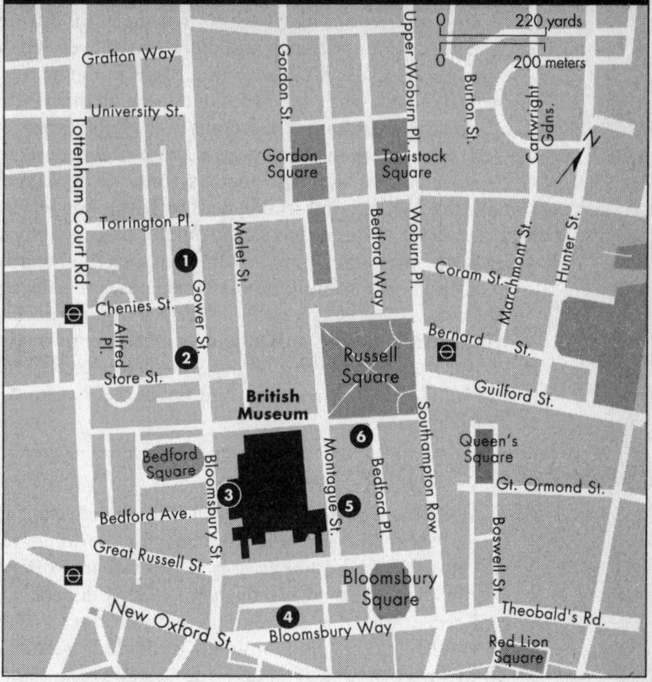

$ ★ **Morgan.** This is a Georgian row-house hotel, family-run with charm and panache. Rooms are small and functionally furnished, yet friendly and cheerful overall, with phones and TVs. The five newish apartments are particularly pleasing: three times the size of normal rooms (and an extra £15/night, placing them in the **$$** category), complete with eat-in kitchens (gourmet cooking sessions are discouraged) and private phone lines. The tiny, paneled breakfast room (rates include the meal) is straight out of a doll's house. The back rooms overlook the British Museum. ✉ *24 Bloomsbury St., WC1B 3QJ,* ☎ *0171/636–3735. 15 rooms with bath or shower, 5 apartments. Breakfast room. No credit cards. Tube: Russell Square.*

$ ★ **Ridgemount.** The kindly owners, Mr. and Mrs. Rees, make you feel at home. The public areas, especially the family-style breakfast room, have a friendly, cluttered Victorian feel. Some rooms overlook a leafy garden, and two now have an ensuite bathroom, for an extra £9/night. ✉ *65 Gower St., WC1E 6HJ,* ☎ *0171/636–1141. 34 rooms, 2 with bath. No credit cards. Tube: Russell Square.*

$ **Ruskin.** Immediately opposite the British Museum, the family-owned Ruskin is both pleasant and quiet—all front windows are double-glazed. The bedrooms are clean, though nondescript; the back ones overlook a pretty garden. Note the bucolic mural (c. 1808) in the lounge. Well-run and very popular. ✉ *23–24 Montague St., WC1B 5BN,* ☎ *0171/636–7388,* FAX *0171/323–1662. 35 rooms, 7 with shower. AE, DC, MC, V. Tube: Russell Square.*

$ **St. Margaret's.** This guest house on a tree-lined Georgian street has been run for many years by a friendly Italian family. You'll find spacious rooms and towering ceilings, and a wonderful location close to Russell Square. The back rooms have a garden view. ✉ *24 Bedford Pl., WC1B 5JL,* ☎ *0171/636–4277. 64 rooms, 10 with bath. No credit cards. Tube: Goodge Street.*

Docklands

$$ **Scandic Crown.** This Swedish-owned place is Scandic by name and by nature, with efficiency and blond wood everywhere. It has its peculiarities, because it's split in two. Block 2 comprises a modern apartment building, while Block 1, containing all the bars and fun stuff, is a converted warehouse. Bedrooms in the latter (prefixed by a "1") are 10 times nicer than the new ones, with rich exposed-brick walls, recessed spotlights, and big windows, some overlooking the Thames. All have the "Most Comfortable Beds In Town," on which you're offered a free night if you fail to sleep soundly (improbably, nobody's taken them up on it). A separate building houses a fine health club with pool, and the dining options (you need them out here—the courtesy bus into town stops early) include the lower deck of a dry-docked three-masted bark, a smörgåsbord buffet, and summertime riverside terrace barbecues. ✉ *265 Rotherhithe St., SE16 1EJ,* ☎ *0171/231–1001,* FAX *0171/231–0599. 386 rooms. 2 restaurants, 2 bars, indoor pool, health club. AE, DC, MC, V.*

Hampstead

$$ **Swiss Cottage Hotel.** It's a little out of the way on a peaceful street behind Swiss Cottage tube stop, but this charming, family-run hotel will suit those who like to stay in a residential district, save a little on the check, and still have their home comforts. The lounge, bar, and reception area are stuffed with antiques and reproductions, cheerfully lighted, and smilingly staffed. In summer, French windows open from the bar and the downstairs restaurant—which serves an old-fashioned Anglo-French menu—onto the garden. Bedrooms off the creaky, labyrinthine corridors are in Victorian style, and most are good-sized. (Note that the elevator doesn't reach the 4th floor.) Executive rooms have bathrooms with pretty painted ceramic sinks and brass fittings. ✉ *4 Adamson Rd., NW3 3HP,* ☎ *0171/722–2281,* FAX *0171/483–4588. 80 rooms. Restaurant, bar. AE, DC, MC, V. Tube: Swiss Cottage.*

$ **La Gaffe.** Another find, a short walk from the Hampstead tube stop. Italian Bernardo Stella has been welcoming the same guests back to these early 18th-century shepherds' cottages for more than a decade. Make no mistake, rooms are tiny with showers only, and the predominantly pink and beige decor isn't luxurious, but the popular wine bar and restaurant, which (naturally) serve Italian food, are yours to lounge around in at all hours—there's a shelf of assorted books to borrow. Between the two "wings" is a raised patio for summer, and each room has TV and phone. You'll love the place if you're a fan of quaint. ✉ *107–111 Heath St., NW3 6SS,* ☎ *0171/435–8965,* FAX *0171/794–7592. 14 rooms with shower. Restaurant, wine bar/café. AE, MC, V. Tube: Hampstead.*

Bed-and-Breakfast Agencies

$$ **Bulldog Club.** You must join Amanda St. George's *very* exclusive B&B club before being eligible to book a stay with some of London's grandest families. Many have converted their now grown-up children's rooms; others have newly built guest annexes; all offer total comfort, with breakfast included and TV and tea/coffee facilities in your room. Most houses revolve around a Knightsbridge/Belgravia axis, though other areas are covered, too. *Further details from:* ✉ *35 The Chase, SW4 0NP,* ☎ *0171/622–6935,* FAX *0171/491–1328. Facilities vary. Most rooms have private bath/shower. AE, MC, V.*

$$ 🏠 **Uptown Reservations.** As the name implies, this B&B booking service accepts only the tonier addresses, and specializes in finding hosted apartments and homes for Americans, often executives of small corporations. Nearly all the 50 or so homes on their register are in Knightsbridge, Belgravia, Kensington, and Chelsea, with a few lying farther west in Holland Park and Maida Vale. The private homes vary, of course, but all are good-looking and have private ensuite bathrooms for guests. ✉ *50 Christchurch St., SW3 4AR,* ☎ *0171/351–3445,* FAX *0171/351–9383. Facilities vary. Payment by bank transfer or U.S. check; 20% deposit required. No credit cards.*

$ 🏠 **Primrose Hill B&B.** A small, friendly bed-and-breakfast agency that's genuinely "committed to the idea traveling shouldn't be a rip-off." Expatriate American Gail O'Farrell has family homes (to which guests get their own latchkeys) in or near villagey Hampstead on her books, and all are comfortable or more than comfortable. So far this has been one of those word-of-mouth secrets, but now that everyone knows, book well ahead. ✉ *14 Edis St., NW1 8LG,* ☎ *0171/722–6869. 15 rooms with varying facilities. No credit cards.*

4 Nightlife and the Arts

rants, is this showcase venue for the healthy British jazz scene, with the emphasis on advanced, free, and improvised work. ✉ *Stoke Newington Church St., N16,* ☎ *0171/254–6516.* 🎫 *£4–£7.* ⏲ *Most nights 8–11 PM. MC, V.*

Rock

The Astoria. Very central, quite hip, this place hosts bands that there's a buzz about, plus late club nights. ✉ *157 Charing Cross Rd., W1,* ☎ *0171/434–0403.* 🎫 *Around £8–£12. Check listings for opening times. No credit cards.*

The Forum. This ex-ballroom with balcony and dance floor packs in the customers and consistently attracts the best medium-to-big-name performers, too. Get the tube to Kentish Town, then follow the hordes. ✉ *9–17 Highgate Rd., NW5,* ☎ *0171/284–2200.* 🎫 *Around £8–£12.* ⏲ *Most nights 7–11. AE, MC, V.*

The Roadhouse. True to its name, this pays homage to the American dream of the open road, with a Harley behind the bar and much memorabilia. Music fits into the feel-good, tuneful, middle-of-the-road end of the R&B/blues/rock/soul spectrum. ✉ *Jubilee Hall, Covent Garden, WC2,* ☎ *0171/240–6001.* 🎫 *£3–£6.* ⏲ *Mon.–Wed. 5:30 PM–1 AM; Thurs.–Sat. 5:30 PM–3 AM, Sun. 12:30–5:30 PM. AE, MC, V.*

Shepherd's Bush Empire. Converted from the BBC TV theater, where Terry Wogan, the United Kingdom's Johnny Carson, recorded his show for years and years, this now hosts the same kind of medium-big names as the north London Forum. ✉ *Shepherd's Bush Green, W12,* ☎ *0181/740–7474.* 🎫 *£8–£12.* ⏲ *7:30–11. AE, MC, V.*

Subterania. Home of Notting Hillbillies everywhere—that is, the hip and cool bohemians of the neighborhood—this large, medium-tech balconied club never welcomes mainstream bands but books the top musicians in any alternative genre from all over the world. ✉ *12 Acklam Rd., W10,* ☎ *0181/960–4590.* 🎫 *£6–£10. Call for hours; bands play Tues.–Thurs. MC, V.*

Clubs

Always call ahead, especially to the dance and youth-oriented places, because the club scene changes constantly.

Camden Palace. This big old place has been top-to-toe refurbished, but it's still difficult to find a facial wrinkle, even if you could see through the laser lights and find your way around the three floors of bars. There's often a live band. ✉ *1A Camden High St., NW1,* ☎ *0171/387–0428.* 🎫 *£3–£9.* ⏲ *Tues.–Sat. 9 PM–3 AM. No credit cards.*

Gardening Club. Next door to the Rock Garden, but far hipper than that ancient dive, this club has different music, ambience, and groovers on different nights, but is consistently the place to be, especially if you're not yet 30. There's also a much bigger Gardening Club 2. (☞ The Gay Scene, *below.*) ✉ *4 The Piazza, WC2,* ☎ *0171/497–3154.* 🎫 *£4–£12.* ⏲ *Mon.–Wed. 10 PM–3 AM, Fri. and Sat. 11 PM–6 AM. AE, MC, DC, V.*

Heaven. London's premier (mainly) gay club is the best place for dancing wildly for hours. A state-of-the-art laser show and a large, throbbing dance floor complement a labyrinth of quieter bars and lounges and a snack bar. (☞ The Gay Scene, *below.*) ✉ *Under the Arches, Villiers St., WC2,* ☎ *0171/839–2520.* 🎫 *£4–£10 depending on night. Call for opening times (Tues.–Sat. approx. 10 PM–3:30 AM). AE, DC, MC, V.*

Hippodrome. A neon horseman marks Peter Stringfellow's second-string club. Much like his first-string one (☞ *below*), this one has lots of sparkly black and silver, several tiers of expensive bars, a restaurant, and lots of enthusiastic lighting around a large dance floor. Very middle-of-the-road. ✉ *Hippodrome Corner, Cranbourn St., WC2,* ☎

NIGHTLIFE

Nighttime London has rejuvenated itself in the past f tangible new spirit of fun abroad on the streets, and ne out opening at an unprecedented rate. Whatever your p somewhere to go. Are you a club animal? London's l mously hip, hot, and happening. Music? From indie ba resident orchestras, free jazz to opera, it's everywhere. traditional torch song sort is undergoing a little revival, never slowed down in the first palce, and remains one o vorite ways to wind down. Our gay section is small, but you need to find the scene, and there is a fabulous scene. remember when you hit the town at night is that regular without special extended licences) stop serving alcohol after 1 on Sundays), and the tubes stop around midnight.

Jazz

100 Club. The best for blues, trad, and Dixie, plus the straight rock-and-roll, this Oxford Street subterranean has t paint-peeling, smoke-choked, dance-inducing atmosphere. Ther counter most nights. ✉ *100 Oxford St., W1,* ☎ *0171/636– £4–£10, depending on the night.* ⏲ *Mon.–Wed. 7:30–m Thurs.–Sat. 8:30–1 AM, Sun. 7:30–11:30. No credit cards.*

Jazz Café. This palace of high-tech cool in a converted bank in b Camden remains an essential hangout for fans of the mainstre of the repertoire and younger crossover performers. It's way no steps from Camden Town tube. ✉ *5–7 Pkwy., NW1,* ☎ *017 6000.* 🎟 *£7–£12, depending on the band.* ⏲ *Mon.–Sat. 7 PM–lat varies). AE, DC, MC, V.*

Pizza Express. It may seem strange, since Pizza Express is the ca best-loved chain of pizza houses, but this is one of London's prin jazz venues, with music every night except Monday in the base restaurant. The subterranean interior is darkly lit, the line-ups (o featuring visiting U.S. performers) are interesting, and the Italian-s thin-crust pizzas are great! ✉ *10 Dean St., W1,* ☎ *0171/437–95* 🎟 *£6–£9, depending on band.* ⏲ *From noon for food; music fro 9:30 PM to 1 AM Tues.–Sun. AE, DC, MC, V.*

The Rhythmic. Another one a little out of the way, but certainly wort the trip, this civilized restaurant/club on an Islington street that's a produce market by day, gets great line-ups, from Jimmy Smith to the Master Musicians of Joujouka. ✉ *89–91 Chapel Market, N1,* ☎ *0171/713–5859.* 🎟 *£7–£12 nonmembers.* ⏲ *Mon.–Sat. 8:30–3 AM. MC, V.*

Ronnie Scott's. The legendary Soho jazz club that, since its opening in the early '60s, has been attracting all the big names. It's usually packed and hot, the food isn't great, service is slow—because the staff can't move through the crowds, either—but the atmosphere can't be beat, and it's probably still London's best. ✉ *:47 Frith St., W1,* ☎ *0171/439–0747.* 🎟 *£10–£15 nonmembers.* ⏲ *Mon.–Sat. 8:30 PM–3 AM, Sun. 8–11:30 PM. Reservations essential. AE, DC, MC, V.*

South Bank. A certain kind of really big name (such as Carla Bley, Jan Garbarek, Richard Thompson) ends up here, at the Royal Festival Hall, or the Queen Elizabeth Hall. What you lose in atmosphere, you gain in accoustical clarity, and you save wear and tear on the shoe leather. ✉ *Waterloo,* ☎ *0171/928–8800.* 🎟 *£7.50–£24. Jazz concerts usually start 7:30 PM; call for this week's events. Reservations essential. AE, MC, V.*

The Vortex. In the wilds of Stoke Newington, a very happening, liberal-arts neighborhood, with tons of vegetarian/Asian–type restau-

0171/437–4311. 🎫 *Mon.–Thurs. £8, Fri. £10, Sat. £12 (half price before 10:30).* ⏲ *Mon.–Sat. 9 PM–3:30 AM. AE, DC, MC, V.*

Ministry of Sound. This is more of an industry than a club, with its own record label, line of apparel, and, of course, DJs. Inside, there are chill-out rooms, dance floors, promotional Sony Playstations, Absolut shot bars—all the club kid's favorite things. ✉ *103 Gaunt St., SE1,* ☎ *0171/378–6528.* 🎫 *£10–£15.* ⏲ *Wed.–Sat. 11 PM–8 AM. MC, V.*

Palookaville. Conveniently close to Covent Garden tube, this basement restaurant/bar charges a cover only after 9 PM, or 11 PM early in the week. It's popular with office people for after-hours drinks. You won't write home about the food or the undemanding music—usually there's a jazz trio or similar live band—but you might about the friendly, mellow ambience. ✉ *13A James St., WC2,* ☎ *0171/240–5857.* 🎫 *£2 Mon.–Wed., £3 Thurs., £4 Fri., Sat.* ⏲ *Mon.–Wed. 5:30 PM–12:30 AM, Thurs.–Sat. 5:30 PM–1:30 AM. MC, V.*

Stringfellows. Peter Stringfellow's first London nightclub is not at all hip, but it *is* glitzy, with mirrored walls, the requisite dance-floor light show, and an expensive art deco–style restaurant. Suburbanites and middle-aged swingers frequent it. ✉ *16–19 Upper St. Martin's La., WC2,* ☎ *0171/240–5534.* 🎫 *Mon.–Wed. £8; Thurs. £10; Fri.–Sat. before 10, £10, after 10, £15.* ⏲ *Mon.–Sat. 8 PM–3:30 AM. AE, DC, MC, V.*

The Wag. This tenacious representative of Soho's club circuit takes on a different character according to which night it is and which DJ is spinning. One extremely loud, sweaty floor houses bars and dance spaces, and a quieter, cooler one a restaurant serving dinner and breakfast. ✉ *33–35 Wardour St., W1,* ☎ *0171/437–5534.* 🎫 *£5–£10, depending on the night.* ⏲ *Mon.–Thurs. 10:30 PM–3 AM; Fri. and Sat. 10:30 PM–6 AM. No credit cards.*

Bars

The Atlantic. This vast, glamorous, wood-floored basement caused a revolution when, in early 1994, it became the first central London bar to be granted a late, late alcohol licence. Although there are now others, it's still popular, so that the only way to get a table on a weekend night is to book it for dinner—luckily the food's fine. ✉ *20 Glasshouse St., W1,* ☎ *0171/734–4888.* ⏲ *Mon.–Sat. noon–3 AM, Sun. noon–11 PM. AE, MC, V.*

Beach Blanket Babylon. In Notting Hill, close to Portobello market, this always packed singles bar is distinguishable by its fanciful decor—like a fairy tale grotto, or a medieval dungeon, visited by the gargoyles of Notre Dame. ✉ *45 Ledbury Rd., W11,* ☎ *0171/229–2907.* ⏲ *Daily noon–11 PM. AE, MC, V.*

The Library. In this very comfortable, dress-code-free, but self-consciously "period" (doesn't matter which as long as it looks old) bar at the swanky Lanesborough Hotel, Salvatore Calabrese offers his completely eccentric collection of ancient cognacs, made in years when something important happened. A shot of this "liquid history" can set you back £500. Don't ask for brandy Alexander. ✉ *Hyde Park Corner, SW1,* ☎ *0171/259–5599.* ⏲ *Mon.–Sat. 11–11, Sun. noon–2:30 PM and 7–10:30. AE, DC, MC, V.*

Cabaret

Comedy Café. Talent nights, jazz, and video karaoke, but mostly stand-up comedy, take place at this popular dive in the City. Admission charges are occasionally waived. There's food available in the evening and usually a late license (for alcohol). ✉ *66 Rivington St., EC2,* ☎ *0171/739–5706.* 🎫 *Free–£7.* ⏲ *Wed.– Thurs. 7:30 PM–1 AM, Fri.–Sat. 7:30 PM–2 AM. MC, V.*

Comedy Store. This is the improv factory where the United Kingdom's funniest standups cut their teeth, now relocated to a bigger and better place. The name performers and new talent you'll see may be strangers to you, but you're guaranteed to laugh. ✉ *Haymarket House, Oxendon St., SW1,* ☎ *0171/344–4444, or 01426/914433 for information.* 💳 *£8–£10. Shows Tues.–Thurs., Sun. at 8, Fri.–Sat. at 8 and midnight. AE, MC, V.*

Casinos

The 1968 Gaming Act states that any person wishing to gamble *must* make a declaration of intent to gamble at the gaming house in question and *must* apply for membership in person. Membership usually takes about two days. In many cases, clubs prefer for the applicant's membership to be proposed by an existing member. Personal guests of existing members are, however, allowed to participate.

Charlie Chester Casino. The drawing cards here are an international restaurant and a modern casino with blackjack, roulette, craps, and Punto Banco. ✉ *12 Archer St., W1,* ☎ *0171/734–0255. Membership £5 for life.* ⏲ *Daily 2 PM–4 AM. Jacket and tie.*

Crockford's. This is a civilized club, established 150 years ago, with none of the jostling for tables that mars many of the flashier clubs. It has attracted a large international clientele since its move from St. James's to Mayfair. The club offers American roulette, Punto Banco, and blackjack. ✉ *30 Curzon St., W1,* ☎ *0171/493–7771. Membership £150 a year.* ⏲ *Daily 2 PM–4 AM. Jacket and tie.*

The Golden Nugget. This large casino just off Piccadilly has blackjack, roulette, and Punto Banco. ✉ *22 Shaftesbury Ave., W1,* ☎ *0171/439–0099. Membership £3.50 for life.* ⏲ *Daily 2 PM–4 AM. Jacket required.*

Palm Beach Casino. In what used to be the old ballroom of the Mayfair Hotel, this is a fast-moving and exciting club attracting a large international membership. It has a red-and-gold interior, with a plush restaurant and bar. You can choose from American roulette, blackjack, and Punto Banco. ✉ *30 Berkeley St., W1,* ☎ *0171/493–6585. Membership £10.* ⏲ *Daily 2 PM–4 AM. Jacket and tie.*

Sportsman Club. This one has a dice table as well as Punto Banco, American roulette, and blackjack. ✉ *3 Tottenham Court Rd., W1,* ☎ *0171/637–5464. Membership £3.45 a year.* ⏲ *Daily 2 PM–4 AM. Jacket and tie.*

The Gay Scene

Since February 1994, with the long-overdue lowering of the age of consent from 21, 18-year-old gay men in Britain have had the blessing of the law in doing together what they've always done together. (Westminster mooted 16, the boys-and-girls age, but British MPs could not quite deal with that). The change did not extend to lesbians, nor did it need to, since there has never been any legislation that so much as mentions gay women—a circumstance that, believe it or not, dates from Queen Victoria's point-blank refusal to believe that women did it with women. AIDS is, of course, a large issue, but the epidemic hasn't yet had quite as devastating an impact as it has on San Francisco and New York.

There are signs of a gay renewal in London. Soho, especially Old Compton Street, has something of a pre-AIDS Christopher Street atmosphere, with gay shops, bars, restaurants, and even beauty salons (get your chest waxed here) jostling for space. The lavender pound is a desirable pound. Though lesbians are included in the "Compton" scene (as are anyone's straight friends), it's predominantly men-for-men. The dyke scene certainly exists, and lesbian chic is as trendy in London as it is in New York or Los Angeles, but it has a lower profile, generally, than the male equivalent, and also tends to be more politically strident. Any women-only event in London attracts a large proportion of gay women.

Check the listings in *Time Out,* the weekly *MetroXtra* (*MX*), and the monthly *Gay Times* for events.

Bars, Cafés, Pubs

The Box. On two floors, one bright, one dark, there's good, light food and (at least at press time) the Sunday night Girl Bar, which wows all London dykes. ✉ *Seven Dials, Monmouth St., WC2,* ☎ *0171/240–5828.*

Comptons. This pub, which has been here forever, is run by Bass Charrington, one of the big U.K. breweries. It's a useful rendezvous for the Soho strip. ✉ *53 Old Compton St., W1,* ☎ *0171/437–4445.*

Crews Bar. As it sounds: a big West End pub with a swanky, New Yorky look, and testosterone on tap. ✉ *14 Upper St. Martin's La., W1,* ☎ *0171/379–4880.*

Drill Hall. A woman-centric arts center with a great program of theater/dance/art events and classes, plus a popular bar, which is women-only Monday. ✉ *16 Chenies St., WC1,* ☎ *0171/631–1353.*

The Edge. Poseurs welcome at this hip Soho hangout, where straight groovers mix in, and there are sidewalk tables in summer. Risk the vodkas infused with candy. ✉ *11 Soho Sq., W1,* ☎ *0171/439–1223.*

First Out. A relaxed, fairly long-established café/bar in the shadow of Centrepoint. Fridays are women-only. ✉ *52 St. Giles High St., WC2,* ☎ *0171/240–8042.*

The Village. A cavern of a fashionable three-floored bar/restaurant/café/disco, whose name makes explicit the similarities between New York a decade back and London now. ✉ *81 Wardour St., W1,* ☎ *0171/434–2124.*

The Yard. This is Soho's best-looking and biggest bar/café, centered around the stunning Courtyard restaurant. ✉ *57 Rupert St., W1,* ☎ *0171/437–2652.*

Cabaret

Madame Jo Jos. By no means devoid of straight spectators, this place has long been one of the most fun drag cabarets in town—civilized of atmosphere, with barechested bar boys. There are various club events too, including London's first drag king night: Naive on Mondays. ✉ *8 Brewer St.,* ☎ *0171/287–1414.* 🎫 *Mon.–Thurs. £6, Fri. and Sat. £8. Doors open at 10 PM; shows at 12:15 and 1:15.*

Vauxhall Tavern. This venerable, curved pub had a drag cabaret before the Lady Bunny was born. Sometimes it's full of gay mafia, other times local media folk having a different night out, and Friday is the night for the lesbian cabaret, Vixens. ✉ *372 Kennington La., SE11,* ☎ *0171/582–0833.* 🎫 *Free.* ⏲ *Mon. 8 PM–1 AM, Tues., Thurs.–Sat. 8 PM–2 AM, Wed. 8 PM–midnight, Sun. 7–10:30 PM.*

Clubs

Heaven. Aptly named, it has by far the best light show on any London dance floor, is unpretentious, *loud,* and huge, with a labyrinth of quiet rooms, bars, and live-music parlors. If you go to just one club, this is the one to choose. Thursday is straight night. ✉ *The Arches, Villiers St., WC2,* ☎ *0171/839–2520.* 🎫 *£4–£8.* ⏲ *Tues.–Sat. 10:30 PM–3:30 AM.*

One-nighters

Some of the best gay dance clubs are held once a week in mixed clubs. The following are well-established, and likely still to be going, but it's best to call first.

Jo's Original Tea Dance. A longtime fave with the girls, this is a very camp and very fun Sunday ballroom, line dance, time warp disco, now in a new home after many years. ✉ *BJ's White Swan, 556 Commercial Rd., E14,* ☎ *0171/780–9870.* 🎫 *£4.* 🕔 *5 PM–midnight.*

Love Muscle. A steaming mixed gender Saturday-night party, with eight hours of dance classics at a big Brixton club. ✉ *The Fridge, Town Hall Parade, Brixton Hill, SW2,* ☎ *0171/326–5100.* 🎫 *£8 before midnight with flyer, £10 midnight–3 AM, £7 after 3 AM.* 🕔 *10 PM–6 AM.*

Queer Nation. This Sunday club is adorable for its laid-back, high-fashion friendliness, with hordes of gay and straight men and women recovering from the weekend together. ✉ *The Gardening Club, 4 The Piazza, Covent Garden, WC2,* ☎ *0171/497–3153.* 🎫 *£6.* 🕔 *9 PM–3 AM.*

THE ARTS

There isn't a "London arts scene"—there are lots of them. As long as there are audiences for Feydeau revivals, drag queens, obscure teenaged rock bands, hit musicals, body-painted Parisian dancers, and improvised stand-up comedy, someone will stage them in London. Commercial sponsorship of the arts is in its infancy here compared to what it is in the United States, and most major arts companies, as well as those smaller ones lucky enough to be grant-aided, are dependent, to some extent, on (inadequate) government subsidy. This ought to mean low ticket prices, but it doesn't necessarily work that way. Even so, when you consider how much a London hotel room costs, the city's arts are a bargain.

We've attempted a representative selection in the following listings, but to find out what's showing now, the weekly magazine *Time Out* (it comes out every Wednesday—Tuesday in central London) is invaluable. The *Evening Standard* also carries listings, especially the Friday edition, as do the "quality" Sunday papers and the Friday and Saturday *Independent, Guardian,* and *Times.* You'll find racks overflowing with leaflets and flyers in most cinema and theater foyers, too, and you can pick up the free fortnightly *London Theatre Guide* leaflet from hotels and tourist information centers.

Theater

Although the price of a seat rarely falls below a tenner, London's West End theaters still pull in enough punters to cause a mini traffic jam each night before the house lights dim and the curtain rises. From Shakespeare to the umpteenth year of *Les Misérables* (or *The Glums,* as it's affectionately known), the West End has what visitors think of as London's theater. But there's more to see in London than the offerings of Theaterland and the national companies.

Of the 100 or so legitimate theaters in the capital, 50 are officially "West End," while the remainder go under the blanket title of "Fringe." Much like New York's Off- and Off-Off-Broadway, Fringe Theater encompasses everything from off-the-wall "physical theater" pieces to first runs of new plays and revivals of old ones. At press time, on the Fringe alone, you could catch two Strindbergs, a Sartre, a Kafka, an Anouillh, an Ionesco, and two Molière productions. There was a production of Sheridan's *School for Scandal* in far-off-off-off Ealing, and a feminist staging of *Ben Hur* in even further Croydon. You could choose between *The Thirty Nine Steps,* or a Canadian adaptation of Bukowski's prose whose title is unprintable, a warts-and-all theatrical portrait of Maria Callas, or an Austrian recasting of *Cosí Fan Tutti* set in a motorway service station. You could catch such diverse offerings as Fassbinder's *The Bitter Tears of Petra von Kant* in a pub in Camden, *The Complete History of America (abridged)* by the *other* RSC (the Reduced Shakespeare Company), an amateur production of *Godspell*, or a long-running show in which tube passengers are the unwitting actors, as the audience secretly follows a lone performer posing as a klutzy commuter. That's just the fringe.

Most theaters have matinees twice a week (Wednesday or Thursday and Saturday) and evening performances that begin at 7:30 or 8; performances on Sunday are rare, but not unknown. Prices vary, but in the West End you should expect to pay from £8 for a seat in the upper balcony to at least £20 for a good one in the stalls (orchestra) or dress circle (mezzanine). Tickets may be booked at the individual theater box offices or over the phone by credit card (some box offices or agents have special numbers for these marked "cc" in the phone book); most theaters still charge no booking fee for the latter. You can also book through ticket agents, such as **First Call** (☎ 0171/240–7941) or **Ticketmaster** (☎ 0171/413–3321 or 800/775–2525 from the U.S.), though these usually do charge a booking fee. **Keith Prowse** has a New York office (✉ 234 W. 44th St., Suite 1000, New York, NY 10036, ☎ 212/398–1430 or 800/669–8687), as does **Edwards & Edwards** (✉ 1 Times Sq. Plaza, 12th Floor, New York, NY 10036, ☎ 212/944–0290 or 800/223–6108). If you're a theater junkie, and want to put together a West End package, the *Complete Guide to London's West End Theatres* has seating plans and booking information for all the houses. It costs £9.95 (plus postage) from the Society of London Theatres (☞ *below*). Alternatively, the Half Price Ticket Booth (no phone) on the southwest corner of Leicester Square sells half-price tickets on the day of performance for approximately 25 theaters (subject to availability). It's open Monday–Saturday 1–6:30 and from noon on Sundays and matinee days; there is a £1.50 service charge, and only cash is accepted. All the larger hotels offer theater bookings, but as they tack on a hefty service charge, you would do better visiting the box offices yourself. You might, however, consider using one particular booking line that doubles the price of tickets: **West End Cares** (☎ 0171/867–1111) donates half of what it charges to AIDS charities.

Warning: Be *very* careful of scalpers outside theaters; they have been known to charge £200 or more for a sought-after ticket. In recent years, there has been another problem: unscrupulous ticket agents, who sell tickets at four or five times their price from the ticket box offices. While a service charge is legitimate, this type of scalping certainly isn't, especially since the vast majority of theaters have some tickets (returns and "house seats") available on the night of performance. If you have a bad experience with a scalper, contact the Development Officer at the **Society of London Theatres** (✉ Bedford Chambers, The Piazza, Covent Garden, WC2E 8HQ, ☎ 0171/836–3193). They probably can't get you a refund, but your letter will help stamp out scalpers in the future.

WEST END

The **Royal Shakespeare Company** and the **Royal National Theatre Company** perform at London's two main arts complexes, the **Barbican Centre** and **The Royal National Theatre** respectively. Both companies mount consistently excellent productions and are usually a safe option for anyone having trouble choosing which play to see.

The following is a list of West End theaters:

Adelphi, ✉ *Strand, WC2E 7NA,* ☎ *0171/379–8884*
Albery, ✉ *St. Martin's La., WC2N 4AH,* ☎ *0171/867–1115*
Aldwych, ✉ *Aldwych, WC2B 4DF,* ☎ *0171/836–6404*
Ambassadors, ✉ *West St., WC2H 9ND,* ☎ *0171/836–6111*

Theaters and Concert Halls

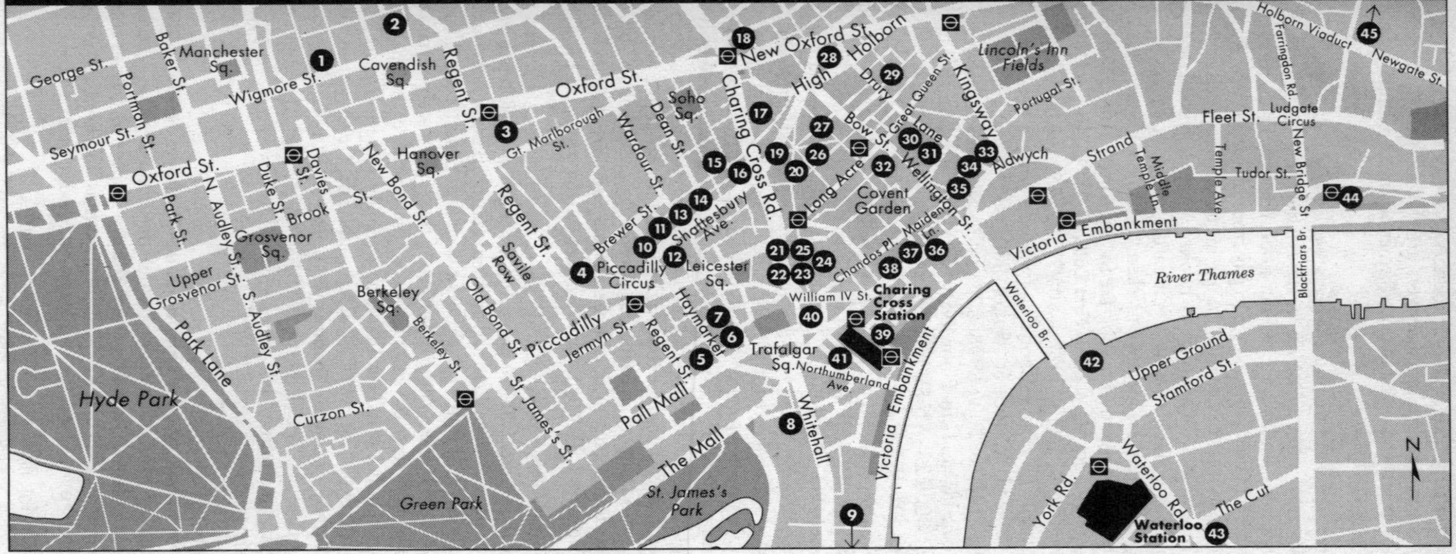

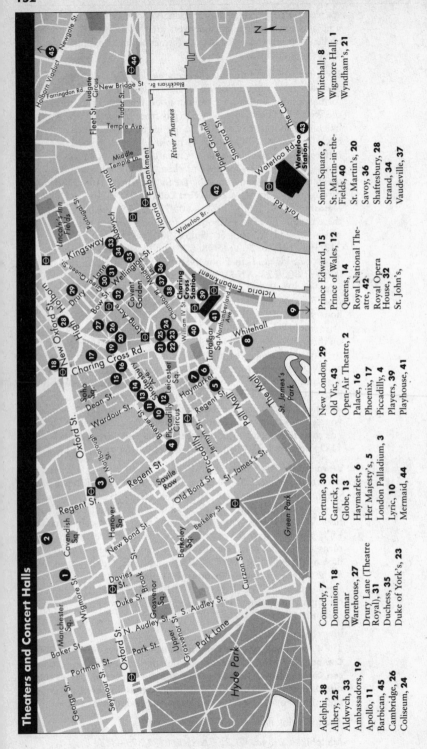

Adelphi, **38**
Albery, **25**
Aldwych, **33**
Ambassadors, **19**
Apollo, **11**
Barbican, **45**
Cambridge, **26**
Coliseum, **24**
Comedy, **7**
Dominion, **18**
Donmar Warehouse, **27**
Drury Lane (Theatre Royal), **31**
Duchess, **35**
Duke of York's, **23**
Fortune, **30**
Garrick, **22**
Globe, **13**
Haymarket, **6**
Her Majesty's, **5**
London Palladium, **3**
Lyric, **10**
Mermaid, **44**
New London, **29**
Old Vic, **43**
Open-Air Theatre, **2**
Palace, **16**
Phoenix, **17**
Piccadilly, **4**
Players, **39**
Playhouse, **41**
Prince Edward, **15**
Prince of Wales, **12**
Queens, **14**
Royal National Theatre, **42**
Royal Opera House, **32**
St. John's, Smith Square, **9**
St. Martin-in-the-Fields, **40**
St. Martin's, **20**
Savoy, **36**
Shaftesbury, **28**
Strand, **34**
Vaudeville, **37**
Whitehall, **8**
Wigmore Hall, **1**
Wyndham's, **21**

5 CENTS
CANADA 1978
PESOS
LIBERTY
VINGT FRANCS

Apollo, ✉ *Shaftesbury Ave., W1V 7HD,* ☎ *0171/494–5070*
Apollo Victoria, ✉ *Wilton Rd., SW1V ILL,* ☎ *0171/416–6042*
Arts Theatre, ✉ *6–7 Great Newport St., WC2H 7JB,* ☎ *0171/836–2132*
Barbican, ✉ *Barbican, EC2Y 8DS,* ☎ *0171/638–8891*
Cambridge, ✉ *Earlham St., WC2H 9HU,* ☎ *0171/379–5299*
Comedy, ✉ *Panton St., SW1Y 4DN,* ☎ *0171/494–5080*
Dominion, ✉ *Tottenham Court Rd., W1 0AG,* ☎ *0171/416–6060*
Donmar Warehouse, ✉ *41 Earlham St., WC2H 9LD,* ☎ *0171/867–1150*
Drury Lane (Theatre Royal), ✉ *Catherine St., WC2B 5JF,* ☎ *0171/494–5001*
Duchess, ✉ *Catherine St., WC2B 5LA,* ☎ *0171/494–5075*
Duke of York's, ✉ *St. Martin's La., WC2N 4BG,* ☎ *0171/836–5122*
Fortune, ✉ *Russell St., WC2B 5HH,* ☎ *0171/836–2238*
Garrick, ✉ *Charing Cross Rd., WC2H 0HH,* ☎ *0171/494–5085*
Globe, ✉ *Shaftesbury Ave., W1V 8AR,* ☎ *0171/494–5067*
Haymarket, ✉ *Haymarket, SW1Y 4HT,* ☎ *0171/930–8800*
Her Majesty's, ✉ *Haymarket, SW1Y 4QR,* ☎ *0171/494–5400*
London Palladium, ✉ *8 Argyll St., W1V 1AD,* ☎ *0171/494–5020*
Lyric, ✉ *Shaftesbury Ave., W1V 7HA,* ☎ *0171/494–5045*
Lyric Hammersmith, ✉ *King St., W6 0QL,* ☎ *0181/741–2311*
Mermaid, ✉ *Puddle Dock, EC4 3DB,* ☎ *0171/410–0000*
New London, ✉ *Drury La., WC2B 5PW,* ☎ *0171/405–0072*
Old Vic, ✉ *Waterloo Rd., SE1 8NB,* ☎ *0171/928–7616*
Open-Air Theatre, ✉ *Inner Circle, Regent's Park, NW1 4NP,* ☎ *0171/935–5884*
Palace, ✉ *Shaftesbury Ave., W1V 8AY,* ☎ *0171/434–0909*
Phoenix, ✉ *Charing Cross Rd., WC2H 0JP,* ☎ *0171/867–1044*
Piccadilly, ✉ *Denman St., W1V 8DY,* ☎ *0171/867–1118*
Players, ✉ *The Arches, Villiers St., WC2N 6NQ,* ☎ *0171/839–1134*
Playhouse, ✉ *Northumberland Ave., WC2N 6NN,* ☎ *0171/839–4401*
Prince Edward, ✉ *Old Compton St., W1V 8AH,* ☎ *0171/734–8951*
Prince of Wales, ✉ *31 Coventry St., W1V 8AS,* ☎ *0171/839–5972*
Queens, ✉ *51 Shaftesbury Ave., W1V 8BA,* ☎ *0171/494–5041*
Royal Court, ✉ *Sloane Sq., SW1W 8AS,* ☎ *0171/730–1745* (☞ *Theatre Upstairs under Fringe, below*)
Royal National Theatre (Cottesloe, Lyttelton, and Olivier), ✉ *South Bank Arts Complex, SE1 9PX,* ☎ *0171/928–2252*
St. Martin's, ✉ *West St., WC2H 9NH,* ☎ *0171/836–1443*
Savoy, ✉ *Strand, WC2R 0ET,* ☎ *0171/836–8888*
Shaftesbury, ✉ *Shaftesbury Ave., WC2H 8DP,* ☎ *0171/379–5399*
Strand, ✉ *Aldwych, WC2B 5LD,* ☎ *0171/930–8800*
Vaudeville, ✉ *Strand, WC2R 0NH,* ☎ *0171/836–9987*
Victoria Palace, ✉ *Victoria St., SW1E 5EA,* ☎ *0171/834–1317*
Westminster, ✉ *12 Palace St., SW1E 5JA,* ☎ *0171/834–0283*
Whitehall, ✉ *14 Whitehall, SW1A 2DY,* ☎ *0171/867–1119*
Wyndham's, ✉ *Charing Cross Rd., WC2H 0DA,* ☎ *0171/867–1116*

FRINGE

Shows can be straight plays, circus, comedy, musicals, readings, or productions every bit as polished and impressive as those in the West End—except for their location and the price of the seat. Fringe tickets are always considerably less expensive than tickets for West End productions. The following theaters are among the better-known fringe venues:

Almeida, ✉ *Almeida St., N1 1AT,* ☎ *0171/359–4404*
BAC, ✉ *176 Lavender Hill, Battersea SW11 1JX,* ☎ *0171/223–2223*
Bush, ✉ *Shepherds Bush Green, W12 8QD,* ☎ *0181/743–3388*
Canal Café Theatre, ✉ *Bridge House, Delamere Terr., W2,* ☎ *0171/289–6054*
Drill Hall, ✉ *16 Chenies St., WC1E 7EX,* ☎ *0171/637–8270*

The Finborough, ✉ *Finborough Arms, Finborough Rd., SW10 9ED,* ☎ *0171/373–3842*

The Gate, ✉ *The Prince Albert, 11 Pembridge Rd., W11 3HQ,* ☎ *0171/229–0706*

Hackney Empire, ✉ *291 Mare St., E8 1EJ,* ☎ *0181/985–2424*

Hampstead, ✉ *Swiss Cottage, NW3 3EX,* ☎ *0171/722–9301*

ICA Theatre, ✉ *The Mall, SW1Y 5AH,* ☎ *0171/930–3647*

Kings Head, ✉ *115 Upper St., N1 1QN,* ☎ *0171/226–1916*

Grace Theatre at the Latchmere, ✉ *503 Battersea Park Rd., SW11 3BW,* ☎ *0171/228–2620*

Lyric Studio, ✉ *Lyric Theatre, King St., W6 9JT,* ☎ *0181/741–2311*

Man in the Moon, ✉ *392 Kings Rd., SW3 5UZ,* ☎ *0171/351–2876*

New End Theatre, ✉ *27 New End, NW3 1JD,* ☎ *0171/794–0022*

Orange Tree, ✉ *1 Clarence St., Richmond, TW9 1SA,* ☎ *0181/940–3633*

Riverside Studios, ✉ *Crisp Rd., W6 9RL,* ☎ *0181/748–3354*

Theatre Royal, ✉ *Stratford East, E15 1BN,* ☎ *0181/534–0310*

Theatre Upstairs, ✉ *Royal Court, Sloane Sq., SW1W 8AS,* ☎ *0171/730–2554*

Tricycle Theatre, ✉ *269 Kilburn High Rd., NW6 7JR,* ☎ *0171/328–1000*

Watermans Arts Centre, ✉ *40 High St., Brentford, TW8 0DS,* ☎ *0181/568–1176*

Young Vic, ✉ *66 The Cut, SE1 8LZ,* ☎ *0171/928–6363*

Concerts

The ticket prices to symphony-size orchestral concerts are fortunately still relatively moderate, usually ranging from £5 to £15. If you can't book in advance, then arrive at the hall an hour before the performance for a chance at returns.

The London Symphony Orchestra is in residence at the **Barbican Centre,** although other top orchestras—including the Philharmonia and the Royal Philharmonic—also perform here. The **South Bank Arts Complex,** which includes the **Royal Festival Hall,** the **Queen Elizabeth Hall,** and the small **Purcell Room,** forms another major venue; the Royal Festival Hall is one of the finest concert halls in Europe. Between the Barbican and South Bank, there are concert performances almost every night of the year. The Barbican also features chamber music concerts with such celebrated orchestras as the City of London Sinfonia.

For a different concert-going experience, as well as the chance to take part in a great British tradition, try the **Royal Albert Hall** during the Promenade Concert season: eight weeks lasting from July to September. Special "promenade" (standing) tickets usually cost half the price of normal tickets and are available at the hall on the night of the concert. Another summer pleasure is the outdoor concert series by the lake at **Kenwood** (✉ Hampstead Heath, ☎ 0181/348–6684). Concerts are also part of the program at the open-air theater in **Holland Park** (☎ 0171/602–7856). Check the listings for details.

You should also look for the lunchtime concerts that take place all over the city in smaller concert halls, the big arts center foyers, and churches; they usually cost under £5 or are free and will feature string quartets, singers, jazz ensembles, or gospel choirs. **St. John's, Smith Square** and **St. Martin-in-the-Fields** are two of the more popular locations. Performances usually begin about 1 PM and last an hour.

CONCERT HALL BOX OFFICE INFORMATION

Barbican Centre, ✉ *Barbican, EC2Y 8DS,* ☎ *0171/638–8891 (reservations); 0171/638–4141 (information)*

Royal Albert Hall, ✉ *Kensington Gore, SW7 2AP,* ☎ *0171/589–8212*
St. John's, Smith Square, ✉ *SW1P 3HA,* ☎ *0171/222–1061*
St. Martin-in-the-Fields, ✉ *Trafalgar Sq., WC2N 4JJ,* ☎ *0171/839–1930*
South Bank Arts Complex, ✉ *South Bank, SE1 8XX,* ☎ *0171/928–8800 (reservations); 0171/928–3002 (information)*
Wigmore Hall, ✉ *36 Wigmore St., W1H 9DF,* ☎ *0171/935–2141*

Opera

The main venue for opera in London is the **Royal Opera House,** which ranks with the Metropolitan Opera House in New York—in every way, including expense. Prices range from £5 in the upper slips ("the gods"—views are often partial from here) to well over £100 for the best seats. Performances are divided into booking periods and sell out early, although returns and standing spaces are sold on the day. (Conditions of purchase vary—call the box office for information.) The Opera House is undergoing a massive rebuilding program, and is moving into temporary accommodation for some of 1996.

English-language productions are staged at the **Coliseum** in St. Martin's Lane, home of the **English National Opera Company.** Prices here are lower than at the Royal Opera House, ranging from £8 to £45, and productions are often innovative and exciting.

Ballet

The Royal Opera House is also the home of the world-famous **Royal Ballet,** although the multi-million pound rebuilding project includes a separate theater for the ballet. Prices are slightly more reasonable for the ballet than they are for the opera, but bookings should be made well in advance, as tickets sell out fast. The **English National Ballet** and visiting international companies perform at the Coliseum and the Royal Festival Hall from time to time. **Sadler's Wells Theatre** also hosts various other ballet companies and regional and international modern dance troupes. Prices here are much cheaper than at Covent Garden.

OPERA AND BALLET BOX OFFICE INFORMATION

Coliseum, ✉ *St. Martin's La., WC2N 4ES,* ☎ *0171/632–8300*
Royal Opera House, ✉ *Covent Garden, WC2E 9DD,* ☎ *0171/304–4000*
Sadler's Wells, ✉ *Rosebery Ave., EC1R 4TN,* ☎ *0171/713–6000*

Modern Dance

Contemporary dance thrives in London, with innovative young choreographers and companies constantly emerging (and then, it often seems, moving to New York). Michael Clark was one of the first of the new wave; Yolanda Snaith and choreographer Lea Anderson's troupe, the Cholmondeleys (pronounced "Chumleys"), are two more examples of home-grown talent. In addition to the many Fringe theaters that produce the odd dance performance, the following theaters showcase contemporary dance:

The Place, ✉ *17 Duke's Rd., WC1,* ☎ *0171/387–0031*
Riverside Studios (☞ Fringe Theater, *above*)
Sadler's Wells (☞ Opera and Ballet, *above*)

Movies

Despite the video invasion, West End movie theaters continue to do good business. Most of the major houses (Odeon, MGM, etc.) congregate in the Leicester Square/Piccadilly Circus area, where tickets average £7. Mondays and matinees are often cheaper at around £4, and there are also fewer crowds. Prices drop to around £5 as you get out of the West End, and are even lower in the suburbs, but unless you're staying there, any savings could be eaten up by transportation costs.

The few movie clubs and repertory cinemas that still exist screen a wider range of movies, including classic, Continental, and underground, as well as rare or underestimated masterpieces. Some charge a membership fee of under £1. The king is the **National Film Theatre** (⊠ South Bank Arts Complex, ☎ 0171/928–3232), where the London Film Festival is based in the fall; there are also lectures and presentations. Daily memberships cost 40p. Also worth checking out are the **Everyman** (⊠ Hollybush Vale, Hampstead, ☎ 0171/435–1525; membership 60p/year), the **Rio** (⊠ Kingsland High St., Hackney E8, ☎ 0171/254–6677), though it's a bit of a trek, and the **Riverside** (☞ Fringe Theater, *above*).

The **Institute of Contemporary Arts** (⊠ the Mall, ☎ 0171/930–3647) contains two cinemas (one is tiny), while the **French Institute** (⊠ 17 Queensbury Pl., SW7, ☎ 0171/589–6211) and the **Goethe Institute** (⊠ Princes Gate, SW7, ☎ 0171/411–3400) show French and German films respectively. Films are also shown irregularly at many of the national museums.

5 Outdoor Activities and Sports

THERE ARE THE WIMBLEDON TENNIS CHAMPIONSHIPS, and there's cricket, and then there's soccer, and that's about all there is for the sports fan in London, right? Wrong. London is a great city for the weekend player of almost anything. It really comes into its own in summer, when the parks sprout nets and goals and painted white lines, outdoor swimming pools open, and a season of spectator events gets underway. The listings below concentrate on facilities available to the casual visitor in a whole range of sports and on the more accessible or well-known spectator events. Bring your gear, and branch out from that hotel gym.

PARTICIPANT SPORTS AND FITNESS

If your sport is missing from those listed below, or if you need additional information, **Sportsline** (☎ 0171/222–8000, weekdays 10–6) supplies details about London's clubs, events, and facilities. It's a free service.

Aerobics

You don't need to buy a membership at any of the following studios, which offer a range of classes for all levels of fitness and are open daily. The average price for an hour's worth of sweating is £5.

Go West Studio (✉ Porchester Centre, Queensway, W2, ☎ 0171/792–2919. Tube: Bayswater). About seven daily classes are graded from beginner to pro, with step, yoga, circuit training and aquaerobics included in the mix.

Jubilee Hall (✉ 30 The Piazza, Covent Garden, WC2, ☎ 0171/379–0008. Tube: Covent Garden). Many are addicted to Jamie Addicoat's "Fatbuster" classes, but there are plenty more, from body sculpting and step to Pilates and jazz dance.

Portobello Green Fitness Centre (✉ 3–5 Thorpe Close, W10, ☎ 0181/960–2221. Tube: Ladbroke Grove). It's under the Westway overpass, and you'll have to battle through flea-market shoppers on weekends to reach the bargain (£3) classes.

Seymour Leisure Centre (✉ Seymour Pl., W2, ☎ 0171/402–5795. Tube: Marylebone). The best classes in the "Move It" program here—especially Julie Corsair's amazing hip-hop rave classes—fill to the brim, but the spacious studios can take the pressure. Arrive early for step; you'll need a ticket (classes cost around the £5 mark).

Bicycling

London is reasonably cycle-friendly for a big city, with special lanes marked for bicycles on some major roads, but it is never safe to ride without a helmet. **Bikepark** (✉ 14 Stukeley St., WC2, ☎ 0171/430–0083. Tube: Covent Garden) can rent anything you want—mountain, hybrid or road bike—from £10/day, £30/weekend, or £30/week, plus a deposit (MC, V) of 75%–100% of the bike's value. All machines are new and issued complete with locks; accessories are available too. Reserve ahead in summer.

Boxing

All Stars Gym. The "KO Circuit" at Isola Akay's friendly gym in a converted church is a two-hour intensive workout, with shadowboxing, heavy bags, pad work, rope jumping, weights, and a lengthy warm-up, cool-down, and stretch. It pulls in both serious fighters and dilettantes, and an average male-to-female ratio of 4 to 1. Total beginners are shown the ropes, too. ✉ *576 Harrow Rd., W10,* ☎ *0181/960*

7724. ⏲ Mon.–Thurs. 7:30 PM, Sat. 10 AM, 12:30 AM. Tube: Westbourne Park.

Dance

There's a lot of dance action around, but only space to list a few of the more general studios. Check the listings in *Time Out* for specialized classes.

Danceworks (✉ 16 Balderton St., W1, ☎ 0171/629–6183. Tube: Bond Street). You'll find what is probably the widest-ranging program of classes here, catering to all standards from beginner to professional. Ballet, jazz, flamenco, Egyptian, and tap are regulars, but there's more.

Pineapple (✉ 7 Langley St., WC2, ☎ 0171/836–4004. Tube: Covent Garden). This is where the '80s fitness boom was launched in London, though modern dance has always been its real business. Classes are highly regarded by the sort of dancers who appear a lot on MTV. There's also a "KO Circuit" here.

The Place (✉ 17 Dukes Rd., WC2, ☎ 0171/388–8430. Tube: Euston). It really *is* the place for modern dance, since it houses the Contemporary Dance Trust and the London Contemporary Dance School, plus a dance theater, in addition to holding all grades of class.

Golf

Golf is as huge in England as it is in the States, but if you want to play a round in London, you'll have to hit the outer boroughs.

Regent's Park Golf and Tennis School (✉ Outer Circle, Regent's Park, NW1, ☎ 0171/724–0643. Tube: Regent's Park). You don't have to travel far to get here—it's just by the zoo—but driving ranges and putting greens are all you'll get. The instructors have a good reputation.

Richmond Park (✉ Roehampton Gate, SW15, ☎ 0181/876–1795. Tube: Richmond). There are two well-kept but very busy 18-hole courses here. You don't have to be a member of anything, and can hire half or full sets of clubs, plus buggies and trollies.

Trent Park Golf Club (✉ Bramley Rd., Southgate N14, ☎ 0181/366–7432. Tube: Oakwood). Here you do have to pay a modest fee to join, but it's worth considering for regular visitors; the setting of this countrified 18-hole course is beautiful, and it's easily reached on the Piccadilly line to Oakwood.

Horseback Riding

Rotten Row and the surrounding network of Hyde Park sand tracks make up the only place to ride in central London—better for posing in the saddle than serious maneuvers, and no galloping allowed. Outer London offers more scope, plus lessons.

Hyde Park Riding Stables (✉ 63 Bathurst Mews, W2, ☎ 0171/723–2813. Tube: Lancaster Gate). One of the very few public stables left for riding in Hyde Park keeps a range of horses from those for beginners to those wanting to brush up their dressage skills.

London Equestrian Centre (✉ Frith Manor Farm, Lullington Garth, N12, ☎ 0181/349–1345; call for directions). This big, bustling north London stable caters to all stages of rider, even nervous beginners. Cross-country, dressage, jumping, and even side-saddle lessons are available, too. You must submit to a half-hour assessment first.

Trent Park Stables (✉ East Pole Farm, Bramley Rd., N14, ☎ 0181/363–8630. Tube: Oakwood). You'll think you've left London as you hack through 300 acres of near-rural Middlesex. You can't ride alone because of insurance restrictions, but all standards are accommodated, and indoor and outdoor lessons, from beginners' to dressage and jumping, are available.

Ice Skating

Hockey is actually becoming pretty popular, but professional and leisure skating has a slight image problem in Britain, where it's perceived as downscale.

Broadgate Arena (✉ 3 Broadgate, EC2, ☎ 0171/588–6565. Tube: Liverpool Street). It's a tiny circle, but it's outdoors—and therefore unique in London. Open from November to April, it's a fun place to skate because of the audience of City workers and the silly team games you can join. Skate rental is available.

Queens Ice Skating Club (✉ Queensway, W2, ☎ 0171/229–0172. Tube: Queensway). A figure-skating rink with disco tendencies, this is central London's only serious ice venue, and you can take a lesson should your outside edge be rusty. You can rent skates here, too. Queensway tube is next door.

Martial Arts

You can learn everything from *ba gua zhang* (a Chinese internal martial art) to *silat perisai diri* (Indonesian self-defense), and karate too.

The Academy (✉ 16 Hoxton Square N1, ☎ 0171/729–5789. Tube: Old Street). Fancy some Jeet Kune Do? Bob Breen's converted school building is one of the best martial arts schools in London.

Jubilee Hall (✉ 30 The Piazza, Covent Garden, WC2, ☎ 0171/379–0008. Tube: Covent Garden). This venue offers regular tai chi chuan, tae kwon do, and karate classes, plus *wu shu* (Chinese boxing).

Rock Climbing

This is getting increasingly popular in London, with several (somewhat hard to find) "mountains" around town, good for all standards of rock fan.

NLRC (✉ Cordova Rd., Bow, E3, ☎ 0181/980–0289. Tube: Mile End). Here are four buildings with every possible rockface—transverse, vertical, and completely upside-down—plus abseiling in the Tower. Classes and equipment are available, and there are usually impressive experts to watch for pointers when you're exhausted.

Sobell Sports Centre (✉ Hornsey Rd., N7, ☎ 0171/609–2166. Tube: Finsbury Park). Islington's all-purpose, council-owned center has three walls, plus instruction and equipment.

Westway Sports Centre (✉ 1 Crowthorne Rd., W10, ☎ 0181/969–0992. Tube: Latimer Road). London's only outside climbing space includes a 15-meter tower, 30 meters of transverse wall, plus boulders, and it's inexpensive too.

Running

London is just perfect for joggers. If you're after a crowd, the more popular routes include **Green Park,** which gets a stream of runners armed with maps from the Piccadilly hotels, and—to a lesser extent—adjacent **St. James's Park.** Both can get perilous with deck chairs during summer days. **Hyde Park** and **Kensington Gardens** together supply a 4-mile perimeter route, or you can do a 2½-mile run in Hyde Park alone if you start at Hyde Park Corner or Marble Arch and encircle the Serpentine. Most Park Lane hotels offer jogging maps for this, their local green space. **Regent's Park** has probably the most populated track because it's a sporting kind of place; the Outer Circle loop measures about 2½ miles.

Away from the center, there are longer, scenic runs over more varied terrain at **Hampstead Heath,** connecting with **Kenwood** and **Parliament Hill,** London's highest point, where you'll get a fabulous panoramic sweep over the entire city. **Richmond Park** is the biggest green space of all, but don't run into the deer during rutting season (Oct.–Nov.). Back in town, there's a rather traffic-heavy 1½-mile riverside run along **Victoria Embankment** from Westminster Bridge to Embankment at Blackfriars Bridge, or a beautiful mile among the rowing clubs and ducks along the Malls—Upper, Lower, and Chiswick—from **Hammersmith Bridge.**

GROUP RUNS

If you don't want to run alone, call the **London Hash House Harriers** (☎ 0181/995–7879). They organize noncompetitive hour-long runs round interesting bits of town, with loops and checkpoints built in. Cost: £1.

Softball

Control your mirth—the sport is huge here; in fact, it's the fastest-growing participatory sport in England. Pick up a game Sunday afternoon in **Regent's Park,** or on the south edge of **Hyde Park.**

Squash

While squash is a popular English sport, its American cousin, raquetball, isn't played here. Most clubs restrict court use to club members, but the facilities listed are open to non-members as well.

Ironmonger Row (✉ Ironmonger Row, EC1, ☎ 0171/253–4011. Tube: Old Street). There are 10 courts in this popular City sports center. You can't book by phone without a membership, but you're likely to get a court if you show up to play during Londoners' office hours or on weekends when courts are less busy.

Portobello Green Fitness Centre (✉ 3–5 Thorpe Close, W10, ☎ 0181/960–2221. Tube: Ladbroke Grove). Only three courts here, but they're inexpensive.

Sobell Sports Centre (✉ Hornsey Rd., N7, ☎ 0171/609–2166. Tube: Finsbury Park). This is a popular place, but you can usually get court time.

Swimming

London does not lack for public swimming pools—clean, lifeguarded, and usually open long hours.

INDOOR POOLS

Chelsea (✉ Chelsea Manor St., SW3, ☎ 0171/352–6985. Tube: South Kensington). This renovated turn-of-the-century 27-by-10-yard pool is just off the King's Road, so it's busy, and packed with kids on weekends.

Seymour Leisure Centre (✉ Seymour Pl., W2, ☎ 0171/402–5795. Tube: Marylebone). There's usually a lane roped off for laps at this very central 44-by-20-yard pool, unless the aquaerobics class has taken over.

Swiss Cottage (✉ Winchester Rd., NW3, ☎ 0171/586–5989. Tube: Swiss Cottage). A little out-of-the-way (but next to the Swiss Cottage tube), this is one of the largest (37 by 16 yards) and best for serious lap swimming. There's a shallow children's pool, too.

INDOOR/OUTDOOR POOLS

Oasis (✉ 32 Endell St., WC2, ☎ 0171/831–1804. Tube: Covent Garden). And it is just that, with a heated pool (open May–Sept.) right in Covent Garden, and a 30-by-10-yard one indoors. Needless to say, they both get packed in summer.

SPA POOLS

Ironmonger Row (☞ *above*). This 33-by-12-yard City pool is in a '30s complex that includes a Turkish bath, not quite as beautiful as Porchester's (☞ *below*). There are separate sessions for men and women.

Porchester Baths (✉ Queensway, W2, ☎ 0171/229–9950. Tube: Queensway). Here there's a 33-by-11-yard pool for serious lap swimmers, plus a 1920s Turkish bath, sauna, and spa of gorgeous, slightly faded grandeur. It, too, has separate sessions for men and women.

BEACHES

Serpentine Lido (✉ Hyde Park, W2, ☎ 0171/262–5484. ⏲ May–Sept. Tube: Knightsbridge). Okay, so it's a beach on a lake, but a hot day in Hyde Park is surreally reminiscent of the seaside. There are changing facilities, and the swimming section is chlorinated.

Hampstead Ponds (co-ed: ✉ East Heath Rd., NW3, ☎ 0171/435–2366; women only: ✉ Millfield La., N6, ☎ 0171/348–1033. British Rail: Hampstead Heath). These Elysian little lakes are surrounded by grassy lounging areas. The women's one is particularly secluded—and crowded in summer, though it's open all year. The "Mixed Pond" is open May through September. Both have murky-looking, but clean, fresh water.

Tennis

Poor England never wins its own Grand Slam tournament. Some blame that circumstance on its being a nation of mere park players, which, for the visitor, has obvious benefits.

Holland Park (✉ Kensington High St., W8, ☎ 0171/602–2226. Tube: Holland Park). This is the prettiest place to play, with six hard courts available April through September.

Islington Tennis Centre (✉ Market Rd., N7, ☎ 0171/700–1370. Tube: Caledonian Road). It's about the only place where you don't need membership to play indoors (year-round), though you need it to reserve by phone. There are four outdoor courts, too, and coaching is available.

Paddington Sports Club (✉ Castelain Rd., W9, ☎ 0171/286–4515. Tube: Maida Vale). A surprisingly large and busy green space provides a set of eight hard courts where you compete for attention with track runners and soccer, cricket, and softball players.

Weight Training

If your hotel lacks a gym, these are central and sell either daily or monthly temporary membership.

Albany Fitness Centre (✉ St. Bede's Church, Albany St., NW1, ☎ 0171/383–7131. Tube: Great Portland Street). This is a deconsecrated church (buy a "Work Off Thy Last Supper" T-shirt), which means tons of space. There's Keiser equipment, free weights, cardio machines, and aerobics/sculpting classes. The cost is around £15/day, with lower weekly rates negotiable.

Central YMCA (✉ 112 Great Russell St., WC1, ☎ 0171/637–8131. Tube: Tottenham Court Road). As you'd expect from the Y, this place boasts every facility and sport, including a great 25-meter pool and a very well-equipped gym. Weekly membership costs around £35.

Jubilee Hall (✉ 30 The Piazza, Covent Garden, WC2, ☎ 0171/379–0008. Tube: Covent Garden). The day rate is £6, monthly £45 at this very crowded but very happening and super-well-equipped central gym.

The Peak (✉ Hyatt Carlton Tower Hotel, 2 Cadogan Pl., SW1, ☎ 0171/235–1234. Tube: Sloane Square). This hotel club is expensive (£30/day) but has top equipment, great ninth-floor views over Knightsbridge, and a sauna—with TV—in the full beauty spa. The 20-visit pass for £400 is fully transferrable, so a whole family could share one—almost a bargain.

Seymour Leisure Centre (✉ Seymour Pl., W2, ☎ 0171/723–8019. Tube: Marylebone). You must complete an hour-long introductory session to use the excellent gym and the cardio center overlooking a hall full of soccer, b-ball, or badminton players, but that and a full membership for a month costs a bargain £31.

Yoga

This discipline is becoming very popular in London, as it is in the United States.

The Life Centre (✉ 15 Edge St., W8, ☎ 0171/221–4602. Tube: Notting Hill Gate). London's newest, and without a doubt best, yoga school specializes in the dynamic, energetic Vinyasa technique imported through Germany by chief instructor Godfrey Devereux. Beautiful premises enhance the experience. A huge range of holistic health therapies are given upstairs.

SPECTATOR SPORTS

Boating

One of London's most beloved sporting events (since 1845) is also the easiest to see, and it's free. The only problem with the late-March **Oxford and Cambridge Boat Race** is securing a position among the crowds that line the Putney-to-Mortlake route (mostly at pubs along the Hammersmith Lower and Upper Malls, or on Putney Bridge). The Saturday start time varies from year to year according to the tides. The **Head of the River Race** is the professional version, only this time up to 420 crews of eight row the university course in the other direction. It usually happens the Saturday before the university race, or sometimes later the same day.

Cricket

Lord's (✉ St. John's Wood, NW8, ☎ 0171/289–1611) has been hallowed turf for worshipers of England's summer game since 1811. The World Series of cricket, the Tests, are played here, but tickets are hard to procure. One-day internationals, though, can usually be seen by lining up on the day, and top-class county matches are similarly accessible—whether the rules are is quite another matter.

The Oval (✉ Kennington Oval, SE11, ☎ 0171/582–6660) is a far easier place to witness the *thwack* of leather on willow. At London's second-string ground, you can see county games of very high standard.

Equestrian Events

It's one of those clichés based in truth that, from the queen down, the English are in love with the horse, as proved by the United Kingdom's Olympic medals. If you require further proof, attend one of the many parades, races, or show jumping exhibitions.

PARADES

You can see all the city's working horses at the Easter Monday **London Harness Horse Parade** (✉ Inner Circle, Regent's Pk., NW1; 9:30 AM–1 PM). The show competitions have categories like "Heavy Horse" and "Single Horsed Commercial Van." Something similar happens to recreational animals at the **London Riding Horse Parade,** on the first Sunday in August in (where else?) Rotten Row.

RACING

The main events of "the Season," as much social as sporting, occur just outside the city. Her actual Majesty attends **Royal Ascot** (✉ Grand Stand, Ascot, Berkshire, ☎ 01344/22211) in mid-June, driving from Windsor in an open carriage, and processing before the plebs daily at 2. **Derby Day** (✉ The Grandstand, Epsom Downs, Surrey, ☎ 01372/726311), on the first Wednesday in June, is the other big one. One of the world's greatest races for three-year-olds, it kicks off at 3:45.

SHOW JUMPING

The **Horse of the Year Show** (✉ Wembley Arena, ☎ 0181/900–1234) in late October is the top international competition, with lots of fun events alongside the serious. Best of all are the Pony Club Games, where child riders perform virtual gymnastics on horseback.

Marathon

Starting at 9 AM on the third Sunday in April, some 25,000 runners in the huge **London Marathon** race from Blackheath or Greenwich to Westminster Bridge or the Mall. Entry forms for the following year are available starting in May (☎ 01891/234234).

Rugby

This is not a million miles from gridiron, but players are unpadded. It raises the British (and especially Welsh) blood pressure like no other sport, and has recently undergone a revolution, with the amateur Rugby Union, and the professional Rugby League, once distinct, more or less merging with the advent of major sponsorship of the amateur game. The **Rugby League Final** has always been played at Wembley Stadium (✉ Wembley, Middlesex, ☎ 0181/900–1234) on the last Saturday in April, while the Rugby Union **Pilkington Cup** is traditionally fought a week later at the Twickenham Rugby Football Ground (✉ Whitton Rd., Twickenham, Middlesex, ☎ 0181/892–8161). Tickets for both are more precious than gold. But you can see international matches at Twickenham during the September-to-April season or catch the home games of the London teams at the spectacular **Saracens** (✉ Dale Green Rd., N14, ☎ 0181/449–3770) and **Rosslyn Park** (✉ Priory La., Upper Richmond Rd., SW15, ☎ 0181/876–1879).

Soccer

To refer to the national winter sport as "soccer" is to blaspheme. It is Football, and the British season culminates in the televised Wembley Stadium **FA Cup Final,** for which tickets are about as easy to get as they are for the Superbowl. International matches at Wembley during the August-to-May season are easier to attend (☎ 0181/900–1234).

For a real taste of this British obsession, though, nothing beats a match at the home ground of one of the three London clubs competing in the Premier League. More than likely you won't see a hint of the infamous hooliganism but will be quite carried away by the electric atmosphere only a vast football crowd can generate. **Tottenham Hotspur,** or "Spurs" (✉ White Hart Lane, 748 High Rd., N17, ☎ 0181/808–3030), and **Arsenal** (✉ Avenell Rd., Highbury, N5, ☎ 0171/359–0131) have north Londoners' loyalties about equally divided, while **Chelsea** (✉ Stamford Bridge, Fulham Rd., SW6, ☎ 0171/385–5545) is adored by the slightly more genteel west London fan.

Tennis

The Wimbledon Lawn Tennis Championships—famous among fans for the green, green grass of Centre Court, for strawberries and cream, and for rain, which always falls, despite the last-week-of-June/first-week-of-July high-summer timing—comprise, of course, one of the top four Grand Slam events of the tennis year. Whether you can get tickets is literally down to the luck of the draw, because there's a ballot system for advance purchase. To apply, send a self-addressed, stamped envelope between October and December to All England Lawn Tennis & Croquet Club, Box 98, Church Rd., Wimbledon SW19 5AE (☎ 0181/946–2244), then fill in the application form, and hope.

But there are other ways to see the tennis. A block of Centre Court tickets is kept back to sell each day, but fanatics line up all night for these, especially in the second week. Each afternoon, though, tickets collected from departed spectators are resold (profits go to charity). These can provide grandstand seats (with plenty to see—play continues till dusk), because those who care so little about tennis are often on expensive business freebies or company season tickets. You can also buy entry to the grounds to roam matches on the outer courts, where even the top-seeded players compete early in the fortnight. For up-to-date information, the London Tourist Board operates a **Wimbledon Information Line** (☎ 01839/123417; cost: 49p/min, 39p cheap rate) from the beginning of June.

6 Restaurants and Pubs

LONDON IS NOW—and longtime absentees must suspend disbelief here—among the top places in the world for dining out. It has long been possible to get a good meal in London, especially by spending big bucks or going ethnic, but it's more than that. A new generation of chefs has emerged, weaned in restaurants and familiar with the cuisines of six continents. They watch each other's work and cross-pollinate. Collectively they've precipitated a fresh style of cooking, which you could call "London," though most have dubbed it "Modern British." Everyone's got an opinion on it, because newspapers now devote pages to food columns and restaurant reviews, which everyone reads. Everyone dines out. England has become a nation of foodies.

Even before the current healthy restaurant scene crystallized, successive waves of immigrants had done their best to help the city out. There are a handful still extant of the venerable French and Italian places that were once the last word in fancy; and there are still the thousands of (mostly northern) Indian restaurants that have long ensured that Londoners see a good tandoori as their birthright. Chinese—Cantonese, mostly—places in London's tiny Chinatown have been around a long time, too, as have Greek tavernas; Thai restaurants have proliferated. Malaysian, Spanish, a hint of Japanese (with more on the way?), Russian, and Korean places have also been opening. After all this, traditional British food, lately revived from its deathbed, appears as one more exotic cuisine in the pantheon.

These listings comprise a taste of London's variety. Largely absent are those aforementioned Indian restaurants, not because they're no good, but because they're nearly all good, and inexpensive, too. Try your local one, or go to Brick Lane in the East End (the **Clifton** is recommended); take a Brit along to do the ordering.

As for cost, the democratization of restaurants means lighter checks than during the '80s, with many experiments in fixed-price menus, but still London is not an inexpensive city. Damage-control methods include making lunch your main meal—the very top places often have bargain lunch menus, halving the price of evening à la carte—and ordering a second appetizer instead of an entrée, to which few places should object. (Note that an appetizer, usually known as a "starter," or "first course," is sometimes called an "entrée," as it is in France, and an entrée in England is dubbed "the main course.") Seek out fixed-price menus, and watch for hidden extras on the check: "cover," bread and vegetables charged separately, and service.

Many restaurants exclude service charges from the menu (which the law obliges them to display outside), then add 10%–15% to the check or else stamp SERVICE NOT INCLUDED along the bottom, in which case you should add the 10%–15% yourself. Don't pay twice for service—unscrupulous restaurateurs may add service, then leave the total in the credit card slip blank, hoping for more.

One final caveat: Beware of Sunday. Many restaurants are closed on this day, especially in the evening; likewise public holidays. Over the Christmas period, London shuts down completely—only hotels will be prepared to feed you. When in doubt, call ahead. It's as well to book a table anyway. After all, everyone eats out nowadays.

CATEGORY	COST*
$$$$	over £45
$$$	£30–£45
$$	£15–£30
$	under £15

**per person for a three-course meal, excluding drinks, service, and VAT*

Mayfair

AMERICAN

$$ ✕ **Smollensky's Balloon.** This American-style bar restaurant is useful for those with children in tow, especially on weekends, when the young are fed burgers, fish sticks, and "Kids' Koktails," and taken off your hands by sundry clowns and magicians. The grown-ups' menu is absolutely committed to red meat, with several cuts of steak the specialty, all served with fries and a choice of sauces. There are also a handful of weekly specials, a single vegetarian pick, and a salmon steak, though you should not travel far for these. ✉ *1 Dover St., W1,* ☎ *0171/491–1199. AE, DC, MC, V. Closed Dec. 24–26, Jan. 1. Tube: Green Park.*

$ ✕ **The Chicago Pizza Pie Factory.** Enormous deep-dish pies with the usual toppings are served in a wood-floored basement, loud with the sounds of WJMK, the Windy City's oldies station. The rest rooms are labeled "Elton John" and "Olivia Newton John." ✉ *17 Hanover Sq., W1,* ☎ *0171/629–2669. AE, MC, V. Closed Dec. 25–26. Tube: Oxford Circus.*

BRITISH

$$$ ✕ **The Greenhouse.** Tucked away behind the Mayfair mansions in a cute, cobbled mews is this elegant salon for people who like their food big and strong. You sit among extravagant topiary and men in ties to partake of famous-from-TV-chef, Gary Rhodes's much-praised British food. Alone, he handles the P.R. for faggots (a type of meatball, once reviled) and braised oxtails; but he invents new things, too, like smoked eel risotto, and he is the master of the stew—venison and bacon in red wine, perhaps. This is the place for stodgy, sticky English desserts like bread-and-butter pudding and steamed syrup sponge. Mr. Rhodes is also behind the People's Palace (☞ *below*). ✉ *27A Hay's Mews, W1,* ☎ *0171/499–3331. Reservations essential. AE, DC, MC, V. Closed Sat. lunch, Sun. dinner, Dec. 25. Tube: Green Park.*

FRENCH

$$$$ ✕ **Chez Nico at Ninety Park Lane.** Those with refined palates and very deep pockets would be well advised not to miss Nico Ladenis's exquisite cuisine, served in this suitably hushed and plush Louis XV dining room next to the Grosvenor House Hotel. Autodidact Nico is one of the world's great chefs, and he's famous for knowing it. The menu is in French and untranslated; vegetarians and children are not welcome. There is no salt on the table—ask for some at your peril. It's all more affordable in daylight, proffering set menus from £29 for three courses. ✉ *90 Park La., W1,* ☎ *0171/409–1290. Reservations essential. Jacket and tie. AE, DC, MC, V. Closed weekends, public holidays, 3 wks in Aug. Tube: Marble Arch.*

$$$$ ✕ **Four Seasons.** This, one of Great Britain's great hotel dining rooms, came to fame under the aegis of Bruno Loubet, now at L'Odéon, who is also responsible for the wonderful Bistrot Bruno (☞ *below*). Young star Jean-Christophe Novelli now holds the reins in this opulent salon complete with park view, and most reports are unequivocal raves. His style is not unrelated to Loubet's *cuisine de terroir,* and although his trademark *assiette des saveurs* (pig's trotter and tail, calf's liver and kidneys, and oxtail) turned out to be too visceral for the clientele, and was banished from the menu, dishes like chicken leg stuffed with ox cheek still surprise. The expensive ingredients of haute cuisine are also present and correct, however, and his skill with game has been noted. Here also, there's a "bargain" £25 set lunch. ✉ *Four Seasons Hotel, Hamilton Place, Park La., W1,* ☎ *0171/499–0888. Reservations required at least 2 days in advance. Jacket and tie. AE, DC, MC, V. Tube: Hyde Park Corner.*

$$$$ ★ ✕ **Le Gavroche.** Albert Roux has handed the toque to his son, Michel, who retains many of his father's capital-C-Classical dishes under the heading "*Hommage à mon père,*" and who has added his own style to the place that many still consider London's finest restaurant. The basement dining room is comfortable and serious, hung with oil paintings, its darkness intensified by racing-green walls. Yet again, the set lunch is relatively affordable at £37 (for canapés and three courses, plus mineral water, a half-bottle of wine, coffee, and petit fours, service *compris*). In fact, it's the only way to eat here if you don't have a generous expense account at your disposal—as most patrons do. ✉ *43 Upper Brook St., W1,* ☎ *0171/408–0881. Reservations advised at least 1 wk in advance. Jacket and tie. AE, DC, MC, V. Closed weekends, 10 days at Christmas, national holidays. Tube: Marble Arch.*

$$$ ✕ **Criterion.** This palatial neo-Byzantine mirrored marble hall, which first opened in 1874, is firmly back on the map, with the arrival of a new regime led by the somewhat self-promoting, but super-talented Marco Pierre White. He doesn't cook here, but some of his well-known and often copied dishes appear on a menu whose divisions include one headed "Farinaceous Dishes"–where you'll find his black, buttery risotto of squid ink, for instance. The glamour of the soaring golden ceiling, peacock blue theater-size drapes, oil paintings, and attentive gallic service adds up to an elegant night out. ✉ *Piccadilly Circus, W1,* ☎ *0171/930–0488. AE, DC, MC, V. Closed Dec. 25. Tube: Piccadilly Circus.*

$$–$$$ ✕ **L'Odéon.** This contribution to London's mania for giant restaurants overlooks Regent Street in a former airline office, its long, low dimensions peculiarly reminiscent of an aircraft, despite the gauzy partitions throughout. Bruno Loubet's French terroir/modern Brit food is startling and satisfying—invention without pretention. Tables by the huge arched windows are fun for people-watching. ✉ *65 Regent St., W1,* ☎ *0171/287–1400. AE, MC, V. Tube: Piccadilly Circus.*

FRENCH/TRADITIONAL ENGLISH

$$$$ ★ ✕ **The Connaught.** This charming and very grand mahogany-paneled, velvet-upholstered, and crystal-chandeliered dining room belongs to the absolutely exclusive eponymous hotel (☞ Chapter 6, Lodging). Waiters wear tails, tables must be booked far in advance, and prices are fearsome; but the restaurant remains London's most respected traditional dining room, with famed French chef Michel Bourdin still in charge of the kitchens after many years. This is the place for game—venison, guinea fowl, pigeon (not local birds)—presented with traditional trimmings or perhaps with some confection of wild mushrooms. "Luncheon dishes" change according to the day of the week (if this is Friday, it must be oxtail) and are not as exorbitant as they seem at first, because the price includes a starter and dessert. The Connaught is by no means a fashionable place, but it is never out of fashion. ✉ *Carlos Pl., W1,* ☎ *0171/499–7070. Reservations essential. Jacket and tie. MC. Closed weekends and national holidays. Tube: Bond Street.*

INTERNATIONAL

$$ ✕ **Bullochs.** The recently refreshed Atheneum Hotel is the least stuffy of the Piccadilly grands, so it's no shock that its restaurant is laid back too. Surrounded by a weird Jerusalem stone, trompe l'oeil bookcase

London Dining *(Boxes Refer to Detail Maps)*

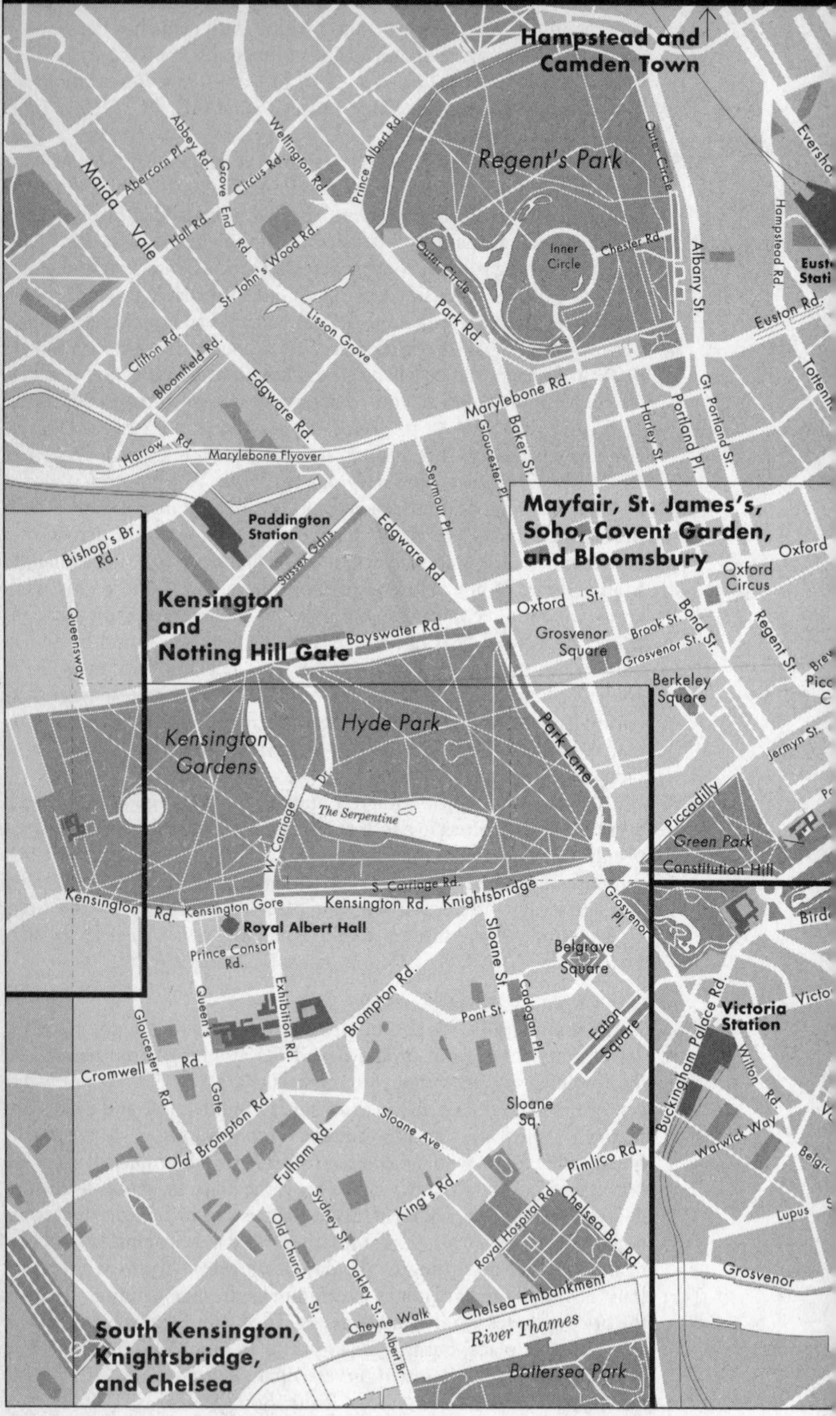

Hampstead and Camden Town
Regent's Park
Inner Circle
Outer Circle
Chester Rd.
Albany St.
Hampstead Rd.
Euston Rd.
Maida Vale
Abercorn Pl.
Abbey Rd.
Grove End Rd.
Circus Rd.
Wellington Rd.
Prince Albert Rd.
Hall Rd.
St. John's Wood Rd.
Lisson Grove
Park Rd.
Clifton Rd.
Bloomfield Rd.
Edgware Rd.
Harrow Rd.
Marylebone Flyover
Marylebone Rd.
Baker St.
Gloucester Pl.
Harley St.
Portland Pl.
Gt. Portland St.
Seymour Pl.
Paddington Station
Sussex Gdns.
Bishop's Br. Rd.
Queensway
Mayfair, St. James's, Soho, Covent Garden, and Bloomsbury
Oxford St.
Oxford Circus
Grosvenor Square
Brook St.
Bond St.
Grosvenor St.
Regent St.
Berkeley Square
Kensington and Notting Hill Gate
Bayswater Rd.
Hyde Park
Kensington Gardens
The Serpentine
W. Carriage Dr.
Park Lane
Jermyn St.
Piccadilly
Green Park
Constitution Hill
S. Carriage Rd.
Kensington Rd.
Kensington Gore
Knightsbridge
Royal Albert Hall
Prince Consort Rd.
Grosvenor Pl.
Belgrave Square
Sloane St.
Cadogan Pl.
Pont St.
Eaton Square
Victoria Station
Buckingham Palace Rd.
Wilton Rd.
Warwick Way
Lupus St.
Grosvenor
Exhibition Rd.
Queen's Gate
Gloucester Rd.
Cromwell Rd.
Brompton Rd.
Old Brompton Rd.
Sloane Ave.
Sloane Sq.
Pimlico Rd.
Fulham Rd.
King's Rd.
Sydney St.
Old Church St.
Oakley St.
Royal Hospital Rd.
Chelsea Br. Rd.
Chelsea Embankment
Cheyne Walk
Albert Br.
River Thames
Battersea Park
South Kensington, Knightsbridge, and Chelsea

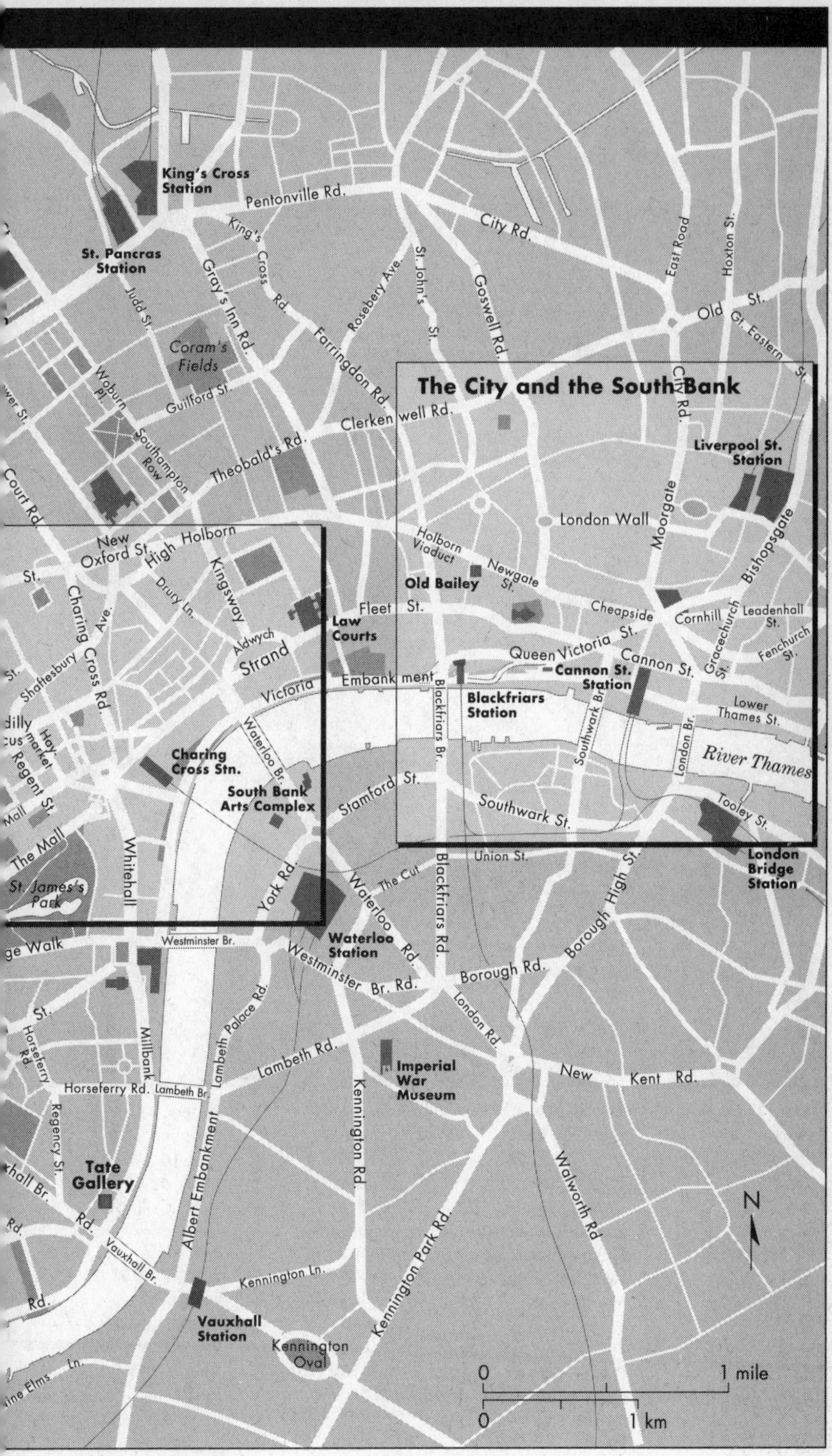
King's Cross Station
Pentonville Rd.
St. Pancras Station
City Rd.
King's Cross Rd.
Gray's Inn Rd.
Judd St.
St. John's St.
Goswell Rd.
Rosebery Ave.
Farringdon Rd.
East Road
Hoxton St.
Old St.
Gt. Eastern St.
Coram's Fields
Woburn Pl.
Guilford St.
The City and the South Bank
City Rd.
Clerken well Rd.
Southampton Row
Theobald's Rd.
Liverpool St. Station
Court Rd.
London Wall
Moorgate
New Oxford St.
High Holborn
Kingsway
Holborn Viaduct
Newgate St.
Bishopsgate
Charing Cross Rd.
Drury Ln.
Old Bailey
Shaftesbury Ave.
Aldwych
Fleet St.
Law Courts
Cheapside
Cornhill
Leadenhall St.
Gracechurch St.
Strand
Queen Victoria St.
Cannon St.
Fenchurch St.
Victoria
Embank ment
Cannon St. Station
Blackfriars Station
Blackfriars Br.
Southwark Br.
London Br.
Lower Thames St.
Hay market
Regent St.
Waterloo Br.
River Thames
Charing Cross Stn.
South Bank Arts Complex
Stamford St.
Southwark St.
Tooley St.
The Mall
Whitehall
St. James's Park
York Rd.
Union St.
The Cut
London Bridge Station
Waterloo Rd.
Blackfriars Rd.
Borough High St.
Westminster Br.
Waterloo Station
Westminster Br. Rd.
Borough Rd.
Lambeth Palace Rd.
London Rd.
Horseferry Rd.
Millbank
Lambeth Rd.
Imperial War Museum
New Kent Rd.
Horseferry Rd.
Lambeth Br.
Kennington Rd.
Regency St.
Albert Embankment
Tate Gallery
Walworth Rd
Kennington Park Rd.
Vauxhall Br.
Kennington Ln.
Vauxhall Station
Kennington Oval
N
0
1 mile
0
1 km

Dining in Mayfair, St. James's, Soho, Covent Garden, and Bloomsbury

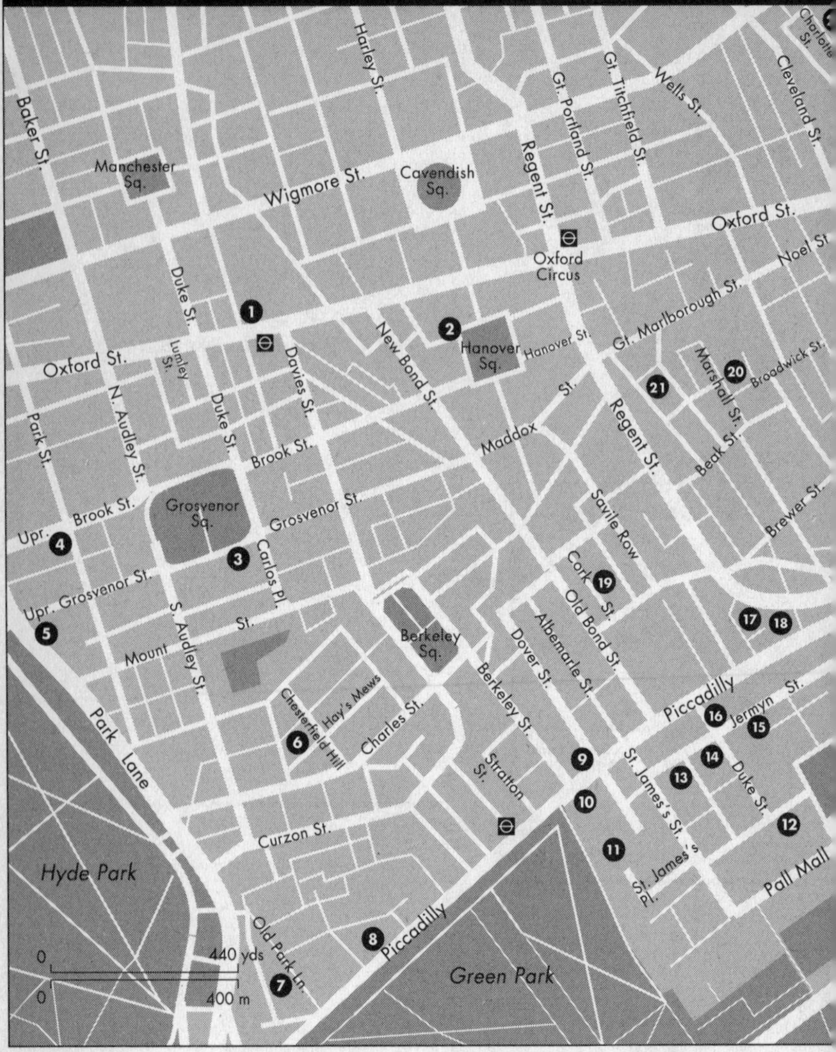

Alastair Little, **30**
Bahn Thai, **33**
Belgo Centraal, **40**
Bertorelli's, **43**
Bistrot Bruno, **34**
Bullochs, **8**
Café Fish, **37**
Café Flo, **42**
Café Piazza, **45**
Chez Gerard, **23**
Chez Nico at Ninety Park Lane, **5**
Chicago Pizza Pie Factory, **2**
Connaught, **3**
Crank's, **20**
Criterion, **36**
Deal's West, **21**
dell'Ugo, **29**
Down Mexico Way, **17**
Elena's L'Etoile, **22**
Fatboy's Diner, **50**
Food for Thought, **39**
Fountain, **16**
Four Seasons, **7**
Fung Shing, **35**
Greenhouse, **6**
Green's Restaurant and Oyster Bar, **14**
Ivy, **38**
Joe Allen's, **49**
Le Caprice, **11**
Le Gavroche, **4**
Le Palais du Jardin, **41**
L' Escargot, **32**
L'Odeon, **18**
Mandeer, **25**
Maxwell's, **44**
Mezzo, **28**
Mulligans, **19**
Museum Street Café, **27**
North Sea Fish Restaurant, **52**
Orso, **46**
Porters, **48**
Quaglino's, **13**
Ritz, **10**
Rules, **47**
Savoy Grill, **51**
Smollensky's Balloon, **9**
Soho Soho, **31**
Square, **12**
Wagamama, **26**
White Tower, **24**
Wilton's, **15**
Zoe, **1**

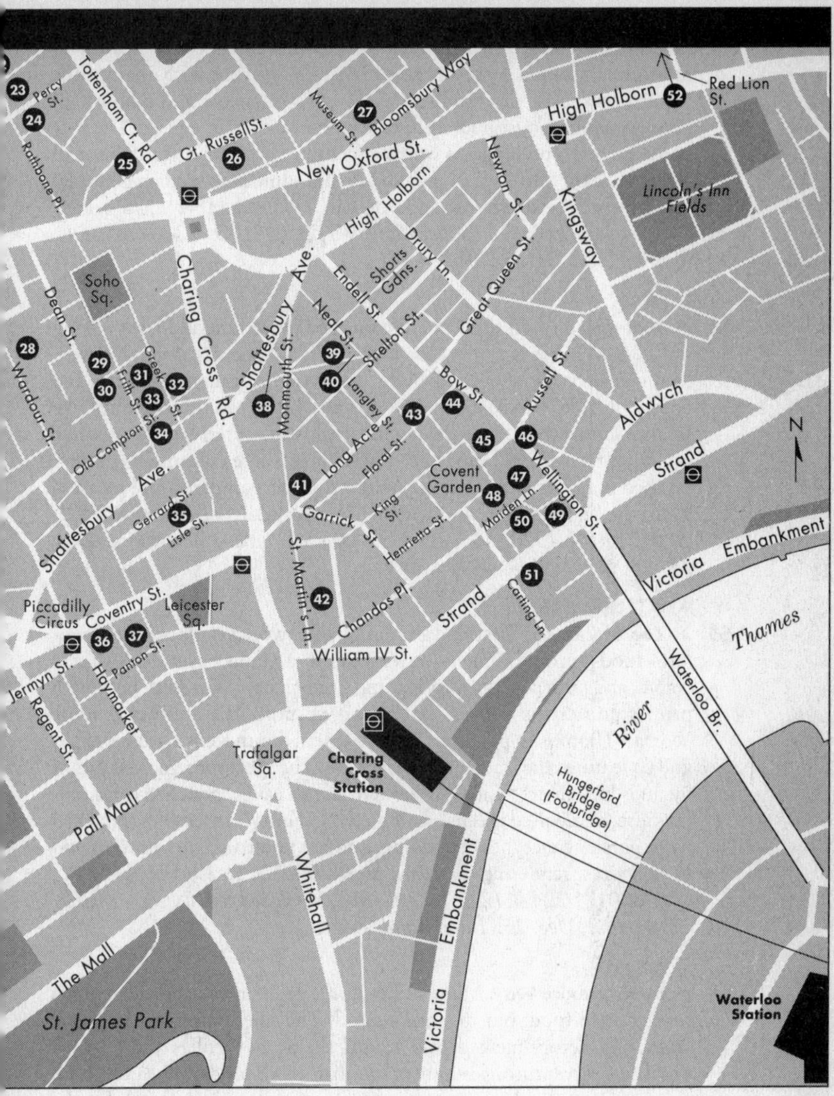

Tottenham Ct. Rd.
Percy St.
Rathbone Pl.
Gt. Russell St.
Museum St.
Bloomsbury Way
New Oxford St.
High Holborn
Red Lion St.
Lincoln's Inn Fields
Newton St.
Kingsway
High Holborn
Drury Ln.
Shorts Gdns.
Endell St.
Great Queen St.
Soho Sq.
Dean St.
Charing Cross Rd.
Shaftesbury Ave.
Neal St.
Shelton St.
Monmouth St.
Wardour St.
Greek St.
Frith St.
Old Compton St.
Langley
Bow St.
Russell St.
Aldwych
Long Acre St.
Floral St.
Covent Garden
Wellington St.
Strand
Shaftesbury Ave.
Gerrard St.
Lisle St.
Garrick St.
King St.
Henrietta St.
Maiden Ln.
St. Martin's Ln.
Victoria Embankment
Piccadilly Circus
Coventry St.
Leicester Sq.
Chandos Pl.
Strand
Carting Ln.
Thames
William IV St.
Jermyn St.
Panton St.
Haymarket
Regent St.
River
Waterloo Br.
Trafalgar Sq.
Charing Cross Station
Hungerford Bridge (Footbridge)
Pall Mall
Whitehall
Victoria Embankment
The Mall
St. James Park
Waterloo Station
N
23
24
25
26
27
28
29
30
31
32
33
34
35
36
37
38
39
40
41
42
43
44
45
46
47
48
49
50
51
52

and mirror decor, try London's most generously anchovied and Parmesaned Caesar salad, then something Mediterranean (tuna steak with ratatouille), Italian (osso bucco), French-ish (turbot with champagne and lemon sauce), or even British (calves liver, bacon, and onions), all good, unpretentious food, and, conveniently, all at one price. The best of the English puddings is a warm and intensely citrus custard they call a Lime Cream "Brûlée." A meal from this admirable kitchen is special enough for a celebration—and you can still get a table when nearby Caprice is booked. ✉ *116 Piccadilly, W1,* ☏ *0171/499–3464. AE, DC, MC, V. Tube: Green Park.*

IRISH

$$ ✕ **Mulligans.** You'd think there would be more Emerald Isle cooking in London, but it is a very rare commodity, especially done this well. Mulligans is straight out of Dublin, down to the draught Guinness and copies of *The Irish Times* in the upstairs bar. Traditional dishes like steak, Guinness and oyster pie, and Irish stew avoid heaviness while retaining flavor, and homey accompaniments like colcannon (buttery mashed potatoes with cabbage) make you feel pampered and pleased, as do the big puddings and friendly service. ✉ *13–14 Cork St., W1,* ☏ *0171/409–1370. AE, MC, V. Closed Sat. lunch, Sun. dinner, Dec. 25–26, Jan. 1. Tube: Green Park.*

MEDITERRANEAN

$$ ✕ **Zoe.** Handy for West End shopping, this two-level place serves two-level food—proper dinners downstairs in a sunlit basement of jazzy colors; and posh cocktails, coffee, and sandwiches ("hot spicy pork with prunes and crispy bacon" is typical) upstairs. It's another Antony Worrall Thompson place (☞ Bistrot 190 in South Kensington, *below*) and so features the trademark heartiness. The schizophrenic restaurant menu is half smart "City" dishes (corn crab cakes, poached eggs, hollandaise, and wilted greens), half huge "Country" ensembles (poached ham, parsley sauce, pease pudding, and hot potato salad), most offered in two sizes, rendering decisions impossible. ✉ *St. Christopher's Pl., W1,* ☏ *0171/224–1122. AE, DC, MC, V. Closed Sat. lunch, Sun. (bar open daily), Dec. 25. Tube: Bond Street.*

MEXICAN

$ ✕ **Down Mexico Way.** Many of London's proliferating Mexican joints serve horrid food, but this one's good. The fine lumpy guacamole is fresh, not factory-packed, and among the usual tortillas and burritos are a few adventurous numbers like fish in almond-chili sauce, with sides of cheese and jalapeño muffins or spiced spinach. Look for the beautiful Spanish ceramic tiles. Avoid evenings here if you want a quiet night out—the place is often taken over by party animals. ✉ *25 Swallow St., W1,* ☏ *0171/437–9895. AE, MC, V. Closed Dec. 25–26. Tube: Piccadilly Circus.*

St. James's

FRENCH

$$ ✕ **Café Fish.** Just to the east of St. James's proper, this cheerful, bustling restaurant has an encyclopedic selection of fish (shark and turbot join the trout, halibut, salmon, and monkfish, some brought daily from Normandy), arranged on the menu according to cooking method: chargrilled, steamed, meunière; smoked fish pâté is brought with the bread to help you choose. Downstairs there's an informal wine bar with a smaller selection of dishes. ✉ *39 Panton St., SW1,* ☏ *0171/930–3999. AE, DC, MC, V. Closed Sat. lunch, Sun., Dec. 25–26, Jan. 1. Tube: Piccadilly Circus.*

FRENCH/TRADITIONAL ENGLISH

$$$$ ✕ **The Ritz.** Constantly accused of being London's prettiest dining room, this Belle Epoque palace of marble, gilt, and trompe l'oeil would moisten even Marie Antoinette's eye; add the view over Green Park and the Ritz's secret sunken garden, and it seems obsolete to eat. But David Nicholls' British/French cuisine stands up to the visual onslaught with costly morsels (foie gras, lobster, truffles, caviar, etc.), superrich, all served with a flourish. Old retainers take great pride in this smooth operation, and are still here, despite the hotel's change of ownership. Englishness is wrested from Louis XVI by a daily roast "from the trolley," and a "British speciality" like Irish stew or braised oxtail. A three-course prix fixe lunch at £28 and a dinner at £33 make the check more bearable, but the wine list is pricey. A Friday and Saturday dinner dance sweetly maintains a dying tradition. ✉ *Piccadilly, W1,* ☎ *0171/493–8181. Reservations essential. Jacket and tie. AE, DC, MC, V. Tube: Green Park.*

MODERN BRITISH

$$$ ★ ✕ **Le Caprice.** Secreted in a small street behind the Ritz, Caprice may command the deepest loyalty of any London restaurant, because it gets everything right: The glamorous, glossy black Eva Jiricna interior, the perfect pitch of the informal but respectful service, the food, halfway between Euro-peasant and fashion plate. This food—crispy duck and watercress salad; seared scallops with bacon and sorrel; risotto nero; Lincolnshire sausage with bubble-and-squeak (potato-and-cabbage hash); grilled rabbit with black olive polenta; and divine desserts too—it has no business being so good, because the other reason everyone comes here is that everyone else does, which leads to the best people-watching in town. (Also try its sister restaurant, the Ivy; ☞ Covent Garden, *below.*) ✉ *Arlington House, Arlington St., SW1,* ☎ *0171/629–2239. Reservations essential. AE, DC, MC, V. Closed Sat. lunch. Tube: Green Park.*

$$$ ✕ **Quaglino's.** Sir Terence Conran—of Bibendum, Mezzo, and Pont de la Tour fame—lavished £2.5 million doing up this famous pre–World War II haunt of the rich, bored, and well connected. Now past its fifth birthday, "Quags" is *the* out-of-towners' post-theater or celebration destination, while Londoners like its late hours. The gigantic sunken restaurant boasts a glamorous staircase, "Crustacea Altar," large bar, and live jazz music. The food is fashionably pan-European with some Oriental trimmings—crab with mirin and soy; noodles with ginger, chili and cilantro; rabbit with prosciutto and herbs; roast crayfish; plateaux de fruits de mer. Desserts come from somewhere between the Paris bistro and the English nursery (raspberry sablé, parkin pudding with butterscotch sauce), and wine from the Old World and the New, some bottles at modest prices. ✉ *16 Bury St., SW1,* ☎ *0171/930–6767. Reservations essential. AE, DC, MC, V. Closed Dec. 25. Tube: Green Park.*

$$$ ★ ✕ **The Square.** For sublime dining in St. James's, here's your third opportunity. Young chef Philip Howard's sophisticated food is matched by an understated tall white room, punctuated with gold and primary-color squares. The menu changes every five minutes, but features a lot from the sea, and game fowl, all with its soul mate on the side: sweet and sour scallops and spiced squid; saddle of rabbit and tarte fine of onions; then roast Tuscan pigeon paired with trompettes and balsamic vinegar; roasted salmon with asparagus risotto. Desserts are subtle—vanilla cream with red fruit compote, or a pile of crème brûlée with its sugar crust balanced on top, in a perfect square. Worldwide wines are grouped by grape and are not overpriced; waitstaff is knowledgeable, likeable, and efficient. ✉ *32 King St., SW1,* ☎ *0171/839–8787.*

Reservations essential. AE, MC, V. Closed weekend lunch, Dec. 24, 25. Tube: Green Park.

TRADITIONAL ENGLISH

$$$$ ✕ **Green's Restaurant and Oyster Bar.** The oyster side of things and the comfy-wood-paneled-restaurant angle are in equal balance at this reliable purveyor of the British dining experience, complete with the whiff of public (meaning private and exclusive) school, and its former inmates. Oysters, of course, are served (and they're not only in season whenever there's an "R" in the month), in two varieties, "small" or "large," alongside smoked fish, lobster cocktail, grilled sole, fish cakes, and so on, but there are comforting English unfishy dishes, like shepherd's pie, too, and—the proper ending to a nanny-sanctioned meal—warm and fattening "nursery puddings," like steamed sponge with custard, and treacle tart. The wine list is notable, especially from the champagne region. ✉ *36 Duke St., St. James's, SW1,* ☎ *0171/930–4566. Reservations essential. Jacket and tie. AE, DC, MC, V. Closed Sun. dinner, national holidays. Tube: Green Park.*

$$$$ ✕ **Wilton's.** The search for the British Establishment stops here, among Edwardian booths full of politicians in a restaurant that traces its pedigree back to 1742 and offers a taste of the adjacent gentlemen's clubs—for which you pay through the nose. Fish is the mainstay of a plainspeaking menu, from which grilled Dover sole is probably ordered most often, with sherry trifle for afters, and an old-fashioned savory like angels on horseback (crisp bacon wrapped around oysters) with the port. Service is buttoned to the neck; one feels one ought to ask permission to use the bathroom. ✉ *55 Jermyn St., SW1,* ☎ *0171/629–9955. Jacket and tie. AE, DC, MC, V. Closed Sat., last wk in July and first 2 wks in Aug., 10 days at Christmas. Tube: Green Park.*

$ ★ ✕ **The Fountain.** At the back of Fortnum and Mason's is this old-fashioned restaurant, as frumpy and as popular as a boarding school matron, serving delicious light meals, toasted snacks, sandwiches, and ice-cream sodas. During the day, go for the Welsh rarebit or cold game pie; in the evening, a no-frills fillet steak is a typical option. Just the place for afternoon tea and ice-cream sundaes after the Royal Academy or Bond Street shopping, or for pre-theater meals. ✉ *181 Piccadilly, W1,* ☎ *0171/734–4938. AE, DC, MC, V. Closed Sun., national holidays. Tube: Green Park.*

Soho

CHINESE

$$ ★ ✕ **Fung Shing.** This comfortable, cool green restaurant is a cut above the Lisle/Wardour Street crowd in both service and ambience, as well as in food. The usual Chinatown options are supplemented by some exciting dishes. Salt-baked chicken, served on or off the bone with an accompanying bowl of intense broth, is essential, and the adventurous might try intestines—deep-fried cigarette-shape morsels, far more delicious than you'd think. ✉ *15 Lisle St., WC2,* ☎ *0171/437–1539. AE, DC, MC, V. Closed Dec. 25. Tube: Leicester Square.*

FRENCH

$$ ✕ **Bistrot Bruno.** Bruno is Bruno Loubet, who earned three Michelin stars at the Four Seasons, opened this, then went on to his posher, more ambitious L'Odéon. He is one of London's most dedicated and original chefs. Though Loubet doesn't cook here, the menu is unmistakably his work, dotted with bits of animals you wouldn't want in your freezer, which in his hands become balanced, beautiful *cuisine du terroir* dishes. His fromage de tête, or brawn (a pâté from the Lorraine made from pig's head in aspic), or tripes Niçoise (cow's stomach, frankly) may not sound appetizing, but on the plate, they are irresistible. Cowards can order smoked fish cannelloni; sautéed rabbit with Swiss chard, olives, and rosemary; salt cod on minestrone vegetables, then an iced meringue and cherry slice. Next door is the bargain Café Bruno. ✉ *63 Frith St., W1,* ☎ *0171/734–4545. Reservations essential. MC, V. Closed Sat. lunch, Sun., Dec. 25. Tube: Leicester Square.*

$–$$$ ✕ **Mezzo.** What does one do after opening London's biggest glamour restaurant? Open an even bigger one of course. This is what Sir Terence Conran did after Quaglino's; in fact, the 700-seater Mezzo isn't only the biggest in London; it's the most gigantic restaurant in all of Europe. Downstairs is the restaurant proper, with its huge glass-walled show kitchen, its Allen Jones murals, its grand piano and dance floor, and its typically Conran-French menu of things like seafood, rabbit stew, steak-frites, fig tart. Upstairs, the bar overlooks a canteen-style operation called Mezzonine, where bowls of coconut-galangal fish soup and grilled squid salad and red duck curry are Asian style. Finally, a late-night café/patisserie/newsstand has a separate entrance next door. The place was a London landmark from day one, with a see-and-be-seen bustle, despite its low celebrity count. ✉ *100 Wardour St., W1,* ☎ *0171/314–4000. AE, DC, MC, V. Closed Dec. 25, Jan. 1. Tube: Leicester Square.*

MEDITERRANEAN

$$ ✕ **dell'Ugo.** At this three-floor Mediterranean café-restaurant from the stable of Antony Worrall Thompson (☞ Bistrot 190 in South Kensington, *below*) you can choose light fare—bruschetta loaded with marinated vegetables, mozzarella, Parmesan etc., Tuscan soups, and country bread—or feast on wintry, warming one-pot ensembles and large platefuls of such sunny dishes as spicy sausages and white bean casserole with onion confit. The place gets overrun with hormone-swapping youth some weekends, but trendiness, on the whole, doesn't mar pleasure. ✉ *56 Frith St., W1,* ☎ *0171/734–8300. Reservations essential for restaurant, not accepted for café. AE, MC, V. Closed Sun., Dec. 25. Tube: Leicester Square.*

$$ ✕ **Soho Soho.** The ground floor is a lively café bar with a (no booking) rotisserie, while upstairs is a more formal and expensive restaurant. Inspiration comes from Provence, both in the olive-oil cooking style and the decor, with its murals, primary colors, and pale ocher terracotta floor tiles. The rotisserie serves omelets, salads, charcuterie, and cheeses, plus a handful of such bistro dishes as Toulouse sausages with fries; herbed, grilled poussin; and tarte tatin. Or you can stay in the café-bar and have just a kir or a beer. ✉ *11–13 Frith St., W1,* ☎ *0171/494–3491. AE, DC, MC, V. Closed Sun., Sat. lunch upstairs, Dec. 25–26, Jan. 1. Tube: Leicester Square.*

MODERN BRITISH

$$$ ✕ **Alastair Little.** Little is one of London's most original—and most imitated—chefs, drawing inspiration from practically everywhere—Thailand, Japan, Scandinavia, France—and bringing it off brilliantly. His restaurant is starkly modern, so all attention focuses on the menu, which changes not once but twice daily in order to take advantage of the best ingredients. There will certainly be fish, but other than that it's hard to predict. Anyone truly interested in food will not be disappointed. Look out also for his newer, smaller, cheaper version—but with the same name—just by Ladbroke Grove tube. ✉ *49 Frith St., W1,* ☎ *0171/734–5183. No credit cards. Closed weekends, national holidays, 2 wks at Christmas, 3 wks in Aug. Tube: Leicester Square.*

$$ ✕ **L'Escargot.** This ever-popular media haunt serves Anglo-French food in its ground floor brasserie and its more formal upstairs restaurant. A comprehensive, reasonably priced wine list sets off a robust ragout of spiced lamb or a simple, fresh poached or grilled fish. This place is reliable and relaxed. ✉ *48 Greek St., W1,* ☎ *0171/437–2679. AE, DC, MC, V. Closed Sun., public holidays. Tube: Leicester Square.*

THAI

$$ ✕ **Bahn Thai.** Many people find this the best of London's many Thai restaurants (you can see at least four others from the door), better still now that its ancient, gloomy decor has been excised. An immensely long menu features little chili symbols for the nervous of palate, plus easy options like char-grilled poussin marinated in honey and spices with a plum dipping sauce. Other Thai dishes are well explained. ✉ *21A Frith St., W1,* ☎ *0171/437–8504. AE, MC, V. Closed Dec. 25–26. Tube: Leicester Square.*

THAI/AMERICAN

$$ ✕ **Deals West.** Viscount Linley, Princess Margaret's son, and his two partners have hit on a winning formula here (and in the two other Deal's, at Chelsea Harbour and Hammersmith): an unlikely sounding merger between America and Thailand. Off Carnaby Street in a relaxed, barn-like diner with exposed brick walls, wooden floors and beams, loud-ish music accompanies ribs, salads, and burgers—as well as Thai curries. Cocktails, extended hours, and live soul and funk on week-ends make this popular with a young, after-work crowd. ✉ *14–16 Fouberts Pl., W1,* ☎ *0171/287–1001. AE, DC, MC, V. Closed Sun. dinner, public holidays. Tube: Oxford Circus.*

VEGETARIAN

$ ✕ **Crank's.** This is a popular vegetarian chain (there are other branches at Covent Garden, Great Newport Street, Adelaide Street, Tottenham Street, and Barrett Street), bought out by the management in 1992, and still serving similar meatless meals to the '60s menu that made their name. They remain always crowded and, irritatingly, insist on closing at 8. ✉ *8 Marshall St., W1,* ☎ *0171/437–9431. Reservations not accepted. AE, DC, MC, V. Closed Sun., national holidays. Tube: Leicester Square.*

Covent Garden

AMERICAN

$$ ★ ✕ **Joe Allen's.** Long hours (thespians flock after the curtain falls in theaterland) and a welcoming, if loud, brick-walled interior mean New York Joe's London branch is still swinging after nearly two decades. The fun, California-inflected menu helps: Roast, stuffed poblano chili, or black bean soup are typical starters; entrées feature barbecue ribs with black-eyed peas and London's only available corn muffins, or roast monkfish with sun-dried-tomato salsa. There are the perennial egg dishes and huge salads, too, and Yankee desserts like grilled banana bread with ice cream and hot caramel sauce. It can get chaotic, with long waits for the cute waiters, but at least there'll be famous faces to ogle in the meantime. ✉ *13 Exeter St., WC2,* ☎ *0171/836–0651. Reservations essential. No credit cards. Closed Easter, Dec. 25–26. Tube: Covent Garden.*

$ ✕ **Fatboy's Diner.** One for the kids, this is a 1941 chrome trailer transplanted from the banks of the Susquehanna in Pennsylvania and now secreted, unexpectedly, in a backstreet, complete with Astroturf "garden." A '50s jukebox accompanies the dogs, burgers, and fries. ✉ *21 Maiden La., WC2,* ☎ *0171/240–1902. Reservations not accepted. No credit cards. Closed Dec. 25. Tube: Covent Garden.*

$ ✕ **Maxwell's.** London's first-ever burger joint, 21 in '93, cloned itself and then grew up. Here's the result, a happy place under the Opera House serving the kind of food you're homesick for: quesadillas and nachos, Buffalo chicken wings, barbecue ribs, Cajun chicken, chef's salad, a real

NYC Reuben, and a burger to die for. ✉ *8–9 James St., WC2,* ☎ *0171/836–0303. AE, DC, V. Closed Dec. 25. Tube: Covent Garden.*

BELGIAN

$–$$ ✕ **Belgo Centraal.** The wackiest dining concept in town started in Camden (☞ *below*), and was so adored, it was cloned uptown in a big basement space you have to enter by elevator. Have mussels and fries in vast quantities, served with your choice of 100 Belgian beers (fruit-flavored, Trappist-brewed, white, or light) by people dressed as monks in a hall like a refectory in a Martian monastery. Also eat *stoemp* (mashed potato and cabbage) with steak; wild boar sausages; lobster or roast chicken. The luxury index is low, but so is the check. ✉ *50 Earlham St., WC2,* ☎ *0171/813–2233. AE, DC, MC, V. Closed Dec. 25, Jan. 1. Tube: Covent Garden.*

BRITISH

$$ ✕ **Porters.** British food, an Olde Worlde public house interior, a nob owner (the Earl of Bradford), and a reasonable check, with vegetables and service included—no wonder Americans invariably like this place. Pies star on the menu—lamb-and-apricot or chicken-and-chili alongside the traditional fish or steak-and-kidney—with steamed sponges and custard for afters. The budget alternative to Rules (☞ *below*). ✉ *17 Henrietta St., WC2,* ☎ *0171/836–6466. Reservations essential for weekend dinner. AE, MC, V. Closed Dec. 25. Tube: Covent Garden.*

FRENCH

$$ ✕ **Le Palais du Jardin.** This does a fair imitation of a Parisian brasserie, complete with a seafood bar offering lobsters for a tenner, though there's plenty else—duck confit with apples and prunes; coq au vin; tuna with a black olive potato cake. It's not quite as chic as it looks, but neither is it as expensive, which accounts for why it is always busy. ✉ *136 Long Acre, WC2,* ☎ *0171/379–5353. AE, DC, MC, V. Closed Dec. 25. Tube: Covent Garden.*

$ ✕ **Café Flo.** This useful brasserie serves the bargain "Idée Flo"—soup or salad, *steak-frites* or *poisson-frites,* and coffee—a wide range of French café food, breakfast, wines, *tartes,* espresso, fresh orange juice, simple set-price weekend menus . . . everything for the Francophile on a budget. There are branches in Hampstead, Islington, Fulham, and Kensington. ✉ *51 St. Martin's La., WC2,* ☎ *0171/836–8289. MC, V. Closed Dec. 25, Jan. 1. Tube: Covent Garden.*

FRENCH/TRADITIONAL ENGLISH

$$$$ ✕ **Savoy Grill.** The grill continues in the first rank of power dining locations. Politicians, newspaper barons, and tycoons like the comforting food and impeccably discreet and attentive service in the low-key, yew-paneled salon. On the menu, an omelet Arnold Bennett (with cheese and smoked fish) is perennial, as is beef Wellington on Tuesday and roast Norfolk duck on Friday. Playgoers can split their theater menu, eating part of their meal before the show, the rest after. ✉ *Strand, WC2,* ☎ *0171/836–4343. Reservations essential for lunch, and for Thurs.–Sat. dinner. Jacket and tie. AE, DC, MC, V. Closed Sat. lunch, Sun. Tube: Aldwych.*

INTERNATIONAL

$$$ ★ ✕ **The Ivy.** This seems to be everybody's favorite restaurant—everybody who works in the media or the arts, that is. In a Deco dining room with blinding white tablecloths, and Hodgkins and Paolozzis on the walls, the celebrated and the wannabes eat Caesar salad, roast grouse, shrimp gumbo, braised oxtail, and rice pudding with Armagnac prunes or sticky toffee pudding. ✉ *1 West St., WC2,* ☎ *0171/836–4751. AE, DC, MC, V. Closed Dec. 25. Tube: Covent Garden.*

ITALIAN

$$$ ✕ **Orso.** The Italian brother of Joe Allen's (☞ *below*), this basement restaurant has the same snappy staff and a glitzy clientele of showbiz types and hacks. The Tuscan-style menu changes every day, but always includes excellent pizza and pasta dishes, plus entrées based perhaps on grilled rabbit or roast sea bass and first courses of roquette (arugula) with shaved Parmesan or deep-fried zucchini flowers stuffed with ricotta. Food here is never boring, much like the place itself. ✉ *27 Wellington St., WC2,* ☎ *0171/240–5269. Reservations essential. No credit cards. Closed Dec. 25–26. Tube: Covent Garden.*

$$ ✕ **Bertorelli's.** Right across from the stage door of the Royal Opera House, Bertorelli's is quietly chic, the food tempting, if not innovative: Poached cotechino sausage with lentils; monkfish ragout with fennel, tomato, and olives; and garganelli with French beans, cob nuts, and Parmesan are typical dishes. Downstairs is a very relaxed inexpensive wine bar serving a simpler menu of pizza, pasta, salads, and a few big dishes and daily specials. ✉ *44A Floral St., WC2,* ☎ *0171/836–3969. AE, DC, MC, V. Closed Dec. 25. Tube: Covent Garden.*

$ ✕ **Café Piazza.** It doesn't look like much with its standard-issue bentwood chairs and undressed tables, but on a good day the food at this usefully central brasserie is far better than the low prices suggest. Weekly specials (osso bucco, a smoked cheese and leek risotto, linguine *alla bottarga*—with mullet roe) augment a menu of Italian greatest hits (minestrone, seafood salad, wood-oven pizzas), plus surprises (ricotta and spinach ravioli with walnut sauce, entrecote marinated in juniper and bay). ✉ *16–17 Russell St., WC2,* ☎ *0171/379–7543. AE, MC, V. Tube: Covent Garden.*

TRADITIONAL ENGLISH

$$$ ✕ **Rules.** A London institution, this Edwardian restaurant was a great favorite of Lily Langtry's, among others. After decades the restaurant remains interesting for its splendid period atmosphere, but annoying for its slow service. For a main dish, try the seasonal entrées on the list of daily specials, which will, in season, include game from Rules's own Scottish estate (venison is disconcertingly called "deer"). It is more than a little touristy, but that's because it's so quaint. ✉ *35 Maiden La., WC2,* ☎ *0171/836–5314. AE, DC, MC, V. Closed Dec. 25. Tube: Covent Garden.*

VEGETARIAN

$ ★ ✕ **Food for Thought.** This simple basement restaurant (no liquor license) seats only 50 and is extremely popular, so you'll almost always find a line of people down the stairs. The menu—stir-fries, casseroles, salads, and desserts—changes every day, and each dish is freshly made; there's no microwave. ✉ *31 Neal St., WC2,* ☎ *0171/836–0239. Reservations not accepted. No credit cards. Closed after 8 PM, 2 wks at Christmas, national holidays. Tube: Covent Garden.*

Bloomsbury

FRENCH

$$–$$$ ★ ✕ **Elena's L'Etoile.** Elena Salvoni presided for years and years over L'Escargot in Soho, where she made so many friends among happy customers she was rewarded with her name in lights—at 75 years old. This understated and long-established place, whose only concession to trendiness of decor is a row of bentwood chairs unaccountably roped to the top of one wall, is one of London's few remaining unreconstructed French bistro restaurants. There's duck braised with red cabbage in an individual casserole, there's sole meunière, and poulet rôti, terrines, salade frisée, crème caramel, tarte au citron, and a warm smile

from Elena, whether you're one of the politician/journalist/actor regulars, or just you. Upstairs is a table for sharing—useful for single travelers or business trippers. ✉ *30 Charlotte St., W1,* ☎ *0171/636–7189. AE, DC, MC, V. Closed weekend lunch, Sun dinner, Dec. 25, Jan. 1. Tube: Goodge Street.*

$$ ✕ **Chez Gerard.** One of a small chain of steak-frites restaurants, this one has widened the choice on the utterly Gallic menu to include more for non–red meat eaters—brioche filled with wild mushrooms and artichoke hearts, for instance, plus fish dishes and something for vegetarians, such as stuffed roast onion. Steak, served with shoestring fries and béarnaise sauce, remains the reason to visit, though. ✉ *8 Charlotte St., W1,* ☎ *0171/636–4975. AE, DC, MC, V. Closed Dec. 25. Tube: Goodge Street.*

GREEK

$$$ ✕ **The White Tower.** The White Tower is quite different from the average London Greek restaurant: its three Georgian stories are lined with antique pistols and prints (and a portrait of that most famous Hellenist, Lord Byron), and its menu lists many unusual dishes, like the cracked wheat, fruit, and nut-stuffed duck you must order in advance, or the chicken Paxinou, served with fried banana and aubergine (eggplant). The *taramasalata*—cod's roe dip, which all too often resembles Pepto-Bismol—is the best in town, was the first in town, and is always ordered by the many establishment types who love this place, and continue to do so, despite the restaurant's recent change of hands. ✉ *1 Percy St., W1,* ☎ *0171/636–8141. Reservations essential. Jacket and tie. AE, DC, MC, V. Closed weekends, national holidays, 3 wks in Aug., 1 wk at Christmas. Tube: Goodge Street.*

INDIAN VEGETARIAN

$ ✕ **Mandeer.** Buried in a basement, with tile floors, brick walls, and temple lamps, the Mandeer is useful for being central (off Tottenham Court Road, where there's nothing much else), and extremely cheap at lunchtime, when you help yourself to the buffet. ✉ *21 Hanway Pl., W1,* ☎ *0171/580–3470. Reservations not accepted for lunch. AE, DC, MC, V. Closed Sun., national holidays, 2 wks over New Year. Tube: Tottenham Court Road.*

JAPANESE

$ ★ ✕ **Wagamama.** London's gone wild for Japanese noodles in this big basement. It's high-tech (your order is taken on a hand-held computer), high-volume—there are always crowds, with which you share wooden refectory tables—and high-turnover, with a fast-moving line always at the door. You can choose ramen in or out of soup, topped with sliced meats or tempura; or "raw energy" dishes—rice, curries, tofu, and so on—all at give-away prices and doggy-bag sizes. So successful has this formula proved, there is now an entire range of clothing, so that grateful diners can *wear* Wagamama. Many of them alternate this Wagamama experience with the newer one at 10a Lexington St. (☎ 0171/292–0990), near Oxford Circus. ✉ *4 Streatham St., WC1,* ☎ *0171/323–9223. Reservations not accepted. No credit cards. Closed Dec. 25. Tube: Tottenham Court Road.*

MODERN BRITISH

$$ ✕ **The Museum Street Café.** This useful and reliable restaurant near the British Museum serves a limited selection of impeccably fresh dishes, intelligently and plainly cooked by the two young owners, and charged prix fixe. The evening menu might feature char-grilled, maize-fed chicken with pesto, followed by a rich chocolate cake; at lunchtime you might choose a sandwich of Stilton on walnut bread and a big bowl of soup. Repeat customers, prepare for a shock—the place has doubled in size, and you no longer have to bring your own wine, but there's still an atypical (for London) ban on smoking. ✉ *47 Museum St., WC1,* ☎ *0171/405–3211. Reservations essential for dinner. MC, V. Closed weekends, public holidays. Tube: Tottenham Court Road.*

SEAFOOD

$ ★ ✕ **The North Sea Fish Restaurant.** This is the place for the British national dish of fish-and-chips—battered and deep-fried whitefish with thick fries shaken with salt and vinegar. It's a bit tricky to find—three blocks south of St. Pancras station, down Judd Street. Only freshly caught fish is served, and you can order it grilled—though that would defeat the object. You can take out or eat in. ✉ *7–8 Leigh St., WC1,* ☎ *0171/387–5892. AE, DC, MC, V. Closed Sun., national holidays, Dec. 25. Tube: Russell Square.*

South Kensington

FRENCH

$$$$ ★ ✕ **Bibendum.** Bibendum is in the reconditioned Michelin House, with its Art Deco decorations and brilliant stained glass, Conran Shop (☞ Chapter 4, Shopping), and Oyster Bar. For some years it was home to Simon Hopkinson's enormous talent. He is famous for preparing simple dishes perfectly, which he now explains in print, while still keeping an eye on this restaurant, which he part-owns. New chef, Matthew Harris, continues in a similar vein. Thus you can order herrings with sour cream, a risotto, or leeks vinaigrette followed by steak au poivre or the perfect boeuf bourgignon, or you might try brains or tripe as they ought to be cooked. The £27 set-price menu at lunchtime is money well spent. ✉ *Michelin House, 81 Fulham Rd., SW3,* ☎ *0171/581–5817. Reservations essential. MC, V. Closed Sun. Tube: South Kensington.*

$$ ★ ✕ **Lou Pescadou.** This place is like a little *tranche* of the South of France, with the sea-theme decor and emphatically French staff. The menu changes often and is based on fish—don't miss the *soupe de poisson* with croutons and *rouille* (rose-color, garlicky mayonnaise) if it's on—but there are other dishes, too, from steak-frites to, perhaps, delicate braised *cervelles*—brains. ✉ *241 Old Brompton Rd., SW5,* ☎ *0171/370–1057. Reservations not accepted. AE, DC, MC, V. Closed Aug., Dec. 25. Tube: Earl's Court.*

MEDITERRANEAN

$$ ✕ **Bistrot 190.** Chef-restaurateur Antony Worrall Thompson (☞ dell'Ugo, *above*) dominates this town's medium-priced eating scene with his happy, hearty food from Southern Europe and around the Mediterranean rim in raucous hardwood-floor-and-art settings. The identifiable feature of an AWT menu is its lists of about 100 loosely related ingredients (pork chop with rhubarb compote, cheese, and mustard mash, for instance), which when read all at once cause you to salivate. Country bread with tapenade and smoked haddock butter are brought first to the table; char-grilled squid with red and green salsa, and a great lemon tart are always in favor. This place, which was his first, is handy to museum or Albert Hall excursions. ✉ *190 Queen's Gate, SW7,* ☎ *0171/581–5666. Reservations not accepted. AE, DC, MC, V. Closed Sat. lunch, Sun., Dec. 25–26, Jan. 1. Tube: Gloucester Road.*

$$ ✕ **Downstairs at 190.** This is a Worrall Thompson creation—this time a good-value fish restaurant (☞ Bistrot 190, *above*). You can choose "Snacking Food," or appetizers, like grilled mussels and clams with garlic crumbs or smoked haddock and salmon carpaccio with anchovy ice cream, or go for lobster ravioli or a cassoulet of fishes, then attempt whisky fudge cake with caramelized oranges. ✉ *190 Queen's Gate,*

Dining in South Kensington, Knightsbridge, and Chelsea

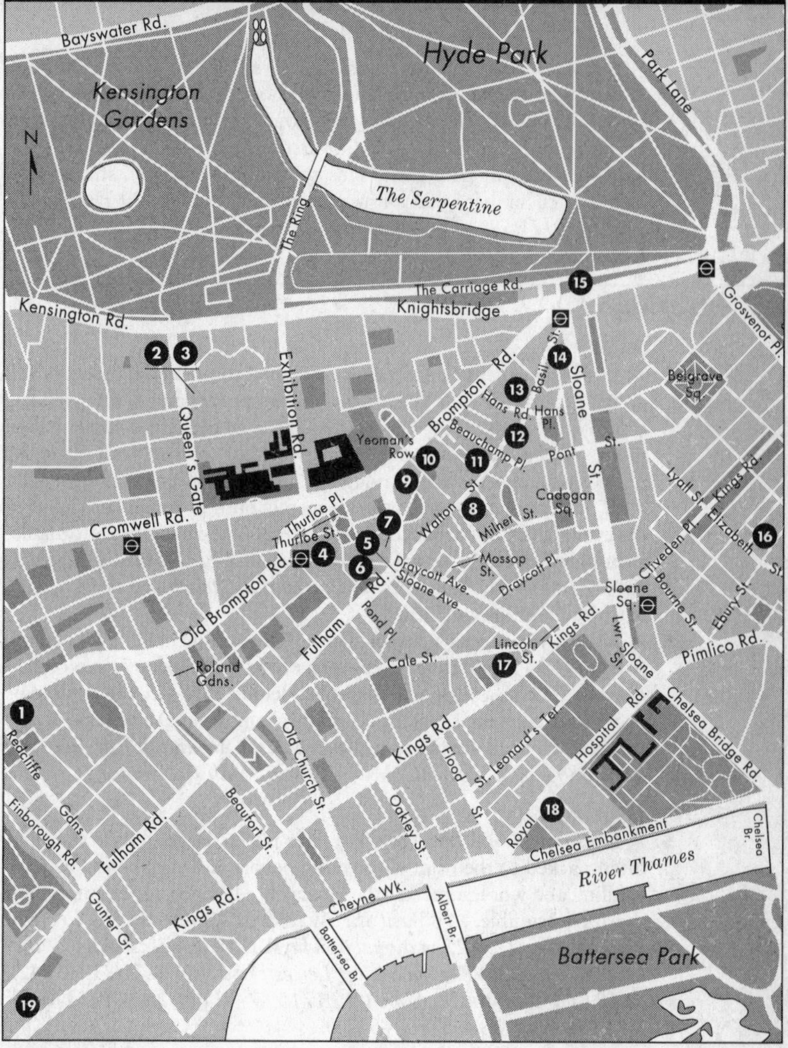

Bibendum, **5**
Bistrot 190, **2**
Capital, **13**
Caravela, **11**
Chelsea Kitchen, **17**
Chutney Mary, **19**
Daquise, **4**
Downstairs at 190, **3**
La Brasserie, **7**
La Tante Claire, **18**
Lou Pescadou, **1**
Luba's Bistro, **10**
Marco Pierre White: The Restaurant, **15**
Mijanou, **16**
PJ's, **6**
St. Quentin, **9**
San Lorenzo, **12**
Stockpot, **14**
Waltons, **8**

SW7, ☏ 0171/581–5666. AE, DC, MC, V. Closed Sun., Dec. 25. Tube: Gloucester Road.

POLISH

$ ✕ **Daquise.** This venerable and well-loved Polish café by the tube station is incongruous in this neighborhood, since it is neither style-conscious nor expensive. Fill your stomach without emptying your pocketbook (or, it must be said, overstimulating your taste buds) on *bigos* (sauerkraut with garlic sausage and mushrooms), stuffed cabbage and cucumber salad, or just coffee and cakes. ✉ *20 Thurloe St., SW7, ☏ 0171/589–6117. No credit cards. Closed Dec. 25. Tube: South Kensington.*

Knightsbridge

FRENCH

$$$$ ✕ **The Capital.** This elegant, clublike dining room has chandeliers and greige rag-rolled walls, a grown-up atmosphere, and formal service. Chef Philip Britten keeps his star bright with perhaps a subtle baked mousse of haddock and ginger, an *emincé* of chicken with olives, or pot-roasted pigeon with Armagnac, then a perfect caramel soufflé with butterscotch sauce. Set-price menus both at lunch (£25) and in the evening (£40—for *six* courses) make it somewhat more affordable, although the best dishes are found à la carte. ✉ *22–24 Basil St., SW3, ☏ 0171/589–5171. Reservations essential. Jacket and tie. AE, DC, MC, V. Tube: Knightsbridge.*

$$ ✕ **St. Quentin.** A very popular slice of Paris, frequented by French expatriates and locals alike. Every inch of the gallic menu is explored—gruyere quiche, escargots, cassoulet, lemon tart—in the bourgeois provincial comfort so many London chains (the Dômes, the Cafés Rouges) try hard yet fail to achieve. ✉ *243 Brompton Rd., SW3, ☏ 0171/589–8005. AE, DC, MC, V. Tube: South Kensington.*

INTERNATIONAL

$ ✕ **Stockpot.** You'll find speedy service in this large, jolly restaurant, often packed to the brim with young people and shoppers. The food is filling and wholesome: try the Lancashire hot pot, for example, and the apple crumble. ✉ *6 Basil St., SW3, ☏ 0171/589–8627. No credit cards. Closed Dec. 25, national holidays. Tube: Knightsbridge. Other branches at ✉ 40 Panton St., off Leicester Sq. (☏ 0171/839–5142); ✉ 18 Old Compton St., Soho (☏ 0171/287–1066); and ✉ 273 King's Rd., Chelsea (☏ 0171/823–3175).*

ITALIAN

$$$ ✕ **San Lorenzo.** This well-established, well-heeled trattoria, with quiet green decor, is nothing special foodwise, but it's just the ticket if you're keen to spot celebrities or royalty, gaze into the world of ladies-who-lunch—or if you are yourself a lady-who-lunches. The usual upscale Italian dishes are here, but they nod to fashion—try wood pigeon with polenta, or any of the veal dishes. ✉ *22 Beauchamp Pl., SW3, ☏ 0171/584–1074. AE, DC, MC, V. Closed Sun. and national holidays. Tube: South Kensington.*

$$$$ ✕ **Marco Pierre White: The Restaurant.** One fears one ought to have read The Book and seen The Movie before patronizing The Restaurant. Actually, if one is from London, one has. Bad boy Marco enjoys Jagger-like fame from his TV appearances and gossip column reports of his complicated love life and random eruptions of fury. He should stick to his pans, say superchef critics, meaning it literally in some cases. But, hype aside, Marco is a great chef and now gets to show off in his most serious setting yet—all valuable oils, starched napery, and batteries of flatware. If you invest in an evening here,

It helps to be pushy in airports.

Introducing the revolutionary new TransPorter™ from American Tourister®. It's the first suitcase you can push around without a fight. TransPorter's™ exclusive four-wheel design lets you push it in front of you with almost no effort–the wheels take the weight. Or pull it on two wheels if you choose. You can even stack on other bags and use it like a luggage cart.

Stable 4-wheel design.

TransPorter™ is designed like a dresser, with built-in shelves to organize your belongings. Or collapse the shelves and pack it like a traditional suitcase. Inside, there's a suiter feature to help keep suits and dresses from wrinkling. When push comes to shove, you can't beat a TransPorter.™ For more information on how you can be this pushy, call 1-800-542-1300.

Shelves collapse on command.

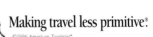

American Tourister

Making travel less primitive.®

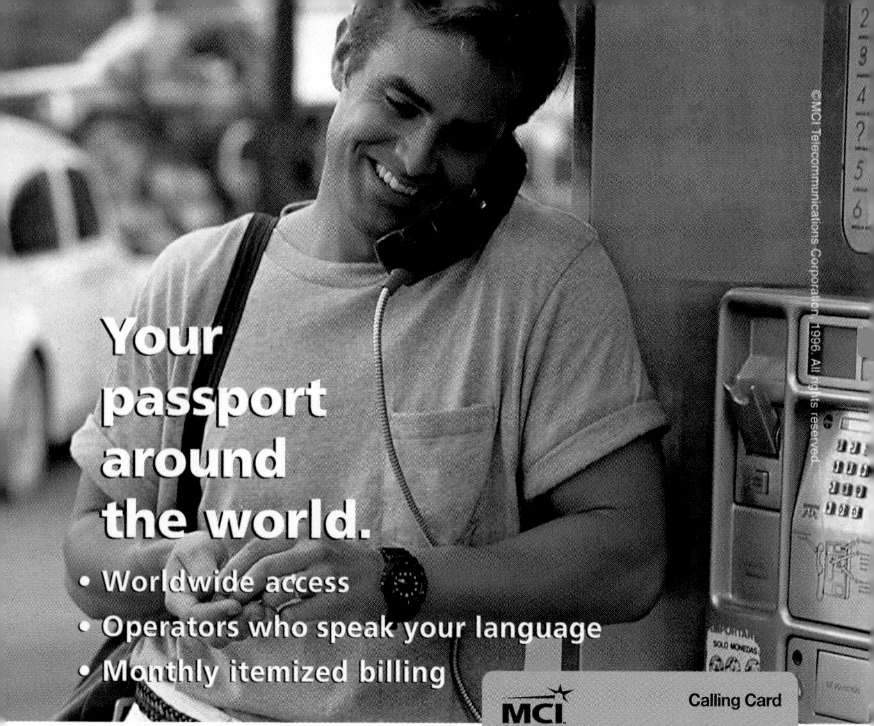

©MCI Telecommunications Corporation, 1996. All rights reserved.
Your passport around the world.
• Worldwide access
• Operators who speak your language
• Monthly itemized billing

MCI
Calling Card
415 555 1234 2244
J.D. SMITH

Use your MCI Card® and these access numbers for an easy way to call when traveling worldwide.

American Samoa	633-2MCI (633-2624)
Antigua †	#2
(Available from public card phones only)	
Aruba ✣	800-888-8
Argentina ★ †	001-800-333-1111
Bahamas (CC) †	1-800-888-8000
Barbados	1-800-888-8000
Belize	815 from pay phones 557 from hotels
Bermuda ✣ †	1-800-888-8000
Bolivia ♦	0-800-2222
Brazil (CC) †	000-8012
British Virgin Islands ✣	1-800-888-8000
Cayman Islands †	1-800-888-8000
Chile (CC) †	
To call using CTC ■	800-207-300
To call using ENTEL ■	123-00316
Colombia (CC) ♦ †	980-16-0001
Costa Rica ♦ †	0800-012-2222
Dominica	1-800-888-8000
Dominican Republic (CC)	1-800-888-8000
Ecuador (CC) ✣ †	999-170
El Salvador ♦	800-1767
Grenada ✣	1-800-888-8000
Guatemala ♦	189
Guyana	177
Haiti (CC) ✣	001-800-444-1234
Honduras ✣	122
Jamaica	1-800-888-8000
(From Special Hotels only)	873
Mexico ▲ †	95-800-674-7000
Netherlands Antilles (CC) ✣ †	001-800-950-1022
Nicaragua (CC)	166
(Outside of Managua, dial 02 first)	
Panama †	108
Military Bases	2810-108
Paraguay ✣	008-11-800
Peru	170
Puerto Rico (CC) †	1-800-888-8000
St. Lucia ✣	1-800-888-8000
Trinidad & Tobago ✣	1-800-888-8000
Turks & Caicos ✣	1-800-888-8000
Uruguay	00-412
U.S. Virgin Islands (CC) †	1-800-888-8000
Venezuela ✣ ♦	800-1114-0

To sign up for the MCI Card, dial the access number of the country you are in and ask to speak with a customer service representative.

MCI

http://www.mci.com

† Automation available from most locations. ✣ Limited availability. ★ Not available from public pay phones. (CC) Country-to-country calling available. May not be available to/from all international locations. (Canada, Puerto Rico, and U.S. Virgin Islands are considered Domestic Access locations.) ♦ Public phones may require deposit of coin or phone card for dial tone. ■ International communications carrier. ▲ When calling from public phones use phones marked LADATEL.

know that he will despise you for ordering his Assiette of Chocolate, which he considers low-class. At press time, after the takeover of the Forte Hotel chain, the future of this, and of Nico at Ninety (☞ *above*), was in some doubt. ✉ *Hyde Park Hotel, Knightsbridge, SW3,* ☎ *0171/259–5380. Reservations essential. Jacket and tie. AE, DC, MC, V. Tube: Knightsbridge.*

PORTUGUESE

$$ ✕ **Caravela.** This narrow lower-ground-floor place is one of London's few Portuguese restaurants. You can get *Caldo verde* (cabbage soup), *bacalhau* (salt-cured cod), and other typical dishes while listening (on Friday or Saturday) to the national music, fado—desperately sad songs belted out at thrash-metal volume. ✉ *39 Beauchamp Pl., SW3,* ☎ *0171/581–2366. AE, DC, MC, V. Closed Sun. lunch, Dec. 25, Easter. Tube: South Kensington.*

RUSSIAN

$ ✕ **Luba's Bistro.** Popular for decades: long wooden tables, plain decor, and authentic Russian cooking—chicken Kiev, beef Stroganoff, etc. Bring your own wine. ✉ *6 Yeoman's Row, SW3,* ☎ *0171/589–2950. Reservations essential. MC, V. Closed Sun., national holidays. Tube: South Kensington.*

TRADITIONAL ENGLISH

$$$$ ✕ **Waltons.** Popular with Americans, this formal, sumptuous, pampering restaurant has strong color schemes, acres of rich fabrics, and flowers. The cuisine is as rich as the surroundings and, though billed as British, is not so easy to categorize—ravioli stuffed with lobster or steamed red mullet on a fondue of tomatoes and fresh basil are as likely as roast lamb. Finish with a "mess" of berries, cream, and meringue. ✉ *121 Walton St., SW3,* ☎ *0171/584–0204. Jacket and tie. AE, DC, MC, V. Closed Dec. 25–26, Jan. 1, and Easter. Tube: South Kensington.*

Chelsea

AMERICAN

$$ ✕ **PJ's.** The decor here evokes the Bulldog Drummond lifestyle, with wooden floors and stained glass, a vast, slowly revolving propeller from a 1940s Curtis flying boat, and polo memorabilia. A menu of all-American staples (soft-shell crab, chowder, gumbo, steaks, smoked ribs), big salads, pecan pie, brownies, and Häagen-Dazs should please all but vegetarians, and portions are big, but this place is more remarkable for ambience than for food—it's open late, it's relaxed, friendly, and efficient, and it has bartenders who can mix anything. The sister PJ's in Covent Garden (✉ 30 Wellington St., ☎ 0171/240–7529) is worth remembering for its excellent weekend "Fun Club" for kids. ✉ *52 Fulham Rd., SW3,* ☎ *0171/581–0025. AE, DC, MC, V. Closed Dec. 25–26, Jan. 1. Tube: South Kensington.*

ANGLO-INDIAN

$$$ ✕ **Chutney Mary.** London's first-and-only Anglo-Indian restaurant provides a fantasy version of the British Raj, all giant wicker armchairs and palms. Dishes like Masala roast lamb (practically a whole leg, marinated and spiced) and "Country Captain" (braised chicken with almonds, raisins, chilies, and spices) alternate with the more familiar North Indian dishes such as roghan josh (lamb curry). The best choices are certainly the dishes re-created from the kitchens of Indian chefs cooking for English palates back in the old Raj days. For this reason, the all-you-can-eat Sunday buffet is not such a great idea, because it leaves those out. Service is deferential, and desserts, unheard of in tandoori places (*kulfi* excepted), are worth leaving room for. ✉ *535 King's Rd.,*

SW10, ☎ 0171/351–3113. Reservations essential. AE, DC, MC, V. Closed Dec. 25 dinner, Dec. 26. Tube: Fulham Broadway.

FRENCH

$$$$ ★ ✕ **La Tante Claire.** Justly famous, but cripplingly expensive. The decor is light and sophisticated, the service impeccable, the French wine list impressive, but the food is the point. From the *carte,* you might choose hot pâté de foie gras on shredded potatoes with a sweet wine and shallot sauce, roast spiced pigeon, or Pierre Koffmann's famous signature dish of pig's feet stuffed with mousse of white meat with sweetbreads and wild mushrooms. As every gourmet expense-accounter knows, the set lunch menu (£26) is a genuine bargain. ✉ *68 Royal Hospital Rd., SW3, ☎ 0171/352–6045. Reservations essential 3–4 wks in advance for dinner, 2–3 days for lunch. Jacket and tie. AE, DC, MC, V. Closed weekends, 2 wks at Christmas, Jan. 1, 10 days at Easter, 3 wks in Aug.–Sept. Tube: Sloane Square.*

$$$ ✕ **Mijanou.** The haunt of politicians and Whitehall civil servants. Chef Sonia Blech claims on the menu that she "merely rearranges the natural ingredients which have always existed," but she's too modest, as such complicated dishes as her quail stuffed with wild rice and pecan nuts or lobster terrine with a mild saffron sauce will prove. Smoking is banned in the entire restaurant, which is just as well, because it's tiny. There is a small patio and a large, brilliant wine list drawn up by the chef's husband, Neville Blech. ✉ *143 Ebury St., SW1, ☎ 0171/730–4099. Reservations essential. Jacket and tie. AE, DC, MC. Closed weekends, national holidays, 1 wk at Christmas, most of Aug. Tube: Sloane Square.*

$$ ✕ **La Brasserie.** This is a convenient spot for South Ken museum visits and has flexible, and long opening hours, a menu of entirely French things, from fish soup to tarte tatin, and a good buzz on a Sunday morning when the entire well-heeled neighborhood sits around reading the papers and sipping *capuccino.* No doing that at peak times, when you must eat, but the food's reliable, if a little overpriced. ✉ *272 Brompton Rd., SW3, ☎ 0171/584–1668. AE, DC, MC, V. Tube: South Kensington.*

INTERNATIONAL

$ ✕ **Chelsea Kitchen.** This café has been crowded since the '60s with hungry people after hot, filling, and inexpensive food. Expect nothing more fancy than pasta, omelets, salads, stews, and casseroles. The menu changes every day. ✉ *98 King's Rd., SW3, ☎ 0171/589–1330. Reservations not accepted. No credit cards. Closed Dec. 25. Tube: Sloane Square.*

Kensington and Notting Hill Gate

AMERICAN

$ ✕ **Tootsies.** A superior burger place, dark but cheerful, decorated with vintage advertisements and playing vintage rock. Alternatives to the burgers, which come with thick, crinkly fries, are big salads, steak, BLTs, and chili in a bottomless pan—they'll give you as much as you can take. The usual ices and pies do for dessert. There are branches in Fulham, Chiswick, and Notting Hill. ✉ *120 Holland Park Ave., W11, ☎ 0171/229–8567. Reservations not accepted. MC, V. Closed Dec. 25. Tube: Holland Park.*

FRENCH

$$$ ✕ **Boyd's.** Boyd Gilmour was a professional percussionist who decided he'd rather rattle the pans, and so built this glass-roofed conservatory garden. It's a soothing, satisfying restaurant, the cooking unpretentious—crab ravioli with ginger and scallions; wood pigeon in a black-currant

All Saints, **6**
Belvedere, **14**
Boyd's, **10**
Chez Moi, **1**
Clarke's, **11**
Costa's Grill, **8**
First Floor, **5**
Geales, **9**
Julie's, **3**
Kalamaras, **7**
Kensington Place, **12**
192, **4**
Tootsies, **2**
Wódka, **13**

Dining in Kensington and Notting Hill Gate

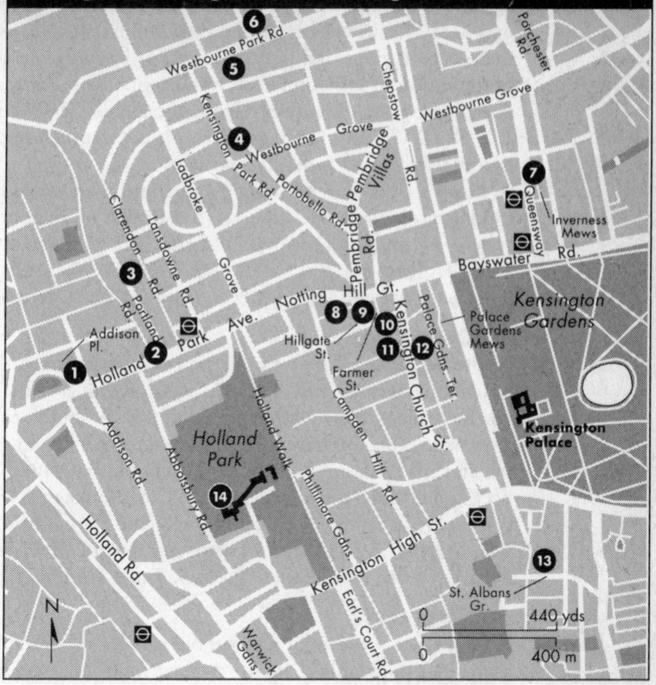

sauce; chocolate terrine—the atmosphere calmer than at near-neighbor Kensington Place (☞ *below*). A 100-bottle wine list includes about 10 to sample by the glass. ✉ *135 Kensington Church St., W8,* ☎ *0171/727–5452. Jacket and tie. AE, MC, V. Closed Sun., Mon., 1 wk at Christmas, Easter. Tube: Notting Hill Gate.*

$$$ ✕ **Chez Moi.** Sophisticated French food is served in a warm, salmon-pink dining room, which, with the tables widely spaced and the lighting low, demands romantic behavior. There are dishes the menu admits are "traditional" that Chez Moi's fans have depended on for a quarter century—things like rack of lamb with garlic and mint and beef tournedos with béarnaise as well as more novel dishes such as the popular "Oursins Chez Moi"—ersatz sea urchins made of shrimp and scallop, with fried angel-hair pasta "spines." The desserts are hit-or-miss, but there are ample chocolates brought with the coffee. ✉ *1 Addison Ave., W11,* ☎ *0171/603–8267. Reservations essential for dinner. AE, DC, MC, V. Dinner only Mon.–Sat., also Sun. lunch. Closed 2 wks over Christmas, 2 wks in Aug., national holidays. Tube: Shepherd's Bush.*

FRENCH/CALIFORNIAN

$$$ ✕ **Clarke's.** There's no choice on the evening menu at Sally Clarke's award-winning restaurant; her dinners feature ultrafresh ingredients, plainly but perfectly cooked, accompanied by home-baked breads. The plant and art–speckled room is similarly home-style, if home is in the big white Kensington houses you see around here. ✉ *124 Kensington Church St., W8,* ☎ *0171/221–9225. Reservations essential. MC, V. Closed weekends, public holidays, 2 wks in Aug. Tube: Notting Hill Gate.*

GREEK

$$ ✕ **Kalamaras.** Here are two small, friendly, authentic Greek restaurants, one "micro" and one "mega," nearly next door to each other. The micro, which doesn't have a liquor license, is cheaper but more cramped than the mega. Menu choice here is wider than at the average Greek restaurant; try a few unusual *mezedes* (appetizers, for sharing), such as artichoke hearts with broad beans and dill, or grilled mussels, then a great moussaka (a rare thing), or kavouri—baked crab. Most of the legion of London Greek restaurants, by the way, are not Greek at all, but Cypriot. This one is Greek, though. ✉ *76–78 Inverness Mews, W2,* ☎ *0171/727–9122. AE, DC, MC, V. Dinner only. Closed Sun., national holidays. Tube: Queensway.*

$ ✕ **Costa's Grill.** Come for good value and such down-to-earth Greek food as grilled fish and *kleftiko* (roast lamb on the bone). The atmosphere is homey and happy, and there's a tiny garden open in summer. ✉ *14 Hillgate St., W8,* ☎ *0171/229–3794. No credit cards. Closed Sun., national holidays, 3 wks in summer. Tube: Notting Hill Gate.*

MEDITERRANEAN

$$ ✕ **The Belvedere.** There can be no finer setting for a summer supper or a sunny Sunday brunch than a window table—or a balcony one if you luck out—at this stunning restaurant in the middle of Holland Park. The menu is big on shaved Parmesan, sun-dried tomatoes, and arugula, which suits the conservatory-like room, but both food and service do occasionally miss the target. Still, with a view like this, who cares about water glasses or bland chicken? ✉ *Holland Park, off Abbotsbury Rd., W8,* ☎ *0171/602–1238. Reservations essential for weekends. AE, DC, MC, V. Closed Sun. dinner, Dec. 25. Tube: Holland Park.*

MODERN BRITISH

$$$ ✕ **First Floor.** A place for well-off but arty locals who know and watch each other, popular both for its inventive food and its ambience—it looks like a bombed church inhabited by distressed nobility. There might be Thai fishcakes or Tuscan lamb stew in the evening, while lunch, at about half the price, consists of such lighter dishes as focaccia with grilled vegetables. ✉ *186 Portobello Rd., W11,* ☎ *0171/243–0072. Reservations essential. AE, MC, V. Closed Dec. 25. Tube: Notting Hill Gate.*

$$$ ★ ✕ **Kensington Place.** Being a favorite among the local glitterati keeps this place always packed and noisy. A huge plate-glass window and mural are backdrops to fashionable food—grilled foie gras with sweetcorn pancake and baked tamarillo with vanilla ice are perennials—but it's the buzz that draws the crowds. ✉ *201 Kensington Church St., W8,* ☎ *0171/727–3184. MC, V. Closed Aug. bank holiday, Dec. 25. Tube: Notting Hill Gate.*

$$ ★ ✕ **192.** A noisy, buzzy wine bar/restaurant just off the Portobello Road, this is as much a social hangout for the local media mafia as a restaurant, especially on weekends, when you'll feel like you've gatecrashed a party, if you manage to get a table, that is. Food likes to keep ahead of fashion, and is best on the appetizer list—many people order two of these instead of an entrée. Try the risottos, the seasonal salad (perhaps romanesco, broccoli, anchovy, and gremolata), the fish (sea bass with fennel, lemon, and rosemary; scallop, chickpea, chorizo, and clam casserole), or whatever sounds unusual. ✉ *192 Kensington Park Rd., W11,* ☎ *0171/229–0482. AE, MC, V. Closed Mon., lunch, public holidays. Tube: Notting Hill Gate.*

$ ✕ **All Saints.** One warms to the wobbly kitchen chairs and spartan plaster walls here after a bottle or two of the inexpensive house wine, and an enormous portion of home-style cooking. Serial chef changes alter the nature of the food, but not of the place, home-away-from-home for young and trendy Notting Hillbillies. Menu staples include roast vegetables with aioli, lamb brochette with tabbouleh and hummus, and a four-inch-high creamy lemon tart. Be warned that this street was not so long ago known as "the front line" in a neighborhood that mixes drug and antique deals on the same block. It's gentrified now, but the non-urban may still find it alarming. ✉ *12–14 All Saint's Rd., W11,* ☎ *0171/243–2808. Reservations essential for dinner. MC, DC, V. Closed Sun. dinner, Dec. 25. Tube: Westbourne Park.*

POLISH

$$ ★ ✕ **Wódka.** This smart, modern Polish restaurant is the only one in the world, as far as we know, to serve smart, modern Polish food. It is popular with elegant locals plus a sprinkling of celebs and often has the atmosphere of a dinner party. Alongside the smoked salmon, herring, caviar, and eggplant *blinis,* you might also find venison sausages or roast duck with *krupnik* (honey-lemon vodka). Order from the separate menu a carafe of the purest vodka in London (and watch the check inflate); it's encased in a block of ice and hand-flavored (with bison grass, cherries, rowanberries) by the owner, who, being an actual Polish prince, is uniquely qualified to do this. ✉ *12 St. Albans Grove, W8,* ☎ *0171/937–6513. Reservations essential for dinner. AE, DC, MC, V. Closed weekend lunch, public holidays. Tube: High Street Kensington.*

SEAFOOD

$ ★ ✕ **Geales.** This is a cut above your typical fish-and-chips joint. The decor is stark but the fish will have been swimming just hours beforehand, even the ones from the Caribbean (fried swordfish is a specialty). Geales is popular with the rich and famous, not just loyal locals. ✉ *2 Farmer St., W8,* ☎ *0171/727–7969. Reservations not accepted. MC. Closed Sun., Mon., 2 wks at Christmas, 3 wks in Aug., national holidays. Tube: Notting Hill Gate.*

TRADITIONAL ENGLISH

$$$ ✕ **Julie's.** This sweet '60s throwback has two parts: an upstairs wine bar and a basement restaurant, both decorated with Victorian ecclesiastical furniture. The cooking is sound, old-fashioned English (salmon-and-halibut terrine, roast pheasant with chestnut stuffing and wild rowan jelly). The traditional Sunday lunches are very popular, and in summer there's a garden for outside eating. ✉ *135 Portland Rd., W11,* ☎ *0171/229–8331. MC, V. Closed Sat. lunch, Dec. 25 and 31, Easter. Tube: Holland Park.*

The City and the South Bank

FRENCH

$$$ ★ ✕ **Le Pont de la Tour.** Sir Terence Conran's place across the river, overlooking the bridge that gives it its name, comes into its own in summer, when the outside tables are heaven. Inside the "Gastrodrome" (his word) there's a vintner and baker and deli, a seafood bar, a brasserie, and this '30s diner-style restaurant, smart as the captain's table. Fish and seafood (lobster salad; Baltic herrings in crème fraîche; roast halibut with aioli), meat and game (venison fillet, port and blueberry sauce; roast veal, caramelized endive) feature heavily—vegetarians are out of luck. Prune and Armagnac tart or chocolate terrine could finish a glamorous—and expensive—meal. By contrast, an impeccable salade niçoise in the brasserie is about £9. ✉ *36D Shad Thames, Butler's Wharf, SE1,* ☎ *0171/403–8403. Reservations essential for lunch, weekend dinner. MC, V. Closed Dec. 25. Tube: Tower Hill.*

ITALIAN

$ ★ ✕ **The Eagle.** If the name makes it sound like a pub, that's because it is a pub, albeit a superior one, with wooden floors, a few sofas, and art on the walls. It does, however, belong in the "Restaurants" section by virtue of the amazingly good-value nouveau Tuscan food, which you choose from the blackboard menu (or by pointing) at the bar. There are about half a dozen dishes, a pasta and/or risotto always among them.

Bill Bentley's, **5**
Eagle, **2**
Moshi Moshi Sushi, **4**
Le Pont de la Tour, **7**
People's Palace, **8**
Quality Chop House, **1**
Sri Siam City, **6**
St. John, **3**

Dining in the City and the South Bank

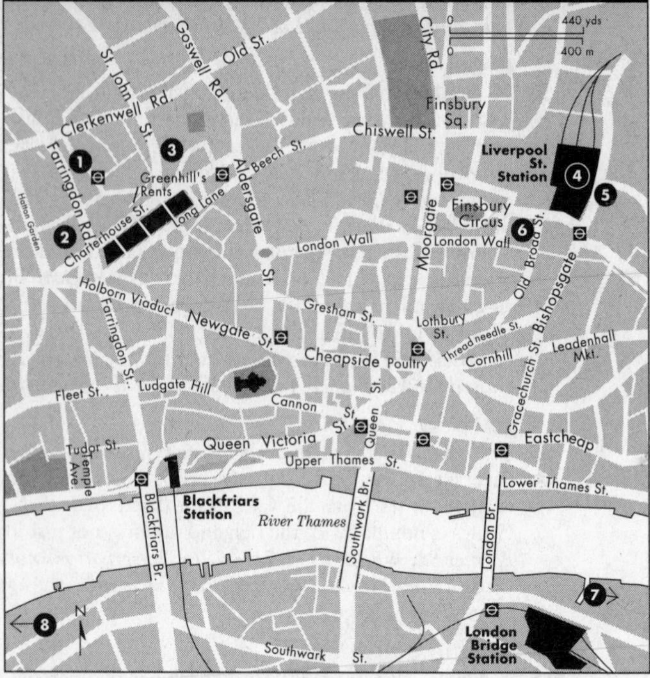

There are currently quite a few places in London charging four times the price for remarkably similar food, as well as a welcome trend toward more and more pubs serving good meals—a trend which The Eagle all but caused. ✉ *159 Farringdon Rd., EC1,* ☎ *0171/837–1353. Reservations not accepted. No credit cards. No food served Sat., Sun. evenings. Tube: Farringdon.*

JAPANESE

$ ✕ **Moshi Moshi Sushi.** London lacks much affordable sushi, but this wacky glass-walled joint above Platform One in Liverpool Street Station may point the way to future sushi bar saturation, because it's proving popular. Pick *tekka* or *kappa maki* (tuna or cucumber seaweed rolls) or the usual sushi suspects—*maguro* (tuna), *sake* (salmon), *saba* (mackerel), etc.—in pairs off a conveyor belt that snakes around the counter. At the end, you count up your color-coded plates to pay. ✉ *Unit 24 Liverpool St. Station, EC2,* ☎ *0171/247–3227. Reservations not accepted. No credit cards. Closed after 9* PM*; weekends; public holidays. Tube: Liverpool Street.*

MODERN BRITISH

$$ ✕ **The People's Palace.** Thank goodness for this place. Now you can finally have a civilized meal during your South Bank arts encounter. With menus by trendy chef Gary Rhodes, of Greenhouse fame (☞ *above*), and run independently (from the Royal Festival Hall et al) by the same owners, this has remarkably low prices considering it has the greatest river view in town. As the baying critics noted around opening time, there are occasional mistakes here, but the more British the dish, the more reliable it proves—roast beef, potted duck, suckling pig sandwich on granary bread, marmalade sponge, sticky toffee pudding—all these are fine. Service is a bit flaky, but the soaring space with its giant windows makes up for everything. ✉ *Royal Festival Hall, Level 3, South Bank, SE1,* ☎ *0171/928–9999. AE, DC, MC, V. Tube: Waterloo.*

$$ ✕ **Quality Chop House.** This was converted from one of the most gorgeous "greasy spoon" caffs in town, retaining the solid Victorian fittings (including pewlike seats, which you often have to share). It is not luxurious, but the food is wonderful. It's almost a parody of caff food—bangers and mash turns out to be home-made herbed veal sausage with rich gravy, light, fluffy potato, and vegetables *à point;* egg and chips (fries) are not remotely greasy. There are also such posh things as salmon fishcakes and steak, and desserts that change with the seasons. ✉ *94 Farringdon Rd., EC1,* ☎ *0171/837–5093. Reservations essential. No credit cards. Closed Sat. lunch, Sun. dinner, public holidays. Tube: Farringdon.*

$$ ★ ✕ **St. John.** This former smokehouse (ham, not cigars), converted by erstwhile architect owner/chef, Fergus Henderson, wowed the town when it opened, with its soaring white walls, schoolroom lamps, stone floors, iron railings, and plain wooden chairs, and its uncompromising fodder. Some find Henderson's chutzpah scary: One infamous appetizer is carrots and egg (a bunch of carrots with green tops intact, and a boiled egg), although the imaginativeness of others—roast bone marrow and parsley salad; smoked eel, beetroot, and horseradish—excuses this silliness. Entrées (roast lamb and parsnip; smoked haddock and fennel; deviled crab) can appear shockingly nude and lumpen on the plate. There are failures, but they're heroic failures. An all-French wine list has plenty of affordable bottles, plus lots of Malmseys and ports. Service is efficiently matey, and the pastry chef's chocolate slice belongs in the brownie hall of fame. ✉ *26 St. John St., EC1,* ☎ *0171/251–0848. Reservations essential. AE, MC, V. Closed Sun. dinner, Dec. 25. Tube: Farringdon.*

SEAFOOD

$$ ✕ **Bill Bentley's.** You can see from the bare walls and the arched ceiling that this was once a wine merchant's vaults. There are four other branches in London, all equally old-fashioned in feel, and all serving Bill Bentley's special oysters and seafood platters. ✉ *Swedeland Ct., 202 Bishopsgate, EC2,* ☎ *0171/283–1763. Reservations essential. Jacket and tie. MC, V. Lunch only. Closed weekends, national holidays. Tube: Liverpool Street.*

THAI

$$ ✕ **Sri Siam City.** The easterly cousin of this well-liked Soho Thai place turns down the chili fire a little, perhaps. The Thai staples—green or red chicken curry, *pad* Thai (noodles stir fried with vegetables and shrimp)—are good, or try an easygoing squid salad with lemongrass, lime, and chili. ✉ *85 London Wall, EC2,* ☎ *0171/628–5772. Reservations advised for lunch. AE, DC, MC, V. Closed weekends; Dec. 25. Tube: Moorgate.*

Camden Town and Hampstead

ANGLO-FRENCH

$$ ✕ **Camden Brasserie.** The perfect neighborhood restaurant, this mellow, brick-walled, wood-floored haven makes its charcoal grill work hard (barbecued corn-fed chicken, salmon fillet, steak, etc., which come with piles of matchstick fries) and offers a daily fish, pasta, soup, and salad, too. Convenient for market, Canal, and Zoo excursions. ✉ *216 Camden High St., NW1,* ☎ *0171/482–2114. MC, V. Closed Dec. 25. Tube: Camden Town.*

BELGIAN

$$ ★ ✕ **Belgo Noord.** To enter what must be London's least normal restaurant, you pass the wavy concrete facade and cross the spotlit "drawbridge" over the brushed-steel open kitchen. Inside, wait staff in

maroon monks' habits sweep over to your refectorylike table to take your order of *moules-frites* (steamed mussels in various sauces with fries), *waterzooi* (a whitefish stew), wild boar sausages, and other authentic Belgian dishes. Try the Kriek, cherry beer brewed by Trappist monks. Of course, this is the older, more handsome, brother of the Covent Garden Belgo Centraal (☞ *above*). ✉ *72 Chalk Farm Rd., NW1,* ☎ *0171/267–0718. Reservations essential, same day only. AE, MC, V. Closed Dec. 25. Tube: Chalk Farm.*

BRITISH

$ ✕ **The Coffee Cup.** A Hampstead landmark for just about as long as anyone can remember, this smoky, dingy, uncomfortable café is lovable, very cheap, and therefore always packed. You can get anything (beans, eggs, kippers, mushrooms) on toast, grills, sandwiches, cakes, fry-ups, etc.—nothing healthy or fashionable whatsoever. There are tables outside in the summer, but no liquor license. ✉ *74 Hampstead High St., NW3,* ☎ *0171/435–7565. Reservations not accepted. No credit cards. Closed Dec. 25. Tube: Hampstead.*

FRENCH

$$ ✕ **Café des Arts.** Every wood-paneled wall in this brasserie housed in a 17th-century cottage on the main street is hung with work for sale—hence the name—and the patrons are just the sort to buy it, too. About half the beautifully presented dishes—tuna tataki (just-seared fillets) with five-spice lentils; Provençale fish stew with rouille; chicken breast with lemon-herb dumplings—come in two sizes, so you can control the check. Don't miss the wicked warm chocolate soufflé. ✉ *82 Hampstead High St., NW3,* ☎ *0171/435–3608. AE, DC, MC, V. Closed Dec. 25. Tube: Hampstead.*

GREEK

$ ✕ **Lemonia.** On a very pleasant street near Regent's Park is this superior version of London Greek—large and light, friendly, and packed every evening. Besides the usual *mezedes* (appetizers), *souvlakia* (kebabs), *stifado* (beef stewed in wine), and so on, there are interesting specials: quail, perhaps, or *gemista* (stuffed vegetables). ✉ *89 Regent's Park Rd., NW1,* ☎ *0171/586–7454. Reservations essential for dinner. No credit cards. Closed Sat. lunch, Sun. dinner, Dec. 25. Tube: Chalk Farm.*

Brunch and Afternoon Tea

It is sometimes suggested that among Londoners, brunch is catching on while the afternoon ritual (often mistakenly referred to as "high tea") is dying out. Tea, the drink, however, is so ingrained in the national character, that tea, the meal, will always have a place in the capital, if only as an occasional celebration, a children's treat, or something you do when your American friends are in town. Reserve for all these, unless otherwise noted.

Brunch

The Belvedere (☞ *above*) in bucolic Holland Park wins hands down for setting, especially if you bag a rare terrace table on a rare sunny day. There is, admittedly no official brunch, but you can fake it from the regular menu. *Lunch served weekends noon–3.*

Butler's Wharf Chop House. At this—yet another Terence Conran (Quaglino's, Pont de la Tour, Bibendum . . .) venture—brunch (£13.50 for two courses) is as British as brunch ever gets, with Dublin Bay prawns, Stilton and celery soup and such, and a fabulous Thames-side setting. ✉ *36E Shad Thames, SE1,* ☎ *0171/403–3403. AE, DC, MC, V. Brunch served Sun. noon–3.*

Christopher's. Imagine you're in Manhattan at this superior Covent Garden purveyor of American food, from pancakes to steak, eggs and fries, via salmon fishcakes and a Caesar salad. Two courses are £12. ✉ *18 Wellington St., WC2,* ☎ *0171/240–4222. AE, DC, MC, V. Brunch served Sun. noon–3:30.*

The Room at the Halcyon. The Halcyon is favored by stars of Hollywood and rock, and is secreted in the leafy neighborhood of Holland Park. An excellent modern British kitchen. ✉ *129 Holland Park Ave., W11,* ☎ *0171/221–5411. AE, DC, MC, V. Brunch served Sun. noon–3:30.*

Joe Allen (☞ *above*) is where to take refuge from the lovely British weather, down some bloody Marys, and maybe a grilled chicken sandwich with Swiss, or a salad of spicy sausage, shrimp, and new potato. Two brunch courses with coffee are a bargain at £10—half the dinner price. *Brunch served weekends noon–4 PM.*

Afternoon Tea

Brown's Hotel does rest on its laurels somewhat, with a packaged aura and nobody around but fellow tourists who believe this the most famous. For £14.95 you get sandwiches, a scone with cream and jam (jelly), and two cream cakes. ✉ *33 Albermarle St., W1,* ☎ *0171/493–6020. Tea served daily 3–6.*

Claridges is the real McCoy, with liveried footmen proffering sandwiches, scones, and superior patisseries (£15.50) in the palatial yet genteel Foyer, to the sound of the resident "Hungarian orchestra" (actually a string quartet). ✉ *Brook St., W1,* ☎ *0171/629–8860. Tea served daily 3–5.*

Fortnum & Mason's. Upstairs at the queen's grocer's, three set teas are ceremoniously offered: standard Afternoon Tea (sandwiches, scone, cakes, £10.50), old-fashioned High Tea (the traditional nursery meal, adding something more robust and savoury, £12.25), and Champagne Tea (£15.75). ✉ *St. James's Restaurant, 4th floor, 181 Piccadilly, W1,* ☎ *0171/734–8040. Tea served Mon.–Sat. 3–5:20.*

Harrods. One for sweet-toothed and greedy people, the Georgian Room at the ridiculously well-known department store has a serve-it-yourself afternoon tea *buffet* that'll give you a sugar rush for a week. ✉ *Brompton Rd., SW3,* ☎ *0171/730–1234. Tea served Mon.–Sat. 3–5:30.*

The Ritz. The Ritz's new owners have put the once-peerless Palm Court tea back on the map, with proper tiered cake stands and silver pots, a harpist, and Louis XVI chaises, plus a leisurely four-hour time slot, all for £17. A good excuse for a glass of champagne. Reservations are taken only to 50% capacity. ✉ *Piccadilly, W1,* ☎ *0171/493–8181. Tea served daily 2–6.*

Savoy. The glamorous Thames-side hotel does one of the most pleasant teas (£16), its triple-tiered cake stands packed with goodies, its tail-coated waiters thrillingly polite. ✉ *The Strand, WC2,* ☎ *0171/836–4343. Tea served daily 3–5:30.*

Pubs

Many Londoners could no more live without their "local" than they could forgo their daily dinner. The pub—or public house, to give it its full title—is ingrained in the British psyche as social center, bolt-hole, second home. Pub culture is still male-dominated, revolving around pints, pool, darts, and sports, but mass redecoration by the major breweries (which own most pubs) in the late '80s transformed so many ancient smoke- and spittle-stained dives into fantasy Edwardian drawing rooms that (on the whole) they feel more congenial to women than ever before. This decade, the fashion has been for modernity, with cocktail lists, distressed paintwork, bare floorboards, and chrome fittings, but the result is similar—these are pubs, but not as we know them. Who cares what they look like though, when there's been such a pub-food renaissance, with others following where the Eagle (☞ *above*) led, and offering more than the antique pub fare of quiche, greasy sausages, and ploughman's lunch (bread, cheese, and pickles).

Arcane licensing laws forbid the serving of alcohol after 11 PM (10:30 on Sunday; different rules for restaurants) and have created, some argue, a nation of alcoholics, obliged to down more pints than is decent in a limited time—a circumstance you see in action at 10 minutes to 11, when the "last orders" bell signals a stampede to the bar. The list below offers a few pubs selected for central location, historical interest, a pleasant garden, music, or good food, but you might just as happily adopt your own temporary local.

Black Friar. A step from Blackfriars tube, this pub has an arts-and-crafts interior that is entertainingly, satirically ecclesiastical, with inlaid mother-of-pearl, wood carvings, stained glass, and marble pillars all over the place, and reliefs of monks and friars poised above finely lettered temperance tracts, regardless of which there are six beers on tap. ✉ *174 Queen Victoria St., EC4,* ☎ *0171/236–5650.*

Bunch of Grapes. A traditional (which means smoky, noisy, and antichic) pub, popular since Victoria was on the throne, in the heart of Shepherd Market, the village-within-Mayfair, and still featuring a full deck of London characters. ✉ *16 Shepherd Market, W1,* ☎ *0171/629–4989.*

The Cow. Oh not *another* Conran. Yes, this place belongs to Tom, son of Sir Terence, though it's a million miles from Quag's and Mezzo. A faux-Dublin back room bar serves oysters, crab salad, and pasta with the wine and Guinness to hordes of the local fabulous people, with a proper restaurant upstairs. ✉ *89 Westbourne Park Rd., W2,* ☎ *0171/221–0021.*

Crown and Goose. A sky-blue-wall, art-bedecked Camden Town local, where armchairs augment the tables, coffee and herb tea the beers, and good food (steak in baguette, smoked chicken salad with honey vinaigrette, baked and stuffed mushrooms) is served to the crowds. ✉ *100 Arlington Rd., NW1,* ☎ *0171/485–2342.*

Dove Inn. Read the list of famous ex-regulars, from Charles II and Nell Gwynn (mere rumor, but a likely one) to Ernest Hemingway, as you queue ages for a beer at this very popular, very comely 16th-century riverside pub by Hammersmith Bridge. If it's *too* full, stroll upstream to the Old Ship or the Blue Anchor. ✉ *19 Upper Mall, W6,* ☎ *0181/748–5405.*

Freemason's Arms. This place is supposed to have the largest pub garden in London, with two terraces, a summerhouse, country-style furniture, and roses everywhere. Try your hand at the 17th-century game of pell mell—a kind of croquet—or at skittles. It's a favorite Hampstead pub, and popular with local young people. ✉ *32 Downshire Hill, NW3,* ☎ *0171/435–2127.*

French House. In the pub where the French Resistance convened during World War II, Soho hipsters and eccentrics rub shoulders now. More than shoulders, actually, because this tiny, tricolore-waving, photograph-lined pub is always full to bursting. ✉ *49 Dean St., W1,* ☎ *0171/437–2799.*

George Inn. The inn sits in a courtyard where Shakespeare's plays were once performed. The present building dates from the late 17th century and is central London's last remaining galleried inn. Dickens was a regular—the inn is featured in *Little Dorrit.* Entertainments include Shakespeare performances, medieval jousts, and morris dancing. ✉ *77 Borough High St., SE1,* ☎ *0171/407–2056.*

Island Queen. Gigantic caricature pirates leer down at you from the ceiling in this sociable Islington (☞ Minogues, *below*) pub, which offers superior home-cooked food (better still in Mojees, the upstairs restaurant), and a fab jukebox. The playwright Joe Orton frequented; he lived—and died—next door, murdered by his lover, Ken Halliwell. ✉ *87 Noel Rd., N1,* ☎ *0171/226–0307.*

Jack Straw's Castle. Straw was one of the leaders of the Peasant's Revolt of 1381, and was hanged nearby. In Tudor times it was a favorite hangout for highwaymen, but by the 19th century it had become picturesque and respectable; artists painted charming views from it and Dickens (inevitably) stayed here. Sadly, it was blitzed during World War II, and rebuilt in the 1960s. You can admire the views over Hampstead Heath and drink (weather permitting) in the large and lovely outside courtyard. ✉ *North End Way, NW3,* ☎ *0171/435–8885.*

The Lamb. Another of Dickens's locals is now a picturesque place for a summer pint, when you can drink on the patio. ✉ *94 Lamb's Conduit St., WC1,* ☎ *0171/405–0713.*

Lamb and Flag. This 17th-century pub was once known as "The Bucket of Blood," because the upstairs room was used as a ring for bare-knuckle boxing. Now, it's a trendy, friendly, and entirely bloodless pub, serving food (at lunchtime only) and real ale. It's on the edge of Covent Garden, off Garrick Street. ✉ *33 Rose St., WC2,* ☎ *0171/836–4108.*

Mayflower. An atmospheric 17th-century riverside inn, with exposed beams and a terrace, this is practically the very place from which the Pilgrims set sail for Plymouth Rock. The inn is licensed to sell American postage stamps. ✉ *117 Rotherhithe St., SE16,* ☎ *0171/237–4088.*

Minogues. A little out of the way in Islington (but perfect for the Almeida theater or Camden Passage antiquing expeditions), this is a friendly, gentrified version of an Irish pub, with Guinness on tap, excellent live traditional folk (Thur.–Sat. when it's opened till midnight), and equally excellent Irish food in the adjoining brasserie. ✉ *80 Liverpool Rd., N1,* ☎ *0171/354–4440.*

Museum Tavern. Across the street from the British Museum, this gloriously Victorian pub makes an ideal resting place after the rigors of the culture trail. With lots of fancy glass—etched mirrors and stained glass panels—gilded pillars, and carvings, the heavily restored hostelry once helped Karl Marx to unwind after a hard day in the Library. He could have spent his kapital on any one of six beers available on tap. ✉ *49 Great Russell St., WC1,* ☎ *0171/242–8987.*

Pheasant and Firkin. David Bruce single-handedly revived the practice of serving beer that's been brewed on the premises (then sold the thriving business), and this is one of his jolly microbrewery/pubs, all named the something and Firkin (a small barrel), serving beers called "dogbolter" or "rail ale," and selling T-shirts printed with bons mots like "I had a Pheasant time at the Firkin pub." Students like this a lot. ✉ *166 Goswell Rd., EC1,* ☎ *0171/235–7429.*

Prospect of Whitby. Named after a ship, this is London's oldest riverside pub, dating back to 1520. Once upon a time it was called "The Devil's Tavern," because of the numbers of low-life criminals—thieves and smugglers—who congregated here. It's ornamented with pewter ware and nautical memorabilia. ✉ *57 Wapping Wall, E1,* ☎ *0171/481–1095.*

Sherlock Holmes. This pub used to be known as the Northumberland Arms, and Arthur Conan Doyle popped in regularly for a pint. It figures in *The Hound of the Baskervilles,* and you can see the hound's head and plaster casts of its huge paws among other Holmes memorabilia in the bar. ✉ *10 Northumberland St., WC2,* ☎ *0171/930–2644.*

Spaniards Inn. This is another historic, oak-beamed pub on Hampstead Heath, boasting a gorgeous rose garden, scene of the tea party in Dickens's *Pickwick Papers*. Dick Turpin, the highwayman, used to frequent the inn; you can see his pistols on display. Romantic poets—Shelley, Keats, Byron—hung out here, and so, of course, did Dickens. It's extremely popular, especially on Sunday when Londoners take to the Heath in search of fresh air. ✉ *Spaniards Rd., NW3,* ☏ *0171/455–3276.*

The Sun. Near the Lamb (☞ *above*) by Coram's Fields, this no-frills pub prides itself on the 20 or so beers from independent breweries it keeps in peak condition. The place tends to be testosterone-heavy, because real ale connoisseurs are not, on the whole, female. ✉ *63 Lamb's Conduit St., WC1,* ☏ *0171/405–8278.*

Three Greyhounds. Usefully Soho-central, this welcoming, reconditioned mock-Tudor pub serves a great bar meal—homemade Scotch eggs (hard boiled, wrapped in sausage meat, and deep fried in bread crumbs), matzo-coated Southern fried chicken, sandwiches of home-cured ham or herring, oysters by the half dozen. Its other claim to fame is its youthful landlady's name—say hi to Roxy Beaujolais. ✉ *25 Greek St., W1,* ☏ *0171/734–8799.*

Windsor Castle. This is one to rest at on a Kensington jaunt, saving a large appetite for the food, especially on Sunday, when they do a traditional roast; other days there are oysters and salads, fishcakes and steak sandwiches. In winter there are blazing fires; in summer, an exquisite walled patio garden. ✉ *114 Campden Hill Rd., W8,* ☏ *0171/727–8491.*

Ye Olde Cheshire Cheese. Yes, it is a tourist trap, but this most historic of all London pubs (it dates from 1667) deserves a visit anyway, for its sawdust-covered floors, low wood-beamed ceilings, the 14th-century crypt of Whitefriars' monastery under the cellar bar, and the set of 17th-century pornographic tiles upstairs. This was the most regular of Dr. Johnson's and Dickens's *many* locals. ✉ *145 Fleet St., EC4,* ☏ *0171/353–6170.*

7 Shopping

Shopping Districts

Camden Town

Crafts and vintage-clothing markets and shops cluster in and around picturesque but over-renovated canalside buildings in this frenetic mecca for the world's youth. Things are quieter midweek. It's a good place for boots and T-shirts, cheap leather jackets, ethnic crafts, antiques, and recycled trendywear.

Chelsea

Chelsea centers on the King's Road, which is no longer synonymous with ultra-fashion but still harbors some designer boutiques, plus antiques and home furnishings emporia.

Covent Garden

A something-for-everyone neighborhood, the restored 19th-century market building features mainly high-class clothing chain stores, plus good-quality crafts stalls and design shops, with additional stalls selling vintage, army-surplus, and ethnic clothing around it. Neal Street and the surrounding alleys offer amazing gifts of every type—bikes, kites, tea, herbs, beads, hats . . . you name it. Floral Street and Long Acre have designer and chain-store fashion in equal measure. It's good for people-watching, too.

Hampstead

For picturesque peace and quiet with your shopping, stroll around here midweek. Upscale clothing stores and representatives of the better chains share the half-dozen streets with cozy boutique-size shops for the home and stomach.

Kensington

Kensington Church Street features expensive antiques, plus a little fashion. The main drag, Kensington High Street, is a smaller, less crowded, and classier version of Oxford Street, with a selection of clothing chains and larger stores at the eastern end.

Knightsbridge

Harrods dominates Brompton Road, but there's plenty more, especially for the well-heeled and fashion-conscious. Harvey Nichols is the top clothes stop, with many expensive designers' *boîtes* along Sloane Street. Walton Street and narrow Beauchamp (pronounced "beecham") Place offer more of the same, plus home furnishings and knickknacks, and Brompton Cross, at the start of Fulham Road, is the most design-conscious corner of London, with the Conran Shop and Joseph leading the field.

Mayfair

Here is Bond Street, Old and New, with desirable dress designers, jewelers, plus fine art (old and new) on Old Bond Street and Cork Street. South Molton Street has high-priced high-style fashion—especially at Browns—and the tailors of Savile Row are of worldwide repute.

Oxford Street

Overcrowded Oxford Street is past its prime and lined with tawdry discount shops. There are some good stores, however—particularly Selfridges, John Lewis, and Marks and Spencer—and interesting boutiques secreted in little St. Christopher's Place and Gees Court.

Piccadilly

Though the actual number of shops is small for a street of its length (Green Park takes up a lot of space), Piccadilly manages to fit in several quintessentially British emporia. Fortnum and Mason is its star, and the arcades are an elegant experience even for shop-phobics.

Regent Street

At right angles to Oxford Street, this wider, curvier version has another couple of department stores, including what is possibly London's most pleasant, Liberty's. Hamley's is the capital's toy center; other shops tend to be chain stores, or airline offices, though there are also shops selling china and bolts of English tweed. "West Soho," around Carnaby Street, stocks designer youth paraphernalia.

St. James's

Where the English gentleman shops. Here are hats, handmade shirts and shoes, silver shaving kits and hip flasks, as well as the Prince of Wales's aftershave supplier and possibly the world's best cheese shop. Nothing is cheap, in any sense.

Specialty Stores

Antiques

Investment pieces or lovable junk, London has lots. Try markets first—even for pedigree silver, the dealers at these places often have the best wares and the knowledge to match. Camden Passage, Portobello Road, and Bermondsey (☞ Street Markets, *below*) are the best, and the former two are surrounded by shops open outside market hours. Kensington Church Street is *the* antiques shopping street, with prices and quality both high. Out of the hundreds of stores, we list five to whet your appetite.

Alfie's Antique Market (✉ 13-25 Church St., NW8, 0171/723–6066) is a huge and exciting labyrinth on several floors, with dealers specializing in anything and everything. You won't be deliberately stiffed, but it's a *caveat emptor* kind of place, thanks to the wide range of merchandise. (☞ Map A.)

Antiquarius (✉ 131–141 King's Rd., SW3, ☎ 0171/351–5353), at the Sloane Square end of the King's Road, is an indoor antiques market with more than 200 stalls offering a wide variety of collectibles, including things that won't bust your baggage allowance: Art Deco brooches, meerschaum pipes, silver salt cellars . . . (☞ Map B.)

Movie art directors do research at the **Gallery of Antique Costume and Textiles** (✉ 2 Church St., NW8, ☎ 0171/723–9981) to get the period just right, because everything here, from bedspreads to bloomers, was stitched before 1930—except for the wonderful range of copycat brocade vests. It lies off our maps, but is easily found three blocks north of the Edgware Road tube.

Gray's Antique Market (✉ 58 Davies St., W1, ☎ 0171/629–7034) and **Gray's Mews** (✉ 1–7 Davies Mews, W1, ☎ 0171/629–7034) around the corner are conveniently central. Both assemble dealers specializing in everything from Sheffield plate to Chippendale furniture all under one roof. Bargains are not impossible, and proper pedigrees are guaranteed. (☞ Map A.)

One of the many specialist stores around here, **Hope and Glory** (✉ 131a Kensington Church St., W8, ☎ 0171/727–8424) has commemorative china and glass from 1887 to the present, with many affordable lesser pieces. (☞ Map B.)

There's nothing small about **LASSCo** (✉ St. Michael's Church, Mark St., EC2, 0171/739–0448), this mad architectural salvage warehouse, where an entire Versaille-like bedchamber abuts, say, Dudley Moore's sparkly red bath, a part of Westminster Bridge, and a pair of Romanesque gargoyles. If you do buy that Italian-tiled floor, you can have it shipped. (Tube: Old St.)

London Silver Vaults (✉ Chancery House, 53–63 Chancery La., WC2, ☎ 0171/3844) is a treasure trove for the average joe from a basement

Shopping A (Mayfair, Soho, and Covent Garden)

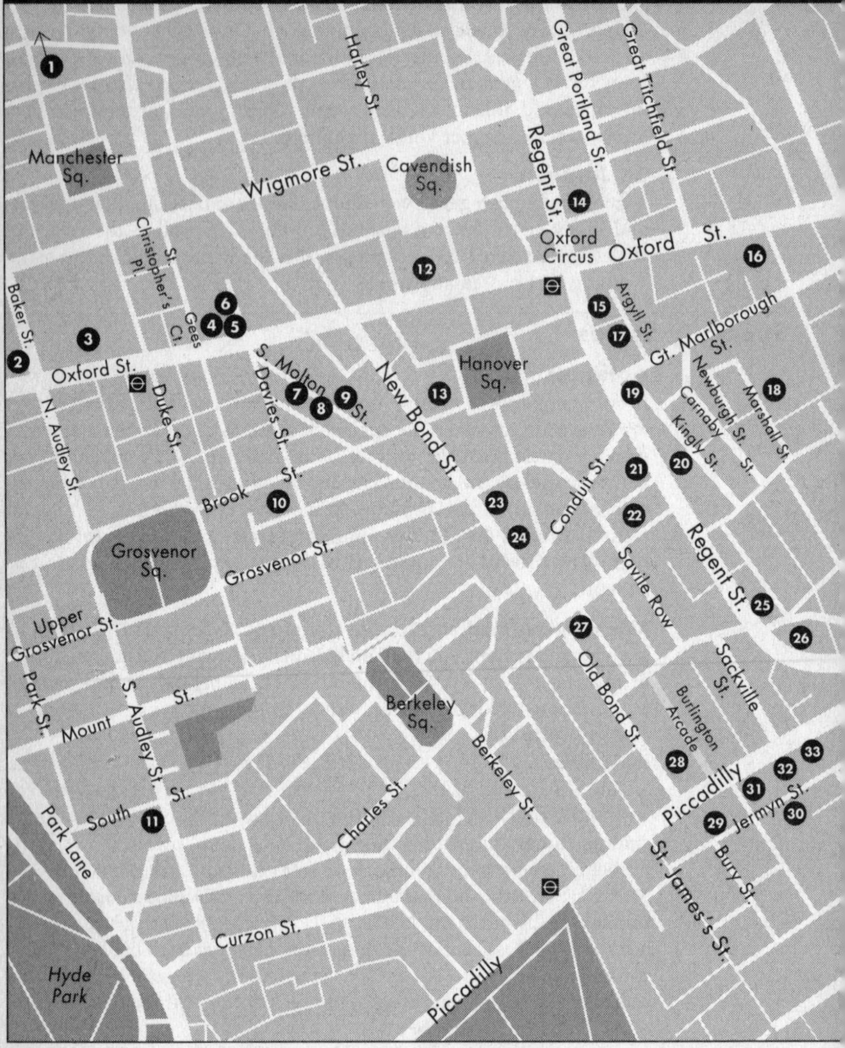

Alfie's Antique Market, **1**
Aquascutum, **26**
Armoury of St. James's, **29**
Asprey's, **24**
Bell, Book and Radmell, **37**
Blazer, **52, 50**
Browns, **7**
Burberrys, **21, 35**
Butler and Wilson, **8**
Cartier, **23**
Contemporary Applied Arts, **56**
Contemporary Ceramics, **18**
Dance Books, **38**
Dillons, **64**
Droopie & Browns, **36**
Duffer of St. George, **57**
Favourbrook, **32**
Forbidden Planet, **63**
Fortnum & Mason, **31**
Foyles, **61**
Garrard, **25**
Gray's Antique Market, **10**
Grosvenor Prints, **55**
Halcyon Days, **13**
Hamleys, **20**
Hatchards, **33**
Hat Shop, **59**
Herbert Johnson, **27**
Irish Linen Co., **28**
Jigsaw, **46**
John Lewis, **12**
Laura Ashley, **17**
Liberty, **19**
Linen Cupboard, **14**
London Silver Vaults, **65**
Lush, **44**
Maison, **53**
Marchpane, **40**
Marks & Spencer, **2, 16**
Mulberry, **4**
Naturally British, **41**
Neal Street East, **51**
Nicole Farhi, **6**
Outlaws Club, **58**
Paddy Campbell, **5**
Paul Smith, **47**
Pellicano, **9**
Penhaligon's, **45**

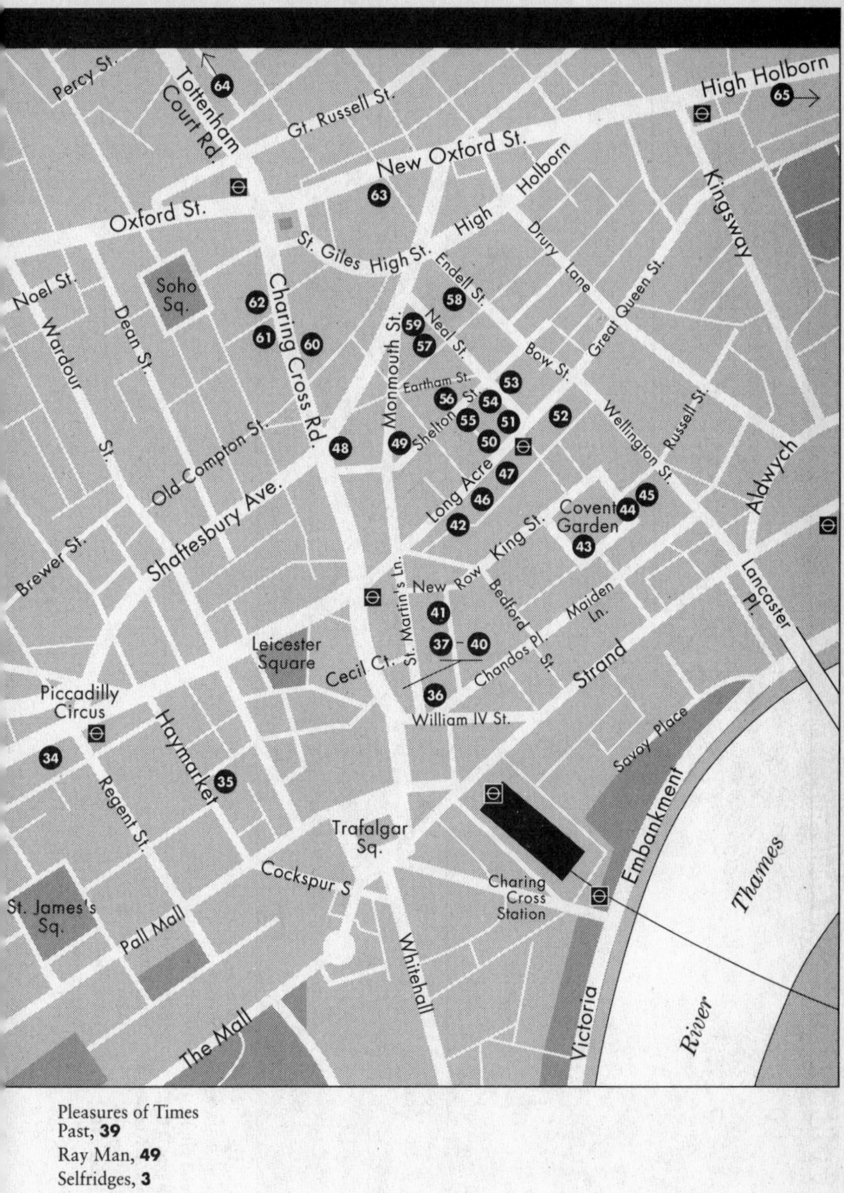

Percy St.
Tottenham Court Rd.
Gt. Russell St.
High Holborn
New Oxford St.
Oxford St.
High Holborn
Kingsway
St. Giles High St.
Drury Lane
Endell St.
Great Queen St.
Noel St.
Soho Sq.
Charing Cross Rd.
Neal St.
Monmouth St.
Bow St.
Wardour St.
Dean St.
Earlham St.
Shelton St.
Wellington St.
Russell St.
Old Compton St.
Long Acre
Aldwych
Shaftesbury Ave.
Covent Garden
King St.
Brewer St.
New Row
Bedford St.
Maiden Ln.
Lancaster Pl.
St. Martin's Ln.
Leicester Square
Cecil Ct.
Chandos Pl.
Strand
Piccadilly Circus
William IV St.
Haymarket
Savoy Place
Regent St.
Trafalgar Sq.
Embankment
Thames
Cockspur S
Charing Cross Station
St. James's Sq.
Pall Mall
Whitehall
The Mall
Victoria
River

Shopping B (Kensington, Knightsbridge, and Chelsea)

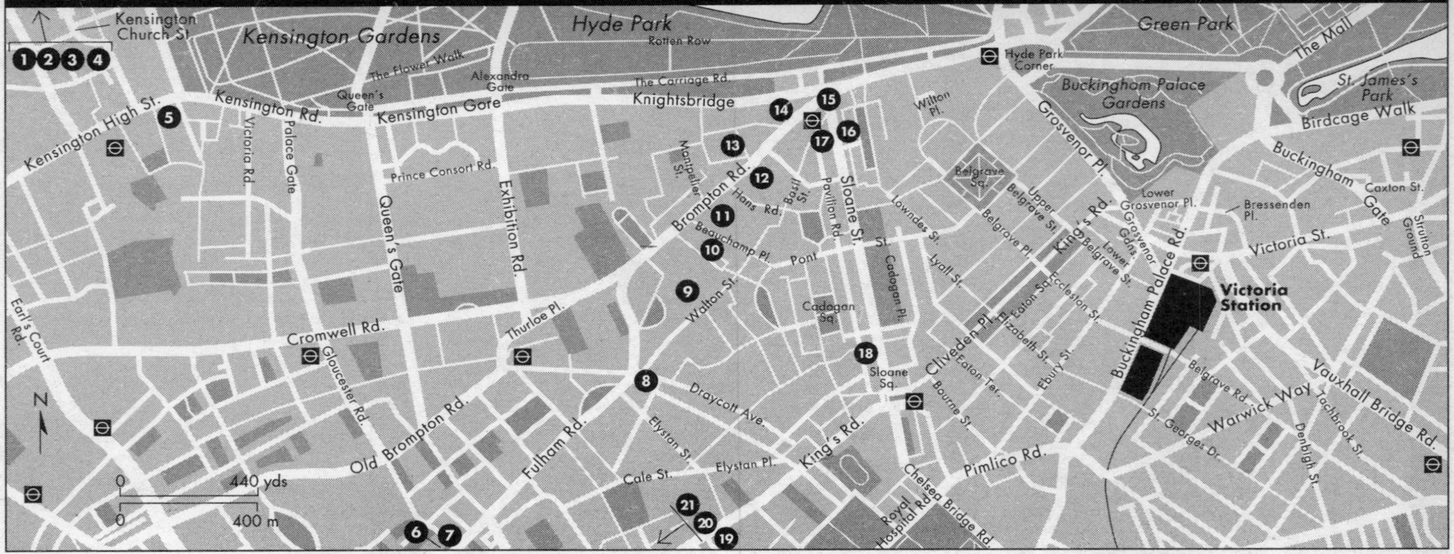

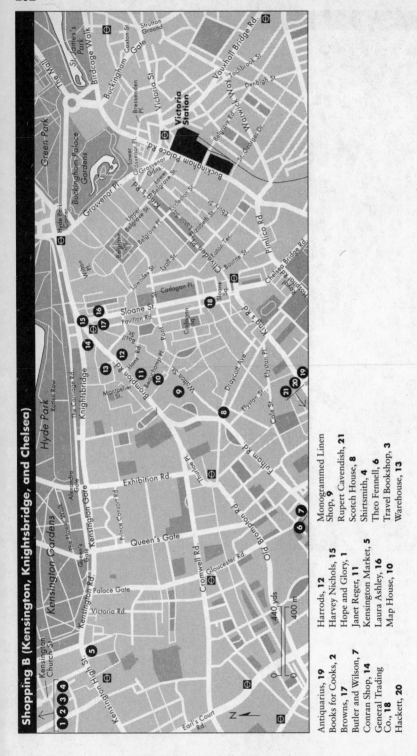

Antiquarius, **19**
Books for Cooks, **2**
Browns, **17**
Butler and Wilson, **7**
Conran Shop, **14**
General Trading Co., **18**
Hackett, **20**
Harrods, **12**
Harvey Nichols, **15**
Hope and Glory, **1**
Janet Reger, **11**
Kensington Market, **5**
Laura Ashley, **16**
Map House, **10**
Monogrammed Linen Shop, **9**
Rupert Cavendish, **21**
Scotch House, **8**
Shirtsmith, **4**
Theo Fennell, **6**
Travel Bookshop, **3**
Warehouse, **13**

conglomeration of around 40 dealers. Some pieces are spectacular, of course, but you can pick up a set of Victorian cake forks or a dented candelabrum for under £50. (☞ Map A.)

Rupert Cavendish (✉ 610 King's Rd., SW6, 0171/731–7041), this most elevated of dealers, has the Biedermeier market cornered, with Empire and Deco bringing up the rear. The shop is a museum experience. (☞ Map B.)

Books

Charing Cross Road is London's booksville, with a couple of dozen stores there or thereabout. The many antiquarian booksellers tend to look daunting (deceptively, as Helen Hanff found by correspondence with No. 84), but there are many new bookshops, too. Especially large, though it has to be the most chaotic and confusing shop in London, is **Foyles** (✉ No. 119, ☎ 0171/437–5660). **Waterstone's** (✉ No. 121–125, ☎ 0171/434–4291) is part of an admirable, and expanding, chain with long hours and a program of author readings and signings. **Hatchards** (✉ 187–188 Piccadilly, WC2, ☎ 0171/439–9921) and **Dillons** (✉ 82 Gower St., WC1, ☎ 0171/636–1577) both have not only a huge stock, but also a well-informed staff to help you choose. (☞ Map A.)

Books for Cooks (✉ 4 Blenheim Cres., W11, ☎ 0171/221–1992) and its near neighbor, **The Travel Bookshop** (✉ No. 13, ☎ 0171/229–5260), are exactly what they say, and worth the trip for enthusiasts. (☞ Map B.) Travel books and maps are the specialty of **Stanfords** (✉ 12 Long Acre, WC2, ☎ 0171/836–1321); art books of **Zwemmer** (✉ 24 Litchfield St., WC2, ☎ 0171/240–4158) just off Charing Cross Road; and sci-fi, fantasy, horror, and comic books of **Forbidden Planet** (✉ 71 New Oxford St., WC1, ☎ 0171/836–4179). (☞ Map A.)

Back on the Charing Cross Road, **Silver Moon** (✉ No. 64, ☎ 0171/836–7906) is an accessible and friendly women's bookshop. Just off the south end, in **Cecil Court**—a pedestrians-only lane where every shop is a specialty bookstore—**Bell, Book and Radmell** (✉ No. 4, ☎ 0171/240–2161) has quality antiquarian volumes and modern first editions; **Marchpane** (✉ No. 16, ☎ 0171/836–8661) stocks covetable rare and antique illustrated children's books; **Dance Books** (✉ No. 9, ☎ 0171/836–2314) has—yes—dance books; and **Pleasures of Times Past** (✉ No. 11, ☎ 0171/836–1142) indulges the collective nostalgia for Victoriana. (☞ Map A.)

China and Glass

English Wedgwood and Minton china are as collectible as they ever were, and most large department stores carry a selection, alongside lesser varieties with smaller price tags. Regent Street has several off-price purveyors, and, if you're in search of a bargain, Harrods's sale can't be beat—but sharpen your elbows first. For vast ranges of formal china and leaded crystal, **Thomas Goode** (✉ 19 S. Audley St., W1, ☎ 0171/499–2823) is one of the world's top shops. (☞ map A.)

Clothing

London is one of the world's four fashion capitals (along with Paris, Milan, and New York), and every designer you've ever heard of is sold here somewhere. As well as the top names, though, London retains a reputation for quirky street style, and many an exciting young designer has cut his or her teeth selling early collections at a London street market. Don't just go by the label, and you could be the first to wear clothes by a future star. Traditional British men's outfitters are also rather well-known. From the Savile Row suit, handmade shirt, and custom shoes to the Harris-tweeds-and-Oxford-brogues English country look that

Ralph Lauren purloined, England's indigenous garments make for real investment dressing.

GENERAL

Aquascutum (✉ 100 Regent St., W1, ☎ 0171/734–6090) is known for its classic raincoats, but also stocks the garments to wear underneath, for both men and women. Style keeps up with the times but is firmly on the safe side, making this a good bet for solvent professionals with an antifashion attitude. (☞ Map A.)

Burberrys (✉ 161–165 Regent St., W1, ☎ 0171/734–4060 and ✉ 18–22 The Haymarket, SW1, ☎ 0171/930–3343) tries to evoke an English Heritage ambience, with mahogany closets and stacks of neatly folded neckerchiefs alongside the trademark "Burberry Check" tartan, which adorns—in addition to those famous raincoat linings—scarves, umbrellas, and even pots of passion-fruit curd and tins of shortbread, in the newish British provisions line. (☞ Map A.)

Favourbrook (✉ 19–21 Piccadilly Arcade, W1, ☎ 0171/491–2337) tailors exquisite, handmade vests and jackets, ties and cummerbunds out of silks and brocades, velvets and satins, embroidered linens and chenilles. There's a range made up for both men and women, or order your own *Four Weddings and a Funeral* outfit. (☞ Map A.)

Herbert Johnson (✉ 30 New Bond St., W1, ☎ 0171/408–1174) is one of a handful of gentleman's hatters who still knows how to construct deerstalkers, bowlers, flat caps, and panamas—all the classic headgear, and Ascot hats for women, too. (☞ Map A.)

Kensington Market (✉ 49–53 Kensington High St., W8, ☎ 0171/938–4343) is the diametric opposite of British stiff-upper-lip anti-fashion. For more than two decades it has been a principal purveyor of the constantly changing, frivolous, hip London street style. Hundreds of stalls—some shop-size, others tiny—are crammed into this building, where you can get lost for hours trying to find the good bits. (☞ Map B.)

Marks & Spencer (✉ 458 Oxford St., W1, ☎ 0171/935–7954, and branches) is a major chain of stores that's an integral part of the British way of life—sturdy practical clothes, good materials and workmanship, and basic accessories, all at moderate, though not bargain-basement, prices. "Marks and Sparks," as they are popularly known, have never been renowned for their high style, though that is changing as they continue to bring in (anonymously) big-name designers to spice up their ranges. What they *are* renowned for is underwear. All of England buys theirs here. This holds true for knitwear as well. This Marble Arch branch has the highest turnover of any shop in the land. (☞ Map A.)

Mulberry (✉ 11–12 Gees Ct., W1, ☎ 0171493–2546) outdoes Ralph Lauren in packaging the English look. Covetable, top-quality leather bags, belts, and cases, wool riding jackets, coats, and sweaters, and corduroy and linen pants are the sort of things found here—at a price. (☞ Map A.)

The Scotch House (✉ 2 Brompton Rd., SW3, ☎ 0171/581–2151), as you'd guess is the place to buy your kilts, tartan scarves, and Argyll socks without going to Edinburgh. It's also well stocked with cashmere and accessories. (☞ Map B.)

Simpson (✉ 203 Piccadilly, W1, ☎ 0171/734–2002) is a quiet, pleasant store with a thoughtful variety of designer and leisure wear, luggage, and gifts. There are a barbershop, restaurant, and wine bar here, plus the most disturbing nonreflective glass in its windows on Piccadilly. (☞ Map A.)

WOMEN'S WEAR

Browns (✉ 23–27 South Molton St., W1, ☎ 0171/491–7833) was the first notable store to populate the South Molton Street pedestrian mall, and seems to sprout more offshoots every time you see it. Well-established, collectible designers (Donna Karan, Romeo Gigli, Jasper Conran, Jil Sander, Yohji Yamamoto) rub shoulder pads here with younger, funkier names (Dries Van Noten, Jean Paul Gaultier, Hussein Chalayan), and Browns also has its own label. Its July and January sales are famed. Also at 6C Sloane St., SW1 (☎ 0171/493–4232). (☞ Maps A and B.)

Droopie & Browns (✉ 99 St. Martin's La., WC2, ☎ 0171/379–4514) features beautifully constructed, extravagantly theatrical frocks and suits, made up in raw silks and fine linens, brocades and velvets. Colors are strong, tailoring is unimpeachable, and kind salespeople don't turn up their noses at larger ladies. (☞ Map A.)

The Hat Shop (✉ 58 Neal St., WC2, ☎ 0171/836–6718) is keeping the art of millinery alive and bringing it within reach of the average pocket. The stock here ranges from classic trilbies, toppers, panamas, and matador hats to frivolous tulle-and-feather constructions, with scores of inexpensive, fun titfers in between. The shop is so tiny that only 10 people are allowed in at a time. (☞ Map A.)

Janet Reger (✉ 2 Beauchamp Pl., SW3, ☎ 0171/584–9360) is still queen of the silk teddy, having become synonymous with the ultimate in luxurious negligees and lingerie many years ago. (☞ Map B.)

Jigsaw (✉ 21 Long Acre, Covent Garden, WC2, ☎ 0171/240–3855, and other branches) is popular for its separates that don't sacrifice quality to fashion, are reasonably priced, and suit women in their twenties to forties. (☞ Map A.)

Laura Ashley (✉ 256–258 Regent St., W1, ☎ 0171/437–9760 and other branches) offers design from the firm founded by the late high priestess of English traditional. Country dresses, blouses, and skirts, plus wallpapers and fabrics in dateless patterns that rely heavily on flowers, fruit, leaves, or just plain stripes, have captured the nostalgic imagination of the world. (☞ Map A.)

Nicole Farhi (✉ 25–26 St. Christopher's Pl., W1, ☎ 0171/486–3416; also at 27 Hampstead High St., NW3, ☎ 0171/435–0866 and other branches), suits the career woman who requires quality, cut, *and* style in a suit, plus weekend wear in summer linens and silks, or winter hand-knitted woolens. Prices are on the high side, but there is some affordable wear as well, especially the sporty, casual Diversion range. Farhi offers an equally desirable men's line. (☞ Map A.)

Paddy Campbell (✉ 8 Gees Ct., W1, ☎ 0171/493–5646) designs elegant matching separates in natural fabrics and subtle colors. Prices are reasonable for this level of workmanship, and the staff will alter garments for a perfect fit. (☞ Map A.)

Pellicano (✉ 63 South Molton St., W1, ☎ 0171/629–2205) stocks only cutting-edge designers, like Brit phenoms Alexander McQueen, Bella Freud, and Sonnentag Mulligan, and the *Vogue*-ier of the internationals (Prada & co) in a salon that virtually opens onto the street. The sales staff can be unbelievably snotty. (☞ Map A.)

The Shirtsmith (✉ 38A Ledbury Rd., W11, ☎ 0171/229–3090) does bespoke and ready made shirts, suits and jackets for women, using fine cottons and Indian silks. Some designs are classic and fitted, others slightly outrageous, like the Chatterton shirt, with more ruffles at the neck than a chrysanthemum. (☞ Map B.)

Warehouse (✉ 19 Argyll St., W1, ☎ 0171/437–7101, and other branches) stocks practical, stylish, reasonably priced separates in easy fabrics and lots of fun colors. The finishing isn't so hot, but style, not substance, counts here, and the shop's youthful fans don't seem to mind. The stock changes very quickly, so it always presents a new face to the world. (☞ Maps A and B.)

Whistles (✉ The Market, Covent Garden, WC2, ☎ 0171/379–7401; also at Heath St., Hampstead, ☎ 0171/431–2395 and other branches) is a small chain stocking its own high-fashion, mid-price label, plus several European (mostly French) designers. Clothes are hung color-coordinated in shops like designers' ateliers. (☞ Map A.)

MEN'S WEAR

Most stores we list above under General Clothing stock excellent men's wear. Try Aquascutum, Burberrys, and Simpson. All the large department stores, too, carry a wide range of men's clothing, Selfridges and Harrods especially.

Blazer (✉ 36 Long Acre, ☎ 0171/379–6258; ✉ 117 Long Acre, WC2, ☎ 0171/379–0456) stocks medium-priced formal wear at the first branch and a casual range at the second. Clothes tend toward the classic, but with style-conscious details and rich colors. (☞ Map A.)

Duffer of St. George (✉ 29 Shorts Gdns., ☎ 0171/379–4660) has a collection of hip designers of street style in several cities, as well as its own label of sporty and dress up lines for clubbing and posing with attitude. (☞ Map A.)

Hackett (✉ 65B New King's Rd., SW6, ☎ 0171/371–7964, and branches) started as a posh thrift store, recycling cricket flannels, hunting pinks, Oxford brogues, and similar Britishwear. Now they make their own, and they have become a genuine—and very good—gentlemen's outfitter. (☞ Map B.)

Paul Smith (✉ 41 Floral St., WC2, ☎ 0171/379–7133) is your man if you don't want to look outlandish but you're bored with plain pants and sober jackets. His well-tailored suits have a subtle quirkiness, his shirts and ties a sense of humor, and his jeans and sweats a good cut. (☞ Map A.)

Tom Gilbey (✉ 2 New Burlington Pl., W1, ☎ 0171/734–4877) is a custom tailor, but the exciting part of his shop is the Waistcoat Gallery, where exquisite vests, some in silk or brocades or embroidered by hand, others marginally plainer, are essential accessories for the dandy. (☞ Map A.)

Turnbull & Asser (✉ 70 Jermyn St., W1, ☎ 0171/930–0502) is *the* custom shirtmaker. Unfortunately for those of average means, the first order must be for a minimum of six shirts, from around £100 each. But there's a range of less expensive, still exquisitely made ready-to-wear shirts, too. (☞ Map A.)

Crafts

With the current interest in alternate ways of living, whole food eating, and preserving the environment, there has been an enormous increase in public awareness of the value of traditional crafts, and London has more than its share of stores that stock the work of traditional and innovative designer-makers.

Contemporary Ceramics (✉ 7 Marshall St., W1, ☎ 0171/437–7605) was formed by some of the best British potters as a cooperative venture to market their wares. The result is a store that carries a wide spectrum of the potter's art, from thoroughly practical pitchers, plates, and bowls to ceramic sculptures. Prices range from the reasonable to way up. (☞ Map A.)

Craftworks (✉ 31 Southend Rd., NW3, ☎ 0171/431–4337) is a haven packed with handmade table- and glassware, ceramics, candlesticks, wall hangings, and mirrors from all over the world—and also from just down the road. (Tube: Hampstead)

Contemporary Applied Arts (✉ 43 Earlham St., WC2, ☎ 0171/836–6993) has a mixed bag of designers and craftspeople displaying their wares over two floors. Anything from glassware and jewelry to furniture and lighting can be found here. (☞ Map A.)

Gabriel's Wharf (✉ Upper Ground, SE1, ☎ 0171/620–0544. Tube: Waterloo) consists of a collection of craftspeople who have set up a cute, brightly-painted village near the South Bank Centre, selling porcelain, jewelry, mirrors, clothes, toys, papier mâché wares and more. In August 1996, the nearby OXO tower gave about 30 more designers workshop and selling space–and London a fabulous river-view restaurant.

The Glasshouse (✉ 21 St. Albans Pl., N1, ☎ 0171/359–8162. Tube: Angel) is off our map, but for indigenous glassware it's about the only place, and you could drop in while visiting nearby Camden Passage. See glass being blown, by several artists, then buy it.

Gifts

Of course, virtually anything from any shop in this chapter has gift potential, but these selections lean toward stores with a lot of choice, both in merchandise and price. Chances are you'll be wanting the recipients of your generous bounty to know how far you traveled to procure it for them, so our suggestions tend toward identifiable Britishness. You should also investigate the possibilities in the shops attached to the major museums, most of which offer far more than racks of souvenir postcards these days. Some of the best are at the **British Museum,** the **V & A,** the **Royal Academy,** and the **London Transport Museum.**

The Armoury of St. James's (✉ 17 Piccadilly Arcade, SW1, ☎ 0171/493–5082) offers perfect playthings for overgrown schoolkids in the form of antique and new painted lead soldiers (most wars with British involvement can be fought in miniature), plus medals, brass buttons, and military prints. (☞ Map A.)

Conran Shop (✉ Michelin House, 81 Fulham Rd., SW3, ☎ 0171/589–7401) is the domain of Sir Terence Conran, of course, who has been informing British middle-class taste since he opened Habitat in the '60s; this is the grown-up, upmarket version. Home enhancers from furniture to stemware, both handmade and mass-produced, famous name and young designer, are displayed in a suitably gorgeous building. (☞ Map B.)

Fortnum & Mason (✉ 181 Piccadilly, W1, ☎ 0171/734–8040), the queen's grocer, is, paradoxically, the most egalitarian of gift stores, with plenty of irresistibly packaged luxury foods, stamped with the gold "by appointment" crest, for under £5. Try the teas, preserves, blocks of chocolate, tins of pâté, or a box of Duchy Originals oatcakes—like Paul Newman, the Prince of Wales has gone into the retail food business with these. (☞ Map A.)

General Trading Co. (✉ 144 Sloane St., SW1, ☎ 0171/730–0411) "does" just about every upper-class wedding gift list, from Charles and Diana's down, but caters also to slimmer pockets with its merchandise shipped from far shores (as the name suggests) but moored securely to English taste. (☞ Map B.)

Halcyon Days (✉ 14 Brook St., W1, ☎ 0171/629–8811) specializes in enamelware. It's best known for its little pillboxes: These can be selected from a range of pastoral scenes or Regency dandies or even plain colors, and personalized with initials or messages, and will add mere ounces to your luggage weight. (☞ Map A.)

Hamleys (✉ 188–196 Regent St., W1, ☎ 0171/734–3161) has six floors of toys and games for children and adults. The huge stock ranges from traditional teddy bears to computer games and all the latest technological gimmickry. Try to avoid it at Christmas, when police have to rope off a section of Regent Street for Hamleys customers. (☞ Map A.)

Lush (✉ 7 The Piazza, Covent Garden, WC2, ☎ 01202/668545; mail order) is crammed with fresh, pure, very wacky, handmade cosmetics. "13 Rabbit" is chocolate and spice for the shower; "Angels on Bare Skin" is divine lavender cleansing mush; soaps ("Banana Moon,"

"Dirty Boy," "Pineapple Grunt") are sliced off huge slabs like cheese, and paper wrapped like in an old-fashioned grocer; Bath Bombs fizz furiously, then leave the water scattered with rosebuds or scented with honey and vanilla. Quite irresistible. (☞ Map A.)

Maison (✉ 47–49 Neal St., WC2, ☎ 0171/240–2822) is a cool, spacious two floors of homage to design. Among the gorgeous goods displayed like museum pieces are lots of witty ideas for presents, from the sublime (Alvar Aalto vases) to the ridiculous (chocolate sardines). (☞ Map A.)

Neal Street East (✉ 5 Neal St., WC2, ☎ 0171/240–0135) isn't big on British, no, but this importer of Oriental everything does carry stock with universal appeal. There are several floors of what you'd expect in the way of woks, chopsticks, bowls, books, kimonos, and toys, but also glorious lacquered boxes, woven baskets, amber and silver jewelry, silk flowers, Japanese kites, and loads of fun gifts for under a fiver. (☞ Map A.)

Penhaligon's (✉ 41 Wellington St., WC2, ☎ 0171/836–2150; also at ✉ 16 Burlington Arcade, W1, ☎ 0171/629–1416, and branches) was established by William Penhaligon, court barber at the end of Queen Victoria's lengthy reign. He blended perfumes and toilet waters in the back of his shop, using essential oils and natural, often exotic ingredients, and you can buy the very same formulations today, along with soaps, talcs, bath oils, and accessories, with the strong whiff of Victoriana both inside and outside the pretty bottles and boxes. (☞ Map A.)

Ray Man (✉ 29 Monmouth St., WC2, ☎ 0171/240–1776), for "Eastern Musical Instruments," is probably the only place in Europe you can buy an *erhhu,* which is, of course, a two-stringed coconut fiddle. It's an amazing place, perfect for gifts for the weird. You can pick up a set of ankle bells or pan pipes for a song. (☞ Map A.)

The Tea House (✉ 15A Neal St., WC2, ☎ 0171/240–7539) purveys everything to do with the British national drink; you can dispatch your entire gift list here. Alongside every variety of tea—including strange or rare brews like orchid, banana, Japanese Rice, and Russian Caravan—are teapots in the shape of a British bobby or a London taxi, plus books, and what the shop terms "teaphernalia"—strainers, and trivets, and infusers, and other gadgets that need explaining. (☞ Map A.)

Jewelry

Jewelry—precious, semiprecious, and totally fake—can be had by just rubbing an Aladdin's lamp in London's West End. Of the department stores, Liberty and Harvey Nichols are particularly known for their fashion jewelry, but here are a few more suggestions for baubles, bangles, and beads.

Asprey's (✉ 165–169 New Bond St., W1, ☎ 0171/493–6767) has been described as the "classiest and most luxurious shop in the world." It offers a range of exquisite jewelry and gifts, both antique and modern. If you're in the market for a six-branched Georgian candelabrum or a six-carat emerald-and-diamond brooch, you won't be disappointed. (☞ Map A.)

Butler and Wilson (✉ 20 South Molton St., W1, ☎ 0171/409–2955; ✉ 189 Fulham Rd., SW3, ☎ 0171/352–8255) is designed to set off its irresistible costume jewelry to the very best advantage—against a dramatic black background. It has some of the best displays in town, and keeps very busy marketing silver, diamanté, French gilt, and pearls by the truckload. (☞ Maps A and B.)

Cartier (✉ 175 New Bond St., W1, ☎ 0171/493–6962) exudes an exclusivity that captures the very essence of Bond Street. It combines royal connections—Cartier's was granted its first royal warrant in 1902—with the last word in luxurious good taste. Many of the Duchess of

Windsor's trinkets were wrought here. The store also sells glassware, leather goods, and stationery. (☞ Map A.)

Garrard (✉ 112 Regent St., W1, ☎ 0171/734–7020) has connections with the royal family going back to 1722 and is still in charge of the upkeep of the Crown Jewels. But they are also family jewelers, and offer an enormous range of items, from antique to modern. (☞ Map A.)

The Outlaws Club (✉ 49 Endell St., WC2, ☎ 0171/379–6940) stocks the work of around 100 designers, with prices ranging from a few pounds up to £200. The dominant style is avant-garde, meaning that this shop has been a favorite with fashion writers for a decade. (☞ Map A.)

Theo Fennell (✉ 177 Fulham Rd., SW3, ☎ 0171/376–4855) designs pieces that are instantly recognizable—exquisitely detailed miniatures, and covetable jewelry (in gold studded with precious stones) that is reminiscent of the ecclesiastical. (☞ Map B.)

Linen

Among the traditional crafts that can still be bought in London, fine linen ranks high. Again, many of the department stores, Liberty and Harrods among them, carry a fair range of linen goods, but here are three specialty stores that you might want to try for more personal service.

The Irish Linen Co. (✉ 35–36 Burlington Arcade, W1, ☎ 0171/493–8949) is a tiny store bursting with crisp, embroidered linen for the table, the bed, and the nose. Exquisite handkerchiefs should be within reach of everyone's pocket. (☞ Map A.)

The Linen Cupboard (✉ 21 Great Castle St., W1, ☎ 0171/629–4062) is stacked with piles of sheets and towels of all sorts and has by far the lowest-priced fine Irish linens and Egyptian cottons in town. (☞ Map A.)

Try **The Monogrammed Linen Shop** (✉ 168 Walton St., SW3, ☎ 0171/589–4033) for a wide range of fine Italian bed linen with matching towels, bathrobes, and nightshirts, as well as tablecloths, place mats, and napkins—all of which you can have monogrammed. Proud grandparents may want to buy a superbly embroidered christening gown here. (☞ Map B.)

Prints

London harbors trillions of prints, and they make great gifts—for yourself, perhaps. We list two West End stores, but try also street markets and Cecil Court (☞ Books, *above*), just north of Trafalgar Square.

Grosvenor Prints (✉ 28–32 Shelton St., WC2, ☎ 0171/836–1979) sells antiquarian prints, but with an emphasis on views and architecture of London—and dogs! It's an eccentric collection, and the prices range widely, but the stock is so odd that you are bound to find something interesting and unusual to meet both your budget and your taste. (☞ Map A.)

At **The Map House** (✉ 54 Beauchamp Pl., SW3, ☎ 0171/589–4325), antique maps can run from a few pounds to several thousand, but the shop also has excellent reproductions of maps and prints, especially of botanical subjects and cityscapes. (☞ Map B.)

Department Stores

London's department stores range from Harrods—which every tourist is obliged to visit—through many serviceable middle-range stores, devoted to the middle-of-the-road tastes of the middle class, to a few cheap jack ones that sell merchandise you would find at a better rate back home. Most of the best and biggest department stores are grouped in the West End around Regent Street and Oxford Street, with two notable exceptions out in Knightsbridge.

You will recognize **Liberty** (✉ 200 Regent St., W1, ☎ 0171/734–1234) by its wonderful black-and-white mock-Tudor facade, a peacock among pigeons in humdrum Regent Street. Inside, it is a labyrinthine building, full of nooks and crannies, all stuffed with goodies like a dream of an eastern bazaar. Famous principally for its fabrics, it also has an Oriental department, rich with color; menswear that tends to the traditional; and women's wear that has lately been spiced up with extra designer ranges. It is a hard store to resist, where you may well find an original gift—especially one made from those classic Liberty prints. (☞ Map A.)

A short distance from Liberty, two blocks west on Oxford Street, is **John Lewis** (✉ 278 Oxford St., W1, ☎ 0171/629–7711), a store whose motto is "Never knowingly undersold," and for sensible goods at sensible prices this store is hard to beat. For the visitor to London who's handy with the needle, John Lewis has a wonderful selection of dress and furnishing fabrics. Many's the American home with John Lewis drapes. (☞ Map A.)

Near the Marble Arch end of Oxford Street—through crowded blocks in the middle of the day or at sale time—lies **Selfridges** (✉ 400 Oxford St., W1, ☎ 0171/629–1234). This giant, bustling store was started early this century by an American, though it's now British-owned. If this all-rounder has an outstanding department, it has to be its Food Hall, or else its frenetic cosmetics department, which seems to perfume the air the whole length of Oxford Street. In recent years, Selfridges has made a specialty of high-profile popular designer fashion and has spent a lot of money sprucing up. Even more important for the visitor to town, there's a branch of the London Tourist Board on the premises, a theater ticket counter, and a branch of Thomas Cook, the travel agent, in the basement. (☞ Map A.)

Harrods (✉ 87 Brompton Rd., SW1, ☎ 0171/730–1234), being the only English department store classed among monuments and museums on every visitor's list, hardly needs an introduction. In fact, its Englishness is tentative, since it is owned by the Egyptian Al Fayed brothers—but who cares? It is swanky and plush and deep-carpeted as ever, its spectacular food halls are alone worth the trip, and it stands out from the pack for fashion, too. You can forgive the store its immodest motto, *Omnia, omnibus, ubique* ("everything, for everyone, everywhere"), because there are more than 230 departments, including a pet shop rumored to supply you with anything from aardvarks to zebras on request, and the toy department—sorry, *kingdom*—which does the same for plush versions. During the pre-Christmas period and the sales, the entire store is a menagerie. (☞ Map B.)

Harvey Nichols (✉ 109 Knightsbridge, SW1, ☎ 0171/235–5000) is just a few blocks from Harrods, but is not competing on the same turf, since its passion is fashion, all the way. There are six floors of it, including departments for dressing homes and men, but the woman who invests in her wardrobe is the main target. Accessories are strong suits, especially jewelry, scarves, and make-up—England's first MAC counter here was 10-deep for months. A reservation at the Fifth Floor restaurant is one of London's most coveted, too. (☞ Map B.)

Street Markets

London is as rich in street markets as it is in parks, and they contribute as much to the city's culture. Practically every neighborhood has its own cluster of fruit-and-vegetable stalls, but we list here the bigger, specialist sort of market, which provides not only (if you luck out) a bargain, but a great day out. A Sunday morning strolling the stalls of Brick Lane and breakfasting on the native bagels (smaller than New York's, but just as good), or a Saturday antiquing in the Portobello Road are

Londoners' pastimes as much as they are tourist activities, and markets are a great way to see the city from the inside out.

Bermondsey (⊠ Tower Bridge Rd., SE1). Also known as the New Caledonian Market, this is London's best antiques market, one of the largest, and the one the dealers frequent. Thanks to their professional presence, the Fridays-only market starts at the unearthly hour of 4 AM, and it's then that the really great buys will be snapped up. You should still be able to find a bargain or two if you turn up a bit later. *Take Bus 15 or 25 to Aldgate, then Bus 42 over Tower Bridge to Bermondsey Sq., or take the tube to London Bridge and walk.* ⏲ *Fri. 4 AM–1.*

Camden Lock Market (NW1). Visit the lock on a sunny August Sunday if you want your concept of a crowd redefined. Camden is actually several markets gathered around a pair of locks in the Regent's Canal, and was once very pretty. Now that further stalls and a new faux warehouse have been inserted into the surrounding brick railway buildings, the haphazard charm of the place is largely lost, although the variety of merchandise is mindblowing—vintage and new clothes (design stars have been discovered here), antiques and junk, jewelry and scarves, candlesticks, ceramics, mirrors, toys . . . But underneath it's really a meat market for hip teens. The neighborhood is bursting with shops and cafés, and further markets, and is a whole lot calmer, if stall-free, midweek. *Take the tube or Bus 24 or 29 to Camden Town.* ⏲ *Shops Tues.–Sun. 9:30–5:30; stalls weekends 8–6.*

Camden Passage (Islington, N1). Despite the name, this one is not in Camden but a couple of miles away in Islington, a neighborhood first gentrified by media hippies in the '60s. Around 350 antiques dealers set up stalls here Saturday and Wednesday, with a curtailed version on Thursday, and it remains a fruitful, fair-priced, and picturesque hunting ground. *Take Bus 19 or 38 or a tube to the Angel.* ⏲ *Wed. and Sat. 8:30–3.*

Greenwich Antiques Market (⊠ Greenwich High Rd., SE10). If you're planning to visit Greenwich, then combine your trip with a wander around this open-air market near St. Alfege Church. You'll find one of the best selections of secondhand and antique clothes in London—quality tweeds and overcoats can be had at amazing prices. The market for antiques is open on weekends only. *Take a British Rail train to New Gate Cross and then Bus 117, or a bus direct to Greenwich.* ⏲ *Antiques, crafts, and clothes weekends 9–5; fruit and vegetables weekdays 9–5.*

Leadenhall Market (EC3). The draw here is not so much what you can buy—plants and food, mainly—as the building itself. It's a handsome late-Victorian structure, ornate and elaborate, with plenty of atmosphere. *Take the tube to Bank or Monument.* ⏲ *Weekdays 9–5.*

Petticoat Lane (⊠ Middlesex St., E1). Actually, Petticoat Lane doesn't exist, and this Sunday clothing and fashion market centers on Middlesex Street, then sprawls in several directions, including east to Brick Lane. Between them, the crammed streets turn up items of dubious parentage (CD players, bikes, car radios), alongside clothes (vintage, new, and just plain tired), jewelry, books, underwear, antiques, woodworking tools, bed linens, jars of pickles, and outright junk in one of London's most entertaining diversions. *Liverpool St., Aldgate, or Aldgate East tubes are the closest.* ⏲ *Sun. 9–2.*

Portobello Market (⊠ Portobello Rd., W11). London's most famous market still wins the prize for the all-round best. It sits in a most lively and multicultural part of town, the 1,500-odd antiques dealers don't rip you off, and it stretches over a mile, changing character completely as it goes. The top (Notting Hill Gate) end is antiques-land (with shops midweek); the middle is where locals buy fruit and vegetables, and hang out in trendy restaurants; the section under the elevated highway called the Westway boasts the best flea market in town; and then it tails off into a giant rummage sale among record stores, vintage clothing boutiques, and art galleries. *Take Bus 52 or the tube to Ladbroke Grove or Notting Hill Gate.* ⏲ *Fruit and vegetables Mon.–Wed. and Fri. 8–5, Thurs. 8–1; antiques Fri. 8–3; both on Sat. 6–5.*

Spitalfields (✉ Brushfield St., E1). Until it eventually becomes shops and offices, the developers of Camden Lock have got hold of the old 3-acre indoor fruit market near Petticoat Lane and installed food, crafts, and clothes stalls, cafés, performance and sports facilities (including an opera house and a swimming pool), and a city farm. There's a different market every day; Saturday is antiques, Sunday a green market. *Directions as for Petticoat Lane, above.* ⏲ *Weekdays 11–3, Sun. 9–3.*

VAT Refunds

To the eternal fury of Britain's storekeepers, who struggle under cataracts of paperwork, Britain is afflicted with a 17½% Value Added Tax. Foreign visitors, however, need not pay VAT if they take advantage of the Personal Export Scheme. Of the various ways to get a VAT refund, the most common are **Over the Counter** and **Direct Export.** Note that though practically all larger stores operate these schemes, information about them is not always readily forthcoming, so it is important to ask. Once you have gotten on the right track, you'll find that almost all of the larger stores have export departments that will be able to give you all the help you need.

The easiest and most usual way of getting your refund is the **Over the Counter** method. There is normally a minimum of £75, below which VAT cannot be refunded. You must also be able to supply proof of your identity—your passport is best. The salesclerk will then fill out the necessary paperwork, Form 407 VAT. (Be sure to get an addressed envelope as well.) Keep the form and give it to customs when you leave the country. Lines at major airports are usually long, so leave plenty of time, and pack the goods you have purchased in your carry-on bags—you'll sometimes need to be able to produce them. The form will then be returned to the store and the refund forwarded to you, minus a small service charge, usually around $3. You can specify how you want the refund. Generally, the easiest way is to have it credited to your charge card. Alternatively, you can have it in the form of a sterling check, but your bank will charge a fee to convert it. Note also that it can take up to eight weeks to receive the refund.

The **Direct Export** method—whereby you have the store send the goods to your home—is more cumbersome. You must have the VAT Form 407 certified by customs, police, or a notary public when you get home and then send it back to the store. They, in turn, will refund your money.

If you are traveling to any other EC country from Britain, the same rules apply, except in France, where you can claim your refund as you leave the country.

However, in 1988 the **Tourist Tax-Free Shopping** service came into operation. This service, which uses special VAT refund vouchers, rather than Form 407, expedites your refund, provided that you make your purchases at a store (identified by the red, white, and blue Tax-Free for Tourists sign) offering the service. If you are going on from Britain to the Continent, you can even get cash refunds. Full details and a list of stores offering the Tax-Free service are available from the British Tourist Authority (✉ 40 W. 57th St., New York, NY 10019, ☎ 212/986–2200, 800/462–2748) and the British Travel Centre (✉ 12 Regent St., London SW1Y 4PQ).

Clothing Sizes

Men

Suit and shirt sizes in the United Kingdom and the Republic of Ireland are the same as U.S. sizes.

Women

DRESSES/COATS

U.S.	4	6	8	10	12	14	16
U.K./Ireland	6	8	10	12	14	16	18

BLOUSES/SWEATERS

U.S.	30	32	34	36	38	40	42
U.K./Ireland	32	34	36	38	40	42	44

SHOES

U.S.	4	5	6	7	8	9	10
U.K./Ireland	2	3	4	5	6	7	8

8 Side Trips from London

SOMETIMES YOU'VE JUST GOT TO GET OUT of the Old Smoke, and just because you're only here for two weeks doesn't mean you, too, won't feel the urge to see trees and sky and stately homes. Take any of these trips, and you'll feel like you added another week to your vacation, such is the change of pace you'll experience. England is so much more than its capital—a fact that Londoners tend to forget.

All five of these places are comfortably within range of London, and are best reached by train, though a bus is a viable alternative to Cambridge and Windsor. Be sure to call ahead for times.

BATH

It is impossible to convey the heartbreaking beauty of Bath, an unsullied Georgian city, which looks for all the world as if its chief architect, John Wood, its principal dandy, "Beau" Nash, and the beloved author who enshrined it in her 19th-century novels, Jane Austen, might still be walking there. Just as in Venice, stepping out of the train station brings you right to the center, and Bath is compact enough to explore easily on foot. A single day is sufficient for you to look your fill on the glorious yellow Bath stone buildings, tour the Roman baths, and stop for tea, though it will give you only a brief taste of the thriving cultural life that still goes on in this vibrant place.

Bath Spa is easily reached by hourly trains from Paddington station (approx. 1 hour 25 minutes journey time), or by National Express coach (☎ 0171/730–0202) from Victoria Coach Station: journey time 3 hours: coaches about every 2 hours. The Tourist Information Centre (☎ 01225/462–831) is on Bath Street in the Colonnades.

The Pump Room and Roman Baths. The first sight you come to, having followed signs from the train station, is the temple to Minerva, goddess of wisdom, that the Romans built when they settled here in AD 43. Legend has it that the first taker of these sacred waters was King Lear's leprous father, Prince Bladud, in the 9th century BC. He was cured. The waters can still be taken and anciently gush at a constant temperature of 46.5° C (116° F). Below the gorgeous and recently restored 18th-century Pump Room (as described in Austen's *Mansfield Park, Emma, Northhanger Abbey,* et al) is a museum of objects found during excavations. ✉ *Abbey Churchyard,* ☎ *01225/461–111.*

Bath Abbey. This is opposite the Roman Baths, and was commissioned by God. Really. The current design came to a bishop in a dream, and was built by the Vertue brothers during the 16th century, although there's been an abbey on this site since the 8th century. In the **Heritage Vaults** is a museum of archeological finds, including an 800-year-old woman, and a model of 13th-century Bath. Look up at the fan-vaulted ceilings in the nave, and the carved angels on the newly restored West Front. *Abbey,* ☎ *01225/446–300; Heritage Vaults,* ☎ *01225/422–462.*

NEED A BREAK? **Sally Lunn's** (✉ North Parade Passage, ☎ 01225/461–634). A tourist trap, but one loved equally by locals, this is possibly the world's only tea room with its own museum. A sally lunn is a sweet cross between an English muffin and a brioche, a foot in diameter, toasted, and dripping with toppings like cinnamon butter, orange curd, coffee-walnut, or herbed goat's cheese.

The Circus. Reached from Bath Abbey by heading north up Union Passage, to Milsom Street and Gay Street, this is a perfectly circular ring of Bath stone houses, designed by John Wood, and completed after his death by his son.

Royal Crescent. The most famous sight in Bath, and you can't help but see why, was designed by John Wood the younger. Perfectly proportioned and beautifully sited, the views sweep over parkland. **Number 1 Royal Crescent** is reconstructed inside exactly as Beau Nash would have had it circa 1765. It is closed from Dec. 12–Mar. 1 and on Mondays. ☏ *01225/428–126.*

Assembly Rooms. On the east side of The Circus are more thrills for Austen readers, these much-mentioned rooms, which now contain the self-explanatory Museum of Costume. ✉ *Bennett St.,* ☏ *01225/461–111.*

Pulteney Bridge. This was the great Georgian architect Robert Adam's sole contribution to Bath, and is, in its way, as fine as the only other bridge in the world with shops lining either side: the Ponte Vecchio in Florence. Find it on the River Avon back down the hill, after wandering around up at the top, exploring the many nooks and crannies, the surprising secret passageways and cobbled streetlets.

CAMBRIDGE

Cambridge is one of the most beautiful cities in Britain, and the celebrated Cambridge University, an academic center since the end of the 13th century, sits right at its heart. The city center is lively and compact: One of the special pleasures of Cambridge is that in just a few yards one can pass from the bustle of the shopping streets to the cloistered seclusion of the halls of academe. As at Oxford, Cambridge university is based on colleges, each of which is an autonomous institution with its own distinct character and traditions. Students join an individual college and receive their education from the dons attached to it, who are known as "fellows." Each college is built around a series of "courts," or quadrangles. As students and fellows live in these courts, access is often restricted (especially during examination weeks in early summer). Visitors are not normally allowed into college buildings other than chapels and halls (dining rooms).

Trains to Cambridge leave Liverpool Street or King's Cross stations every hour, and take an hour. By National Express coach (☏ 0171/730–0202) from Victoria Coach Station, the journey takes 2 hours; coaches hourly. Cambridge Tourist Information Centre is in Wheeler Street, an extension of Benet Street, off King's Parade (☏ 01223/322–640).

King's College. Probably the best known of all the colleges, thanks partly to its choir, which gives the Festival of Nine Lessons and Carols every Christmas Eve, broadcast all over the world. The chapel in which this takes place is a masterpiece of late Gothic (1446) architecture, with a great fan-vaulted roof supported only by a tracery of soaring side columns. Behind the altar hangs Rubens's painting *The Adoration of the Magi.* Behind King's are the famous "Backs," the gardens that run down to the River Cam, onto which many of the colleges back.

Trinity College. From King's, make your way along the river and through the narrow lanes past Clare College and Trinity Hall to the river, and this, the largest of all the colleges. It has a handsome 17th-century Great Court and a library by Christopher Wren. The massive gatehouse houses "Great Tom," a large clock that strikes each hour with high and low notes. Prince Charles was an undergraduate here during the late 1960s. Beyond Trinity lies **St. John's,** the second largest college.

Queen's College. Reached by going along the Backs from King's, this is where Isaac Newton's **Mathematical Bridge** crosses the river. This arched wooden structure was originally held together by gravitational force alone, but when it was dismantled for clues as to how Newton did it, nobody managed to figure it out, and it had to be reconstructed using nails. In from the river, on Trumpington Street, stands **Pembroke College,** with some 14th-century buildings and a chapel by Wren, and **Peterhouse,** the oldest college.

NEED A BREAK? **The Pickerel** (✉ 30 Magdalene St., by the bridge) is a pleasant pub with a small courtyard.

The Fitzwilliam Museum. Lying beyond Peterhouse, this museum contains outstanding collections of art, including several Constable paintings, and antiquities–starring some objects from ancient Egypt). ✉ *Trumpington St.,* ☎ *01223/332–900.* *Free.* *Tues.–Fri., Lower galleries 10–2, Upper galleries 2–5, Sat. both galleries 10–5, Sun. both galleries 2:15–5; closed Good Friday and Christmas–Jan. 1.*

Grantchester. The pretty village made famous by the poet Rupert Brooke is reachable by punt (hired at Silver Street Bridge or Mill Lane) upstream along the Cam, or you can walk along the Backs past St. John's. On a sunny day, there's no better way of absorbing Cambridge's unique atmosphere—you will seem to have all the time in the world.

OXFORD

The best thing to do in Oxford is to wander around the tiny alleyways that link the honey-colored stone buildings beneath those "dreaming spires," exploring the colleges where the undergraduates live and work. Like Cambridge, Oxford University is not a single body but a collection of 35 independent colleges; most are open to visitors, including many magnificent chapels and dining halls.

Get here by hourly train from Paddington station. The journey takes 55 minutes, or 1 hour 40 minutes by coach from Victoria Coach Station. Several companies operate services, so buses leave every 20 minutes or so. The Oxford Information Centre is in St. Aldate's, opposite the Town Hall, ☎ 01865/726–871.

Magdalen. Pronounced "Maudlin," this is one of the most impressive of the Oxford colleges, with 500-year-old cloisters and lawns leading down to the River Cherwell.

St. Edmund Hall. One of the smallest and most picturesque quadrangles has an old well in the center.

Christ Church. This college has the largest quadrangle, known as Tom Quad. Portraits of former pupils, including John Wesley, William Penn, and no less than 14 prime ministers, hang in the impressive dining hall.

Balliol College. The doors between the inner and outer quadrangles of Christ Church's neighbor still bear the scorch marks from the flames that burned Archbishop Cranmer and Bishops Latimer and Ridley at the stake in 1555 for their Protestant beliefs.

The Oxford Story. This is a multimedia presentation of the university's 800-year history, in which visitors travel through depictions of college life. ✉ *6 Broad St.,* ☎ *01865/728–822.* *£4.50 adults, £3.95 senior* *citizens and students, £3.25 children.* ⏲ *Apr.–June, Sept., and Oct., daily 9:30–5; July and Aug., daily 9–6:30; Nov.–Mar., daily 10–4.*

Sheldonian Theatre. The Sheldonian was Christopher Wren's first building, which he designed like a semicircular Roman amphitheater. Graduation ceremonies are held here. ✉ *Sheldonian Theatre, Broad St.,* ☎ *01865/277–299.* ⏲ *Mon.–Sat. 10–12:45, 2–4:45; closes at 3:45 Dec.–Feb.*

Ashmolean Museum. The Ashmolean is Britain's oldest public museum. Here are priceless collections of Egyptian, Greek, and Roman artifacts, Michelangelo drawings, and European silverware. ✉ *Ashmolean, Beaumont St.,* ☎ *01865/278–000.* 🎫 *Free.* ⏲ *Tues.–Sat. 10–4, Sun. 2–4, bank holiday Mons. 2–5; closed Mon. and some holidays.*

STRATFORD-UPON-AVON

It goes without saying that Stratford is a must for Shakespeare enthusiasts. But even without its most famous son, the town would be worth visiting. Its half-timbered buildings show how prosperous it was during the 16th century, when it was a thriving craft and trading center. There are also attractive 18th-century buildings.

Try to catch the direct train each morning from Paddington Station (☎ 0171/262–6767 for times), or else you'll be doomed to at least one change, at Leamington Spa. There are two direct trains back from Stratford each afternoon too, and journey time is 2 hours 20 minutes. It takes no longer to go by National Express (☎ 0171/730–0202) from Victoria Coach Station, and there are three coaches daily, though the fastest route is by train *and* bus: from Euston Station to Coventry, then switching to a Guide Friday bus. The trip takes 2 hours, and there are four departures daily (☎ 0171/387–7070 for information). Stratford Tourist Information Centre is at Bridge Foot, by the bridge, (☎ 01789/293–127).

Shakespeare. The **Shakespeare Centre** and **Shakespeare's Birthplace** are where to start your Bard odyssey. Among the exhibits are many of the costumes used in the BBC's dramatization of the plays and various articles relating to his life and work. The other Shakespeare shrines are **Anne Hathaway's Cottage**—the early home of the playwright's wife, in Shottery, on the edge of town—and **Holy Trinity Church,** where Shakespeare, his wife, and several of their family are buried. *Shakespeare's Birthplace,* ✉ *Henley St.,* ☎ *01789/204–016.* 🎫 *Combined admission for Shakespeare Birthplace Trust properties: £7.50 adults, £7 senior citizens and students, £3.50 children, or individual tickets £2.60 adults, £1.20 children.* ⏲ *Mar.–Oct., Mon.–Sat. 9–5:30, Sun. 10–5:30; Nov.–Feb., Mon.–Sat. 9:30–4, Sun. 10:30–4; closed Dec. 24–26, New Year and Good Friday mornings.*

NEED A BREAK? **Mistress Quickly** in Henley Street serves light refreshments and meals throughout the day; an unusual feature is the jigsaw tree sculpture.

World of Shakespeare. This multimedia exhibit illustrates the playwright's times by describing Queen Elizabeth's royal progress from London to Kenilworth Castle in 1575. ✉ *13 Waterside,* ☎ *01789/269–190.* 🎫 *£3.50 adults, £2.50 students, children, and senior citizens, £8 family (2 adults and 2 children).* ⏲ *Daily 9:30–5; closed Dec. 25.*

Hall's Croft. This fine Tudor town house was the home of Shakespeare's daughter Susanna and her doctor husband. It has contemporary furniture, and the doctor's dispensary and consulting room can also be seen. ✉ *Old Town,* ☎ *01789/292–107.* 🎫 *£1.80 adults, 80p* *children.* ⊙ *Mar.–Oct., Mon.–Sat. 9:30–5, Sun. 10:30–5; Nov.–Feb., Mon.–Sat. 10:30–4, Sun. 1:30–4.*

The Royal Shakespeare Theatre. Perfectly positioned on the banks of the Avon, this is where the Royal Shakespeare Company (known as the RSC) lives outside London, mounting several productions each season. The design of the smaller **Swan Theatre,** in the same building, is based on the original Elizabethan Globe. Its construction was funded by an Anglophile American millionaire, Frederick Koch. It's best to book well in advance, but day-of-performance tickets are always available. ✉ *Stratford-upon-Avon, CV37 6BB,* ☎ *01789/295–623.*

WINDSOR

The star sight of this quiet Berkshire town is, without a shadow of a doubt, Windsor Castle, although its Great Park shouldn't be forgotten, and Eton College, England's most famous public school is also here. There's also now a brand-new attraction to add to the Windsor value: the kid's paradise of Legoland.

Windsor Castle is the most impressive and the longest-serving of all England's royal palaces. It's the only royal residence to have been in continuous royal use since the days of William the Conqueror, who chose this site to build a timber stockade soon after his conquest of Britain in 1066. It was Edward III in the 1300s who really founded the castle, building the Norman gateway, the great round tower, and new state apartments, then subsequent monarchs added new buildings or improved existing ones according to their tastes and their finances. Charles II restored the state apartments during the 1600s, and during the 1820s George IV, that most extravagant of kings with a mania for building, converted what was still essentially a medieval castle into the royal palace you see today.

The queen uses Windsor a lot, spending most weekends here, often joined by family and friends. She's here when the Royal Standard is flown above the Round Tower, but not when you see the Union Jack.

Windsor is easy to reach by train, either from Waterloo direct to Windsor and Eton Riverside (50 minutes), or from Paddington to Windsor Central, changing at Reading (45 minutes); there are 2 trains per hour on each route. The Green Line bus (☎ 01737/242–411) leaves from Eccleston Bridge, behind Victoria train station, *not* from the Coach Station itself. Make sure you catch the fast direct service, which takes 45 minutes and runs hourly; the stopping services take up to 1 hour 15 minutes. Windsor's Tourist Information Centre (☎ 01753/852–010) is in Central Station.

Windsor Castle. The massive citadel occupies 13 acres, but the first part you notice on entering is the massive **Round Tower** on top of which the standard is flown, and at the base of which is the 11th century Moat Garden, which you can occasionally visit in summer. Passing through the portcullised **Norman Gate,** you reach the **Upper Ward,** the quadrangle containing the State Apartments—which you may tour when the queen is out—and the sovereign's Private Apartments, which you may not. Big ceremonies, like processions for foreign Heads of State, go on here, as does the Changing of the Guard, when the queen is in. Next you reach the **Lower Ward,** where the star sight is the magnificent **St. George's Chapel,** symbolic and actual guardian of the Order of the Garter, the highest Chivalric Order in the land, founded in 1348 by Edward III. Ten sovereigns are buried in the fantastic Gothic Perpendicular, 230 feet long Chapel, with its gargoyles, buttresses, and pinnacles, its banners, swords, and choir stalls, with enamelled plates displaying arms of the Knights of the Order of the Garter.

The **State Apartments** are grander than Buckingham Palace's, and have the added attraction of a few gems from the queen's vast art collection: choice canvasses by Rubens, Rembrandt, Van Dyck, Gainsborough, Canaletto, and Holbein; da Vinci drawings; Gobelin tapestries, and limewood carvings by Grinling Gibbons. The views across to Windsor Great Park, the remains of a former royal hunting forest, are magnificent too.

One unmissable treat—and not only for children—is **Queen Mary's Dolls' House**, a 12:1 scale, seven-story palace, complete with electricity, running water, and working elevators, designed in 1924 by Sir Edwin Lutyens. The detail is literally incredible—for example, some of the miniature books in the library are by Kipling, Conan Doyle, Thomas Hardy, and G.K. Chesterton—written by the great authors in their own hand.

The terrible fire of November 1992, which started in the queen's private chapel, totally gutted some of the State Apartments. A swift rescue effort meant that, miraculously, hardly any works of art were lost. However, parts of the castle will remain closed while repairs and rebuilding are in progress—probably at least until the year 2000. ✉ *Windsor Castle,* ☎ *01753/868–286.* 🎫 *£8 adults, £5.50 senior citizens, £4 children under 17. Call 01753/831–118 for opening times.*

Eton. Windsor's equally historic neighbor, and home of the famous public school. (Public, of course, meaning ultra-private in this context) is a short walk away, across the river. Classes at Eton College are held now, as always, in the distinctive redbrick Tudor-style buildings; the oldest buildings are grouped around a quadrangle called School Yard. The **Museum of Eton Life** has displays on the school's history, and a guided tour is also available. ✉ *Brewhouse Yard,* ☎ *01753/671–177.* 🎫 *£2.20 adults, £1.50 children under 16.* ⏲ *Daily during term 2–4:30, 10:30–4:30 on school vacations; closed 1st Sun. in Oct.–Apr. 1. Guided tours daily at 2:15 and 3:15; charge £3.20 adults, £2.70 children under 16, including admission to museum.*

Legoland. Really of interest only to children, unless you have particularly powerful nostalgia for the "legos" of your youth, this is a landscaped theme park that recreates the great cities of Europe in trillions of plastic bricks, offers a driving school for underage drivers, adventure trails with pirates and castles, and a "Duplo" (big bricks) area for small kids, with a fairy tale ride and puppet theater. ✉ *Winkfield Rd.,* ☎ *01753/626–364.* ⏲ *Apr.–Sept. Daily 10–6, Oct. weekends 10–6.*

9 Portraits of London

LONDON AT A GLANCE: A CHRONOLOGY

THIS DATE TABLE parallels events in London's history with events in the world at large, especially in the Americas, to give a sense of perspective to the chronology of London. The dates of British kings and queens are those of their reigns, not of their lives.

c. 400 BC Early Iron Age hamlet built at Heathrow (now London airport)

54 BC Julius Caesar arrives with short-lived expedition

AD 43 Romans conquer Britain, led by the emperor Claudius

60 Boudicca, queen of Iceni, razes the first Roman Londinium

c. 100 The Romans make Londinium center of their British activities, though not the capital

410 Romans withdraw from Britain

410–500 Anglo-Saxon invasion and settlement

700s Viking invasion and settlement begins

856 Alfred the Great (871–99), king of the West Saxons, "restored London and made it habitable"

1042 Edward the Confessor (1042–66) moves his court to Westminster and begins the reconstruction of the abbey and its monastic buildings

1066 William the Conqueror (1066–87), duke of Normandy, wins the battle of Hastings

1067 William grants London a charter confirming its rights and privileges

1078 The Tower of London begins with the building of the White Tower

1097 Westminster Hall completed under William II, Rufus (1087–1100)

1123 St. Bartholomew's Hospital founded by Rahere

1132 Charter of Liberties granted by Henry I (1100–35), giving London the right to choose its own sheriffs

1136 Fire destroys London Bridge (new one built 1176–1209)

1185 Knights Templar build the New Temple by the Thames

1191 First mayor of London elected

1265 First Parliament held in Westminster Abbey Chapter House

1314 Old St. Paul's Cathedral completed

1327 Incorporation of first trade guilds (which govern the City for centuries)

1348–58 The Black Death strikes London; one-third of the population dies

1382 The Peasants' Revolt destroys part of the city

1411 The Guildhall (already centuries on the same site) rebuilt

1476 William Caxton (1422–91) introduces printing to England in Westminster

c. 1483 London's population estimated at around 75,000

1515 Henry VII's tomb in Westminster Abbey completed

1529 Hampton Court given by Cardinal Wolsey to Henry VIII; it becomes a favorite royal residence

1568 Royal Exchange founded

1588 Preparations at Tilbury to repel the Spanish invasion; the Armada defeated in the Channel

1599 Shakespeare's Globe Theatre built on the South Bank

1603 Population of London over 200,000

1605 Unsuccessful Gunpowder Plot to blow up the Houses of Parliament

1619–22 Banqueting House built

1640s New fortifications for the defense of the capital built at the start of the Civil War between the Crown and Parliament forces

1649 Charles I (1625–49) beheaded outside the Banqueting House on Whitehall

1658 Oliver Cromwell (Lord Protector) dies

1660 Charles II (1649–85) restored to the throne (the Restoration) after exile in Europe

1665 The Great Plague; deaths probably reach 100,000 (official figure for one week alone was 8,297)

1666 The Great Fire burns for three days; 89 churches, 13,200 houses destroyed over an area of 400 streets

1675 Sir Christopher Wren (1632–1723) begins work on the new St. Paul's Cathedral

1682–92 Main work on the Royal Hospital Chelsea

1688 William III (1689–1702) transfers royal residence from Whitehall Palace to Kensington Palace

1694 The Bank of England founded

1698 Whitehall Palace destroyed by fire

1732 Number 10 Downing Street becomes the prime minister's official residence

1739–53 Mansion House built

1755 Trooping the Colour first performed for George II

1762 George III (1760–1820) makes Buckingham Palace the royal residence

1773 Stock Exchange founded in Threadneedle Street

1792 Bank of England built

1801 Population just under 1,000,000 (first census)

1802 First gaslights on the London streets

1805 Spectacular funeral of Horatio Nelson (1758–1805), who was killed at the battle of Trafalgar

1812 Regent's Park laid out

1817 First Waterloo Bridge built

1827 Marble Arch erected (in 1851 moved to the northeast corner of Hyde Park)

1829–41 Trafalgar Square laid out

1834 The Houses of Parliament gutted by fire; 1840–52 the present Westminster Palace built

1835 Madame Tussaud settles in Baker Street

1836 London's first railway begins operation, London Bridge to Deptford

1837 Victoria (1837–1901) comes to the throne

1838 National Gallery opens in Trafalgar Square

1845 British Museum completed

1851 The Great Exhibition, Prince Albert's brainchild, held in the Crystal Palace, Hyde Park

1863 Arrival of the Underground (the tube), first train on the Metropolitan Line

1869 Albert Embankment completed, first stage in containing the Thames's floodwaters

1870 The Albert Hall opens

1878 First electric street lights

1894 Tower Bridge constructed

1897 Queen Victoria celebrates her Diamond Jubilee

1901 Victoria dies, marking the end of an era; London's population reaches around 4,500,000

1914–18 World War I—London bombed (1915) by German zeppelins; (355 incendiaries, 567 explosives; 670 killed, 1,962 injured)

1926 General Strike; London is partly paralyzed

1935 London County Council establishes a Green Belt to preserve the city's outer open spaces

1939–45 World War II—air raids, between Sept. 1940 and July 1941, 45,000–50,000 bombs (including incendiaries) are dropped on London; 1944 Flying Bomb (Doodlebug) raids; 1945 V2 raids; during the latter two series of raids 8,938 killed, 24,504 injured. Total casualties for the whole war, about 30,000 killed, more than 50,000 injured

1946 Heathrow Airport opens

1951 The Festival of Britain spurs postwar uplift

1953 Coronation of Queen Elizabeth II (born 1926)

1956 Clean Air Act abolishes open fires and makes London's mists and fogs a romantic memory

1965 Sir Winston Churchill's funeral, a great public pageant; the Post Office Tower—now the Telecom Tower—one of Britain's tallest buildings, opens

1973 New Stock Exchange opens

1974 Covent Garden fruit-and-vegetable market moves across the Thames; the original area is remodeled

1976 National Theatre opens on the South Bank

1977 Queen Elizabeth celebrates her Silver Jubilee

1979 Margaret Thatcher elected prime minister

1981 National Westminster Tower, Britain's tallest building, opens in the City; Prince Charles marries Lady Diana Spencer in St. Paul's Cathedral

1982 The Barbican Centre opens

1983 The first woman lord mayor takes office

1984 The Thames Barrier, designed to prevent flooding in central London, is inaugurated

1986 The Greater London Council (the city's centralized municipal government) is abolished by Parliament; London's population now stands at approximately 6,696,000

1990 Margaret Thatcher resigns as prime minister

1991 Cesar Pelli's Tower—1 Canada Square—opens at Canary Wharf and becomes Britain's tallest building

1994 The Channel Tunnel opens a direct rail link between Britain and Europe

WREN AND THE GREAT FIRE OF LONDON

SINCE ENGLAND AS A WHOLE IS SO RICH in medieval churches, the perceptive visitor to the City of London may wonder why there are none around. Except for five on the northern edge of the City, there seems to be nothing earlier than the late 17th century. The answer lies in the four terrible days and nights, between September 2 and 5, 1666, when fire destroyed five-sixths of the mainly timber-built, medieval city. Those four days did three to four times as much damage as did Hitler's bombs and rockets in the six years of World War II. This was how it happened.

On the night of Saturday, September 2, 1666, the king's own baker, Master Robert Farynor, put out the oven fire in his bake house in Pudding Lane near the north end of London Bridge and went to bed. He was quite certain that he had extinguished his stove, but in the small hours of the morning his manservant was awakened by smoke and, realizing that the house was on fire, roused the household, whose members crept to safety across the roof to the house next door, with the exception of a maid who, scared of heights, died in the flames.

For the next four days, the fire raged. A steady wind blew from the northeast, the Essex side, of the city, driving the flames through the narrow streets of timber-framed houses. The flames were carried toward Thames Street, the riverside area, where stocks of oil, coal, hay, timber, and hemp lay piled on the quayside; the fire could not have been given a surer foothold. At first, the severity of the danger was not realized; Samuel Pepys, civil servant and diarist, roused by his servant who was working late, looked out of the window "but being unused to such fires as followed, I thought it far enough off, and so went to bed again and to sleep." At about the same time, some wary citizens had called the lord mayor, Sir Thomas Bludworth, from his bed. He dismissed the danger. "Pish! a woman might piss it out," he was reported as having said; and the opportunity to control the fire was lost. Before morning, St. Magnus Church was destroyed and the Thames water house on the north end of the bridge, which could throw a jet of water over the steeple of the church, was gone, too. People began, desperately, to evacuate their goods; some threw their treasures into the Thames in the hope that they might be washed back on a later tide. Samuel Pepys dug a hole in his back garden to bury state papers—his home served as the admiralty's office—and his much-valued Parmesan cheese.

The fire began to work its way into the heart of the City; it destroyed the Royal Exchange, took the medieval Guildhall, whose oak timbers were so stout that for hours they glowed "in a bright, shining coale, as it had been a palace of gold or a great building of burnished brass." At last the fire reached St. Paul's Cathedral, crowning the western hill of the City. The old cathedral had been one of the great wonders of medieval Europe. The City booksellers, convinced that the sanctity of the cathedral and the thickness of its stone walls would be proof even against this fire, had filled the crypt with their books. Their faith was ill founded, for the flames took hold of St. Paul's and gutted it. The lead of the roof flowed in volcanic torrents down Ludgate Hill.

The king, Charles II, and his brother, the duke of York, alerted by Pepys, organized fire-fighting teams from among the panic-stricken citizens; houses were blown up to create firebreaks, thatched roofs torn down to prevent sparks from igniting them. But it was not till Wednesday night that the wind dropped, and a light fall of rain, early on Thursday morning, made it possible to gain some sort of control over the disaster. In those four days, the fire had swept from close to the eastern boundary of the City, near to London Tower, as far westward as Fleet Street, to within a hundred yards of the Temple Church. Some 400 streets containing 13,200 houses were wiped out; London lost St. Paul's Cathedral, 87 churches, the Guildhall, the Royal Exchange, the Custom House, the Leadenhall, and 44 City Company Halls. All that remained was a paring around the northeastern and northern edges. Five medieval churches remained unscathed, as did St. Bartholomew-the-Great farther north. Samuel Pepys's house was safe, too.

THE PERSON WHO BEST KEPT HIS HEAD was the king himself. On September 13, he issued a proclamation declaring that London would be rebuilt of stouter, less combustible materials, that the streets must be wider, that a proper survey should be made so that no man should lose what was rightly his, that he himself would be responsible for the rebuilding of the Custom House, and that those who rebuilt in an approved manner would be rebated the hearth tax (domestic rates) for seven years. Others reacted to the king's lead with equal speed and efficiency; within a week of the fire's ending, the king received a plan from a young mathematician, Dr. Christopher Wren of Oxford University, demonstrating how the city might be newly laid out in an ideal, geometric manner. Within the following week, four more such plans reached the monarch. Charles, who had spent his years of exile during and after the Civil War as a poor relation at the magnificent court of Louis XIV, wanted to seize this chance to emulate France. But he was a realistic man. A commission was set up—six men, three chosen by the king and three by the City, two of whom had already put forward plans of their own. Wren was one of the king's team. Commendably prompt, the commission announced its finding on October 24. London must be rebuilt on the old street plan, with such road widenings and improvements as could be made without causing too much disturbance. Speed in rebuilding and the restoration of trade were imperative.

It is fashionable to lament the rejection of Wren's plan as London's great lost opportunity. I myself doubt this. A great city evolves gradually; its streets and buildings represent the needs, concerns, ambitions, and dreams of its citizens. Overall plannings or redevelopments, whether they be the product of one man's vision or a committee's consensus, are apt to disregard the human needs of those who are going to live there. London may well have been wise to retain its medieval street plan.

In this emergency, 17th-century society—the king, the City authorities, Parliament—moved with a speed almost unbelievable in the 20th century. By February 1667, a series of bills had been drafted, debated, and passed to become the Fire Acts. They laid down that houses of standard types were to be built of noncombustible materials with flat, uniform frontages. The picturesque timber-framed, lathe-and-plaster dwellings, one floor jutting out above another, possibly with a thatched roof as crown, were banished from the City. A special Fire Court was set up to resolve disputes about land and tenure, the judges and lawyers volunteering to work without fees in this unparalleled emergency; it sat for six years and gave judgment in some 1,500 cases which, considering that 13,200 houses had been destroyed, many of them held in multiple tenancies, suggests that most parties exercised common sense and restraint in building claims. When all was settled, the City authorities, by way of thanks and recognition of services, commissioned full-length portraits of the 22 judges, which are still in the possession of the Guildhall.

The homeless citizens were instructed to pay half a mark (37½p) for a hastily sworn-in surveyor to stake out the limits of their former houses so that the land could be cleared and rebuilding begin. The great shortages were of money, men, and materials. But a tax to be levied on coal entering the Port of London was authorized to pay for the reconstruction of St. Paul's, the churches, and public buildings; the City authorities and the Livery Companies dug into their resources and, in days when prudent people kept a good part of their substance in gold pieces in a money chest under their own roofs, neighbor lent to neighbor and the great rebuilding began. The new houses were built from London's own earth; the clay of the Thames basin, once fired, made excellent bricks. The Guild laws, restricting labor to local residents, were relaxed so that help could come in from all over the country. By 1671, within five years, more than 7,000 houses—95% of what was to be rebuilt—were completed or well under way; the new Custom House was finished, and the Royal Exchange enlarged and reopened. In that year, Lord Mayor's Day was once again celebrated with ceremony and pageantry.

The coal tax came in slowly at first, and this, coupled with lack of stone, meant that the cathedral and city churches remained unbuilt, though sites were cleared and men worshiped in temporary "tabernacles." Eighty-seven churches had been destroyed, 51 were rebuilt, many parishes being amalgamated. For all of these, Wren provided the designs, though inevitably the detailed working-out was undertaken by other hands, and site supervision was necessarily the responsibility of others. Fourteen churches were begun in 1670; between the mid-1670s and the early 1680s, there were some 30 under construction. By 1685, the main structures of most had been completed; towers and spires were added or finished in the early 1700s, after half a generation's breathing space. In creating these churches, Wren—the son of a dean, the nephew of a bishop—had to decide what an Anglican church should look like. The great medieval Catholic tradition of church building had fallen into abeyance with the Reformation; then, the emphasis had been on the altar, and an impenetrable screen often separated the priest from his flock. Now communion was to be celebrated in the sight of all, since all would participate, and a greater importance would be given to the sermon, which would have to be audible—in short, the need was for a church for *congregational* worship. Wren advanced no single solution, but in almost all his churches he placed the emphasis on the body of the nave and brought the chancel well within the church.

WREN WAS, IN MOST CASES, WORKING on cramped and irregularly shaped sites and, at the beginning, it was still uncertain how large and how steady an income would be produced by the coal tax. The exteriors of Wren's churches are very plain; sometimes, in London's busy streets, it is possible to walk past and, unless you are observant, miss the entrance—St. Peter, Cornhill, is a good example. But one feature stands out, even today: To each church, Wren gave a distinctive tower, spire, or steeple, and by them you can still pilot your way around the City's streets. Inside the church the provision of fittings was the responsibility of the parish and so, from examining the altar, the pulpit, the organ, the font, and the woodwork in general, we can deduce a good deal about the wealth and taste of each 17th-century parish.

Of those 51 churches, time, chance, the developer, and wartime damage have taken their toll. Between 1781 and 1939, 19 of Wren's churches were destroyed; another seven were lost to the bombs and were not restored after the war. Of those that remain, most are in excellent condition, well looked-after, and well loved. Some remain as parish churches; others, owing to dwindling congregations, have become Guild churches with special weekday responsibilities toward London's daytime, working population, or toward particular religious or social needs. Many of them depend upon voluntary help with supervision, and so are not open all the time. But they are still there, playing their part in the religious, social, and ceremonial life of the City.

All the time that he was planning or supervising the City churches, Wren was thinking about St. Paul's. Even before the fire, he had been called in by the dean and chapter to advise on how the cathedral should be restored after the damage and decay of the Civil War and the Commonwealth years. After the disaster, when it proved impossible to improvise a temporary church because of the calcined condition of the remaining fabric, Dean Sancroft, later archbishop of Canterbury, wrote to Wren, "You are so absolutely and indispensably necessary to us that we can do nothing, resolve on nothing, without you." After several rejected plans, Wren undertook the Great Model, which can still be seen in the crypt of St. Paul's. It is over 18 feet long, cost over £500 to make—a first-class house on a main street could then be had for £400. It was to be a single-story building in the shape of a Greek cross with arms of equal length, with a giant portico, and a dome 120 feet wide—eight feet wider than the present dome and only 17 feet smaller than St. Peter's in Rome. But the design was too revolutionary, too great a departure from the traditional Latin cross of the old cathedral, and the clergy rejected it. Their reaction was not all prejudice; there was a practical need to choose a building that could be completed a part at a time. Wren resolved to "make no more models, or publicly to expose his Drawings" but, patient as always, produced a compromise design: Latin cross in shape with a cupola surmounted with a spire. Nine years of deliberation and argument had slipped by since the fire; it was time for work to begin. The king gave his Warrant to this hybrid plan in May 1675, authorizing Wren, whom he had knighted two years before and who had been surveyor-general since 1669, to make "variations, rather ornamental than essential, as from time to time he should see proper." Wren took advantage of this liberty to return much closer to his preferred design, and to give us the masterpiece that is St. Paul's.

WHEN THE SITE WAS CLEARED and they began to set out the foundations, Wren told a workman to find a sizable piece of stone to use as a marker. The man brought, at random and by chance, a piece of an old gravestone with one word upon it: RESURGAM—the Latin for "I shall rise again." Everyone took this to be a good omen. And rise the cathedral did—520 feet long and 365 feet in height, from the crown of the lantern over the dome to the ground—and all in a comparatively short space of time, the first service being held in the choir on December 2, 1697. Even so, there were criticisms and disagreements: At one stage, hoping to speed matters, Parliament tried to hold back half of each of Wren's annual payments of £200 until the work was completed. There were also agitations for the dome to be clad in copper rather than in somber and dignified lead. Despite everything, Wren and his team of craftsmen and skilled laborers worked on steadily. His son, the younger Christopher, placed the last stone on the lantern late in October 1708, watched by old Edward Strong the mason, whose brother Thomas had laid the foundation stone in June 1675. It had taken 120 years and 13 architects to build St. Peter's in Rome; St. Paul's was the work of one man, completed in half a lifetime.

Wren lies buried in the crypt, with the proudest epitaph that any architect could ever have: *Lector, si monumentum requiris, circumspice*—Reader, if you seek his monument, look around you.

— Ann Saunders

Author of Art and Architecture of London, *Dr. Saunders lectures to visiting American students on London history and costume. She is a leading figure in the London Topographical Society.*

THE TRUE HEART OF LONDON

MOST PEOPLE who become theater goers in adult life have, I believe, a distinct memory of the first time they ever saw a live performance. And I suspect that many of those people, wherever they happen to have been born, will remember equally clearly the first time they went to the theater in London.

For myself, it was Christmas 1965, when my parents took me to see *The Wind in the Willows* in Her Majesty's Theatre. Five years old, I sat in wide-eyed wonder among a hushed, attentive audience, responding together to the enchantment of the bright lights and the strange costumes. Today, Her Majesty's Theatre houses *The Phantom of the Opera,* the most famous musical in the world; it has become a landmark among London sights for visitors from all over.

And yet Her Majesty's Theatre is only one of the 50-odd historic theaters in London's West End, with which the history of London has been bound up since Shakespeare gathered his company together at Bankside's Globe. London's theaters have always been at the center of its public life, and as a visitor to London, heading to the West End perhaps for that unforgettable first time, you join 11 million others who attend the city's theaters every year—without even counting the Fringe, London's equivalent of Off-Broadway. Of that 11 million, about a third come from abroad, theater high on their list of must-sees. So, welcome to the ranks of London theater goers: You take your place in a noble tradition.

After the great age of Shakespeare and Jacobean drama came the 17th-century pleasure gardens, the theaters and bear pits of the South bank; these in their turn gave way to the fiercely competitive Theatres Royal in 18th-century Covent Garden, dominated by the Theatre Royal, Drury Lane (home of *Miss Saigon* today), the Theatre Royal Covent Garden, and a frisky newcomer, the Little Theatre in the Haymarket. By virtue of an exclusive royal license to present plays for public entertainment, the mighty Theatre Royal, Drury Lane, had enjoyed a monopoly since the restoration of the monarchy in 1660; in 1729, the Little Theatre gained "royal" status, initiating a wave of competition that finally crested at the end of the 19th century—by which time central London was thoroughly alive with theaters.

In the latter part of Queen Victoria's reign, from the 1870s until her death in 1901, the theater district was thick with the dust, noise, and clatter of bizarrely ornate theaters going up as fast as audiences could fill them. Although it is now nearly 30 years since the last new theater went up in the commercial West End, we enjoy today the legacy of that extraordinary turn-of-the century outburst of building activity, which exchanged the debris of part of Victorian slum London for a gleaming new theater district.

A walk along Shaftesbury Avenue from Piccadilly Circus to Cambridge Circus provides a model education in fin de siècle British theater style. Seen during the daytime, when the avenue is bustling, or at night when the theaters light up, the theater district is as much the heart of London as the royal palaces, cathedrals, and parks for which the city is universally famous.

Shaftesbury Avenue begins on the north side of Piccadilly Circus, and its five theaters line its left side like sentinels. But before you set off along the avenue, seek out the Criterion, a tiny jewel box of a theater on the southern edge of Piccadilly Circus. Built in 1873 by Thomas Verity (who also built the Comedy Theatre in nearby Panton Street), the Criterion's Rococo entrance opens onto a dazzling staircase lined with mirrors and brightly colored ceramic tiles. This staircase takes you down to a pink-and-white auditorium, almost as far below ground as the tube trains that can be heard rumbling nearby during the quieter moments of a performance. When it first opened in 1874, the Criterion was considered a miracle of subterranean engineering—particularly for the system by which fresh air was pumped down into the auditorium to save the audience from asphyxiation. Nowadays the air-conditioning is more conventional, but the theater remains a must-see on your tour.

BACK ON SHAFTESBURY Avenue proper, the first theater is the oldest: the Lyric, built in 1888 by C. J. Phipps, a fine red stone building with a broad, handsome front. By contrast, the neighboring Apollo, opened in 1901, presents a creamy-white facade, with corner domes supported by graceful muses. If you look carefully to the right of the front entrance you can see the eccentric family crest of the first owner, Henry Lowenfield: a silver chain and buckle with a flying lizard, supported by lions.

Continue a few paces farther and you'll come to the Queen's and the Gielgud, built between 1906 and 1907 to balance the two corners of a block by prolific theater architect W.G.R. Sprague. Together they make one of London's trio of twin theaters. From the outside, the similarity between the Queen's and the Gielgud has been lost since the Queen's lost its facade to a bomb during the blitz. Inside, however, below street level, the auditorium still presents a perfect mirror image of its twin. Sprague was fond of this effect: You can see it again in the Aldwych and Strand theaters, which flank the Waldorf Hotel block in the Aldwych, and again at St. Martin's Court, near the southern end of Charing Cross Road, where the Albery and Wyndham's theaters stand back to back like friendly rivals.

Shaftesbury Avenue saves its greatest glory for last. As you walk from Queen's toward Cambridge Circus, you'll sense the shadow of a towering monolith rising on your left, the side wall of which takes up the whole block from Greek Street onward. Only when you cross to the other side of Cambridge Circus can you turn to take in the whole, magnificent view of the Palace Theatre, a flagship of Theaterland and a London landmark. The Palace was built in 1891 by architect G. H. Holloway for the great impresario Richard D'Oyly Carte, who intended it as a Royal Opera House for the presentation of British opera. Unfortunately D'Oyly Carte had overlooked the fact that, apart from his own favorites Gilbert and Sullivan, there were few British composers whose work could fill such a mighty edifice and attract the audiences to make it pay. Speedily renamed the Palace Theatre of Varieties, it quickly became popular: a monument both to late-19th-century theater architecture and to the resourcefulness of a producer quick to get himself out of an unprofitable enterprise!

Indeed, it was variety theater, successor to the music-hall entertainment of the late 19th century, that proved the great moneymaker of the early 1900s and the raison d'être of a number of the larger theaters that make their living today as venues for megamusicals or opera. One man, the architect Frank Matcham, was chiefly responsible for the gargantuan Empires, Hippodromes, and Coliseums that sprang up not only in London but across England between the 1890s and 1910s. Much of Matcham's work has been lost, but central London still boasts two of his masterpieces: the London Palladium, which you'll find tucked away in Argyll Street, an unlikely-looking side street east of Oxford Circus, and the London Coliseum in St. Martin's Lane.

The London Coliseum is one of the wonders of London. Its noteworthy features are many: a rosy-hued Italianate facade; a spacious foyer with a gloriously decorative mosaic domed ceiling; a well-proportioned 2,000-seat auditorium (the box office here can truthfully claim "there is no bad seat in the house"); one of the largest stages in the entire country; and the famous Coliseum lions leaping in gilded rampage from either side of the proscenium arch. The Coliseum was the first theater in the world to have a revolving stage, and royal guests in the early half of the century were transported from front door to royal box in a private curtained carriage that ran on rails still preserved beneath the foyer carpet! Anything was possible in this queen of theaters: ice shows, variety, musicals, pantomime, opera, or ballet. Today it makes a fitting home for the English National Opera, and at night its famous rooftop globe illuminates the sky and is visible from Covent Garden to Trafalgar Square. Its nearby friendly rival, the Royal Opera House in Covent Garden, may have a longer history, a royal pedigree, and a more classically beautiful interior, but the Coliseum remains uniquely impressive.

THE HISTORY OF THEATERLAND is a history of people, too, and, as you wander the area's streets and alleyways, you'll learn about the men and women who have shaped commercial West End theater over the decades. It isn't hard to find the most famous among them. Noël Coward is honored with his very own bar at the Phoenix Theatre; composer and musical actor Ivor Novello is remembered with a sign on the wall outside the Strand Theatre; and a solemnly optimistic legend above the stage door of the Prince Edward Theatre in Soho's Greek Street observes that "the world's greatest artistes have passed, and will pass, through these doors." If you take a backstage tour of the Theatre Royal, Drury Lane, you'll be treated to the history behind many of London's most famous theatrical greats—from the leading Shakespearean actors of the 18th and 19th centuries, such as Garrick, Kean, and Mrs. Siddons, to the more recent roll call of 20th-century musicals to which Drury Lane has played host. Along the way, you will hear about some less-substantial personalities, among them the ghostly Man in Grey, who haunts the staircase above the Royal Circle.

Some of the most famous names are honored in surprising places. The image of Sir Henry Irving, the first theatrical knight, hangs over the door to the Lyceum Public House, on the corner of The Strand and Wellington Street, just a few paces from the front steps of his own theater, the Lyceum. Irving, whose agent Bram Stoker wrote the horror classic *Dracula,* was the actor responsible for rescuing Shakespeare from the 19th-century rhetorical school of acting (better known as overacting).

Amid the serious lore of London theater life, you'll find some oddities, too: Did you know that the entrance that the Savoy Theater shares with its neighbor, the Savoy Hotel, is the only piece of road in the United Kingdom where cars drive on the right? The Adelphi, whose severe black Art Deco facade now faces the Savoy across The Strand, stands on the site of a dairy that once supplied the royal household with milk and butter. Dairy owner John Scott first built a theater here in 1806 to indulge the theatrical talents of his daughter Jane, and there has been a theater here ever since.

Today the West End is run by some 100 producers, theater owners, and managers. Some of them are newcomers, and some are themselves descendants of theatrical predecessors. It is here, perhaps, that the secrets of the West End's success lie: its continuity from one generation to the next, and its ability to reinvent itself along the way. From time to time, new technologies bring new competition—cinema, television and multimedia home entertainment—but there is always an audience for live theater. It helps that the British have an uncanny capacity for producing an unending stream of gifted performers. But London also excels at large-scale musicals, à la Sir Andrew Lloyd Webber and Cameron Mackintosh, and at farces and thrillers, which are regularly exported to the United States. London theater is equally adept at reinterpretations of classic drama, and—although the cry goes up at regular intervals that the West End is dying, that new work by unheard-of writers is too risky—at theatrical analysis of contemporary social issues. Look around, and you'll find a half-dozen plays that have crossed into the commercial theater from the Fringe, nurtured by producers who believe that important new work should reach a wider audience. You'll also see an entirely new generation of directors, whose name on a bill guarantees a stimulating evening: Stephen Daldry, Nicholas Hytner, Phyllida Lloyd, Sam Mendes, Deborah Warner. Look out for these names, and strike out into new theatrical territory.

No other city in the world can offer you so stunning a variety. Whatever you choose, I can promise you won't forget it—as a child of five or as a seasoned adult culture addict. Welcome to the true heart of London.

—Jane Moss

Ms. Moss has contributed to many publications in London and the U.K. Since 1988, she has been Information Officer for the Society of the London Theatre and has a reputation as a walking encyclopedia on British theater, past and present.

INDEX

✕ = *restaurant*, ▣ = *hotel*

A

B

C

E

F

G

H

T

U

V

NOTES

NOTES

NOTES

Fodor's

Special Series

Affordables

Caribbean

Europe

Florida

France

Germany

Great Britain

Italy

London

Paris

Fodor's Bed & Breakfasts and Country Inns

America

California

The Mid-Atlantic

New England

The Pacific Northwest

The South

The Southwest

The Upper Great Lakes

The Berkeley Guides

California

Central America

Eastern Europe

Europe

France

Germany & Austria

Great Britain & Ireland

Italy

London

Mexico

New York City

Pacific Northwest & Alaska

Paris

San Francisco

Compass American Guides

Arizona

Canada

Chicago

Colorado

Hawaii

Idaho

Hollywood

Las Vegas

Maine

Manhattan

Montana

New Mexico

New Orleans

Oregon

San Francisco

Santa Fe

South Carolina

South Dakota

Southwest

Texas

Utah

Virginia

Washington

Wine Country

Wisconsin

Wyoming

Fodor's Citypacks

Atlanta

Hong Kong

London

New York City

Paris

Rome

San Francisco

Washington, D.C.

Fodor's Español

California

Caribe Occidental

Caribe Oriental

Gran Bretaña

Londres

Mexico

Nueva York

Paris

Fodor's Exploring Guides

Australia

Boston & New England

Britain

California

Caribbean

China

Egypt

Florence & Tuscany

Florida

France

Germany

Ireland

Israel

Italy

Japan

London

Mexico

Moscow & St. Petersburg

New York City

Paris

Prague

Provence

Rome

San Francisco

Scotland

Singapore & Malaysia

Spain

Thailand

Turkey

Venice

Fodor's Flashmaps

Boston

New York

San Francisco

Washington, D.C.

Fodor's Pocket Guides

Acapulco

Atlanta

Barbados

Jamaica

London

New York City

Paris

Prague

Puerto Rico

Rome

San Francisco

Washington, D.C.

Mobil Travel Guides

America's Best Hotels & Restaurants

California & the West

Frequent Traveler's Guide to Major Cities

Great Lakes

Mid-Atlantic

Northeast

Northwest & Great Plains

Southeast

Southwest & South Central

Rivages Guides

Bed and Breakfasts of Character and Charm in France

Hotels and Country Inns of Character and Charm in France

Hotels and Country Inns of Character and Charm in Italy

Hotels and Country Inns of Character and Charm in Paris

Hotels and Country Inns of Character and Charm in Portugal

Hotels and Country Inns of Character and Charm in Spain

Short Escapes

Britain

France

New England

Near New York City

Fodor's Sports

Golf Digest's Best Places to Play

Skiing USA

USA Today The Complete Four Sport Stadium Guide

Fodor's Vacation Planners

Great American Learning Vacations

Great American Sports & Adventure Vacations

Great American Vacations

Great American Vacations for Travelers with Disabilities

National Parks and Seashores of the East

National Parks of the West